TWENTY-TWO HUNDRED DAYS TO PULO WE:

My education in the Navy

by

Jack Edwards

Published by
MELROSE BOOKS
An Imprint of Melrose Press Limited
St Thomas Place, Ely
Cambridgeshire
CB7 4GG, UK
www.melrosebooks.com

FIRST EDITION

Cover designed by Ross Hilton and Bryan Carpenter

ISBN 1 905226 39 X

Printed and bound in Great Britain by:
Bath Press Limited, Lower Bristol Road,
Bath, BA2 3BL, UK

Dedication

I would like to dedicate this book to my late wife who urged me to write about my schooldays and the Navy. I didn't know that she had joined the staff at Bletchley Park as Wren Joyce Dyster – she never told me even when she became Joyce Edwards. She kept her contract with them and only mentioned it when the Official Secrets Act had run its course.

Acknowledgements

There are so many people I want to thank for helping me to put this book together and I am grateful to them all.

I am particularly indebted to Keith Hill for reading through the draft copies, correcting faults, checking up on facts and encouraging me when I was flagging. He has been a tower of strength.

Many thanks are due to Yvonne Sandwell for starting the typing on her electric typewriter; to Anna Bellingham for her patience in designing the layout for the book and producing the typewritten pages with the diagrams on the computer; and to Chris Pudsey who took over some way through. All were persevering in their work, typing and retyping seemingly endless pages of notes and draft copies.

I am indebted to Eileen Bainbridge for her skilful drawings; to Ron Moor, ex-Royal Marine from HMS *Nigeria*, who advised me on RN duties on board or ashore; and to Commander W.E. Chick DSC RN (Ret'd) for technical advice and photographs with regard to the repairs he supervised to get the badly-damaged ship back to safety.

My thanks are also due to the Portsmouth Naval Museum who found Mr Richard Noyce (Medals); Mr David Allport, Warrant Officer I (Communications) RN; Maritime Welfare School; HMS *Collingwood* who answered queries about my 1937 signal card; and Commander Bruce Nicholls OBE RN (Ret'd) with Mr C.D. Rickard RN (Ret'd) who both supplied me with information about signal flags, despite being busy with preparations for the celebration of the bicentenary of the Battle of Trafalgar.

Others I would like to mention are Pam Cooper for her encouragement after reading an early draft copy of my book and Gill Lumb who worked with me at Whipsnade Zoo and kept me in contact with her father, Commander W.E. Chick.

Photographs: I am indebted to Naval Airman H.C. Johnson for giving me the photos of HMS *Nigeria* which he took with his RN camera on board or in the air all those years ago, and others who have contributed photographs. Also Bletchley Park Trust, www.bletchleypark.org.uk, who gave permission to reproduce the photograph of the Enigma machine.

Last, but not least, I must thank all those people I have written about in this book who helped me to get through the difficult times and survive the war; those recent friends and members of my badminton club who have been supportive and encouraging during the writing of this book; and to my wife Barbie for putting up with everything when the book took over.

Every reasonable effort has been made to acknowledge the ownership of copyrighted material. Any errors that may have occurred are inadvertent and will be corrected in any subsequent editions provided notification is sent to the author.

Contents

Author's Introduction

Take a look at the photograph taken in 1939. It is of the thirty-three boys (out of the original forty – not including the two instructors and a dog!) who completed the five-week course at HMS *St Vincent*, the stone frigate at Gosport, and who reached the end of the assessment stage. At the same time as we were completing our course at *St Vincent*, two other groups, each of forty boys of a similar age, were being assessed at Shotley and Rosyth. They later completed training with us on the Isle of Man.

These 120-odd sixteen-year-olds from *St Vincent*, Shotley and Rosyth were trained for seven months (at that time the war had started). They were divided into six school classes of twenty boys, plus the teacher. Each group was sent to a different RN ship. My group, already reduced by illness to seventeen, was sent to HMS *Nigeria*. These young boy seamen were quickly snapped up by officers who knew that these well-trained technicians were familiar with radar and had been trained to use it. Radar was going to be vitally important.

Radar was new then and not all ships were equipped with it at that time. But because *Nigeria* was brand new she was fitted with it and qualified 'specialists' – however young – were needed to operate it. Although very young, the only person who regarded himself as a 'boy' was the boy himself – who was amazed to find he was treated with such respect by his elders – but in spite of this he still only received one shilling (5p) per week and was only allowed ashore on Saturday and Sunday afternoons!

The boy seamen were treated like adults and were regarded as being capable of doing the same tasks as anyone else on the ship. They became specialists; they were courageous, well-educated seamen who were respected by the rest of the ship's crew – they also became energetic and disciplined *Nigerians*. The situation they found themselves in forced them to grow up quickly and in the early days

ix

of their naval service they soon encountered the harsh realities of war, seeing starving Russians bombed almost to destruction, and the hardships of enemies who were suffering even more than they were.

I can still vividly recall the feelings I had when I was eighteen and stood by our Navy schoolteacher watching the pupils leaving the ship – one way or another. Sadly, a considerable number were committed to the deep. We seventeen boy seamen are still waiting for the Admiralty medal for the Russian campaign.

The boy seamen showed great courage. They looked after one another, retained their spirit of fun and adventure and were always willing to volunteer for difficult jobs to play their part in winning the war. I never heard any of them complain or say that it was unfair or that they should have been sent to serve in the war at that age; they just did their jobs to the best of their ability.

Jack Edwards

St. Vincent Class

I

A 29 Bus to Whitehall

The letter arrived with the early post on the 30th November 1987 and was addressed to 'The participant on the occasion of the 40th Anniversary of the Victory in the Great Patriotic War 1941–1945'. This had taken two years to catch up with me. It requested this participant to contact the Russian Ambassador in London to be honoured with a gold medal and a citation. Gorbachev had arrived with Glasnost and Perestroika. All this came as a complete surprise.

I immediately wrote to the ambassador expressing my appreciation for the honour they had bestowed upon me. It also wound back my memory clock to that thin young fifteen-year-old boy seaman second class, who became so embroiled in events on the Russian/Finnish border with all its terrible weather and consequences. I felt that perhaps this was an unusual experience and as such could be of interest to the modern generation. History, I think, is recorded by the victors but not necessarily by those that were at the sharp end. Perhaps, also, today's so different youngsters may find the contents of interest by comparing their lot in life today with that of 1939 when I was just fifteen years old. Also, I feel it should at least be an unusual yarn. So where does one start? I suppose where everyone does, right at the beginning.

There is no evidence to suggest I was a beautiful baby but I most certainly was born with a silver spoon in my mouth. My mother had married late in life and had produced three children in a hurry by the time she was forty-two, two boys and a girl.

Our father was a serving lieutenant in the Royal Artillery, whose peacetime job was to tour the country planning and organising gymkhanas and horse shows.

He was a good horseman and our family life was spent moving from place to place and enjoying horses, which for me also meant moving from private school to private school and, even though it was beginning to show that I was possibly dyslexic (a condition not officially

1

Photo 1. Brother and Sister and me

recognised in those days), my inability to spell never put me under any pressure, possibly because in about four years I attended twelve different private schools. Then without any warning this lovely lifestyle came to an abrupt end as my father was pensioned off on half pay. He obtained a position as a manager of a London nightclub, which had its fair share of chorus girls, and I suppose it was inevitable that he should be taken in by their obvious charms and it was not long before he and my mother parted. The last time I saw my father was when I was playing in the front garden at our Shooters Hill, London, home. He turned up in his car, complete with a female passenger, with a package for my mother. Obviously he would have been better thought of if had he come alone.

It was a magnificent beast of a car, a bull-nosed green job of 1930 vintage (Bentley type). It had a brass honeycomb radiator grill, together with big brass headlights, with its hood down on that sunny day when I was seven years old. By holding the warm radiator top, I could just see this lady through the narrow

Photo 2. My Father

2

windscreens sitting quietly minding her own business in the passenger seat, her large-brimmed hat held securely on her head by a green silk scarf. I remember everything was green – the privet hedge outside the house, the car and the grass verge. It was indeed a green day.

She was very pretty but her face held for me a hard expression, perhaps she was a chorus girl. My attention was taken by my father coming down the front garden path followed by my mother. She looked so distressed, I remember that look well. She threw something to the ground, shouted "keep your money" and then calling to me to follow, retreated to the house. My father climbed aboard the car and I became aware that he was staring down at me. He looked serious and I felt uncomfortable as I moved towards the gate between the two halves of the hedge. He started the engine with a roar, looked at me again, and with a wave of his arm drove off. That was the last time I ever saw him.

My mother wrote to me some thirteen years later whilst I was serving in Burma. It was short, simple and to the point: "Your father has died after a long illness." She did not say what it was and in the years later I never asked. She had added that he had asked to see me before he died.

I felt it was sad; the mail as always was three months late and there was not the time to mourn even though he was my father. Fellow servicemen were dying around me and had been doing so in large numbers for some time and I was indeed a possible candidate to share the same fate. I do know that all through my life I tried hard not to act like him. I suppose really I was ashamed of him; perhaps I have been unfair to him.

After my father left us, money was short and life became dreadful. Mother was forced to take a position at a large restaurant washing up, which meant that she did not arrive home until after midnight and the house was always cold. I remember my mother looking worried and awful as she hurried us to school in the mornings. Then one day our Auntie Wyn (her sister) turned up and took us all home with her in a beautiful black motorised cab to Winchmore Hill, N21, and from that point onwards I regarded my Auntie Wyn as my fairy godmother.

Auntie was unmarried and lived in a big, comfortably heated house with Grandpa and Grandma (both nearly ninety years old). Auntie Wyn owned and ran a large corner shop selling knitting wools, tapestries and art needlework.

Auntie Wyn was especially kind to me. She was always pleasant and even when she was being strict she somehow or other managed to be nice about it. She read to us every night, lots and lots of fiction

Photo 3. Family group, comprising Uncle Jim, Mother and Uncle Gilbert, Grandpa, Grandma and Auntie Wyn

and I remember particularly the stories of the *Three Midshipmen* and most of Dickens' novels. I eagerly looked forward to going to bed in our beautiful large bedroom where all three of us slept, with its well-guarded coal fire and its flickering reflections on the ceiling which we could watch when she tucked us up for the night and turned off the lights.

We spent all our school holidays in a small, recently-built bungalow at Swalecliffe, Kent. Either Grandpa paid for it to gain some peaceful moments without children or Auntie picked up the bill; I do not know which. I do know that as a child it was my idea of paradise. The bungalow was situated opposite a small farm, where I was allowed to help with the animals. It was also close to a nice sandy beach and in close proximity to the Southern Railway station.

4

It was a day of great excitement when we were asked to pack our holiday clothes in the commodious shared green trunk which was sent (luggage in advance) by Carter Patterson's lorry. Either Mother or Auntie would take us down by train to the bungalow called 'Wyndoon' and the other came down a week later on a cheap day-return ticket to relieve the first, who would then return to London on the same ticket. In this way they kept the wool shop open throughout the school holidays.

It was whilst we were enjoying an autumn half-term holiday that the elephant turned up. It was about six one morning when my brother woke me up with "there's an elephant in the front garden eating Auntie's flowers". "Oh, go back to sleep," I replied. "No," he said, "there really *is* an elephant." Reluctantly I got up from my bed and there in the small front garden was an elephant happily eating Auntie's cabbages (Auntie always planted vegetables in every available spot in that very small garden). At that stage we both panicked and rushed into Auntie's bedroom.

"Wake up Auntie, there's an elephant in the front garden", and despite the rude awakening she saw the joke immediately. That's what she liked about little boys' humour. "Yes," she said, "that's very funny." At that stage we grasped her hands and with some force pulled her from her bed shouting to her "come and see – come and see the elephant". Seeing this joke had more to it than most she good-naturedly came, despite the early hour and chilly morning. We urged her to hurry to the front-room window. The elephant in the meantime had made a 180-degree turn, so what Auntie saw at first was a large grey elephant's bottom with a small tail. It was quite a long time before she murmured "oh my", and "my word, it *is* an elephant". There was another long pause. Then she said, as only my aunt would: "We must get dressed straightaway, we can't deal with an elephant in our nighties and don't forget your shoes and socks." Then she was off to dress herself. Once more she came into the front room and looked out. The elephant was still there but had been joined by a slightly-built young man with the standard droopy moustache and armed with a short stout stick. Auntie saw he was holding the elephant's ear so she ventured out to the front porch. The man, seeing a fully-dressed Auntie with her shoes on, apologised for the damage the elephant had done to the garden. "You see, ma'am, she got out of her paddock at the circus' winter quarters," which he explained was just up the road past the farm. Seeing Auntie's worried expression he said: "She wouldn't hurt a fly, even the children can touch her, if you've got a bun they could feed her." We did not have any buns but we had some of Auntie's home-made scones which the man with the stick assured us were just as good.

At 6.30 in the morning, after two very nervous children and an equally frightened Auntie had fed this young female Asian elephant with three home-cooked scones and had given her three tentative pats, the elephant quietly left the garden with her keeper, but not before depositing a medium-size cannon ball on our lawn! After waving the elephant and keeper goodbye we all retreated back into 'Wyndoon' to enjoy one of Auntie Wyn's 'bacon-and-egg specials'.

It was a story we all told time and time again and how we did laugh even though nobody ever believed us! Auntie Wyn brightened up my life considerably in those days. I wonder how many children were as lucky as we were to have such an aunt?

All along, poor Mother had been having a hard time. Also, she had not been at all well and had to live down the stigma of the divorce. The vicar and all the relations, with the exception of Auntie Wyn and Uncle Gilbert, had treated her as though she was a sort of pariah. As soon as it was obvious that she was a permanent resident at Elm Park, Auntie Annie and Uncle Jim, her brother, ceased to call, although they lived less than half a mile away.

One day when we were about ten years old, my brother and I found ourselves outside Uncle Jim's palatial residence and after betting each other we wouldn't do it, one of us plucked up courage to ring the bell and the two of us waited nervously for someone to come. It was not long before Auntie Annie appeared. Neither of us knew what to say. Auntie Annie gave us little time to think then she snapped sharply: "What do you want?" I could think of nothing to say but my young brother did and at the time I thought it was incredibly clever of him to say: "We're thirsty, can we have a drink please?" We had discussed this situation before ringing the bell and thought that Auntie would, after inviting us in, provide us on this hot day with a glass each of lemonade together with a cake and, after asking about our health, send us on our way with a sweet or two. We both smiled our best smiles. What happened was, "wait" and the door closed before after a minute or two re-opening to reveal Auntie Annie with two old cups full of water. "When you've finished leave the cups on the step." She said "good day" and closed the door. (That was the last we saw of Auntie Annie except, that is, until we were grown up and she was a hundred years of age). When we arrived home and told Mother she was upset and annoyed. We were instructed not to call there again.

Uncle Gilbert, who died young, had apparently been fond of his young sister, our mother, and had been most generous with his financial support which ceased with his demise. There was no such thing then as Government Family Support.

Mother gradually overcame the difficulties of living as a divorcée, her sense of humour began to return slowly and she began to join in and enjoy all our garden and park sports. She was a fair hand at badminton, tennis and cricket but, unlike Mother, Auntie Wyn was never much of a sportswoman. Everybody in the immediate family joined in our indoor games – snakes and ladders, cards, tiddly-winks, ludo, jigsaws, draughts and chess – but most of all Mother loved music. She was a talented pianist (and had a beautiful singing voice). She played whilst Auntie Wyn played the violin, and singsongs were a top priority for us all.

Auntie Wyn taught us all how to sew, embroider, work tapestries and make home-made wool carpets; she did not expect boys to knit. She provided us with nice clothes and she gave me 6d a week for looking after the garden, which I enjoyed. Another of the gifts was a large painting box and drawing materials. She taught me about the technicalities of art in all its forms for which I am extremely grateful.

There was only one crisis that I remember generating, all over a half crown i.e. 2/6d or 12½ new pence (don't forget in those days 12½p would take two adults to the cinema as well as buying some chocolates). This coin appeared to live permanently on the kitchen mantelpiece, seen only when descending to that level from the hall and what I had failed to note was that it was changed every Saturday after the milkman had called. One Thursday, on my way to choir practice at Holy Trinity Church in Green Lanes, I quietly paused at the mantelpiece, slipped this half crown into my pocket and, being by nature a great entertainer, invited the whole boys' choir to the coffee shop opposite the church to buy some coconut iced fairy cakes. It was whilst I was paying for these with my newly obtained 2/6d coin that the local bobby came in. It was when all the choir boys had quietly left that this 'gentleman in blue' knew something was up (old-fashioned bobbies had that second sense). "Come on lad, where did you get it?" and with both him and the coffee shop owner looking at me, "from my mum," I lied. "Pay up," he said, "let's go and ask her; where do you live?" I knew I was doomed and that the whole thing had got out of hand. I had no choice but to tell him. "Elm Park Road," I whispered. With that his hand arrived securely on my collar and off we went. It was about a two-hundred-yard journey and everybody (I mean everybody) stopped and looked. I recognised some of the faces and I knew at that point I would never ever steal again. My mother opened the door with a shocked expression. She was obviously horrified but, fortunately, Auntie was in the shop. The policeman made his report to my mother. She looked as if she was going to faint; at that point she was joined by my grandpa. Mother admitted that she had not given the coin to me and that the milk money was missing from the kitchen. The policeman looked pleased: "Will you deal with it then?" "We most certainly will," said my grandpa, who by now had caught on. I also realised that I had dragged the law to our front door by my disgrace and there was worse to follow. Grandpa had armed himself with his large smooth-handled mahogany clothes brush, a weapon that I had always been threatened with but up to now had not received. With Mother as a witness, I was instructed to take off my trousers down to my underpants, told to kneel, bend over my bed and receive six of the best from my grandpa (it was always six of the best), whilst Mother looked on and wept. Although this was the worst beating I had ever had, it was all the events around it that worried me most of all. The biggest lesson I learnt was that when punishment was administered quickly after the crime, for the punisher and the receiver it always worked; to delay the punishment ends in stalemate. Stealing had definitely been crossed off my lifestyle; it also made me become more mature. Also I learnt that when you were punished by Grandpa, Mother or Auntie, the other two kept out of it and the matter was never raised again. Auntie never ever mentioned the policeman.

Grandpa and Grandma died within a year of one another (peacefully and in their nineties), which meant their two rooms became vacant, so we three children ended up with a bedroom apiece; I stayed where I was. In this large house it appeared at the time as though we children were not only sleeping further apart but also growing apart, whether it was our maturing or the sad demise of our nice grandparents or for other unexplainable reasons. There was a noticeable difference for me, the feeling of guilt because my poor spelling meant I was unable to pass the dreaded 11-plus after two attempts. Being left behind at the Council School helped to subscribe to a doubt. I never felt inferior, even when my brother and sister both passed the scholarship exams for Grammar School entrance. I think Auntie's kindness had a lot to do with suppressing that form of guilt with the statement: "There's an old Chinese proverb, two's company, three's a crowd." How or why either my mother or aunt or both made the decision for me to take up a commercial education at Pitmans College, Palmers Green, at the age of twelve years I shall never know. Between them, they signed me up for four years at the Palmers Green College.

At first I was a young boy feeling that I should get up on my own two feet and do something about it but I didn't know what to do. I used to daydream that there were one or two beautiful unspoilt Pacific islands or some unknown lost paradise in South America: there might be a way to trek overland or sail the seas back to unspoilt nature that would cure all the woes I was feeling. I felt I wanted to run away to feed these fantasies where semi-naked women dwelt and would fill my life with innocent happiness until I was old, but alas this never happened. I was an innocent, immature, healthy young boy and wanted to run away from my responsibilities.

I must admit that joining the college was a pleasant surprise and free at first from all pressures. I remember that I took to shorthand like a duck to water and had no particular pressing problems with geography, French, arithmetic, history, commerce or typing. It was only when I started my typing and shorthand speed tests that I suddenly became aware that, in decoding my shorthand, the words produced with my spelling ability resulted in another type of code instead of the English language!

That awful feeling of letting down my guardian ladies, who were paying £4 a week for my tuition, once more returned as I was aware they could ill afford such a sum. England, during my early teens, had emerged from a depressing slump. Employment possibilities were improving and Auntie Wyn's business was on the up-and-up. My friends and I were finding so many interesting things to do with our leisure time.

As a mixed group of students from Pitmans, known as 'the mob' (after the gangster films), we were enjoying a carefree lifestyle.

Suddenly we were too old to go roller-skating in the streets; we had just changed into long trousers and had turned to ice-skating at the new Harringay Ice Rink on a Saturday morning, after abandoning the Saturday kids' sixpenny flicks. Now, at fourteen, we were able to go to the evening or afternoon cinema, easily pretending to be eighteen in our long trousers or perhaps they let in anyone provided it was a 'C' rating – I do not think we ever tried our luck at an 'A' movie.

Photo 4. Me with my bicycle

9

Auntie and Mother provided me with a new Raleigh bicycle to get me to college "without having to pay the bus fares", so they said, but it might have been that all fourteen-year-olds at Pitmans had bikes and they did not want me to be the odd one out. Whatever the reason, I had a new feeling of freedom; I had wheels, which enabled me to bike to weekend picnics and enjoy bike rides into the local country areas.

Pitmans students were subject to a number of rules, all of which so far as I can recollect were kept, possibly because of the respect we all had for Mr Warner, the headmaster, and our fee-paying parents. The number one mandatory rule I am sure all students will remember was "Thou shall not fraternise with the opposite sex within a one mile radius of the school".

Living in close proximity to Elm Park Road was one Joyce Dyster, a very nice-looking girl with gorgeous blue eyes who cycled past my house on her way to school and who, to my surprise and delight, allowed me to join her. However, due to rule No.1, we had to part company or join at St John's Church, Palmers Green, which is one mile from Pitmans College. It is true to say that at the age of fourteen we had become attracted by the opposite sex, as a result of which both sexes seem to have entered into a mutual respect and automatically into a new and sophisticated method of communication, which was both pleasant and adult. I have to say that whilst sex was in the background somewhere, I knew of no boy or girl in that school group who crossed that line into an advanced sexual relationship. Such behaviour would not have occurred at that time but would have come when we were at least eighteen or more.

These were trouble-free happy days. Friendships between these boys and girls were not serious bonding contracts and it was not uncommon to change friendships regularly. Amid all this freedom and enjoyment nobody free-wheeled, we all took our studies seriously.

While still only fourteen I plucked up courage to have a confab with Mother and Auntie to discuss this insurmountable spelling problem I was experiencing at Pitmans, where it was rearing its ugly head in geography, history, commerce and French, as well as shorthand and typing. I pointed out that it would be more sensible for me to try another educational tack.

The whole family had enjoyed a trip to London to see the Royal Tournament a few weeks previously and whilst there Mother, Auntie and myself had taken the opportunity to sound out the recruitment sergeant who pointed out the advantages of a service special education, which of course he said all boys enjoyed. If you chose the Navy, you would travel all over the world too.

Mother remembered that being married to a career soldier had certain financial advantages but neither she nor Auntie had any desire to see me become a boy soldier. However, both of them showed a lukewarm interest in me becoming a naval writer using shorthand and typing for general office duties when I reached eighteen. We came away with the necessary address of where to contact the Navy should we change our minds.

I could see that joining the Royal Navy was an opportunity to lighten my family's financial responsibilities to me. Sailing round the world had a ring to it. It sounded like a great adventure from the cinema. For the next few months I did all in my power to try to get Mother and Auntie to change their way of thinking.

A once-a-week treat from Auntie Wyn was a trip to the Capitol Cinema at the end of the road, all armed with two-pennyworth of self-chosen sweets, purchased from the sweet shop on the way. Auntie enjoyed the cinema and she had her special favourites. She enjoyed seeing Myrna Loy and William Powell in a series called *The Thin Man* with Aster the white wire-haired terrier. She enjoyed epic films like *Mutiny on the Bounty*, *The Six Wives of Henry VIII* and *The Bengal Lancers*. We knew Auntie had a secret crush on Gary Cooper, it was a crush she could not hide. I remember we all giggled at her but she did not seem to mind, these were good and happy days.

She took seriously the Pathé News with its cockerel talisman; we all did. This was the time the Japanese were brutally invading China and had raped and massacred in Nanking; the Italians were attacking semi-naked Abyssinians with mustard gas and there was the Spanish Civil War being aided and abetted by the German and Italian air forces. Dreadful stories were coming out of Europe of the persecution of the Jews. I think both Mother and Auntie were convinced a war was coming and that, whatever happened, we would all end up in it somehow or other.

Despite these dreadful predictions, I found myself at fifteen years of age (with little academic attainment to my credit but with a sound and healthy constitution) on my way to the Admiralty, Whitehall, in a No.29 bus with Mother's and Auntie's blessings to start my naval career as a writer when I reached eighteen years of age. I don't think I had any idea that this journey I was attempting solo was going to rock the world, but I do remember that strange new feeling of self-confidence that I was somehow or other in charge of my own destiny and a general feeling of satisfaction. I suppose that all kids get to this point in their lives; perhaps it's one of those steps we climb when we arrive at puberty. The things I remember about that day, even if they are a bit hazy, was that an elderly petty officer (PO) had taken all my particulars, that a naval schoolteacher had given me a simple test in English and arithmetic, and a doctor had presumably looked through one ear to check that daylight could not be seen from the other.

The most vivid recollection was at the end of the ordeal, the final interview with the ancient PO, in which I was told that if I wanted to be considered for a position as a writer I should re-apply when I was eighteen, on the other hand if I wanted to become a boy seaman I was to take a sealed buff envelope back home for my parents to study. What I remember today as clearly as I did then was the next question: "Are you hungry, boy?" It must have been about 12.30 and I distinctly remember replying with "yes please". At that point I was given what was called the 'chit' on which was printed 'Meal' in heavy lettering. It had a lot of small print which young boys never notice and then again in large print 'Signature'. "You see," said the PO, "if and when you sign this chit, take it into that mess room, give it to the cook and he'll give you a meal, as much as you like to eat." I was hungry and it had been a long trip. I did not hesitate, I took his pen and signed and unknowingly had instantly managed to get myself into debt. After enjoying a first class meal with second helpings I made my way home and presented Mother with the buff envelope.

One day in 1939 the second buff envelope arrived addressed to Mother. I do not recall all the contents, except that it contained a buff travel warrant issued by the Royal Navy for one boy to travel to Portsmouth main station some two months hence. I took a letter written by Mother to the headmaster which explained that I was off to join the Navy. Mr Warner kindly wished me luck. I verbally informed the maths/history teacher who took it in his stride. The typing lady, who had suffered most from my awful spelling, was obviously very relieved, but the French teacher, whom I always liked, asked me to repeat the message before taking my hand and bursting into tears.

I could not understand at the time why neither Mother nor Auntie raised any objections to my going after all the previous resistance they had shown but six years later I learnt the truth. My auntie was beginning a long and fatal illness, which they were keeping from us. Mother must have realised that if I settled in the Navy I would be one less to worry about.

It was not until departure day arrived that the enormity of my decision to face the world alone came home to me. Auntie had decided to say a quick goodbye, before proceeding to open the shop, and I realised that I was about to walk away from a lovely clean, organised and comfortable home and leave two dear and loving ladies who had protected and attended to all my needs, always in my best interests.

There was seemingly no way out of this situation and, like it or not, I had a train to catch from Waterloo. Despite all this I was also nervous as any lad would be travelling such a distance for the first time on his own.

The trolley buses ran like clockwork every ten minutes. They were quiet, clean and fast and I can remember them replacing trams. There I was in my grey school trousers and sports jacket with the travel warrant in the inside pocket, with two shillings' (10p) worth of change and a brown paper bag with waxed string handles containing an apple, an orange and two white bread jam sandwiches.

Perhaps it was ten minutes earlier than necessary but needing to be sure I got away in good time I approached Mother to say goodbye. She looked flustered and said: "I must have a talk with you about those women, they are everywhere." Her face had gone very red. So far I hadn't got a clue, I was only concerned about missing my trolley bus and then perhaps my Waterloo train. "What women?" I asked. "Oh," she replied, "be careful of these women, do be very careful." "Mother," I said, "I must go or I'll miss my train." "Of course," she said, "but do be careful," to which I responded "don't worry, of course I will". I gave her a hug, it was the biggest hug I had ever given her, and as I kissed her I saw the tears, and off I went. Auntie was serving in the shop and I gave her a friendly wave. I was halfway to Wood Green underground station in the trolley bus before the penny dropped. I could not help smiling to myself as I thought about poor Mother. 'Us boys' at Pitmans knew about 'those women', I quietly mused to myself, even if we hadn't ever seen one let alone touched one!

The ticket office clerk at Waterloo mainline station took my travel warrant, looked at me with a smile, stamped my warrant and passed it back to me with "Platform 5 son, ten minutes past ten". I made my way to an empty third-class carriage on the train standing at Platform 5.

I arrived at Portsmouth mainline station minus my apple, orange and white home-made jam sandwich. It had been a long and lonely journey with nobody else to share the carriage with. On descending from the train I nervously approached a sailor and showed him my travel warrant. "Do you know where I should go?" I asked, to which he responded: "Where you should go to sail the seven seas and drink the eighth bastard? Why, only over there, lad," he smiled, "by that blue lorry." He then produced a bigger, friendlier smile. By the side of the lorry stood a PO with a list who looked up and said "Name?" "Edwards," I replied. "Edwards, *Sir.* Jump aboard," he ordered. I climbed aboard the highly-polished blue lorry and found myself in the company of a crowd of motley youngsters dressed in every type of mufti, who sat in complete silence as we were driven to the Gosport Ferry on our way to HMS *St Vincent*.

II

On Trial

We arrived at HMS *St Vincent* (known in the Navy as a stone frigate) which comprised large separate blocks of Victorian buildings named after famous long-gone admirals. Each block had a brightly painted ship's figurehead outside, all built at the water's edge. In the middle was a large parade ground sporting a 182-foot-high white-painted mast.

We were too late for lunch. I thought "thank goodness for Mother's home-made jam sandwiches". We were marched as a group to the clothing store where we were issued with some twenty-five to thirty items of sailor's kit, including blankets, together with a large brown paper container to pack our civilian clothes in. These paper bags of clothes would be stored here until the five weeks or less were up. We queued in half-a-dozen lines to enable each article of this new issue to be stamped with our name in half-inch black print.

We were then ushered into a so-called instruction room by a tall beefy PO who explained what was expected of us in the coming five weeks. He said we would be required, using single chain stitches, to sew over the black printed names with either black cotton or blue wool, in so doing completely covering the printed dye. If I remember correctly, this amounted to nineteen half-inch names, which did not include the three extra one-inch names on the two thick wool blankets and mattress cover. At the end of this month we were to have a 'tidy' kit muster when each article had to be rolled up into eleven-inch rolls tied by string with the sewn name showing in the centre between the two strings.

This muscular PO made it quite clear, as he issued each one of us with a 'housewife', which he called a 'Huz'if', that the cotton and wool provided should be sewn in a neat and tidy way and 'homeward bounders' (long stitches for a faster job) would not be accepted. This complete change from most boys' norm became an instant cultural shock. It is doubtful if any of these boys had ever sewn a button on, let alone threaded a tapestry needle with wool; all would have left that sort of thing to a mother or sister.

Worse was to come, this sewing was to be completed in our evening time. Individuals began to realise that to be named Cox had a tremendous advantage over a Macpherson. I was able to assist a South African boy named van der Merve who was well in arrears with his needlework. When I was on leave, Auntie Wyn was pleased to hear that some of her training had come into its own and had assisted my friend as well as myself.

Having collected our kit duly stamped we were chased off to our three-storey block where we were instructed to strip off and shower, after which each and every one of us was inspected by a doctor who explained, with a broad Scottish accent, that he was hunting for wee beasties which he called 'crabs'; up till then I had always understood that crabs were crustacea captured on the sea-shore and served up with salad dressing for Sunday tea. I had to go through this indignity again with another doctor because of a chest rash, the result of which was that I was advised to ask mother for proper toilet soap rather than use the naval soap known as 'pusser's hard', which was a standard soap supplied for cleaning floors and clothes washing. These two undignified inspections, scrutinising *every* corner of my body, were not enjoyable. At the end of this ordeal we were told to don our new uniforms and we then realised that we were beginning to look like sailors, even if we were not as yet. After returning our brown paper wrapped civilian clothes we were sent exhausted to enjoy our first naval meal of tea, bread, tinned butter and tinned jam labelled 'red' and generous lumps cut from a large, almost two-foot-square, fruit cake. Whilst we were eating this late but satisfying meal (boys from the north and west who had travelled long distances that day had not eaten since breakfast), a PO gave us each a sheet of headed writing-paper and an envelope with instructions to write home to our guardians to inform them we had arrived safely at HMS *St Vincent*. Those who did not have a stamp could buy one from this PO and those who did not have any money could sign for one, the cost of which would be deducted from their first week's pay.

It was a lot of tired boys who fell asleep that first night away from home. I was lying there on an uncomfortable lower section of a two-tiered iron bed between two new coarse, hairy, heavy blankets and sleeping in unwashed freshly-issued vest and underpants which smelt strongly of cotton. I remember this night and it was only one day on from the middle class comfort I was used to in freshly-ironed pyjamas between crisp sheets to the harsh reality of the Royal Navy night. There was an even bigger step to take the next day and the day after and so forth for months to come. I am sure that some of the noises I heard on that first night included a few gentle sobs of despair. That same night, or so it seemed, the bugle sounded off – it was already 0545 hours. The duty PO walked past all the iron beds giving each upper foot rail a hefty blow with a piece of 4ft x 2in wood whilst reciting at the top of his voice "wakey, wakey, rise and shine". On this morning we all got up as fast as we could, dressed in our new, stiff, freshly issued white duck uniforms which felt strange and uncomfortable. The PO herded us to the mass bathroom on the lower floor, housing rows of open-fronted toilets, hand basins and shower units, all without any privacy to perform a mass face wash and teeth-cleaning exercise with the exception of one boy who also had to shave. After the wash and prior to starting work before breakfast we were offered a china mug of pleasant-tasting hot, strong cocoa named 'kye', made from a solid bar of greasy-looking chocolate which had been brought to the boil in equal amounts of tinned milk and water and left brewing. Also on offer were concrete-hard ship's biscuits which could be broken only by placing them in the palm of your hand and slamming them down hard on the base of a wooden table. Although most of us took advantage of this early morning cocoa drink, which was also available on Saturdays and Sundays, I noticed that, like me, there were few takers for the biscuits.

It was pointed out by our PO that we were 'nozzers', new entries, and as such were the lowest form of naval life who would call *all* the staff for the next five weeks 'Sir'. Further, when told to fall in we should automatically form our lines four deep with the tallest on the right and shortest on the left. Everywhere we went, either singly or as a party, we would do so at the double (a steady run).

At 0630 that morning we were to 'double' to the drill hall (assembly point), it was approximately ten yards wide and forty yards long. Ten boys, including myself, were each allocated a two-yard-wide strip of the rough concrete floor which was twenty yards long. We were each armed with a heavy galvanised bucket full of cold water, a 2in x 2in x 6in bar of soap and a large hand scrubber. The PO warned us that dirty white duck suits had to be scrubbed with the same soap and brush in our own spare time, therefore kneeling down on the wet floor was 'out'. He then instructed us how to scrub concrete:

We were further reminded that breakfast was between 0745 and 0830 hours, and that the work would be supervised. As soon as the job of scrubbing had been finished we could go to breakfast. There was of course a catch. The Navy used the stick-and-carrot method; individuals could not go to breakfast alone, it had to be the entire

EB.

Figure 1. How to scrub concrete

group, therefore it was in the interest of the early finishers to assist the slower scrubbers. Concrete is hard stuff to scrub and harder to dry and takes time, it never seemed to be dry. With the exception of Saturdays and Sundays, this was to be my early morning task for the next five weeks. Others claimed they had worse jobs, particularly my South African friend who had won ten toilets, ten hand basins and ten showers to clean.

Breakfast consisted of one hard-boiled egg, without an egg cup, two pieces of bread half an inch thick with butter and a mug of tea, which was not as good as the soft-boiled egg with a touch of butter served at home in an egg cup with salt, pepper and 'soldiers'. When boys get up at 0545 hours and scrub a concrete floor they will eat anything! After breakfast we were 'doubled' to the barber's shop, manned by four chatty and friendly barbers who, while asking "where do you come from son?", quickly and efficiently cut *all* your hair off before you could answer – the Navy's way of ensuring that head lice had no quarters to breed in. I felt like Convict 99. "There you are," remarked my barber, "don't forget to keep your hat on when they take your photo."

On this first full day in the Navy, known as the 'Andrew', it was barely 1000 hours and here I was completely worn out and as bald as a coot. I did not think much of it.

Before we could recover, our PO (who seemed to have 'won' us as a class) suggested that as the weather was warm and sunny we should go swimming. We were separated into swimmers and non-swimmers; I joined the swimmers group who were in the minority. The PO then enquired of the swimmers if they could swim twenty feet under water without diving off the side; all those that felt this was beyond their capabilities were then asked to join the non-swimmers.

The outdoor swimming baths were not large and were seven-feet deep without a shallow end. All swimmers were asked to don one of the many wet duck suits, plus a pair of canvas deck shoes from an already soaking wet heap. In the meantime we watched with some interest, standing there in our recently-donned and uncomfortable wet duck suits, a sour-faced swimming pool physical training instructor slotting an eighteen- to twenty-foot-long bamboo rod into a two-foot-high iron fulcrum (see Figure 2). The non-swimmers had in the meantime disappeared into an adjacent building, presumably for swimming instructions. When I looked at all the apparatus of cork ropes, bamboo and life jackets I could not help feeling lucky and thankful for the swimming experience obtained whilst swimming off the beach at Swalecliffe during those holidays at Auntie Wyn's bungalow. When my turn came, the sour-faced PO ordered me to jump into the pool and grab the rail. These POs always shouted, in fact they nearly deafened you every time they opened their mouths. They never spoke normally. I assumed that only people who had the ability to shout louder than anyone else were selected for this training establishment. Once I was in the water, the PO threw a canvas-covered house brick into the centre of the pool. "Swim along the bottom of the pool, pick up the brick and bring it back to me while still swimming along the bottom," he bellowed. I don't remember having any problems with this request and followed his orders. Next he yelled: "Out you get, you'll do, put your clothes on and fall in at the end of the pool." It had by now become obvious that we were not going to attend any form of schooling or instruction classes. The whole emphasis of this initial five weeks' training was to introduce us to the famous naval discipline and to see how we stood up to it.

None of this prepared me for what I observed after 'falling in' with the first few lads who had satisfactorily completed their swimming. Opposite us was the bamboo pole resting on the fulcrum.

The two PO physical training instructors were briefing a tall, incredibly thin and undernourished-looking lad who had not even been swimming before and who was concentrating on the instructions on how to move his arms and legs in the water. As soon as he nodded his head he was picked up bodily and thrown into the centre of this

E.B.

Figure 2. Learning to swim

seven-foot-deep pool then, before he disappeared completely under the water, the bamboo pole manned by the two POs was thrust under him and, using the iron fulcrum, they flicked this poor thin lad clear of the surface whilst at the same time shouting further instructions on how to use his arms and legs. It was obvious that the lad was terrified: after six such flicks a third PO physical training instructor retrieved the boy from the pool using another bamboo pole with a leather ring on its end, which landed half round his neck and arm. The boy was then dragged out of the water by all three POs. The poor lad was spitting, coughing and gasping for breath and looking more dead than alive. The water held no terror for me and was pleasantly warm on that sunny day but must have been a nightmare for that lad.

All non-swimmers went through this ordeal and were given three chances to learn to swim. I do not know if this lad was sent home but he disappeared from the class. Most of the other less proficient swimmers managed to learn this art and later in life were probably more than pleased they did.

After the swimming we were marched off to lunch which everyone ate without hesitation. The daily routine did not vary very much from day to day, with the exception of Sunday which introduced us to the church parade. Time between events was taken up by so-called drills; like the Grand Old Duke of York's men we were marched up and then down again with a promise to do so with .303 Lee Enfield rifles during our last two weeks. The radio in the dormitory had mentioned Munich and Neville Chamberlain several times – not that we were taking much notice of it at all, we had far too much on our minds

Photo 5. St Vincent class

what with sewing and trying to keep up with our many chores. One Sunday we had our photo taken as a group.

Smoking and drinking alcohol were illegal for all ratings under eighteen, as in civil law. I assume the Navy took notice of this as there was nowhere at *St Vincent* to buy such goods even if you had any money, your shilling (5p) a week would have hardly gone far in this direction. There was a canteen that sold sweets and chocolates but more importantly stamps to enable you to write home.

It was just after breakfast on a Saturday that we were told to fall in and were then marched off to the large oblong gymnasium and told not to talk before being ushered in to join the ranks of some hundred and fifty boys from other classes, all neatly lined up down one of the long walls. We heard a hissed 'nozzers' from the boys already there but we didn't know why we were there. After a while, two physical training instructors came in carrying a vaulting horse about four feet high. We then immediately knew that the vaulting horse was the stage and we were the audience. The senior gunnery officer arrived with three gold rings on his sleeves, with black shiny gaiters and a whistle on a string round his neck. He stood very still on the left of the box. At that moment two masters-at-arms (senior naval police officers) marched in with a boy, dressed in clean white ducks, between them. They stopped at the vaulting horse. One of the physical training instructors led the boy to the box and made him lie across the vaulting horse, tummy down, at the same time smoothing

21

the wrinkles out of the seat of his duck trousers. The other physical training instructor went to the back of the stage and produced a large cane fitted with a half-round handle. At that moment the doctor came in, the same man that recommended proper soap for my skin rash, and it was not until then that I realised that I was about to witness a flogging. It was the utter silence of the place that made it seem so terrifying. The gunnery officer called us to attention and read out the charge against this boy seaman who had been caught smoking and who was to receive six strokes as punishment under Admiralty Order number so-and-so, he then blew his whistle and shouted "commence punishment". One of the masters-at-arms laid on six of the best, none of which landed in the same place. After the sixth, the whistle blew again and I heard "punishment completed, stand at ease". Everybody stayed quiet whilst the doctor examined the boy, who had not made a sound. At that point we were all marched out. I found it awful, I felt as if I had attended an execution, as bad as if someone had had his head cut off. I also learnt then that smoking could have a painful effect on your health.

It was only two or three days after this episode, whilst sewing our name tags, that one of the older boys produced a cigarette and pondered how to get hold of a match when one of the boys, whom I had considered to be as thick as two planks, came up with the suggestion that they used the light switch.

The boy who owned the cigarette decided that he did not want to get near the light switch and reluctantly passed the cigarette over

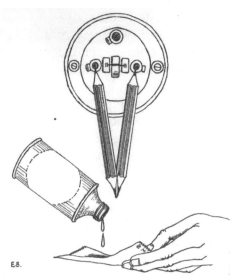

to our friend of the 'two planks' to ignite. Sentries were posted in case of a visit from a stray PO, perhaps it was to escape the boredom of that evening's sewing that everyone entered into the spirit of the quest for this Aladdin's light. I was asked to find a pencil whilst others were requested to find some toilet paper and a tin of Bluebell metal polish. I could not find a complete pencil but produced a lead pencil with about a quarter of its original length missing. "Cut it in half," ordered the boy with the cigarette now in his mouth, "and sharpen each half at

Figure 3. How to light a cigarette

both ends." At this point he began to unscrew the light switch brass cover plate, exposing the two holes with negative and positive wire connections. I gave him the two small half pencils duly sharpened at each end. After telling the boy holding the piece of toilet paper to soak it in the metal polish he, without hesitation, inserted each pencil into the two holes holding them by the wooden shafts, the resultant sparks instantly ignited the toilet paper which regrettably burnt to nothing before the cigarette could be lighted. We all saw that this could work. "There," he said to me, "you hold the pencils and I'll get near to the toilet paper." Another piece of toilet paper was prepared with metal polish. I suppose from time to time most people do silly things! I loaded the two small pencils as before and brought the two ends together, perhaps I was nervous, someone had mentioned 440 volts, anyway I produced an arc with a blinding flash, the wood at the ends of the two pencils caught alight. I felt two crushing blows, one under each armpit, and I fell to the floor because of the effect of the electric shock. The paper had lit, as had the cigarette. This was proof enough to me that smoking was indeed detrimental to your health and a dreadfully painful pastime. I also came to the conclusion that I was as thick as three planks and would wait until I was eighteen before considering taking up smoking.

We were finding out that to try to manage on a shilling a week was almost impossible, pay-days never came quickly enough. Perhaps I should explain: the total week's salary came to five shillings and thru'pence. This was made up of a payment of one shilling and ninepence for kit upkeep allowance, available for replacement articles like socks and underpants (if you lost or damaged an article of kit which could not be met by this one shilling and ninepence then you had to pay for it yourself), so your salary was calculated thus – five shillings and thru'pence, less your one shilling weekly personal payment leaving four shillings and thru'pence which was made up of one shilling and ninepence kit upkeep and two shillings and sixpence which was the pledge I had made for my mother's allowance. The Navy matched your parent's allowance so there was every incentive to make it as high as you could and I am sure Mother was more than happy to receive a one-pound note every month. On reaching eighteen years of age, all the kit upkeep allowance that had not been used would be credited to you together with any other monies that were with the paymaster, but as I had made arrangements for Mother to receive the two shillings and sixpence this eighteen-year-old sailor's payout did not look as if it was going to be very high.

Before receiving our first payment, we were trained on the intricacies of how to collect our weekly shilling. It was explained that we would be lined up in alphabetical order in front of the paymaster's table, which would be staffed by him and a PO writer who would call us forward by name when our turn came. This was our cue to shout out our service number followed by "Sir". We would then move smartly to the pay table, come to a halt and, using our right hand, quickly remove our hat and hold it flat side up at arm's length to enable the paymaster to place our shilling on the top of our hat. As soon as the shilling was in position and the commander had removed his hand, we were taught to quickly place our left hand firmly on the shilling, thus holding it securely, to turn left and double away with our hat, shilling and hand all clamped together, and rejoin the ranks. There we pocketed our shilling in our money-belt pocket and replaced our hat. Should we drop the shilling in front of the table the PO writer would confiscate it until we had collected it from his office the next day, in our own time. The drill was practised using a flat stone with the class PO acting as the 'paybob'.

Pay-day turned up and we were all confident that we had mastered the art of collecting our weekly 'bob'. Having lined up in the correct alphabetical order, my turn eventually came with "Edwards J.A." being called by the PO writer. I very properly and smartly marched forward, halted in front of the table (laden with a smart polished wooden box designed like a croupier's game-tray fitted with channels loaded with the King's shillings) whilst removing my hat and shouting "CJX 163760 Sir", at the same time thrusting forward my hat to receive that small round shining object which seemed a long time coming. The PO writer seemed occupied in reading the large ledger-type book, with pages that looked like graph paper, as though he couldn't find what he was looking for. "Ah," he said at last, "Edwards J.A. 163760 tuppence." The paymaster placed two large copper penny coins on the top of my hat. "But Sir," said I, and got no further as the master-at-arms (commonly known as the 'crusher' or 'jaunty') standing near the table bellowed "silence, don't talk back to an officer, left turn and double back to your class, any queries will be dealt with at the pay office". I turned left to move off and in my confused state dropped the two pennies. "Pick 'em up," came from the jaunty again, "and double off." "Next," he said. I rejoined my class. "What was that all about?" roared the class PO. "They only gave me tuppence, Sir," I said, as I heard a murmur of sympathy from the class. To give the PO his due, he was as confused as I was and immediately ordered me to report to the paymaster's office where I met a chief PO writer who looked at my records. "Oh yes," he said, "I have a chit signed by you for the tenpence you spent during your visit to the recruiting office to cover the food you ate, you shouldn't have been such a little pig and said yes to a meal." I felt there was no answer to that so I jogged back to rejoin my class, a sadder but wiser boy, contemplating why none of the other boys had been made to cough up as well. I had to admit for someone who had been taught Pitmans book-keeping that there were no flies on this Navy's accounts.

The class was instructed on the importance of tidiness aboard ship, with particular reference to the correct storage of personal clothing in the lockers provided and also the correct housing of properly made-up hammocks. Loose clothing would immediately block pumps if the ship was damaged and taking on water. We were to find out that the lockers provided in some ships were not only on the small side but also often damp. We also had a day of hammock drill: how to pack it into a large stowable sausage shape, hang it up and get into it and out of it which caused many a laugh.

As usual there were unwritten laws in the Royal Navy, one was that no-one would tolerate a thief. Throughout my whole time in the sea-going service I never remember anybody being accused of stealing anything belonging to another shipmate. I must admit that on that particular pay-day, I could not help feeling that the Navy itself carried out a bit of petty larceny on me. This was going to mean that I would have only enough money to write home to Mother and Auntie to let them know that all was well.

You tended to think of these things at 2115 hours (lights out time) but generally you were too tired and fell asleep before you could work up a worry. The next day brought fresh worries anyway.

There were murmurs of Munich on the wireless. The next morning we were introduced to the gym which was well supplied with climbing ropes, wall bars and vaulting horses. We were met by two muscular PO physical training instructors dressed in tight-fitting blue slacks and short-sleeved vests that made them look super fit. Having fallen us in, in four neat rows, as was the habit of all class POs, one of the POs began to explain the purpose of our visit to the gym. "You may have noticed the high mast at the edge of the parade ground," he paused at this point, "possibly you may have thought it is there as a prestige object for our senior officers, on the other hand perhaps you lads have been told that it is used to fly a pennant during Cowes week so that their commodore can see it from the Isle of Wight, but the truth of the matter is that from that crows-nest up there at 182 feet you can see the whole of the Isle of Wight. Well, my lucky lads, it is my pleasure to inform you that all of you will be experiencing the joy of that view from 182 feet next week. What's more you'll be spending three whole days here learning how to climb the rigging."

During the three days spent learning to master the vaulting horse, drills on the wall bars and rings together with muscle-building exercises on the floor mats and of course rope climbing, it did not take long for me to master the vaulting horse which had been set up longways at about four and a half feet high. I was told by the physical training instructor to take a good long run and leapfrog over. Obeying, I ran and leapfrogged but landed like a stranded whale sitting astride the centre of the vaulting horse. "You seem to have got the right idea," said the physical training instructor in a kindly way, "go back and run faster this time, go and try again." I took an extra long run and just as my feet had left the ground I felt this push and pain on my rear end and, much to my amazement, soared through the air to land squarely on my two feet. "See-e-e, you can do it," said the physical training instructor, shaking the canvas implement.

Both these PO physical training instructors carried a canvas tube about a foot long and one inch in diameter. The canvas was neatly stitched into a round tube with sailmaker's yarn (thin prepared string). The inside was packed hard with sharp sand, kept there by two round pieces of canvas also stitched on. This was what had hit me. I was to learn that there was a great art in using this canvas tube. It inflicted pain on a moving human target which was already going in the right direction and more pain if you were not moving fast enough. The boys had nicknamed this weapon a 'Stonickee', a mixture of the following words – satanic, stricken and stinker, I believe, used by ancient press gangs.

The same routine was used with rope climbing. We were first instructed by a rope-climbing demonstration, given by both of the physical training instructors who made it look so easy. They literally jumped up two or three feet and grasped the rope with both hands thereby taking their own weight, at the same time twisting their right leg once round the rope and edging it over their right foot. The left foot was then placed sole down on the top of the right foot with the rope between and whilst in this locked position they moved their arms one at a time to a higher position and thus by slackening their feet were able to relock their feet in a higher position. Using this method of hands and feet they were quickly brought to the ceiling. After being told, "you see how easy it is," we were invited to try our luck at the rope climbing. Likewise, it did not take me long to master the art of climbing ropes. I jumped and hung on until I had locked my feet in the correct fashion. When the physical training instructor arrived, he said "good, now go higher," and, as I started to move, out came the sand and canvas 'persuader'. Before I had realised it, my head had bumped the ceiling. Again, "see-e-e you can do it," said my tormentor. After three days in the gym, we all seemed to have grown muscles like Tarzan. Our two PO physical training instructors at last decided that we were now in fair enough shape to tackle that 182-foot stick at the edge of the parade ground.

I looked with more interest than usual on that morning as I was about to climb this huge white mast which loomed above the buildings that surrounded it; it had a couple of relic cannons near its base. It was constructed like a mast on a Nelson ship of the line with spreading shrouds and devil's elbows.

At the top of this was a large golden sphere which looked enormous even from 182 feet below. We had been doubled to the parade ground as a class of thirty-odd, but on arrival found we were joining some two hundred or so boys from other classes, who had already started to ascend one side. The sight of all these white-canvas-clad boys clinging to the rigging gave me an awful sinking sensation which I think has lived in the pit of my stomach ever since. When it finally came to my turn to join this constantly moving line of tiny canvas-covered lads clinging for their lives aloft, there was some comfort in the fact that there was a lad above you as well as one below you.

At the bottom of the mast were short railway lines embedded into the ground at an angle of 45 degrees all the way round and stretched across them a net, made of tarred one-inch rope (which, by the way, was as hard as concrete) with a mesh of about one foot square. If a boy ever fell, and should he miss the central platform and survive the actual fall, I would imagine the hardness of the net would kill him or at the very least cut him to pieces. There was an incident that day, one of the boys lost his nerve halfway

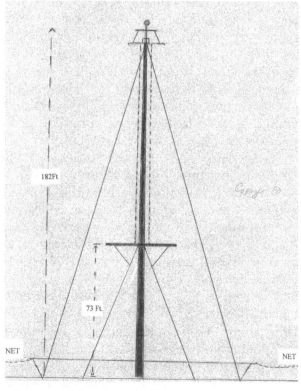

Figure 4. Mast

between the platform and the masthead. The lads following him came to a halt and those in front of him had kept moving, thus producing an ever-increasing gap. "What's up?" shouted the PO. "It's no good, Sir," replied the frightened boy, "I can't go on." "Well," shouted the PO, "then come down." "It's no good, Sir," replied the boy, gripping hard to the shaking Jacob's rope ladder, "I can't come down either." At this point, two physical training instructors swarmed up to the now vacant space and literally pulled him from the swaying ladder and manhandled him to the lower platform where four POs carried him to *terra firma* and all was well. I had found that on our arrival at the upper crows-nest, a PO with a canvas/sand 'persuader' would not let us put our feet on the platform floor but made us go sideways from one ladder to the other side ladder using, as a support for our feet, an outside half-inch iron tube attached to the platform floor. Even at that height he constantly banged the platform base with his 'Stonickee' to prevent our feet touching the platform floor and straying onto the apparently private space.

Time waits for no man and we were fast approaching our last week and the promised monthly run ashore (i.e. Saturday afternoon leave from 1300 to 1800 hours). I had managed to complete my sewing and my kit muster had been 'passed' and had been a reasonable success. By this time we were all beginning to become accustomed to the daily orders and a different lifestyle. We were used to eating our food served up at tables which had been scrubbed almost white by somebody at 0630 hours. We had also become familiar with providing the nicknames for our food such as 'train smash' for sausages and tinned chopped tomatoes, and 'burgoo' for porridge which you could stand your spoon up in and it would stay there! We had to clean our boots so that you could see your face in them. We played football on Saturday forenoons but never cricket. We kept clean and did our laundry, scrubbing the blue dye from our collars which bled it into our three white stripes at the edge. We had marched with and without rifles, had attended church parades either as a Church of England or Roman Catholic, there was no category for 'no-goists'. I suppose we all considered our class had developed into a team and I think everyone thought that they were taller and fitter since they had arrived at *St Vincent*. The wireless news was ominous, it was of Poland, Czechoslovakia and Austria, with Neville Chamberlain and Hitler performing a never-ending square dance and Mussolini winding the gramophone. General Tojo and the Japanese were also committing terrible crimes in the Far East.

The run ashore was well planned. I would be going with my two friends. We had discussed all the details, our pooled finances seemed satisfactory, we could sport two shillings and tenpence. The plan was simple, we would find three nice girls about fifteen years old that would be hanging around, possibly in the shopping centre at Portsmouth, and of course it was agreed that we would sweep them off their feet and take them somewhere (they would know where) for tea and cakes. Two shillings and ten pence would, we felt, be sufficient, especially as the ferry to Portsmouth was free to the Royal Navy and that was it, except for one thing: under no circumstances would any of us take off our hats. It was generally accepted that no self-respecting fifteen-year-old girl would put up with our lack of hair. At last the time arrived, it was a whole month since we had seen civilisation as we had known it. We caught the ferry and arrived in Portsmouth. What we did not know was that Portsmouth on a Saturday afternoon with the fleet in was a town full of 'proper' sailors with money-belts full to the brim looking for girls. The other circumstance that we had also failed to consider was that any self-respecting father in 1939 would not allow his daughter to hang about by herself, be it in a shopping centre or even outside a police station, when the fleet was in. We reconsidered our position and found that if we went into the front row at the local cinema we would have sufficient funds to pay for the entrance fee and have enough loose change to buy three bags of broken biscuits from the nearby grocer.

We found when we came out of the cinema that these broken biscuits, duly despatched, had left us very dry, so three very dry and broke new sailors called into the Salvation Army Hostel where, after singing two hymns, we were given large mugs of tea and a home-made cake. This we agreed was excellent planning as by the time we had arrived back at *St Vincent* we had missed our tea and would not see any more food until 0815 the next morning. At first, we thought the visit to the Salvation Army was a bit of a lark but on our way back to the ship we discussed the fact that their kindness had enabled us to last out until breakfast without going hungry.

The first five weeks on trial came to an end. The class had done well, thirty or so of us had survived the ordeal and this Jack Edwards was now so altered from the innocent young boy of five weeks earlier. This was decision time too for all of us. We were going on seven days' leave and taking with us a buff envelope inside which was the form for permission (waiting for our guardian's signature) which would be necessary for us to continue our careers in the Royal Navy.

The day before we were due to go on leave, Neville Chamberlain declared war on Germany. Somehow all of these momentous happenings were going over my head, the top priority was to ensure Mother signed the permission note. In the circumstances it seemed the sensible thing to do. Those seven days of leave were going to be the chance to show off my new uniform and talk about my experiences in the Royal Navy. It would be the opportunity to blow my own trumpet and do a bit of showing off but in effect the war and events overtook me. Everyone was talking about the so-called 'phoney' war where nothing much had happened to our country except for the occasional sinkings at sea. People had not really seen much difference in their normal lives.

Before I knew it the seven days were up and, apart from Mother's and Auntie's interest, everyone had ignored me. The general opinion at that time was that it would all be over soon, or perhaps this is what the people wanted to think. For me, all I knew was that under no circumstances did I want to be left out of the war. I remember having very mixed feelings about it all. I had developed a strong dislike for Hitler and Mussolini and all they were doing.

I left Mother and Auntie with the feeling that they thought that I had, as they put it, "grown up a lot". The war was only a few days old and most people I met thought I was some sort of Sea Scout. Mother had signed the necessary document for which I was happy. I still knew nothing of Auntie's illness. I blamed myself a lot in later years for being so selfish and failing at the time to notice this fact. Despite all this, a smiling Mother and Auntie gave me a big hug and kiss, then waved me goodbye. I learnt later that both felt that the Navy would not send a boy of sixteen to sea and that by the time I had grown up to the required age the war would be over. I did have time to see my Pitmans friend, Joyce Dyster, for a brief meeting when she promised to write to me, which she did for the duration. Her father, whom I discovered was a pretty decent type of a chap, ran me up to London Bridge railway station in his 1938 Vauxhall car using his precious petrol. His last words to me about the war were: "This war is going to last a long time, look after yourself young fellow."

III

I Go to a Holiday Camp

On arrival back at *St Vincent* I found the class had mustered. There was only one boy missing and the rest had been successful in obtaining their guardians' signatures.

The programme was for us to complete our training in the next five months at *St Vincent* but this was not to be. Whilst we had been on leave, the German radio service had broadcast a statement about *St Vincent* itself. It was given by Lord Haw Haw, an Irishman who did not like a divided Ireland. (I always wondered what his feelings were concerning the Jews, I knew about them when I was fifteen, why didn't he?) This propaganda wireless broadcast came over one morning: "Germany calling, Germany calling – we know all about HMS *St Vincent* training young boys to fight Germany. This establishment will be getting a visit from Hermann Goering's Luftwaffe." These broadcasts seemed to have little effect on my Royal Navy colleagues, or for that matter me, but they did produce whimsical responses such as follows, by an unknown poet:

> Hitler only had one ball
> Goering two, but very small
> Himmler had something similar
> Poor old Goebels had no balls at all.

Whether the above information is correct I know not!

It was barely a week after this broadcast that the class was informed that we were leaving to join another ship and to our great excitement it was 'top secret'. There were always one or two so-called 'lower-deck lawyers' or 'know-alls' who either dreamed up an answer to the unknown or had 'almost' overheard a 'higher rank' say something that could in their minds be relevant to the situation. Such people would spread a buzz or story of their own making which, once started, spread like a forest fire. In this instance the buzz was that, because of the war and the fact that we had finished our preliminary training, the Royal Navy had decided to send us straight to sea without any further training. Oh how wrong it was! There was a doubt as to where we were going but at least this bit was accurate enough!

At 0600 one morning we packed our kitbags and lashed our hammocks. We were issued with two packs of food, one for lunch and one for tea, which indicated a long journey. We were, together with our baggage and food, transferred by smart blue lorries to a collection point in railway sidings where some two hundred of us were loaded up, twelve boys to each compartment. All railway stations and signposts had had place names removed, in case of invasion, to make it difficult for the enemy to find their way about.

The train pulled out from this nameless place at about 1000 hours. We had been up for some time that morning and as there was no supervision in these compartments, the train movement seemed to be the signal to open the lunch food packs and for us hungry boys to devour the contents, which we did before 1030 hours. The journey was full of stops and starts and changes of direction, making it impossible for us to calculate our position or our destination.

By 1400 hours we had long finished our packed tea rations when the train came to a halt to take on water for the engine and give us a chance to unload our water. A PO came to instruct us to descend with a jump (there was no platform) and walk forward to the carriage sporting a WC compartment.

It was a lovely day and people were in their gardens that ran down to the railway tracks. The sight of two hundred boys dressed like sailors jumping out of the train and moving up towards the engine must have raised a question or two in their minds. It was when about ten of us, followed by a watchful PO, were slowly walking back that a middle-aged lady, not able to contain her curiosity, spoke to the smallest and possibly the youngest of us: "Are you Sea Scouts off to your summer camp?" The little lad was obviously very upset. He pulled himself up to his full height and made a statement: "No, lady, we're not Sea Scouts, we're sailors and we're going to war. I'm fifteen years old and too old to be a Scout." After all, this is what we knew to be true. The lady looked confused, she obviously was not taking any notice of this little boy. By this time the PO had arrived, we were all a little bit upset and had all stopped. "Is he," she said, directing her conversation to the PO, "pulling my leg?" "No, madam," said the PO with a smile as he had seen the funny side of it, "they're all fully signed-up boy seamen in the Royal Navy and will be at sea soon." "But," said the woman, "they're so young," and without any warning began to cry. "It's awful," she said. We all became embarrassed, there was a pause.

"I'll get some sweets," she said, and at a fast rate she had gone to her house. At the word 'sweets' we got rid of our embarrassment and stopped dead in our tracks; sweets seemed a good idea.

There was obviously some delay with the train (for what reason none of us knew) and our smiling PO left us to wait for the promised sweets. As good as her word the lady returned with wrapped toffees, but this time she brought back two companions, one of whom interrogated me, asking my age and why my father and mother had allowed this to happen. I muttered something about not having a father and the shortage of money at home, the shilling a week wage and so on. The lady didn't cry, thank goodness, but hurried back to the houses and returned with even more ladies carrying all sorts of goodies: apples, oranges, biscuits and cakes. The lady I spoke to carried a large tin filled with a freshly-baked cake, which she cut into slices with a knife she produced. People kept coming and several lucky boys were given ice-creams. We were there for some time and I imagine every boy succeeded in receiving something. I have often thought of this occasion and, remembering the dialect, have concluded that it must have been somewhere near Chester. When the train finally pulled out, two hundred well-fed boys waved goodbye to these good Samaritans who in their turn waved back.

It was almost dark when a lot of tired boys finally disembarked from the train to embark on an 'unknown' ship, where we all searched for a place amongst its many benches to sleep. The following morning we awoke to find out that we had travelled on a ferry and were about to disembark at Douglas, Isle of Man, before being marched to Cunningham's holiday camp, next door to the caged-up internees' camp in the Isle of Man. In comparison with HMS *St Vincent*, Cunningham's holiday camp was luxury itself, all so different from Gosport. The impressive glass entrance looked like an 1890's Kew Gardens' tall greenhouse with supporting pillars, housing medium-sized palm trees and tropical shrubs. The floor was covered with glazed tiles. This foyer was where the 'campers' would have 'signed in' under a plaque marked 'Palm Court'. The Navy changed all this and called it the 'Quarterdeck', having arranged another entrance complete with sentries and sentry boxes. The only time you would be called to the 'Quarterdeck' would be for 'Commander's Defaulters'.

The impressive ballroom, with its chandeliers and central rotating two-foot-diameter ball covered with different coloured two-inch-square glass mirrors and the lovely wooden floor, was too good for a gym, assembly room or a venue to hold morning prayers. For all the Navy's name changes, it still resembled a holiday camp.

The chalets looked quite nice. They held three black iron single beds and were constructed of a timber frame covered with three-sixteenths of an inch asbestos/cement sheets painted white outside and either blue, pink or green inside. The roofs were also flimsy. Each chalet had a large window overlooking the sea.

A problem arose with the polished red compo floors. The Navy always scrubbed decks using cold water and 'pusser's hard' soap. Once the polish had been scrubbed off it was found that the red compo underneath was soluble in water and could not be dried with our mopping-up cloths. The sight of a lot of boys with red turn-ups to their white duck suits, together with heavily dyed red feet and socks, forced the senior officers reluctantly to come to the conclusion (and to our eternal delight) that scrubbing these red floors had to be abandoned.

We found out that October was the wrong time of the year to start a five-month holiday camp stay, despite the fact that the Isle of Man enjoyed a reputation for having mild winters. Huts constructed from asbestos cement sheets and devoid of any form of heating proved to be very cold.

Whilst on seven-day Christmas leave, I told Mother and Auntie that I had spent two weeks in hospital with tonsillitis during November. Auntie then provided me with a rubber hot water-bottle. This I was able to get filled with very hot water provided by a very nice mumsy lady in the 'galley', not to use in bed but to enable me to dry my wet laundry by wrapping it round the hot water-bottle. This bottle was in great demand also by my two room-mates.

Huts were arranged in groups with fancy names. The Navy altered the names and called them 'divisions', which they named after long-gone admirals.

This large establishment's dining-room was never called the 'mess deck' during my stay, and as an extra bonus it was decided that the floor and tabletops should not be scrubbed. For once in our naval lives we did not have to get up and scrub living quarters and mess decks; this must have caused some POs to have withdrawal symptoms! Unknown to us, this saved time had already been earmarked. It was also apparent that its attractively clothed female kitchen and serving staff (no such species had ever been employed at *St Vincent*) were to remain *in situ*. These ladies had not had the chance to get used to us and still treated us like holiday-makers.

The food was out of this world and, if you were polite and asked for more, nine times out of ten you got it!

Our ablutions were all carried out in one of the many small unheated washrooms where, except in the early morning rush, you could usually find a vacant toilet and a small hand-basin, some with a hot water tap which you used for bathing (not to be recommended in the winter) or for washing clothes.

A nearby school had been commandeered for our use after its pupils had been evacuated to other Isle of Man schools.

Our school days were broken up into three sessions; the forenoon, 0900 to 1230 hours; the afternoon, 1400 to 1700; and evening, 1830 to 2000; a total of eight hours' schooling every weekday. The subjects taught were English, maths, gunnery (including explosives and the very new top-secret radar), and seamanship including navigation. Depending on the weather, sport was held once or twice a week and included boxing, cross-country running, track events, football and gymnastics. This is how all the saved scrubbing time was taken up. This was shattering news for me; I had thought that I had completely escaped school when I left Pitmans and there were exams to come!

Wherever we went, be it church parade, the school, the playing field or the sea-shore to practise boat pulling (rowing) in a twenty-two-foot naval wooden clinker-built cutter with its heavy sixteen-foot wooden oars, we did so by marching or jogging accompanied by a boy seaman with his kettledrum. During these trips we quite often passed the hotels that housed the foreign internee prisoners who stared at us through the external wire cage which surrounded the hotel gardens. Along the seafront.

To make sure that this was no holiday camp, the entire establishment was renamed HMS *St George* and a twenty-foot-high mast was fixed to the side of one end of a chalet and a naval ensign was run up in the morning and lowered in the evening to the sound of a bugle, accompanied by a colour guard of honour carrying rifles and made up of some of the tallest boys available and the shortest PO.

During my time at HMS *St George*, I had five Saturday afternoons' leave ashore. The Isle of Man was a pleasant place and the people were also very pleasant.

As the end of March approached, I had apparently passed all that was necessary and had managed a 'VG' assessment. I do not know how! The class had done well and we were still all together. Our PO instructor informed us, as we were about to leave HMS *St George*, that both the conduct and the ability of the class to pass *all* subjects, including maths (see sample of maths paper), had made this, his first 1939 Isle of Man class, a pleasure to teach.

Although I did not know it at the time, the radar training I received there was going to saddle me with a tremendous responsibility in the near future. Now my class and some two hundred other boys were to be moved on to other things in the next few weeks.

35

E.D. 2689 — 5

EDUCATIONAL TEST I.

MARCH, 1940

Paper II ENGLISH

Time allowed, 1½ hours after completion of Question 1

1.   Dictation.

2.   Write down the plurals of the following nouns:-
     Watch, Knife, Gas, Sheep, Field- mouse, Court Martial.

Write down the singular forms of the following plural nouns:-

     Geese, Brethren, Cannon, Staves, Oases, Men-servants, Oarsmen.

3.   Insert the necessary stops, quotation and punctuation marks, and capitals in the following three passages, keeping all the words in exactly the same order as given :—

     (a) Hark shouted Tom what was that sound
     (b) The house is on fire the people in the street shouted jump
     (c) Every lady in the land
         Has twenty nails on each hand
         Five and twenty on hands and feet
         This is true and no deceit

4.

  NOTE :—*This question should not exceed thirty-four lines(or one page of foolscap) in length. Read over and correct what you have written. Marks will be given for punctuation, common-sense, good arrangement, clearness and accuracy of expression.*

Composition.   Attempt ONE ONLY of the following:-

     (a) Write an account of a country ramble.

     (b) Describe a visit you have paid to any foreign port or land.

     (c) How can we best commemorate the great work done and the sacrifices freely made by all classes of this country in the various wars in which they have served?

     (d) Write an essay on "Broadcasting and its future."

(5087)   H. & S. Ltd.

EDUCATIONAL TEST I.

MARCH, 1940

Paper I (a) ARITHMETIC

Time allowed, 2½ hours

(Write on both sides of the paper. Show all your rough work in the margin of the paper. Unless you make plain the steps by which your answers are obtained, full marks cannot be earned. Answer not more than EIGHT *questions. The questions may be taken in any order , but must be numbered as below (B1,B2 , etc.)*

B1. (a)   Divide the sum of 1⅛ and ⅞ by the difference between 3¼ and 1⅛ .

   (b)   If one pipe would fill a cistern in 2 hours, while another one would fill it in 3 hours , how long would it take to fill the cistern if the two pipes were working together?

B2. (a)   Simplify $\dfrac{3.842 - 2.035}{1.76}$
   answer to be given to two decimal places only.

   (b)   Find the value of 0.25 of £7 8*s*. 4*d*. + 0.3 of £5 0*s*. 10*d*.

B3. A motorist licenced his car for the period 25th March, 1940 to 30th June 1940, and paid £3 8*s*. 9*d*. road tax , £2 12*s*. 0*d*. insurance and £1 5*s*. 3*d*. for petrol, oil and repairs. For this period he was allowed 6 gallons of petrol only. Find
   (a)   cost of running the car per gallon

   (b)   the average cost per mile to the nearest half penny, assuming that the car travelled 30 miles on 1 gallon of petrol.

B4. A rectangular plot of ground 64 feet long and 25 feet wide has a path 2 feet wide running round it. Find the area of this path and the cost of cementing it at 1*s*. 9*d*. per square yard.

(OVER)

Figure 5. Educational Tests

Photo 6. St. George's (at 'present')

Photo 7. St. George's (at 'slope')

In our Isle of Man chalets we were not given any form of verbal orders within the camp; all internal instructions came by bugle:

Figure 6. Bugle music

Daily or weekly newspapers were not available, neither were there wireless sets. We depended entirely on 'bush telegraph'. The news we were getting this way, that April, was all bad. Of course this was totally ignored by young boys with other things on their minds!

Despite all this, and with the very good spring weather, our lifestyle seemed to be improving. It was as if we were attending a private boarding school during sports week. Classes, except for the large classes of radar instruction, had slowed down and either we had got used to it or discipline had eased some! There we were apparently wasting away April with a series of school sports days. Cross-country runs had become competitive. I had usually performed well in these. The track event of 220 yards had always been my favourite and most successful sport; water polo and football I left to the more energetic.

The sports PO instructor had for some time been feeding me propaganda statistics based, so he said, on my ability to move quickly. This, together with my long reach, made me a natural boxer. He had, without consulting me, entered me for the boxing competition.

When that day arrived and I confronted my opponent, a fair-haired, slight lad of medium height, it was a foregone conclusion that I would half kill him, thus establishing a naval boxing career. It did not quite work out like that. The bell rang, I stepped forward, and this slightly-built boy hit me so many times I can't remember. I do know it hurt a lot, my nose was bleeding badly and I lost. "You'll never make a boxer as long as you live," said the PO instructor as he attempted to stop my nose bleeding. My opponent progressed into the next round, where he met a more experienced boy and had seven bells knocked out of him. The result was I concluded that boxing careers should be kept very short.

Up till now we had almost ignored the news about the war. We were young and had other equally important things to think about and in any case we knew we were going to win this war; there were no ifs or buts.

The end of April 1940 found some two hundred of us filing patiently onto the Isle of Man ferry, each on his way to a different unknown destination. My new group consisted of some forty boys, of which only three had been in my original class. Our group's destination turned out to be Chatham Naval Barracks, HMS Pembroke, known as the stone frigate *Pembroke V*.

There was no way of ignoring the news here, everything was happening. Parliament was in turmoil and we had a new prime minister called Churchill. HM the King had made a BBC broadcast, and our Army in France and Belgium was in serious trouble, as indeed were these countries themselves. I remember Sir Oswald Mosley had been arrested. Things couldn't have looked worse. I expected to be sent somewhere to help save the Empire but instead I was surprised to be given a travelling warrant and sent on fourteen days' leave.

I found both Mother and Auntie to be very worried over the state of the war and listening to every BBC bulletin, but they were very pleased to see me. With the wireless constantly on, I had a 'ringside seat' to the events leading up to the final Dunkirk evacuation. Everyone I spoke to had that 'we've got our backs to the wall at the moment, but that won't last, we'll win in the end' feeling. My school friend's father who had joined the Local Defence Volunteers (the forerunner of the Home Guard) had been issued with a pistol and was talking about shooting his wife and daughter if the Germans came to London. At this time Belgium had surrendered, but he of course would fight to the death.

I found Mother and Auntie's attitude funny. They had always been worried in the past about my safety and the dangers of going to sea in a war, now they felt that a boy safely housed in an armour-plated battleship had got to be in a better environment than all the civilians would be, living with air raids and a possible invasion. Despite all these harrowing and tumultuous times, Mother still had the normal family feelings, she remembered my *St Vincent* sensitive-skin problem and presented me with a large cake of Pears' Golden Glory see-through soap as a going away present as my leave came to an end. Golden Glory soap saved more than my skin!

On arrival back at Chatham railway station, where sailors outnumbered civilian passengers, I asked a fellow matelot where the Gents was. "Just outside, you'll see there's a man pointing," he said. Sure enough there was a large bronze statue, I think of William Cobbett, with his back towards the station with his arm outstretched pointing to a small building marked 'Gentlemen'. William Cobbett tried to join the Royal Marines in 1784 but ended up becoming a soldier earning sixpence a day (a lot more in real terms than I was earning). Sailors always said this statue was erected by the good people of Chatham for the convenience of troubled sailors who had to contend with 366 pubs, one for every day of the year and a spare.

I returned to *Pembroke V*, just in time to be sent on to Dover as the soldiers were evacuating Dunkirk.

IV

Sent to Borstal

Pembroke V, although large, was a crowded place in May 1940 and I kept getting lost. There were a lot of boys in our barrack block, all awaiting a draft to either a ship or shore establishment. It was our duty to report to the drafting section every morning to see if our names were chalked up on a huge blackboard in this factory-like building. It was a chore, a bit like tracing a train time and platform number on Waterloo railway station's mechanical timetable. If you were not mentioned then you returned to your barrack block where you joined a working party or were sent 'square bashing' as you might have done in 1920, not 1940.

Dunkirk did some good in that it gave us some freedom from the binding forces of useless traditions that wasted so much time. On my first morning back from the Draft Office I, with five other boys, was ordered to report, armed with our oilskins, to our duty leading seaman or 'killick' as they were nicknamed. This killick was 'old', possibly as much as forty-five. He had obviously been called back whilst still in the Royal Naval Reserve. His uniform looked threadbare, with its red leading seaman's hook and three good-conduct badges. This killick was not happy. We were whisked off in a tatty blue unpolished lorry to a nearby gunnery school in Gillingham called St Mary's Barracks. To our surprise (and our killick's), on arriving at St Mary's we were issued with a highly-polished brass and metal 1914–18 Maxim machine-gun and nine single rounds of very clean ammunition for which they made the killick sign. This gun had been used as a training aid and had probably been taken apart and reassembled by hundreds of gunnery training recruits. We were impressed. Were we going to fire this shiny brass monster? It was all very exciting. Our killick however was not impressed. "It's old," he said, "it's been taken to pieces so many times it might have pieces missing or there may even be bent bits, perhaps there are wrong parts. Does it work? Only nine rounds?" he asked

42

the young newly-joined 'Wavy Navy' officer as he signed the chit. We were witnessing an old naval salt at his best. He said "never, never volunteer". He did not want us to do any of it.

At this point the sub-lieutenant gunnery officer, complete with his new shiny black gaiters, handed over what appeared to be a circular breadboard screwed onto a large broom handle, making him look like a Chinese acrobat balancing a plate on a stick. The 'breadboard' was marked up with the cardinal points of the compass. "It is intended that your leading seaman will fire the gun," ordered the subby, "two of your boy seamen will assist with the loading and carrying the ammunition whilst two others will man the compass-bearing instrument and call out enemy aircraft positions and complete the log." A small notebook and pencil was passed over to our bemused killick. "Finally," said the subby, "you'll need the other boy seaman as a messenger." With that he handed one of the boys an enemy aircraft silhouette chart. Who had thought this up for us?

At this point our killick organised the loading of these items and us into the lorry and, after saluting the subby, climbed up with the driver and off we went.

It took nearly two and a half hours to get to the outskirts of Dover, to a hill where the killick had been ordered to report. The killick's face showed his concern. Dover now had a reputation synonymous with Dunkirk; we could see lots of small craft heaped up in the harbour. We could hear the noise of bombs and gunfire from France. The lorry had stopped on a grass-covered hill overlooking the harbour and sea. We did not see any soldiers in the town, nor any aircraft (ours or theirs). It all looked a peaceful beautiful afternoon. We unloaded the gun and all the ancillary equipment. The lorry driver drove off the road and switched off his engine, rolled a cigarette, and lit up as if to say all this is nothing to do with me. Our killick decided to give us a lecture on the art of survival. He was not sure, he explained, why we six had been picked for this foolhardy venture, or indeed what we were here for. "This thing looks to me as if it was designed to fit aboard one of them small craft," he said, as he glanced towards the harbour. We sensed that he expected to be sent over the Channel somewhere. "But," he said, "I would make it quite clear that I am in charge and as the senior rating I will do *all* the talking necessary with officers and others, you are not to say anything to anybody, and under no circumstances are you to volunteer for anything be it word, thought or deed that might end up with us six going to France. Do I make it clear?" "Yes, Killick," we all murmured. "Good," said our leader, "now settle down and wait for the officer." But there was no officer and as the time wore on we six boys became hungry. At about

1800 hours one of the boys asked: "When do we eat, Killick?" By now all minds were concentrating on food, even the killick's; we had not had any lunch. This was our leader's plan: the lorry driver would take his lorry into Dover and bring back fish and chips. There would be a kitty, we would all put our share of money in a hat. It was at this point that the killick found himself between a rock and a hard place: who in the annals of naval history had ever heard of a boy seaman second class having any money in his pocket for fish and chips or indeed for anything? We just stared at him. He sighed and gave the driver a one-pound note. "I want a receipt," he said. "What are they going to drink?" asked the driver. Another sigh. "Get them a couple of bottles of Tizer and a bottle of beer for me. You get your own vitals and charge them to your department."

After eating the greasy fish and chips, washed down by a shared bottle of fizzy Tizer (which I had never drunk before), I found I had difficulty ignoring my rumbling tummy and getting to sleep wrapped in my oilskin coat, under the lorry with five other fidgeting boys. The killick and the driver had made themselves comfortable in the driver's cab. The warm night air was also disturbed by aircraft noises. When I awoke the next day I became aware that both my boots were off and one of my socks was missing. Whether I had removed them in the night I could not recall, perhaps the boys had been skylarking because I had slept late, this was a possibility. Search as I might I could not find my sock.

At this point an elderly proper two-ringed officer turned up, possibly also recalled from retirement. All I could hear from his conversation with our killick was that there was no more ammunition available in that calibre, sandbags were short and the gun pit wanted a concrete centre. I heard a "yes, sir" from a cheerful-faced killick and finally the officer told him "get them some breakfast on the way". "Sir," repeated the killick with a smart salute. "Get yourselves and the gear aboard," said our smiling leader as the two-ringer walked away. "I'm not going to have to build a sandbagged gun pit with a concrete floor to become a sitting target for the first marauding Messerschmitt that comes this way, neither am I going to have to wet-nurse you lot on a small boat." "I've lost my sock," I said. "Put your boot on and get yourself a new pair when we get back to *Pembroke V*. Now get a move on," snarled the killick. The driver knew where to go; it was to a café on the way back. It was a breakfast I will never forget: sausages, bacon, eggs, tomatoes and fried bread with lots of warm tea, all devoured well before eight in the morning, served by a smiling, mumsy lady.

We did go back to *Pembroke V* but not to get a new pair of socks, there was no time. I collected my kit, said goodbye to my five new friends and the killick, who I never saw again. I joined the forty-odd new boys with whom I had left the Isle of Man at the gate of *Pembroke V*. Two lorries transferred our kits and us to Maidstone Borstal Institute, which I entered still minus one sock.

With my upbringing it was quite a shock to arrive at this institution and to be shown to my very own cell, in a corridor of cells. This cell, which I think had a number 5 on its iron door, was small with one sturdy single bed. Although the window did not have bars it did have that 'you can't get out of here' look. The heavy door with its iron rivets had a four-inch-diameter 'peep hole', the cover of which could be lifted from the outside by anyone wishing to look in, including our bugle boy who enjoyed this exercise by lifting it up and blowing his bugle through it, and almost deafening us. The two things that stick in my memory concerning this cell were the shaped pillow made of hard wood and that everything except this wooden pillow was painted battleship grey; it most certainly had that grey look. It would have given both Mother and Auntie an awful shock to know that their boy was sleeping in a cell all by himself in a Borstal Institution so I never told them, not even after the war.

To accommodate the Navy, this remand home had been divided into two separate sections by the installation of a high chain-link type of fence. As well as having been allocated cells at ground level for our sleeping quarters, the Navy had also gained what was called the 'parade ground'. The Borstal inmates and staff occupied the second and, I believe, third floors of the buildings, all of which had balconies which enabled all and sundry the opportunity of a ringside seat to all our activities. It was easy to see which boy was which: we were dressed in white duck suits whilst the Borstal lads wore khaki shirts, shorts and knee-high socks. The only shared bit of the real estate was the bathroom which the Royal Navy used pm whilst the khaki boys used it am.

As we 'fell in' on the parade ground the next morning, prior to commencing rifle drill, we were all aware of being watched by the inmates. They gave no call, whistles or shouts, in fact the whole time we were there they were completely silent, they just stood and watched, awestruck, they did not even talk to one another. It was as if they were alien khaki people from another planet.

Having, during that hot summer period, spent four days moving in and out of *Pembroke V* together with a night sleeping out on the Dover Heights, plus a night in the Borstal cell, I became the first bath customer that afternoon. The entrance to the bathroom was close to my cell so, immediately after lunch, wrapped only in my towel and carrying Mother's Pears' Golden Glory soap, I walked into the bathroom to find myself confronted by a middle-aged man dressed in naval stoker's overalls standing by the end wall. The wall was covered with brass-handled gate valves controlling the hot and cold water through a series of surface run overhead pipes to possibly twelve baths fitted in rows of three, giving the appearance, with their pipes hooked to the ceiling, as if at any moment they would drive off like dodgems at the local funfair.

"How," I asked, "do you fill them up?" "Pick a bath," he said, "and I'll fill it up from here." Being awkward, I said "I'll have the one in the middle". The stoker turned the necessary gate valves on and this bath began to fill. By the time I had got to the bath it had about six inches of water in it. "OK," I called and the water stopped. Taking off my towel and hanging it on a vertical pipe with a knot, I placed one foot in the bath to test the temperature. Finding it OK, and with Mother's Pears' soap in my right hand, I was about to put my other foot in when I noticed that the stoker was moving towards me purposefully. Somehow or other I knew he was not coming over for a chat. I was also very much aware that I was at a great disadvantage, standing there with one foot in the bath and one out, totally in the nude. The stoker's face had a look of "I'm not going to do you any good". I was amazed at my instant reaction, as soon as his hand touched my arm I lashed out with my bar of special soap. I missed his jaw but hit him in the throat, whereupon he gave a gasp and let go of my arm, thus giving me the opportunity to run for the door, which I did without worrying to collect my towel; but I had not noticed that he had previously locked the door. I did not hesitate and ran to one of the high open windows. I could not reach it but I found a stool and was about to make my escape when he was there with an even worse mean look on his face. In desperation, using my bar of Golden Glory soap like a stone-age man might have used a large oblong stone, I aimed a blow as hard as I could at his jaw. Again I missed but this time hit his nose. There was blood everywhere. I was able to take advantage of this injury to get through the window. It wasn't until I was outside the window that the reality of my position became clear: there I was, stark naked and standing outside on the window-sill contemplating a six-foot drop onto a shingle path with bare feet, and in full view of our khaki neighbours standing on their upper balconies. Having no other option I jumped, fear will make you do these sort of things. I broke my fall by landing on both feet and hands and, with a very red face and sore feet, ran the necessary seventy-odd yards to my cell, very much aware of all those eyes watching me.

After washing my feet and hands and the oaf's blood off me in a bucket of cold water and drying myself on my underclothes (I had lost my towel forever), I was determined never to enter that bathroom again and made it my business to warn all my immediate naval colleagues of the possible hazards of bathing.

It took something like a year for me to lose the nickname of 'Golden Glory boy' but never again was I assaulted thus, being fair-haired I suppose it was quite a good nickname. I read with interest the advert on the soap's wrapper which stated repeatedly the merits of Pears' soap's purity!

I never found out whether the stoker was part of the Borstal's staff or an on-loan Royal Navy rating. If he was the Borstal's, perhaps some of those boys watching my dash for freedom had suffered similar misery.

The next day I 'fell in' for rifle drill dressed in white ducks but still with only one sock. This was noticed by the PO who ordered me to "go back to your cell and put your other sock on, idiot". I tried to explain why I had only one sock, to which he replied: "Do as I say, put your other sock on," to which I replied that I couldn't. He then retorted: "Don't argue with me, take half an hours' jankers tonight." So there I was, trolling round the parade ground supporting eighteen pounds of Lee Enfield rifle held at arm's length above my head with a fourteen-pound pack, belt and twenty-one-inch bayonet, kept at a steady run by another PO and watched all the time by the khaki fellows. They must have thought it was better to be a 'Borstal boy' than a 'Navy boy'!

Whilst eating my evening meal, I and most of the other boys saw the bathroom stoker, whose nose looked puffy and awful with both nostrils filled with plugs of rolled bandage. It did a lot for my reputation as a tough boy – nobody ever picked a fight with me – but I realised I had made a dreadful enemy and spent some time securing my cell door with string before dropping off into a nervous sleep. The following day was a carbon copy of the previous one, which again ended in half an hour of jankers, this time overseen by the first PO. Despite changing the sock to the other foot I ended up with very sore feet. This sock episode meant that I was more worried about its loss and my sore feet than about the events we were hearing about in Dunkirk.

It was to my great joy and relief that the very next day I was drafted back to *Pembroke V* with a small group of ex-*St George*'s boys (which was possibly due to our radar training). It also meant that I could buy myself a pair of socks or two and a new towel!

I could not help wondering if the two POs and the bathroom stoker (if he was Royal Navy) were all old pals who were set on taking revenge on an upstart boy, or whether the two parade POs were dyed-in-the-wool *St Vincent*-type instructors who were not bright enough to realise that 'slops' (clothes replacements) were not available at Borstal and had punished me for not obeying orders.

Photo 8. The first paybook photograph at the age of sixteen

V

A Brand-New Ship

Pembroke V was full to bursting. There were new entrants who had been called up, naval reservists who had been clawed back (some over forty years of age). There were survivors from lost and damaged convoy escorts, from sunk and damaged Norwegian campaign ships and, of course, from the two hundred-odd Dunkirk shipping casualties.

It is true to say in all this hurly-burly one half hardly knew what the other half was up to. If you could have found an empty cupboard and put a typewriter in it you could have started your own department. The lads already established in the barracks before we arrived advised us to do nothing except check every day for a possible 'draft' to a ship or another establishment. Their recommendation was at all times to wear our gym shoes minus the green gaiters. If we were stopped whilst aimlessly wandering from one point to another and asked what we were doing we should immediately come to a halt, shout "Sir", and then state, "excused boots, Sir", indicating that we were under some medical treatment laid down by a doctor who had relieved us from everyday duties; there were a lot of survivors legally doing just that. I remember at the time feeling very guilty pursuing this path.

This temporary Dunkirk state of affairs did not last long but long enough to benefit me for the next four days until I received my draft to a ship. It did however give me the opportunity to 'go ashore' for those four evenings from 1630 hours to 0800 the next day. Nobody in charge seemed to care whether you were man or boy. The problem was I did not have sufficient money for the necessary fares from Chatham to Winchmore Hill.

This first night's freedom found a group of four boys walking calmly through the main gate past the sentries to a nearby pub. There were supposed to have been 366 pubs available in those days. Although without funds to buy beer, the sounds of singing accompanied by someone strumming on a piano gave us courage to enter and join the jolly (half inebriated) 'Jack Tars'. It was here whilst in general conversation with them that we were educated in the arts of free travel, by bus, train and underground ('the tube' as it was known). We were advised to contact a certain AB (able seaman) who, whilst working in the *Pembroke V* printing section, ran a successful railway ticket forging service and who for six old pence would supply a green monthly return ticket from Chatham railway station to anywhere in the British Isles, date-stamped for whatever month you required. Such a ticket, complete with the Railway's terms and conditions on the back, was an exact copy of the real thing. If you were unable to produce the sixpence fee, then a 'sip' of your daily rum issue would suffice. Perhaps I should explain that the daily issue of 'grog' consisted of one-third neat rum mixed, in front of an officer, with two-thirds water, which nearly filled the average mug and which became as flat as a pancake if not drunk immediately. POs and above drew the same amount of neat rum but without the added water, therefore this could be stored in a bottle and drunk whenever desired.

Boy seamen on the other hand were not allowed hard liquor but were supposed to get the same quantity of lime juice which had no currency value at all. On arrival at your eighteenth birthday, if you opted not to draw your rum you were paid an extra three old pennies a day, almost the same as two weeks of boy's allowance. Lime juice was hard to get, in fact I only got it once. It was too much fiddling about for the store PO to issue it from his stores, if he had troubled to order it in the first place. If it was only half the value of rum based on the extra thru'pence a day, I reckon the Navy owes me at least a 1940-value ten-pound note for not issuing it. Two of the excuses were that it was too cold in the Arctic and that there was not any scurvy. To give a fellow shipmate 'sippers' was to hand him your cup and shout "that's enough". I have watched chaps tilt their cup, mark it with a pencil and hold it level as if they were watching a spirit level; how much the lucky or unlucky fellow got depended on his ability to suck. To offer a fellow seaman 'gulpers' would be bordering on the extreme; such an offer could leave your cup of 'two and one' half empty.

Our railway ticket instructor explained it was important not to get the monthly ticket clipped. It was purely carried as insurance should the ticket checker get on the train. We would have bought (if possible) a cheap workman's ticket from Chatham to Rochester or London Bridge to Woolwich, hopefully as ticket checkers were rare on moving trains you did the bit in between for nothing. On arrival in Chatham at that early time in the morning, and possibly without a workman's ticket, the thing to do was to collect together in as big a crowd as possible and all run past the ticket collector, throwing a sixpence piece and calling out that you had lost your ticket. This crowd-and-sixpence routine was always recommended for dealing with the tube. The aim, on the Chatham double-decker bus, was to overcrowd it, move about up and down, ring the bell and so on. That way, hopefully, nobody ever paid the penny fare. "I always carry," he said, "a piece of official-looking paper with 'Royal Navy' on it, be it a shop chit for clothing issued, a redundant daily order, instructions, or an old disused travel warrant (discretely folded), and say 'travel warrant', flashing it quickly if I am ever asked."

It struck all four of us after this lecture on law-breaking and anti-social behaviour towards bus conductors and the like that, even if we had trod this path to get transported to London, we still needed some ready cash for cheap-day tickets and our weekly shilling had already burnt a considerable hole in our pocket. None of us was entitled to draw grog. We were also uncertain if the information given was accurate. In the end, being I hope sensible boys, we decided to try to scrounge a warrant when we were being interviewed by the draft officer the next morning. The draft officer was an old boy, called back for the war, he looked at our young faces: "So you want to go home to see your mothers," he said, "why not?" and to our great delight issued us with a travel warrant each. He said to me with a nod and a wink as he issued mine "Don't hand it in." "No, Sir," I replied although I did not know what he meant, perhaps Dunkirk had softened his attitude to free travel. That afternoon, with lots of other sailors, we caught the 1645 hours fast train from Chatham to London on the old Southern Railway. We sat in the carriage, read and reread the travel warrant until one of us said: "Mine isn't dated, I can use it over and over again." We were all surprised and delighted to find that all four were undated and proceeded to do a war dance in the carriage.

At London Bridge we observed a crowd of Chatham matelots just in front of the ticket barrier and at a shouted order from someone they rushed through the barrier like children bursting out of school at four o'clock. As the last matelots disappeared into the main station we approached with our legal warrants to find the policeman and ticket collectors were wreathed in smiles; they had obviously seen it all as a huge joke. What were they going to do to a poor sailor only days away from joining a ship and all its dangers? Here he was, short of money and without a ticket, would they arrest him and take him before a magistrate so that he might miss his ship? Some of those sailors might have liked that. At that particular time the next train from Kent could have been full of Germans. What a stupid lot we British are at times!

Sitting in the 'tube' I observed several soldiers who looked totally exhausted. One had his sleeve cut away exposing a wound which had one stitch in it and no dressing. One soldier asked the lady sitting next to him to wake him when the train reached Wood Green. The other passengers were looking at these soldiers in a strange way and nobody tried to speak with them.

On leaving Wood Green tube station, I boarded a waiting trolley bus for Winchmore Hill. When the conductor approached, for what I took to be a request for me to purchase a ticket, I showed him my travel warrant, upon which, in a very loud voice so that all the downstairs passengers could hear, he good-naturedly asked how old I was. Embarrassed, I told him. "How long have you been in the Navy?" "Nine months," I said. "Could you stop at the Capitol Cinema stop, please?" "Where do you live?" he asked. "Elm Park Road," I answered. "For a boy of your age who has been in the Navy for nine months, this bus will take you to your mother's front door even if I have to take the hook off the overhead electric cable and run on the batteries." At this stage all the passengers clapped. "It's only five houses down," I said, terribly embarrassed. Good as his word, he stopped at Elm Park Road where he shook my hand whilst saying "we all wish you good luck", to which there was a chorus of "good luck and come home soon" from the passengers.

The following morning at eight the returning train, loaded with sleepy matelots, arrived back at Chatham station where I joined the queue of sailors passing a policeman on my left who held his helmet upside-down, full to the brim of silver sixpences, and the ticket collector on my right with his hat equally full to the brim with 'tanners'. For my sins I threw in my own sixpence, having made sure my undated travel warrant was safely buttoned up in my Naval-issue money-belt for use the next day.

Although I had been successfully getting home to see Mother and Auntie with my undated travel warrant for three nights running, this way of life was always under threat with the arrival of a Draft Notice or an air raid which were fast becoming a way of life.

Pembroke V was always a possible target as it was so close to the docks. The thing to do was to get clear of the barracks as early as possible. Once you were cleared and had passed the gate sentry, the world was your oyster and with luck you would get to Winchmore Hill. The bombing troubles of London were yet to come. Air raid warnings arrived in three colours, if my memory serves me correctly: 'yellow' indicating it might happen; 'red' stating it was overhead; and 'green' if it was all over. Most of the 'yellow' warnings never developed into a 'red' and could stay at that level of warning for hours before a 'green' was issued. Whilst a 'yellow' state was in being all leave was cancelled until a 'green' arrived, when *Pembroke V* members could vacate the air raid shelters.

All this paled into insignificance when on the fourth day, Edwards J.A. CJX163760 appeared on the Draft Board to report that afternoon to the medical unit attached to the Draft Section. I had been incredibly lucky to have managed these three extra nights at home and to have had a couple of hours of Joyce Dyster's company, when she once again promised to write. I cannot remember her kissing me goodbye but perhaps she did.

I had no idea where I was off to, other than it necessitated a trip to the doctor and yet another 'small-arms inspection' as we now called it, and my first lot of jabs. There we were, dressed only in our underpants, lined up in a queue for the numerous jabs we were to be given when I noticed on the back of the beefy fellow in front of me numerous deep scars which looked as if they had healed with charcoal in them. During the conversation I had with this man, whilst getting ever nearer to the doctor carrying out the injections, I learnt that he had been a miner and had received these cuts whilst dragging himself through narrow openings dressed only in shorts and vest in a stuffy hot mine shaft. He arrived in front of the doctor and put out his arm but before the doctor could inject him the ex-miner simply collapsed to the floor in a dead faint. Although I did not know it at the time, this man was to become one of my mess mates who was to show great courage later. As they carried him away the doctor deposited all his armed needles into both my arms. I was going to end up resembling a pincushion, although I did not know it at the time. I was passed fit and issued with the necessary travel warrant, pukka this time, which read 'South Shields'.

I was up early the next morning with two very swollen and painful arms. I packed my kitbag and hammock and after breakfast fell in on the parade ground with a group of complete strangers of all ages. The injections had left me feeling lousy and it was painful loading my hammock and kitbag onto the lorry at *Pembroke V* and off again at Chatham station. I was not sorry to be leaving *Pembroke V*.

After what seemed a very long train journey via London, we arrived in Newcastle where nice Salvation Army ladies served us tea and buns (no packed lunches on this trip) and, although it wasn't much, we were expected to pay for our tea. We caught a further train that deposited us on the station platform at South Shields. There was a reception committee awaiting us, as we left the train, after we loaded our kit onto yet another dark blue lorry. We were formed up and marched through South Shields and through some sort of tunnel down to the docks.

We then came to a halt beside this great, grey, brand-spanking-new cruiser.

HMS *Nigeria* was built by Vickers Armstrong (Tyne Yard), laid down 8th February 1938, launched 18th July 1939, completed 23rd September 1940. Range 10,200 miles at 12 knots, 1,700 tons fuel oil. Engines: 4 shaft Parsons geared turbines, 4 Admiralty 3-drum boilers, 72,500shp. Maximum speed 31.5 knots, length 555 ft (OA) and beam 62 ft. She weighed ten thousand tons, with eight four-inch and twelve six-inch guns. 8500 Tons

Her masts were fitted with radar aerials which, despite our intensive training, we had never seen before. This ship was probably the most up-to-date the Navy had in commission at that time. In fact it was probably more up-to-date than any other naval ship for its size throughout the world. No other country was as advanced as we were with *our* invention known as 'radar'.

Words are hard to find to describe my boyish feelings as I surveyed this gleaming giant. It looked so big, pride welled up in me. I also felt very nervous as I climbed the gangplank; this was the real thing. I was indeed cutting the bonds which had held me in the safe Mother/Auntie environment for the first fifteen years of my life.

No sooner had I arrived on the quarterdeck than the chief PO shouted: "Salute the flag, state name and number." Having followed his instructions, I was handed a slip of paper. "Your mess and locker number," howled the chief PO. "Where is it?" I asked. "Odd numbers to starboard (right), even numbers to port (left)," replied the frustrated chief PO. My first shipboard seamanship lesson, I suddenly felt I really was going to sea at last. "Find it," he said, "and stow your hammock and gear." "Yes, Sir," I replied. "Don't call me Sir," he growled, "I'm a chief." I quickly learnt that a mess was really a table consisting of a three-foot-wide by twelve-foot-long construction with a soft wood top about two inches thick, hinged to the ship's side at one end and supported by two tubular legs at the other. The legs could be folded up to enable the table to be hooked onto the deck-head (ceiling), thereby making space for scrubbing the deck beneath, a daily chore. Each mess table came complete with long benches with sufficient seating capacity for six seamen on each bench.

I found my mess number thirteen on the starboard side of 'B' Turret's trunk, which also supported the storage nettings for hammocks. Being the first arrival, I was pleased to relieve my aching arms of my heavy hammock. Taking advantage of this quiet moment and the absence of other members, I quickly unpacked my gear and stowed it as tidily as I could in the aluminium locker provided. These lockers were about two feet wide, two feet six inches high and possibly ten inches deep. Although they were fitted with a sturdy latch there was no way of locking them. Locks and keys were never provided and deemed unnecessary, as the Navy would not tolerate thieves.

This area, which supported three such mess tables together with the necessary stools and lockers, was approximately twenty-five feet long by twenty feet wide and was known as the mess deck. Each mess table was positioned by a porthole (not standard throughout the ship) and contained 'air conditioning' supplied by a six-inch-wide square duct with five 'punkah louvre' outlets (see Figure 8). These messes were numbered 9, 11 and 13. It was obvious that with thirty men in such a small space it was going to be crowded. There were some thirty-five messes in the forward part of the ship housing some five hundred seamen, marines and stokers. When added to the complement of officers living in the aft section, it brought the ship's company up to some eight hundred souls.

I did not have to wait long before the expected thirty-odd fellow passengers turned up. The mess deck became suddenly very noisy and claustrophobic. The fact that they were all total strangers did not stop them from exchanging greetings, asking probing questions and settling down comfortably with one another. It was not long before somebody with naval experience had collected the boiling water in a mess kettle (a very large aluminium teapot) from the galley and made the tea.

It didn't take a genius to recognise that the only other young person in this crowd of apparent grown-ups was a fellow boy seaman. It was also to our mutual satisfaction when we realised we were both members of 13 Mess and at that time we were not intimidated by the number 13, but then boys wouldn't be would they?

There was a boys' mess deck but this was only capable of accommodating up to fifteen boys with a resident discipline PO. However, seventeen boys had been drafted to the ship. They came from several different establishments, all of which had given these lads a first-class training over an eight-month period, whilst the 'hostilities only' call-ups had received a bare six weeks' training. Each one of the boys was to be greeted with open arms by the heads of departments. The two of us who had escaped the boys' mess deck and its PO were to realise later how lucky we had been! All sixteen of these boys were complete strangers to me. The nine participants joining 13 Mess is shown in Table 1.

A brief history of the mess members may help readers to understand how 13 Mess members almost became a type of family in the next two years and how, after a while, the mess seemed to have a 'welcome home' feeling when you came down off watch instead of just a place to eat and sleep.

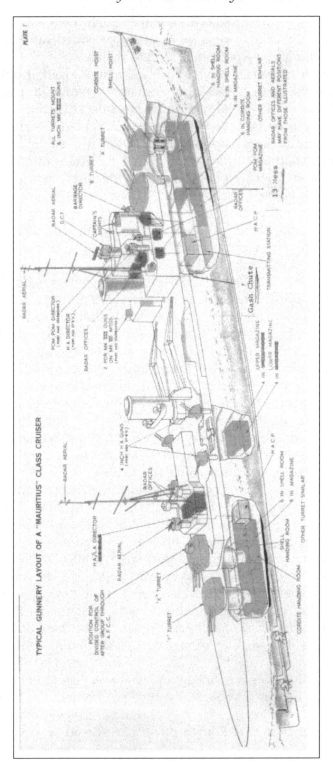

Figure 7. Gunnery layout

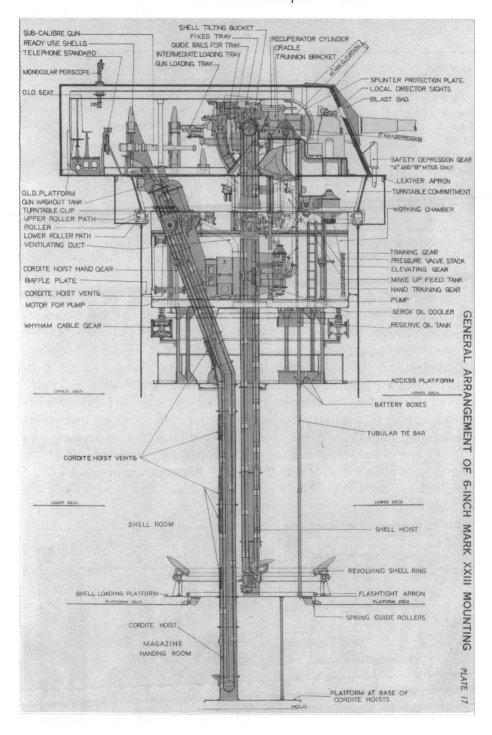

Figure 7a. General arrangement of 6-inch Mark XXIII Mounting

TABLE 1

Nickname	Rating	Age	Qualifications	
Stripey	AB	47	Three good conduct stripes	RN Career
Raggie	AB	35	Two good conduct stripes	RN Career
Tom	AB	32	Two good conduct stripes	RN Career
Sharky	O/S	19	Nil	RN Career
Smithie	O/S	25		HO
Tammy	O/S	32	Asdic Opp.	HO
Forty-Niner	O/S	26		HO
JTB	Boy	17	Nil	
Cutts	Boy	17	Nil	

AB	= Able seaman	HO	= Hostilities only
O/S	= Ordinary seaman	Asdic	= Underwater sonar operator

Stripey had been picked, because of his seniority, to be the member in charge of the mess by the PO in charge of all the seamen's accommodation. This well-built bearded macho PO (who was known as the 'mess deck dodger') was responsible for mess deck discipline, cleanliness and tidiness, which he applied harshly and as a result he was nobody's friend. If during his rounds he found a mess unkempt, with personal items and clothes not stowed away, he had the authority to fine a mess individual a tanner per item or the mess as a whole by confiscating the offending article and only returning it in exchange for a whole bar of pusser's washing soap, which the guilty individual had to purchase from the 'slops' at the cost of sixpence (an amount I could ill afford to give away). Also he had the authority to send individuals

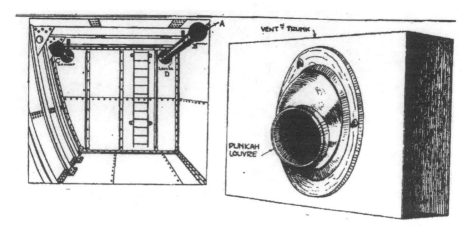

Figure 8. Fresh air outlet in 13 Mess

or the entire mess to attend Commander's Defaulters – loose clothing could cause a problem if it floated off a wet floor and went down and blocked the suction pumps.

Stripey was forty-seven years old, having retired at forty-two. He then became a member of the Royal Fleet Reserve. I suspect he had volunteered to come back, despite the fact that he limped badly. During his twenty-four years' service he had been more interested in sport than promotion and I gathered that he had played rugby for the Navy and was a fair hand at water polo. Some time during his sporting years he had injured his left knee badly and now at forty-seven arthritis had caught up with him. There were times when he was obviously having trouble with his knee but this did not prevent him from doing 'his duty' as they said, and as far as I knew he never went on sick parade with it. Stripey was a cheerful chap, an experienced seaman and well liked by everyone who knew him. He took his mess duties seriously and made certain that everyone enjoyed their rights and obeyed all the rules. He was a surrogate grandfather to us all and never complained about his knee during the roughest of seas or despite the intense cold.

Raggie was short and plump, with a swarthy complexion and a badly pock-marked face which he tried to camouflage with a bushy dark beard. I suppose he collected his quaint nickname because of his 'bundle of rags' appearance. He was also an experienced seaman who always accepted what came. I found him kind and considerate and he had the virtue of minding his own business at all times. He also called everyone Raggie; perhaps this was a regional expression.

The third experienced long-term AB was Tom. He had joined the pre-war 'China Fleet' in 1933/34 (a year after the first aborted Japanese Shanghai landings). His ship had been based mostly at Shanghai and the adjacent coastal waters, the ship finally leaving for Blighty after visiting Hong Kong following the second Japanese landing in late 1937. It was almost a year before Tom told me of his China 'sorrow'. In 1934, whilst visiting the local Shanghai Methodist Church, he had met a very pretty mixed-race Chinese girl who had an English father and a Chinese mother. By the following year Tom had asked this bilingual girl to marry him. After discussing the matter with the ship's padre he applied for seven days' compassionate leave to get married and this was turned down on the grounds of the unsettled situation on the China Station at that time. It was also pointed out that Great Britain could not be responsible for foreign nationals. The unknown whereabouts of the girl's father did not help the situation. The padre advised him against marrying 'unofficially' through the Shore Church Societies (he could be drafted home straightaway and might never get back to China again) and, under naval rules, it would not be possible for him to arrange for a naval marriage allowance. Further advice given by the padre was, as he said, to see the girl as much as possible and set up a flat and return after his service time had expired, when he would be forty years old. By this time it was thought the Japanese problem would be over and he would have saved sufficient funds for the shipping fare back to China and the return fares after having married the girl in Shanghai. They spent two happy years together before the Japs returned to Shanghai and Tom returned to England, leaving the girl and her mother in China. It was the unknown that worried Tom plus the terrible stories that were being reported on the radio and in the newspapers. None of the mess members asked him all the obvious questions such as, what was her name, what had happened to her father and, was she pregnant? Despite all this, he carried out his naval duties as was expected of him without fault. I suppose his determination to return to China as soon as the war was over was what kept him going during the earlier part of the war. We often saw him get out his writing paper, pen and this pretty girl's photograph. Nobody knew what he did with those letters. It was all impossible and sad.

Sharky was Irish, nineteen and a newly-promoted O/S. He had made one trip on a destroyer which had been sunk at Narvik during the short Norwegian campaign and had been wounded in the right shoulder, as a result of which he collected a lot of tiny metal shrapnel pieces, including some on the right side of his head. He had a habit of picking these little pieces of metal out with his finger-nails (mostly, it seemed, at meal times), when he would good-naturedly shout "I've got it", and then show us all a tiny fragment of German iron. I liked him mostly for helping my young imagination to think that getting hit could be a bit of fun and not a tragedy.

Smithie was the first HO rating I had ever met. Before he could catch his breath he had completed his six weeks' training and been drafted to the ship. Smithie was in a daze. It was only seven weeks earlier that he had lived in a comfortable home where he had been spoon-fed by two caring parents who had 'spoilt him rotten'. Smithie was going through a very trying time. I remember Stripey advising him on his ablutions. "Collect a bucket of warm water from the galley tap and wash your underclothes," pleaded Stripey. It was quite true he did smell after being seasick. "Buy some soap powder from the canteen, it'll tell you on the packet how to use it." Stripey's knowledge was endless! Smithie followed orders, collected his bucket, water and soap powder, studied the instructions, emptied half the contents of the soap powder into his bucket of water, stirred the ingredients, placed his dirty underwear in the bucket and left it to soak all night as directed by the manufacturers. The next morning Smithie's clothes were set in a white soapy jelly. We all laughed and found out that Smithie had no sense of humour.

Tammy was the only married member of the mess. He also was fresh from training but had the advantage of having several months at it obtaining his Asdic qualifications. Asdic operators spent most of their time in a small dark room listening to outgoing and incoming 'pings'. Tammy had a great deal of trouble going to sleep after being 'on watch'; he said that when he shut his eyes he could still hear the 'pings'. An Asdic operator had a very responsible job because if he missed a submarine echo then we could all suffer. I think this responsibility weighed heavily on Tammy's shoulders.

The Forty-Niner, also an O/S at twenty-six, was the same miner from Yorkshire who had fainted at the *Pembroke V* medical. Although an HO rating, he had volunteered for the Navy; we all suspected the reason was to escape mining rather than his love of the sea. He turned out to be a most reasonable chap and well stocked up with courage.

JTB and myself were for the next few months going to be the lowest of the low, as far as the members of 13 Mess were concerned. I think it true to say that the two of us were the least worried about the number '13', for me especially because Joyce Dyster's home address was number 13 Little Bury Street. According to our three senior ABs, anyone with the surname of Edwards automatically collected the nickname of 'Cutts', so Cutts I was.

The second morning aboard was taken up with the arrival of a Nigerian chief. He was tall and very black, dressed in what we described as a 'night-shirt and a funny hat'. Some four hundred of us had been told to muster on the quarterdeck, a place that normally was only available for the elite to walk on. Crammed together on these holy wooden planks we watched the ceremony. The Nigerian chief had been invited by the builders, Messrs Vickers Armstrong, and our captain, to christen the ship which he did with due ceremony wearing his robes of state. We watched as a silver bell, about a foot high and ten inches in diameter, suitably inscribed, was presented to the ship on behalf of the people of Nigeria.

The ship carried a loudspeaker system which not only relayed daily orders and official information but which was also used to transmit selected BBC radio programmes and news bulletins. During the dog watches (i.e. between 1600 and 2000 hours) the padre and others ran a music request programme for members of the ship's company (a good selection of twelve-inch records was carried). The padre also had the use of a double cabin about twelve feet by twelve feet which had been converted into a chapel which had a dozen stacked chairs, a portable lectern and an altar. Both the latter could be carried up and used in No. 1 or No. 2 aircraft hangars, after moving the Walrus aircraft out onto the catapult, if we were in harbour on a Sunday, which was not often. I remember being selected once to be a member of the 'church working party' and mustering on the flight-deck. "You two boys," ordered the duty PO, "go below and collect the two 'praying machines' and fix them up in the starboard hangar; don't hang about." The PO knew the padre loved a chat (I think he was a very lonely man). "Tell the Sky Pilot that Jesus may want you for a sunbeam but the jaunty says you can't be spared."

Other than our seamanship manual, gunnery books and the padre's bibles and prayer-books, the Navy had not made any arrangements for a library and, therefore, light reading matter of any type was at a premium, which brings us back to the mess deck dodger. There resided in 12 Mess an incredible knitter of wools and to this end his wife, sister or mother sent him on a regular basis a copy of *Woman's Own*, or a similar magazine, which was eagerly read from cover to cover by all and sundry. It happened that among the adverts in this magazine was a half page extolling the merits of, I think, 'Puritan' soap flakes. Another page had published letters from readers, together with its editor's answers. This prompted a 'wag' to write the following letter: "Dear Editor, I found that 'Puritan' flakes have a delicate fragrance and when used for washing any personal garments it left them with a soft and gentle feel. I would recommend 'Puritan' flakes to all your readers." This was signed M.D. Dodger followed by his address, obviously obtained from the mail office.

It was some months later that our knitter received from home his latest copy of this ladies' magazine in which he discovered the copy of M.D. Dodger's letter and the editor's reply, which read something like this: "Dear M.D. Dodger, you spoke for us all, please accept the manufacturer's free packet of their product for your very own use." This particular incident became the joke of the year, laughter after all was in short supply then. However, the very butch mess deck PO was not amused. I don't know but I imagine his wife was pleased to receive the free packet of soap flakes.

It was during these early days on board that JTB and I realised that to some extent we had jumped out of the frying pan into the fire: the same rules in place in boys' shore establishments had followed us to the ship. Boys had to remain non-smokers and they were not allowed evening local shore leave. We were only allowed out on Saturday or Sunday afternoons up to 1800 hours and the pay was still one shilling a week. Whilst all the grown-up crew would be allowed every other evening off, working as duty watch when on board, boys were duty watch every night including either Saturday or Sunday, this included being 13 Mess cleaners-up after every evening meal, which was called 'tea' at 1730 hours. The returning revellers would also wake us up just as we had dropped off to sleep.

These were the days when you had to keep your wits about you. The continuous stream of verbal instructions from the loudspeaker would often carry your name or watch. You would hear a slight buzz followed by a pipe (a sound made by a bosun's whistle) followed by "do you hear there?" and then the message.

JTB and I were piped and instructed to report to the gunnery officer on the quarterdeck. This sub-lieutenant, who some thirty years previously had joined the Navy as a boy seaman, was obviously pleased to see us. He, like most of us, had a nickname: 'Mickey', we thought possibly 'Mickey Mouse' because of his ears. Both JTB and myself took to him instantly. We found out that because of our radar schooling we were going to be trained to understand the mechanical computer that operated the Gunnery Deflection Unit equipment and plots (see Figures 12, 13, 14). JTB won the low-angled TS (transmission station) position because he had passed Education Test Part 2 and I took over the lesser job of high-angle control position (HACP) because I only had Education Test Part 1 (see Figure 5).

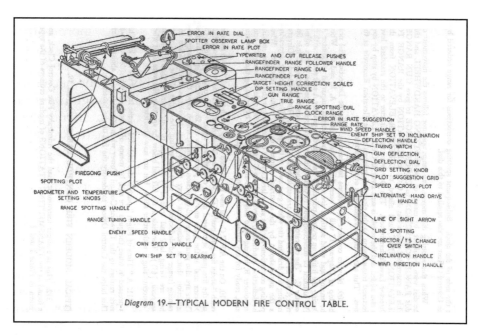

Figure 9. Typical modern fire control table

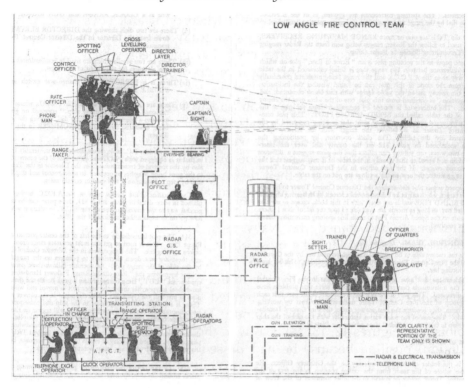

Figure 10. Low angle fire control team

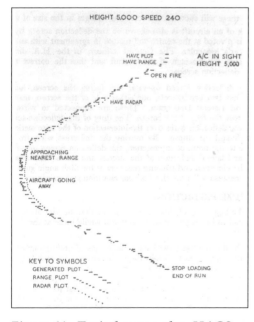

Figure 11. Typical range plot, HACS

Mickey was more than relieved that the two of us were eager to accept both the responsibility and the necessary learning skills required and he acted more like a friend than an officer. He had arranged to relieve both of us from all duties for the next three weeks. He also warned us that we would be responsible for on the job training of the TS and HACP crews. My team turned out to be Royal Marine bandsmen. One of them (a Jewish chap) had volunteered for service whilst employed by one of the BBC orchestras and two more of them were from

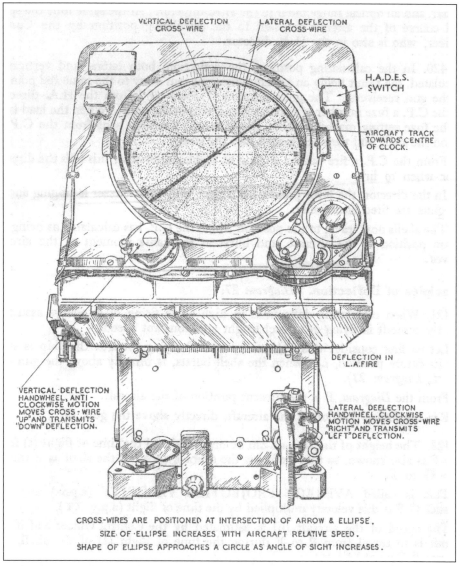

VERTICAL DEFLECTION CROSS-WIRE

LATERAL DEFLECTION CROSS-WIRE

H.A.D.E.S. SWITCH

AIRCRAFT TRACK TOWARDS CENTRE OF CLOCK.

DEFLECTION IN L.A.FIRE

VERTICAL DEFLECTION HANDWHEEL, ANTI-CLOCKWISE MOTION MOVES CROSS-WIRE "UP" AND TRANSMITS "DOWN" DEFLECTION.

LATERAL DEFLECTION HANDWHEEL, CLOCKWISE MOTION MOVES CROSS-WIRE "RIGHT" AND TRANSMITS "LEFT" DEFLECTION.

CROSS-WIRES ARE POSITIONED AT INTERSECTION OF ARROW & ELLIPSE.
SIZE OF ELLIPSE INCREASES WITH AIRCRAFT RELATIVE SPEED.
SHAPE OF ELLIPSE APPROACHES A CIRCLE AS ANGLE OF SIGHT INCREASES.

Figure 12. Deflection screen – HACS Mark IV

the Salvation Army. When I look back on it, I am amazed that they all accepted this situation, of an only just seventeen-year-old telling them what to do and how to do it. They were all nice gentlemen, like Godfrey in Dad's Army, a group of intellectuals. I am equally amazed that I had the gall, at my tender age, to tell them what to do. I never again in my life had such a responsible job.

Relief from all duties did not stop us from having to queue at the galley for the meals for 13 Mess. The PO cook was a very good chef

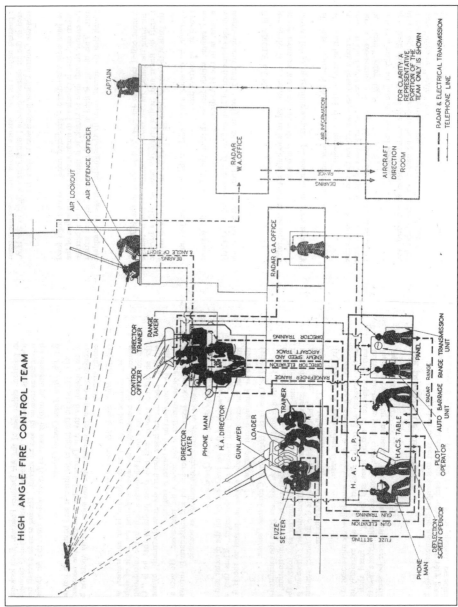

Figure 13. High-angle fire control

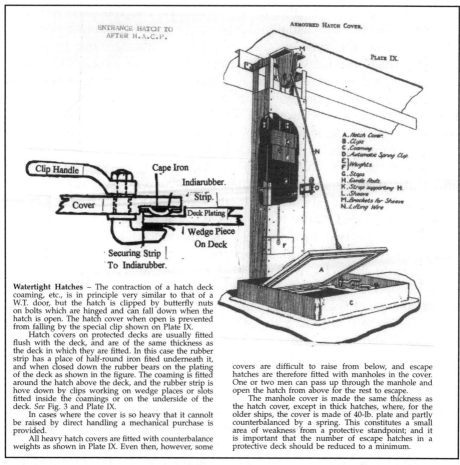

Figure 14. Entrance hatch to after HACP

who had the habit of 'extracting the Michael', as they say. On my first collection day I called him "Sir", a habit that was hard to forget. "Soup for 13 Mess," he said with a twinkle in his eyes, "pea or bean, lad?" I thought for a moment. "Pea, please Sir." He took the mess kettle and with a large ladle filled the kettle with about a bucket full of soup stock, then with due ceremony unhooked a two-foot length of string threaded through a green pea and dragged it through the soup. "Pea soup," he said in a loud voice "for 13 Mess." This was followed by laughter from the galley staff. I found out later that this cook could not go ashore because he was on a course of injections for syphilis that he had caught two years previously. Although this was common knowledge it did not seem to stop anyone from eating his prepared food. These injections were apparently given with a six-inch needle into the base of the spine and were very painful.

We hurried back to the mess to deliver the food as warm as possible, where it was usually shared out in equal portions by Stripey. This was also the time of the grog issue, although not to JTB or myself, which produced a jolly atmosphere with much small talk. On this particular day everyone had learnt of their action station; this was the major topic of conversation. It was when Stripey asked JTB where his action station was that sudden silence reigned. JTB told him shyly he was to be the plot operator in the TS. I can see Stripey's weather-beaten face even now, full of disbelief. "You mean you're working in the TS?" "No," said JTB quietly, "I'm the TS plot operator and Cutts is the same in the after HACP; we're both on a special three-week training session." "Is that right?" said Stripey, looking at me. "Yes," I said, "only in the HACP." Stripey was a most generous man. "We have two mess mates," he announced to all and sundry, "they've got themselves important officer-type action stations, good luck to them I say." From that moment on JTB and I were no longer 'nozzers' and even Smithie became friendly. Neither JTB nor myself felt there was anything unusual about it all nor did we dwell on it. We were two lads acting like all lads would, just carrying out our orders and at that time not getting in any way big-headed about it.

There it was, a brand-new ship at the beginning of a war, tied up to a stone jetty. It carried a mass of complicated weaponry but without ammunition for safety reasons; shells and high explosives could be 'shipped' aboard only from the end of a long special ammunition jetty some way outside the city limits. It was obvious that fuses and high explosives could only be handled and stored by fully trained and experienced crews.

It was the commander's duty gradually to bond together a team out of all these vastly different individuals (including myself) now residing on board. The one aim was to get the ship ready for sea in the shortest possible time. He had to 'bolt' us together like some intricate piece of machinery, wholly in sympathy with the ship. Before the end of those first memorable days we were piped to 'clear lower decks' and assemble on the quarterdeck, where the captain introduced himself and his fellow officers together with the senior lower-deck personalities including the master-at-arms, the chief gunner's mate and the bosun. He ended up by saying: "An efficient ship is a happy ship and I have just one month to achieve this and by George I'm going to do just that whatever it takes!"

Air raids were beginning to happen and some boxes of 'ready use' ammunition had been delivered for both the .5 machine-guns and pom-poms, known as 'Chicago Pianos'.

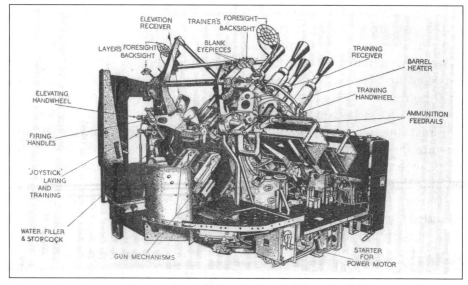

Figure 15. 2-Pdr. Pom-Pom Mark VII Mounting

Not only had we to understand and act on the different bugle calls, piping instructions and watch keeping, but we also had to understand which watch was which. I belonged to the starboard watch, whilst JTB was port watch, which meant we both had to think for ourselves as we hardly ever met at the mess during the day.

The twenty-four hour naval day had been divided into seven watches ever since Nelson's day, if not before. It was divided into the watches which occurred at these times:

1600 to 1800	First dog watch
1800 to 2000	Second dog watch
2000 to 2400	First watch
2400 to 0400	Middle watch
0400 to 0800	Morning watch
0800 to 1200	Forenoon watch
1200 to 1600	Afternoon watch

Figure 16. Different watches

A crew engaged at action stations would be at the first degree of readiness with no watch keeping and unable to leave for any circumstances, not even for attending the toilet. A crew at the second degree of readiness would be unable to leave their place of action, waiting for a possible action to start with no watch keeping and only allowed to leave this post with permission for something urgent like attending the toilet. A crew at the third degree of readiness would be at sea working a four- or two-hour watch (see Figure 16), unable to leave their watch station until relieved by the other watch keeper. This same crew when not on watch during the forenoon watch would be expected to carry out routine ship's maintenance between the hours of 0830 hours and 1130. The half hours at either end enabled these crew members to eat both breakfast and lunch before their next watch.

When the ship was in harbour and not under attack it would assume the fourth degree of readiness when all watch keepers would work when off watch. The fourth degree of readiness was one watch on and three watches off (see Figure 17).

If shore leave occurred it was usually every other night (boys not included), which dovetailed into the watches.

It was in all these circumstances that Stripey trained us to be considerate mess mates. If you were going on watch at 1200 hours you would, as explained, stop work at 1130. One member from the mess would collect the 13 Mess' food tray. Stripey would make sure that we only took our fair share and, before eating, this one member would return the tray to the galley to be kept warm for the late-comers from the forenoon watch. The same rules applied for breakfast and tea. It was also important for those members who were entitled to a grog issue that it was accurately measured and poured into a secured container for each to drink after his watch.

Degrees of readiness

DAY	THIRD DEGREE OF READINESS (4 hours on, 4 hours off)						
	First dog	Second dog	First watch	Middle watch	Morning watch	Forenoon watch	Afternoon watch
One	X		X		X		X
Two		X		X		X	
Three	X		X		X		X
	FOURTH DEGREE OF READINESS						
One	X				X		
Two		X				X	
Three			X				X
Four				X			
Five	X						

Figure 17. Degrees of readiness

The organisation of the watches was complicated. You could not have a hand whose third degree of readiness was masthead lookout but whose action station was 'Y' Turret shell handling room. The estimated minimum time it would take to get from the masthead to 'Y' Turret shell was seven minutes. The sudden appearance of the enemy could cause havoc in that time. As my PO used to say, "there are the quick, and the dead!" The clerical work required to ensure that this sort of situation did not occur was both complex and time absorbing; there were no computers. Everything had to run like a well-oiled expensive Swiss watch.

JTB and I spent a lot of this time with 'Mickey' carrying out exercise after exercise which involved communicating with my control officer, a Canadian who had volunteered to come to Britain to join our Navy. He was 'hostilities only' and therefore his one gold sleeve-ring was curvy instead of straight. All such officers were nicknamed 'Wavy Navy' sub-lieutenants.

Whilst the days were always full of events and very busy, evenings were not (it depended on your watch). When not on watch one evening JTB and I were commandeered by the killick from 9 Mess who was off to collect draught beer and fish and chips for ten watch keepers in 9, 11 and 13 Messes. We were instructed to wash out the mess kettle (the utensil used to collect soup and so on from the galley), which was always used for washing up the mess dishes. Once a week it was polished with Bluebell metal polish inside and out and was always spotlessly clean. It had a capacity of two and a half gallons and sported a strong handle.

To young lads, a ship that cannot be left soon becomes a prison. JTB and I were delighted to volunteer for anything that involved a walk out of the dockyard gate into the mysterious narrow streets beyond. Our first port of call was the pub. I had rarely been in a pub before and was surprised to find it so small; neither had I experienced blackout curtains (used on all outside doors and windows). It meant closing the porch door with its blackout curtain before opening the pub entrance door, to stop light flooding into the street. Every pub window was secondary glazed with a close-woven jet-black cloth made up with laths and drawing pins; these windows could not be opened. This made the well-lit pub stuffy with a strong smell of beer and tobacco smoke, which made our eyes smart.

The worried publican accepted our killick's explanation that these two under-age lads were solely there as mess kettle carriers and would not be drinking or smoking. This done the killick ordered "Twelve pints of the best draught beer please" whilst lifting the kettle over the pub bar to the chorus of loud laughter from the customers. Once filled with a really generous amount (much more than twelve pints), it now took two men to lift it back over the bar for JTB and myself to carry. We left with everybody's good wishes!

Our next port of call was the fish-and-chip shop further up the road. Whilst JTB and I stood guard over the couple of gallons of beer outside the shop, the killick negotiated the purchase of the necessary fish and chips. He rejoined us with two carrier bags full to the brim with food. Whilst this sale was in progress, JTB and I became aware of muffled grunts and sighs coming from the entrance porch of a darkened closed shop front. It took some time for our eyes to become accustomed to the gloom and then we could just about make out a matelot attempting to seduce a woman whilst they were standing up, both were the worse for drink and her skirt had been pulled up by the sailor. They looked as if they might fall over at any time. The funniest part of the whole affair was that the 'lady', who was eating chips from the newspaper wrappings, looked as though she was reading the news columns at the same time. It was a type of circus act! "What's that?" asked a perplexed JTB. "Ah," I said, "I know, my mother warned me about that; it's one of 'those' women. Didn't your mother warn you to be careful with 'those' women?" "No," he said, "do they always eat fish and chips at the same time?" We both laughed about it and pointed the situation out to the killick who joined in with our mirth.

On the way back to the ship, the killick handed a parcel of chips to the 'docky gate policeman' who then dipped his mug into the great can of beer, which I took to be the necessary bribe to let us out in the first place. On arrival back at the ship we slipped quietly up the prow whilst the officer of the watch was out of sight and presented the ten seamen with their fish and chips and beer, which they had paid for. We had not paid, but JTB and I were given an equal share of the chips for our labours, but it was more than the killick would dare do than to let us drink beer so they had a collection between them and gave us five pence each which enabled us to buy two thin red-wrapped bars of Nestlés chocolate and a couple of 'Goffers' from our NAAFI canteen.

The brown-lino-floored canteen, which contained a tied-down piano in one corner, was opposite a small shop and 'Goffer' bar. There were a few canvas stacked chairs, a card table and a fitted dart board. The shop could supply you with sweets, cigarettes, soap and so on. A 'Goffer' is best described as a fizzy drink, the colour of Coca Cola, but there the resemblance ended; it tasted awful and as you drank it caught the back of your throat and made you cough, hence the name 'Goffer' (cougher)!

Although this boat had not moved one single inch I began to settle down to life afloat. I had got used to being called 'Cutts'. My light-blue collar together with my 'action station' and nickname indicated to all and sundry that I was not new to the Navy, despite being just seventeen. The outward sign of a crew member's naval experience was the colour of his collar. It took at least six months' scrubbing to turn a stiff dark blue into a delightful Mediterranean blue soft collar. This knowledge helped inexperienced naval officers to select such a person to carry out an order without the said officer having to explain what he required, particularly as he might not have sufficient knowledge to do the job himself! The obvious way to produce the extra wartime officers needed would have been to promote experienced chiefs and POs but My Lords of the Admiralty felt that chief POs and POs would be too rough to handle a position in the wardroom; hence they produced the white-paper candidate. A selected 'call-up' would be trained in knife and fork use. We saw these people as a by-product of snobbery and nicknamed them 'waste-paper candidates' (with passes in knife and fork drill) and quite often found them to be square pegs in round holes.

Sleeping arrangements were cramped and hammocks were slung twenty-four inches apart with a head-to-feet system that meant whichever way you looked, right or left, there was a pair of feet beside you. Life could be full of surprises, some very humorous, some not.

At 0545 we were noisily woken by the bugled reveilles, followed quickly by a different duty PO every morning usually shouting "wakey, wakey, rise and shine", accompanied by much broomstick banging on the hammock supports.

There were two noticeable variations to the usual wake-up routine. One was delivered by a very Welsh PO with one of those famous Welsh singing voices. He greeted us with: "Beautiful dreamers lash up and stow / Cooks to the galley have gone long ago / Now's the time we all have to pee / Beautiful dreamers wake up for me," all sung to that well-known Bing Crosby song. The 'lash up and stow' was what had to be carried out every morning with hammocks. The bugle call 'cooks to the galley' (see Figure 6) indicated that breakfast had been cooked and awaited collection by duty members from each mess, all of which would not happen until 0730.

The other variation was occasionally used when the jaunty himself came round the mess decks to waken us lads. There was nothing beautiful about his morning greeting: "Wakey, wakey, rise and shine," came his gruff roar, "the sun is over the yard-arm, burning your eyes out." He would be banging the lids of the mess utensils as he walked past and giving your hammock a violent punch whilst adding: "Take your hands off your cocks and put them on your socks." Woe betide you if you were still there when he returned from his mess deck rounds. I was amazed to see the injuries that a seaman received for going back to sleep after the jaunty's initial not so gentle get-up call. Seeing this lonely hammock still slung and with mess mates weaving and ducking underneath, the jaunty bent his body and legs until his shoulder was well under his victim's backside and, using the pressure obtained by straightening his body and legs, sent the poor seaman some two feet into the air, at speed, until his nose and forehead crashed into the cork-and-paint substance which had been applied to the deck-head to help reduce condensation. The victim swung from his hammock, his face and nose bleeding from the embedded tiny bits of painted cork, whilst listening to the jaunty's lecture on the nuisance of an unstowed hammock in a crowded area where space was at a premium. After this episode I felt once again that to 'lay in' in the morning could be another health hazard.

Unable to enjoy Saturday afternoon shore leave with my friends who were all on the opposite watch, and lacking the courage to go alone, I agreed to join a Suffolk lad called Pete from the boys' mess deck. He assured me that if we took the train from the local station just one stop down we would quickly and cheaply arrive at a funfair and beach. Immediately after lunch we walked to the nearby railway station armed with our shilling wages safely hidden in our money-belts, which were buttoned securely inside our bell-bottoms behind the four flap buttons.

We had descended the steps to the platform when my new acquaintance suddenly left me to speak to two girls in their mid-teens. I stopped and observed him from a distance and saw one of the girls terminate the conversation with a swing of her handbag to Pete's head which floored him immediately. After bending over him for a few seconds both the girls ran off at speed. Pete did not get up, I ran to him but by the time I arrived he was sitting up with a hand on his bleeding chin. "What happened?" I asked, as I helped him to his feet. "She hit me with her handbag," he said, "there must have been half a house brick in it." Still holding his bleeding jaw, he added: "But she didn't get my shilling." "Why did you speak to them?" was my next question. "Well," he said, "only to invite them to join us at the funfair. They asked if we had any money. I told them we'd just been paid. This wouldn't have happened in Ipswich," he said. "Idiot," I said, "let's get you back to the ship's sickbay, your face looks awful."

The PO male nurse, known as the sickbay tiffy, met us. "What happened to you," he asked, "been fighting?" "No," said Pete, "I got hit by a handbag." "A *handbag*?" said the tiffy, with a touch of the

Oscar Wildes. "You two should know better than to mess about with little girls' knickers, little girls will bring you nothing but trouble." He applied a single stitch to the side of Pete's jaw. There was no argument there I thought, Mother was right, some of 'those' women could be quite young but still dangerous to your health to boot!

There were two chutes, one attached to the port side and the other to the starboard side of the ship just under the flight-deck (see 'Gash' chute in Figure 7). A chute was half of a thirty-inch diameter pipe welded to the outer side of the ship's side and fitted with a hinged lid. This provided all and sundry with a way of disposing of unwanted dirty water, sometimes referred to as gash, without leaving unsightly stains on the ship's sides. It was advisable to use the chute on the lee side or you could get very wet with the dirty water in one go if the seas or winds were strong enough. It was where JTB or myself would pour the dirty greasy washing-up water after completing our dish-washing duties, when all the adult mess members had gone ashore and left their dirty dishes.

The journey to the chutes (see Figure 7) with a heavy 'fanny' full of greasy water from 13 Mess was considerable and involved negotiating a dangerous fifteen-step iron ladder. JTB and I found, using the rules of Euclid, that the journey from the end of 13 Mess table to the very large porthole provided was a mere ten feet and hence, with nobody to witness our action, we got into the habit of utilising this illegal facility.

Then one night it happened. We were happily chatting as I washed and JTB dried and stowed the plates into their respective mess shelves when, without any effort at all, I heaved the dirty water out of the porthole. It was JTB's instant remark of "Tinkle, tinkle, little spoon, knife and fork will follow soon" that made me realise two things: the lightning wit and speed of JTB's excellent brain and that I had sent overboard nine sets of stainless steel knives, forks and spoons, together with three teaspoons and an aluminium soup ladle, i.e., everybody's eating irons were now lying in the Tyneside mud five fathoms down. The enormity of the crime took some time to register with the pair of us: if Stripey reported us for losing HM Navy's equipment I, at least, was for the high jump. It would mean weeks of 'Jankers', loss of money and, worse still, nasty remarks on my service record.

We decided that the best course of action to take was to report the loss of the cutlery to Stripey when he returned from shore leave that night, rather than try to explain it all in a rush the next morning. Having slung our hammocks we nervously awaited Stripey's return. Sharp on 2330 hours they all returned as a noisy crowd, most of them showing the effects of the local brew. Plucking up courage, and with JTB watching, I approached a really jolly Stripey. "Stripey," I said, "I'm sorry to tell you I've had an accident." "What accident?" slurred Stripey. "After doing the washing up I tipped the dirty water down the chute but I'd forgotten to take the knives and forks out and they've gone over the side," I lied. Well, it was only a small lie. Why, I thought, should I tell him about the porthole and confess to two crimes instead of one? Everybody that was listening roared with laughter and to JTB's and my amazement, so did Stripey. My bad news had been received as though it had been the joke of the year. "Don't worry," said Stripey, who was still chuckling as he swung his hammock. JTB looked at me as if to say "we've got away with that quite nicely".

The next morning, being duty cook of the mess, I was first up and, having stowed my hammock, went to the galley to collect the breakfast of braised lambs' kidneys floating in gravy giving off a delicious aroma, topped with twenty pieces of hard fried bread. When I arrived back at the mess, Stripey and most of my mess mates were sitting down waiting for their grub; some were obviously suffering from headaches arising from the night before. Placing the meat tray on the end of the table, I looked at Stripey awaiting the usual instructions to dish up. "Oh, they look good," stated Stripey. "Who wants kidneys?" he said, passing his plate for a generous helping. Using a piece of fried bread I shovelled kidney and gravy onto his plate, which was passed down to him. After a "ta" from Stripey, he asked, "Where's my knife and fork?" My heart sank; he had not remembered the night before or the confession. JTB gave me a look of sympathy. "I told you last night, Stripey, about throwing them overboard, and you said not to worry." At this stage he went barmy. "You did *what*?" This was a very different Stripey from last night. I had to confess all over again but now with everyone listening, including the members of the other two messes who were well within earshot. I felt dreadful and must have sounded like an idiot. I was worried too about what Stripey was going to do. When he had finally stopped swearing at me, the rest of the mess members waded in with their two pennyworth of caustic remarks and laughter was coming from 9 and 11 Messes. I suppose JTB and I were lucky that morning because half of our mess members were not fond of kidneys and were finding no problem with eating the fried bread using their fingers. For many mealtimes to come I was the most unpopular member of the mess, although JTB took some flack, until our messmates were lucky enough to beg, borrow or buy replacements ashore. JTB and I received more than our just punishment by having to wait six whole months before our mess mates received proper eating irons. In the meantime we had to make do with using our seaman's

> **Mess Utensils. On commissioning, each mess is completed with a full set of mess utensils. The principal items are mess kettle, tea urn, fanny (metal tin, 1½ gallons), meat dishes, tea and sugar canister, pepper dredge, salt jar and mustard pot, plates, cups and saucers, knives, forks, spoons, potato net, dish cloths and a linoleum table cloth. Crockery, dish and table cloths are issued gratuitously every six months. Knives forks and spoons whenever lost can be taken up on repayment from the ship's store. The 'tinned' gear, i.e., kettles, etc., are supplied to last a commission, but can be replaced on special occasions by a board of survey. Whiting is supplied for cleaning tinned gear.**

Figure 18. King's Regs – Mess Utensils

splicing knives, fingers and sipping from tilted plates. We felt we were both lucky and grateful that Stripey never pursued this 'crime' with higher authorities, i.e. the mess deck dodger himself.

Air raids had been mostly during the dog watches and had not, as far as the ship was concerned, advanced past early yellow warnings. On the 4th September 1940 a red had occurred about midday and although close by was not close enough for our pom-poms to be used. Although it was noisy we were unable to see what was happening. The final 'all clear' was sounded by bugle in the early afternoon and by teatime the ship's routine was back to normal. Shore leave had commenced as usual for approximately half the ship's company but not for the duty watch.

It was during the second dog watch that a 'do you hear there?' came over the loudspeakers: "All non-watch keeping spare hands to muster at the aft gangway at the double." As Tom (who was nearly always on board) and I left for the quarterdeck I was more than pleased to go, it sounded exciting. JTB was on watch missing it all. There were some eighteen of us waiting at the gangway when the officer of the watch (a new sub-lieutenant) turned up. He did not waste any time. "A request had been made to the Royal Navy," he said, "to provide a working party to assist the local air raid wardens. You are to help where you can with the damage. There are two lorries alongside to take you. Carry on, leading seaman." "Aye, aye, Sir," roared the killick, while at the same time saluting. He immediately divided us up into two groups of ten and eight. He nominated Tom as leader of the eight, which included me, whilst he took charge of the other ten.

"Sir," shouted the killick, again saluting the one ringer, "what about these two lads?" I expected to be told to return to the mess deck but no: "Put one in each lorry," ordered the officer of the watch. "Don't you lose them, leading seaman." "No, Sir," laughed the killick. The quarterdeck bosun's mate listed our names and we were off. We drove for some distance before we arrived at the scene of the midday air raid.

The lorry driver took us as near as he could to the damaged area. We eight alighted and made our way on foot over the rubble past a double-decker bus which was still on its side obstructing the road. Beyond it, some thirty feet away, was the bomb crater. The explosion had demolished some two or three houses completely. It had also apparently stripped every roof tile in sight as well as breaking all the windows. Firemen were hosing down the last embers of the fire and people were still collecting their belongings. Halfway between the crater and the crossroads at the end of the street was a paved forecourt in front of what appeared to be a warehouse and on that area was a large tarpaulin covering about twenty bodies.

Tom, who was in charge, asked an air raid warden what was happening and if we could help. He replied: "All of the local injured and dead have been removed to hospitals except for the twenty bus casualties, all Chinese seamen, who are waiting for collection." With Tom's background it was not surprising that he went to look under the tarpaulin and returned to confirm that they were Chinamen, probably merchant seamen on their way to join a merchant ship in the nearby docks. I had never seen a dead body before and was not in the mood to volunteer at that moment. It was the warden who suggested that, as there was nothing we could do, would we offer our services to the publican on the street corner? I can still hear the remark "what a good idea" from some of the eight as we approached the corner, passing the publican's wife loading bottles of beer and spirits into the back of a private car which she had been able to drive in from the other direction. Tom approached the worried publican and offered our services. "Thanks," replied the publican, "but what I really need is transport." Tom looked at his team with a look that said keep your big mouths shut. Tom now became a businessman. "I might," he said, "be able to organise some for you, what've you got to move?" "These five big barrels of beer, some smaller ones, the glass mugs and tankards and there's that upright piano and stool. So much," he said with a sigh, "and it's a full three miles to my brother-in-law." "Ah," said Tom, moving closer, "I think I can arrange a lorry quickly but what about my lads here?" at the same time rubbing his nose with his forefinger. "All the beer they can drink," replied the landlord immediately. "And some to take home?" retorted Tom. "Why yes," conceded the landlord. "You're on," said Tom, whilst asking the landlord for the directions back to our lorry and duly dispatching two of the lads to find the lorry driver while the rest of us began moving the merchandise onto the pavement outside. The large barrels came up from the cellar with the aid of a special curved rung ladder that all pubs have as standard equipment. All of this preparatory work was finished by the time the lorry turned up. The driver and messengers were immediately given a pint each to help them catch up. You could see from the looks of pleasure on their faces that they hadn't felt they had been excluded.

It didn't take the sailors long to hoist and lash the barrels aboard the lorry, the barrel ladder having been securely lashed with spare rope provided by the driver. With all hands to the piano, some pulling from the lorry and some pushing and lifting from the road, the piano and stool were lashed and housed safely behind the driver's cab. At this stage one of the eight (a marine musician) settled down on the piano stool, emptied the beer from his glass in one go, gave the empty glass to someone to fill and struck up with 'There'll be bluebirds over the white cliffs of Dover' and other topical songs. We all joined in lustily as we drove the three miles to the brother-in-law's.

Tom had decided that I should be allowed half a pint of this free beer, which all the lads were downing as fast as they could. This was the first beer I had drunk. I really did not think much of it but I did enjoy the singing and waving as we passed spectators. I spent most of the journey holding up the keyboard cover so that it didn't fall on the pianist's hands whilst we were driving along the bumpy road. The landlord and his wife were delighted when we noisily delivered their liquid belongings to their safe haven.

On arrival back at the ship, the bosun's mate was heard to remark "I thought you lot were supposed to be clearing up after an air raid, not getting as pissed as newts" as he ticked our names off the 'ashore list'. This had been my first air raid experience and my first run ashore. I felt guilty; I had enjoyed the whole evening despite feeling very sorry for the dead Chinamen, and had a headache the next morning.

The last I heard on the subject from Tom, as he secretly smuggled a bottle of whisky aboard, was when he whispered into my ear his pet saying "you'se loves the Navy".

During this 1940 September month, the ship was in the area of some fourteen air attacks. We moved to a mooring at Tyne Bell Quay alongside the aircraft-carrier *Victorious* and found its enormous size dwarfed us. We all put to sea the next day to carry out continuous exercises with torpedoes and the Walrus aircraft, both of which had

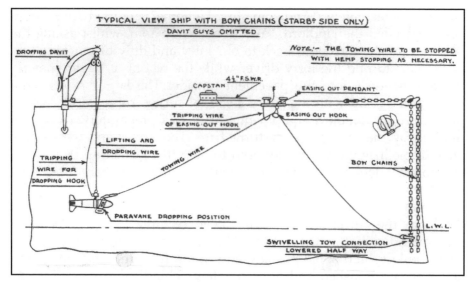

Figure 19. Getting in and out paravanes (PVs)

to be collected using small sea boats with old fashioned oars and hoisted back on board. We returned to the ammunition ship from lighters in the river away from buildings and quays. Hundreds of four- and six-inch shells, weighing almost one hundredweight, had to be manhandled up the ship's side and stowed below-decks in the magazines and shell-handling rooms. The backbreaking work went on day and night non-stop. We were going to find the sea littered with mines, so streaming PVs was to become a way of life.

The BBC issued a bulletin stating that an invasion was always a possibility. We also heard that Buckingham Palace had been bombed. Following an accident, one of our lads died, our first casualty, and although I had never seen this sixteen-year-old I found this very sad. But it did not dampen my excitement at going to sea in this fully loaded, speedy cruiser.

The news and general outlook in October 1940 was anything but good. Our ships (both RN and Merchant) were being sunk by mines, U-boats, and aircraft. Merchant losses alone were some 190,000 tons and I was still being seasick. It was also a month of exercise after exercise and still more exercises. British Summer Time was to continue through the winter and the Government had put up rail fares by 6 per cent but, as there was little chance of us getting any leave for a long time, none of this seemed important.

Many of the ship's company were getting their teeth checked whilst at Scapa Flow (a dreadful place, I thought) on the battle cruiser *Hood*, the hospital ship *Amarapoora*, and the *Dunbar Castle*. We all cleared the lower deck, an order only given to the entire ship's company when there was important information to deliver. This time we were read the 'Articles of War', one of which clearly stated that I could be severely punished for not doing what I was told, or for talking too much when I was ashore. Another article told us that we must never mention the ship's name anywhere but in the dockyard. She carried a code number. If I remember correctly that was 180.

During one of our exercises, my high-angle team actually hit a drogue being towed by our own Walrus aircraft. Our gunnery officer gave us a pat on the back and three cheers, as he put it: "Two today and one tomorrow," if we did as well. However, our pilot had different thoughts, a blown-away drogue was too close for comfort, so he thought. He signalled back: "I'm towing this bastard not pushing it", which shows you cannot please everyone!

At that time the Italians had attacked Greece without warning, although it seemed that the Greeks were giving them a bloody nose. Air raids were increasing in number for the whole of the United Kingdom. A typical BBC bulletin often quoted the number of our aircraft that were shot down that day, but a lesser number of pilots were saved.

Our captain got a ride in one of our Walrus planes which included a catapulted start and a sea landing. We did not think he was impressed as he ordered all three pilots to catapult off and land their planes all through the next day.

Whilst at sea, in an attempt to cure my seasickness I spent every spare hour off watch walking around the upper deck, taking in the fresh air and eating dry biscuits purchased at the canteen (which I could ill afford) and only drinking cold water, a cure recommended by Tom, my mess mate. I couldn't be comforted even when told that it was well known that Nelson himself suffered with the same complaint, and indeed our own admiral aboard was immediately sick as soon as he heard the anchor chain rattle. Another memory of that time was a visit to the 1914 battleship *Iron Duke* before it was sunk at Scapa Flow.

On going to sea we passed the lightship *Cape Wrath*, Wicklow Light at 2334, and exchanged pennants with HMS *Pytchley* and HMS *Chiltern*. Being *en route* to Plymouth without escorts on that dark night gave me a feeling of isolation, not helped by my continued seasickness. This trip also produced a complete mystery, this was the moving plank. The sight of a long-serving naval officer (with two gold rings on his arm) leaving his cabin, which was located above the starboard forward propeller (see Figure 7), carrying a long wooden plank, was bewildering to say the least, a ritual he carried out every time we left harbour. The plank was some five feet five inches long, eight inches wide and three-quarters of an inch thick, with several nicks about an inch deep cut into the edges.

This officer, ignoring all the amazed onlookers, made this journey from his cabin to the DCT (director control tower) (see Figure 7) which, with the exception of the masthead lookout position, was as high as you could go. He had to negotiate several gangways and watertight doors as well as vertical iron-rung ladders. The plank was eventually used as a bed when supported by the rate officers' and spotting officers' stationary stools, with the notched side locking against the central officers' stool support column (see Figure 20). The reverse plank journey occurred on returning to a harbour.

The mystery of why an officer should want to live and sleep like an Indian fakir at his cold action station instead of in his warm cabin (complete with a comfortable leather upholstered horsehair bunk and within easy reach of a hand wash basin) baffled everyone and was the subject of many conversations and conjecture. In the end there were three plausible explanations washing about as buzzes, and they all had one common denominator: fear. The first was he was frightened that he would be late on arrival at his action station (perhaps he had been caught out before). The other two were similar. His last ship was sunk by a 'tin-fish' (torpedo) whilst he had been asleep in his cabin which was over a fuel tank. The explosion had damaged the deck of the cabin and he had been covered with '90 second' fuel oil. The third explanation was slightly worse in so far as the 'tin-fish' explosion had jammed debris against his cabin door

PHONE MAN
SPOTTING OFFICER
CONTROL OFFICER
DIRECTOR TRAINER
DIRECTOR CHANGE-
-OVER PISTOL
RATE OFFICER
DIRECTOR LAYER
CROSS LEVELLING OPERATOR

Diagram 9.—TYPICAL ARRANGEMENT OF D.C.T. CREW.

Figure 20. Typical arrangement of DCT crew

82

and he had had to hack his way out with a knife and sword before abandoning the sinking ship.

Whatever the truth was, he seemed to be a decent sort of a bloke for an officer. He had left his last ship in a hurry and, therefore, had our sympathy. We all accepted his foible which after a while became accepted by the whole of the ship's company, including the captain, as the 'norm' – except of course the fourteen ratings who were expected to keep a watch in the DCT in very cramped positions due to the plank.

There was another officer even stranger than 'The Plank' as we had nicknamed him. That officer was a 'waste-paper' candidate training to become the cable officer. The cable officer was supposed, amongst his other duties, to be in charge of the 'special sea duty men' party which consisted of some twenty-five hands (working seamen), of which I was one. They were piped to muster onto the fo'c'sle some twenty minutes before the ship entered or left harbour. These seamen were required either to cast off or secure wires from or to the jetty or to disconnect or secure the anchor chain to or from the mooring buoy. The special sea duty men were also responsible for streaming or recovering anti-mine PVs after getting underway or on returning to harbour.

When mooring to a buoy, a strong agile person, who was a good swimmer, was required. This job usually fell to a boy seaman in the party and I seemed to get the job almost permanently. The act of mooring to a buoy in an open harbour, with all eyes watching from other anchored and secured ships, according to our captain involved speed and efficiency. He, like all captains of small ships, liked to enter into some unwritten competition with regard to entering harbour and securing as quickly as possible to the buoy without too much concern for the danger involved or for the safety of the seaman employed. He would steam in as fast as he could and stop dead with the ship's bows just touching the buoy by going full astern on all engines at the same time, a highly exciting experience for all concerned, especially for the buoy jumper and the two seamen in the thirty-two-foot motor cutter which was lowered onto the sea before the ship had stopped, a really risky operation.

The buoy jumper's part in this operation was to leap onto the violently bobbing ten-foot-long buoy with a twenty-eight-pound eighteen-inch-long shackle and pin, together with a hammer and marlinspike. The two seamen gathered the end of the heavy anchor cable, minus the anchor, and married it to the round buoy shackle. The buoy jumper would then connect this cable (using the shackle carried onto the buoy) and insert the large pin through the shackle eye, and finally place a lead plug into the pinhole and hammer it home to stop it

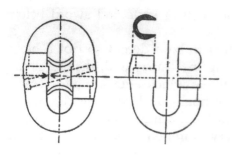

Figure 21. Joining shackle

falling out. One false move could have resulted in the loss of a finger, perhaps a toe or even a tremendous blow on the head from the swinging cable, or one could have fallen off the buoy or been knocked into the water and, loaded as one was with the shackle pin, hammer and iron marlinspike tied to one's belt with a lanyard, it would ensure a quick descent to the sea bed, or if the engines were still in the reverse mode one could be sucked into the four propellers with their twelve sharp blades.

Once you had completed the connection it was a quick leap from the pitching buoy into a moving motor cutter, which then turned round and headed back to the crane hook to be hoisted inboard or made fast to the mooring painter at the boom. Then you had to scramble out of the cutter, up the Jacob's ladder, and scurry out of sight below, away

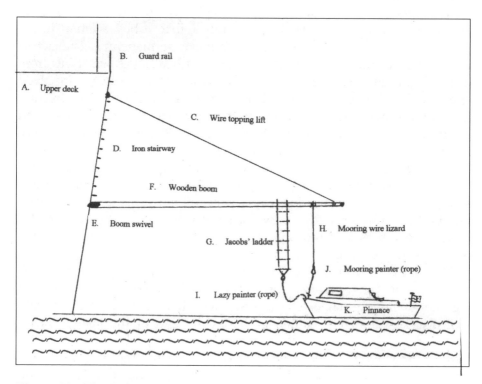

Figure 22. The Boom

from interested telescopes aboard other ships. The captain expected this operation to be completed within ten minutes once the twenty-two-foot motor cutter hit the water. Times were published with the daily orders if it took longer.

On approaching Milford Haven on Thursday, 31st October 1940 it was a surprise to the whole of the ship's company when we came to a sudden halt. Special sea duty men were piped to muster immediately onto the fo'c'sle. Nobody seemed to know what had happened or who was responsible. Was it the officer of the watch, the helmsman or the navigator's course that was at fault? There we were, held hard and fast by our own starboard paravane which had become entangled with a very large navigation buoy marking the 'In' channel to Milford Haven harbour, at 1700 hours, and just before dark. Two very worried officers, the captain and commander, viewing the serious situation, met the special sea duty men. There we all were in one of His Majesty's newest cruisers, completely stopped and almost out of action, presenting a perfect target for a passing U-boat at dusk in waters that were liable to have been mined by German aircraft.

Our L/S counted his men and reported to the commander "special sea duty men mustered and correct, Sir," well before the trainee cable officer had come into sight. Our killick was enjoying the situation; he and the waste-paper candidate had crossed swords on more than one occasion. "You're late," snarled the very worried commander at the cable officer. "Well man, what are you going to do?" asked the even more worried captain in a deadly calm, even voice, whilst acknowledging the cable officer's salute. By this time (out of curiosity) most of the off-watch crew had made their way to the upper deck, joining those already on watch.

The upper deck was the best place to see what was happening and also the safest spot to be if U-boats were about. It was hardly fair on this young man who had been pushed into this position because of the snobbish system of selecting officers from public schoolboys. He was completely out of his depth. He looked over the starboard side in the gathering dusk at what the Navy would term 'a right lot of bastards'. It was a real jumble of PV, chains, wires and tow shackles, pulled through the bow eye from the port side by the sudden jerk produced when the ship came to an immediate halt on its collision with the channel buoy (see Figure 19).

The youngster raised his eyes and became aware that he had more than half of the ship's company, including most of the officers, as an audience. The strain was too much. White-faced he started to say something to the captain, changed his mind and sprinted away to hide in his cabin. The captain seemed to shrug his shoulders and calmly said to the L/S: "Get the motor cutter lowered and take a working party to clear that buoy." "Aye, aye, Sir," replied the killick.

The killick knew that all boys had spent weeks at their training establishments being thoroughly trained on how to stream and recover PVs, so he left me and two new ordinary seamen on board to sort it out whilst he took the rest of the special sea duty men on the motor cutter. It took about twenty minutes for us to clear the tangle on board whilst they cleared the PV from the buoy. Darkness had descended and we were underway again. As I was clearing our tools and tidying the ropes we had used, the commander came across and said "Well done, Edwards". It was not the "well done" bit that mattered, it was the fact that he knew my name that was unusual.

The next morning I was piped to muster on the quarterdeck and told on arrival to go for an audience with the commander in his office. "Your actions last night when the ship was in danger were quick and exemplary, I am therefore recommending you for leading seaman," he said. I thanked him for his kind words and hurried forward to the mess and told Tom. Oh, how he did laugh! "You can't be an ordinary seaman until you're eighteen, an able seaman until you're nineteen or a killick until you're twenty – if you're still alive." To which he added, as usual, "you'se loves the Navy", and we all laughed.

VI

The Barrage Balloon Major

We left Milford Haven with HMS *Garland* and arrived at Plymouth Sound during an air raid on Sunday 2nd November 1940 at 1830 hours. None of us knew at the time that we had been sent to strengthen Plymouth's air defences in the area of the dockyard and the adjacent part of the town. Poor Plymouth was being pounded with thousands of tons of German bombs. There were a hundred and thirty air raids, some continuous both night and day, during the thirty-three days we were there.

Before we had arrived at the Sound a meeting had been arranged between the adjacent Royal Artillery ack-ack section and our gunnery department. JTB and I were ordered to attend. The Army had sent a mature sergeant and wartime major, possibly an ex-territorial. We were to discuss and organise co-operation between the Army and ourselves to enable the local ack-ack units to take advantage of our superior firepower and sophisticated radar fire-control system. This would enable the Army and the Navy to engage more targets and extend the box barrage during mass air raids. Mickey explained to our Army guests that we were capable of firing specially fused six-inch shells some four miles out to sea, thus engaging approaching enemy aircraft before they crossed the coast from our twelve low-angle main armaments. The ship's low-angle six-inch guns could not be used to fire at overhead targets, as it was impossible to elevate them higher than forty-five degrees. However, he said, pointing to our eight four-inch high-angle guns, "Our gunners are capable of firing eighty rounds a minute from them". The sergeant was impressed. Mickey then gave particulars of our radar control systems (see Figures 11 and 12), which, he said, would enable our plot operators to supply the enemy aircraft's speeds, heights, bearing and position for their ack-ack gun emplacements and then to give them the order to open fire. Mickey reminded the major that to maximise the combined Navy and Army effort it was important that the major informed the ship controlling plot operations that his guns were on the bearings given by us and he was ready to open fire when ordered. The major promised the Army would co-operate and fulfil its obligations. There were smiles all round; that is until Mickey introduced him to the plot operators who he described as recently promoted boys first class (myself and JTB, together with a junior Royal Marine bandsman who, Mickey explained as an afterthought, was a fine trumpet player). The major's face was a picture. He was obviously very confused and could not adjust to the idea of taking orders from two seventeen-year-olds and an eighteen-year-old musician, even if he could play the trumpet well. He said nothing, whilst the sergeant could not control his smile. Without further ado, Mickey pointed out that the telephone lines would all be connected by 1800 that evening, and the major and sergeant then left the ship. Mickey dismissed us with: "Don't you three let us down: we're all part of a team; we're all depending on you."

We went into action with the Army using the agreed routine that very evening. During that first action it became clear that, whilst the ship was moored out on the exposed Sound, without any camouflage, it had become a sitting duck for any passing enemy aircraft. In the circumstances those in command decided to move to a safer mooring. We embarked the local pilot early next morning whilst a large tug (I think named *Samson*) was secured for towing us forward and the ship proceeded to Devonport, where communication was once again established with the major's unit.

Much to my delight we were informed that the starboard watch could take eight days' leave. When the after HACP (see Figure 14), who were all starboard watch, were away, the forward HACP, all port watch, took over the HA guns and *vice versa*. The leave was to start at noon. Just before we were all due to go, and waiting for our

Figure 23. Depends on you

travel warrants, all hell broke loose in the form of a very heavy air raid. This was followed by thirty more such raids which, as we had to return to normal for the rest of that day, brought us down to seven days' leave. Before leaving the ship, the captain apologised for the delay and warned us of our obligation, under the Articles of War, to return on time even if there were air raids. Being late would be read as desertion and that had dire consequences. I was beginning to get used to the Luftwaffe and to understand what war was about for the citizens of Plymouth. Despite the air raids, the train got off almost on time and had been making good progress when it came to an abrupt halt: it had hit a slow goods train using the same line. The engine, together with the three front carriages of our train, had been derailed and the last two goods wagons of the other train were also damaged, as was part of the line. Although the train was packed with sailors and other service men and women, so far as I remember, nobody was hurt, but it took all day to rectify so that by the time I arrived home to Mother and Auntie I had lost another day of my leave.

I was unable to see either my sister Joan or brother Peter during this leave. Joan had decided on a nursing career and was training at the Royal Free Hospital and Peter had been sent to boarding school on the Isle of Wight. It was going to be some years before I clapped eyes on them again.

I spent an afternoon on a cycling outing with Joyce Dyster and was invited to afternoon tea with her family on another day. The five days rushed past and, remembering the captain's warning, I made sure I allowed myself ample time to return to the ship, arriving early. During the tearful goodbyes from Mother and Auntie, I was given some money to get my likeness copied as they had not got an up-to-date photograph. I became very depressed on the journey back thinking: "Don't they expect me to return, is that why they need my photograph?" But the train was packed with sailors all reminiscing about their leave, which soon cheered me up. I had no idea that my dear aunt was going into hospital to have her first operation due to cancer.

The starboard watch returned to the ship on Saturday 9th November during one of Plymouth's bad air raids. Enemy planes were dropping sea mines on the harbour. Our torpedo department, which understood all about mines, was in the process of being lowered over the side in all available small boats to try to locate these mines and blow them up. This was a very dangerous operation. The port watch were glad to take their eight days' leave. The following Saturday afternoon I was given boy's local leave. This gave me sufficient time to locate a photographic studio, which was open despite the air raids. The chap

Photo 9. Taken in Plymouth for Mother and Auntie

took my photograph and kindly promised to post it home to Mother and Auntie. I thanked him and paid with the money they had given me. It was some years before I saw this photograph; I remember thinking it didn't look bad for a 'nozzer' (see Photo 9).

Since my return from leave, the major and I had been communicating reasonably successfully until one night, in the middle of a very heavy raid, I dropped a 'clanger' and sent the major's lads a wrong control bearing with the result that 'me and the Army' shot down one of our own barrage balloons. At first I thought it was a great joke until I was informed that there was to be an enquiry into this error, which wiped the smile from my face; then I was very worried. Mickey had said that I was part of a team and not to let the Navy's side down, which I felt I had. This was the first time that I began to understand about the responsibility that went with the job. JTB was very sympathetic about it and, after listening, Tom made a statement, which I have remembered all my life. "Today's problem will fade into insignificance when tomorrow's crisis arrives." This was the only type of counselling I was ever to receive! Despite this moral support I could not help remembering what Mickey had said: "Remember you're part of the Navy team."

It seemed that everybody was at this inquest; Mickey smiled at me when he arrived. I must have looked very worried, I felt panicky and unsure. The major and his sergeant turned up on time. Our senior gunnery officer ('Guns') started the meeting off by greeting everyone and stating how well we had all performed but that there was room for improvement. He never mentioned the balloon. It was at this point that the major hijacked the meeting by actually apologising for the Army's error in 'downing' the barrage balloon. Further, he added, he

Figure 24. 'Part of the Navy team'

had urged the ATS (Auxiliary Territorial Service, the Army's female branch) ladies manning this balloon unit to do their best to get it repaired and get it airborne as soon as possible. He suggested that the Navy and the Army should carry out extra drill to ensure *his* unit did not make the same mistake again.

Everybody on the naval side, including myself, was delighted with this result and agreed wholeheartedly with the extra drill suggestion. 'Guns' then invited the major to the wardroom for a gin or two. I could not understand why the now-smiling major had 'taken the rap'. I was over the moon with the results. When I went to the major to thank him for covering up for me, the major replied that he wasn't going to let the whole world know that he had been taking instructions from a schoolboy! When I asked Mickey why this chap had taken the blame, Mickey said that he had done it purposely so that it appeared that he had been in charge. "After all," he added, "shooting down one of our barrage balloons gets you noticed and might even lead to promotion. Wars are like that!"

At 0920 hours on Saturday forenoon on 16th November whilst we were still moored, the destroyer HMS *Mistral* accidentally collided with our unusual square stern. The modern theory then was that a square stern gave a ship more mobility, which I believe Drake understood and it still holds good today. As a result of this blow we were left with a sizeable dent. We had scarcely caught our breath when at 0940 we were hit a second time in almost the same spot by the yacht *Ralletta*. Counting the bumps on the train, three knocks in one month seemed to be enough for me. As a result of these two collisions the dockyard commander-in-charge (who had come aboard) ordered us to carry out sea trials to ascertain whether they had damaged the rudder or propellers.

Whilst leaving harbour to make these tests we sailed close to one of the German magnetic mines (recently dropped) which went off with a colossal bang, fortunately causing no casualties or damage to the ship. Enemy air-strikes were becoming more frequent and closer to the ship, we knew when they were overhead because the pom-poms and .5 machine-guns opened up. It was useless for them to fire unless the target was less than two thousand feet.

On the 18th, the submarine HMS *Clyde* moored alongside us so that she could receive the required stores at the same time as we provisioned ship. The packages of stores were collected from lorries on the quayside and we carried them across the ship and down over the other side for the *Clyde*. All this work was carried out 'at the double' (as the Navy put it) during an air raid. I was getting used to hard labour!

The next day the port watch returned from their eight days' leave, again during an air raid, as we were embarking depth charges – not to be recommended in these circumstances!

The 21st was the day selected for the extra gun drill, volunteered for by the major. Another naval saying was, one volunteer was better than ten pressed men, but I had been taught that you never volunteered for anything.

We had been using 'ammo' very quickly and spent the next day ammunitioning ship, again during an air raid. As Tom said, "November is Guy Fawkes month".

So far as I can remember, we were in Plymouth to support the shore-based anti-aircraft units and provide moral support to its citizens. It is certain that we made a lot of noise which must have given the townspeople the feeling that they were hitting back but the pressure waves from our guns were also shaking the tiles off the nearby house roofs, which made us think that they hoped that 'My Lords of the Admiralty' might send this fast cruiser of some ten thousand tons, with its four seventy-five-hundred horse power engines and its twelve six-inch and eight four-inch guns, back to sea where it could be better employed and away from their houses. I shall never forget the hundred and thirty air raids during the month or so we were there, the barrage balloon incident, and watching a third of the city's buildings being totally destroyed and realising that a lot of people (mostly women and children) were being maimed or killed.

On the 24th we changed our mooring and prepared to go to sea to check the operation of our rudder and propellers to ensure that the collisions with the destroyer HMS *Mistral* and the yacht *Ralletta* had not damaged them.

VII

The First Convoys

After the sea trials to test our stern, we left Devonport during heavy air raids. This was the first time that I was ordered to 'swing the lead'. This did not mean having a loaf to dodge some work but to take a sounding to find the depth that was continuously changing as we left land. This old-fashioned method was used to check that our electronic equipment was working accurately and had not been damaged by our recent collisions. This meant standing in one of the 'chains' (generally fitted in most RN ships), which is a small platform each side of the fo'c'sle. The weight of the lead was 14 lbs and it was of leg-of-mutton shape. The bottom of the lead was hollowed out and filled with tallow. This procedure was called arming the lead. When sand or seaweed stuck to the tallow it indicated the nature of the seabed. The eighth-inch-thick line attached to the lead was twenty-five fathoms in length (a fathom being six feet) and marked in the following way:

2 fathoms	two strips of leather
3 fathoms	three strips of leather
5 fathoms	a piece of white bunting
7 fathoms	a piece of red bunting
10 fathoms	a piece of leather with a hole in it
13 fathoms	a piece of blue bunting
15 fathoms	a piece of white bunting
17 fathoms	a piece of red bunting
20 fathoms	a small piece of string with two knots

All these were reported at the top of your voice. "By the mark, 3 (or whatever), Sir!" Fathoms at 1, 4, 6, 8, 9, 11, 12, 14, 16, 18 and 19 are not marked but called 'deeps', therefore you would shout "by the deep, 9, Sir". You always spun the lead underhand and forward in an ever-widening circle above your head and let it go just before it hit the water, calling out "by the mark a deep, Sir". It was an awful job in the dark; you always got wet and cold, day or night. If you shouted "sandy bottom, Sir" after looking at the tallow, and if the navigation officer's chart showed rocky bottom, you would be ordered to recharge the lead with new tallow and start all over again. Years later I remember receiving a telegram on my wedding day saying "please report position and depth and the nature of the bottom at midnight!"

We sighted our first convoy in the Irish Sea and joined their particular zigzag formation. Officers of the watch had a zigzag instruction book giving the angles for at least ten zigzags which were referred to by number. I expected to find these grey shapes of ships bunched together in a small group of about ten ships surrounded by an almost equal number of escort naval ships. Instead, there were about fifty merchantmen distributed over an enormous area of sea protected by only ten escorts, mostly trawlers.

Convoys, besides being dangerous, were hard work, forced long hours without sleep and were always cold and often sad with the many casualties. We also hated travelling at speeds of between six and eight ship knots (seven to nine miles per hour), the speed of the slowest ship and, because of the zigzags, a hundred miles turned into a hundred and eighty miles. A convoy acted as if it was a single living homogenous mass. The ships apparently spread out higgledy-piggledy over the ocean were sailing on a predetermined course and an exact distance from their neighbours, having just sufficient space to obey the convoy 'supremo's' (the commodore's) course instructions and zigzag alterations without colliding with the other ships, particularly at night or in a fog.

I never fully understood why we would, from time to time, catch up with and join a convoy only to leave it after a couple of days when we sailed off in a different direction to the destination that we were originally bound for. The merchantmen always blamed the Navy for deserting them. A convoy was a very frightening place to be.

Whether it was by chance that we were going in the same direction or whether there was some fantastic Admiralty control that knew exactly where every RN ship was and maximised that ship's movements to help reinforce the convoy's protection, even if it was only for two days, we were moved from one hotspot to another. So it was on that December day that we parted company from this convoy and headed for Scapa Flow.

These instructions carried out accurately and with speedy discipline made it very difficult for a single U-boat to carry out a successful attack. All these ships by now (including the fifty merchantmen) carried heavy and light anti-aircraft guns. Should an aircraft carry out an attack on a single ship or a section of the convoy all these ships could open up together. Because of the pre-planned box-barrage system, controlled by the commodore's ship, these attacking aircraft would receive heavy fire from all the fifty-plus guns. The convoy was so arranged that there were empty corridors down the centre and we, the Navy, could sail in spurts down these to assist in the defence of the convoy.

On arriving at Scapa Flow, we lads were allowed to go ashore in the motor cutter with the rest of the off-watch crew for an afternoon to watch a football match between two teams provided from a battleship and a County Class cruiser moored in the 'Flow'. Draped in a heavy coat and wearing black wellies to protect us from the cold and mud, we were landed on one of the many wind-blown islands near our ship. Scapa in the winter was a grey, bleak depressing place, as far as I was concerned, but as there was nothing else on offer a considerable number of spectators had turned up from various ships in the anchorage.

Before half-time had arrived I was suddenly aware that there was a slow movement of spectators deserting the match in the direction of a low dry-stone wall, the boundary of a nearby farm. On the other side of this boundary I could see a muffled figure looking like the Michelin man leading a large, slow-moving brown bull towards several cows grazing in the shelter of a small hillock. From where I stood it was like looking at a film in slow motion. As if sensing something unusual was about to happen, the spectators one by one abandoned the match and slowly descended without any apparent noise to the low dry-stone wall; there must have been some five hundred of them. It was the full-backs that were the first to abandon the match, slowly followed by the rest of the two teams, although at that moment they were unable to see what it was all about. The abandoned referee, provided by the local RAF station, was the last solitary person on the pitch and stuck to his post with the whistle still in his mouth looking very forlorn; he obviously did not understand matelots.

Those five hundred pairs of eyes belonging to the sailors (who had probably not seen the opposite sex for at least twelve months), presumably out of envy of the bull, kept a respectful silence, omitting only an occasional low murmur which sometimes sounded like a sigh of appreciation and admiration as the bull went about his work. The football match ended as a draw as the competition (between the two teams) seemed to have disappeared.

On the way back to the motor cutter, JTB and I stopped to watch two illegal crown and anchor schools being played on the grass – both had attracted players in the hundreds – where the lowest bet was a one-pound note; nothing for boy seamen there. From the edge of the crowd we watched enormous amounts of money changing hands; notes were everywhere being weighed down by large stones to stop them flying away in the wind. JTB and I quickly learnt that you could not beat a crown and anchor board. I suppose both events were part of our growing up but it was and still is an amusing memory. I had, without realising it, grown up in that month at Plymouth; naval growing up, that is, not boy growing up, which gave me more confidence and a newly matured naval outlook which meant living on one's nerves, a good way to lose weight. However, when it came to everyday events like this I was still a seventeen-year-old.

During the next two weeks or so we were moving in and out of Scapa carrying out exercise after exercise and experiencing my first Christmas at sea.

It was a sad Christmas for us lads as we 'lost' another companion. This was the 'communication number' in the after control position, situated on the top of 'Y' Turret (see Figure 7). This cramped position hardly gave sufficient room to house the after control officer, the range finder operator and the boy seaman. There was no room to stand up in this claustrophobic place and only just enough room for one person to enter or leave at a time. You could not 'change over' once in. The boy seaman had to be the first in, followed by the officer and then the range finder. One never knew when a call to 'action station' would occur and if the boy was the last to arrive he would find a queue, this must have been a worry. The position could also get very stuffy.

It was during one of these on-and-off training exercises (sometimes held at night) that this young lad, a Scot, threw an epileptic fit whilst closed up at his action station. To say this caused a panic is to put it mildly. The whole after control night exercise had to be cancelled, just as if the turret had been hit by an enemy shell; all turrets had to be switched to local firing to complete the exercise. It was obvious that a sailor with this complaint could not hold down a job in the Navy and our young Scot was discharged from the service.

Poor young Jock was distraught; he did not want to leave the 'Andrew' but had no option. One wondered about his home life, why did he with an obviously good education join up for a shilling a week? Perhaps he did not want to go home. It's funny how we all missed him and why I always remember him from our short acquaintance; perhaps it was because he was the second of the original twenty boys to leave the ship at sea. The first had been killed on one of our first sea journeys – he was hit by a heavy object which had not been secured properly and fell on him.

On 10th December, Rear Admiral Burrough transferred his flag to HMS *Kenya* whilst we returned to Nuir Skerry Gate. Perhaps the admiral had a good friend on the *Kenya*; only an admiral could choose his Christmas companions.

We weighed anchor for Pentland Firth on 13th December 1940 where we carried out exercises with six-inch and four-inch close-range weapons and fired and recovered torpedoes. Christmas day, which fell on the Thursday, was ignored except for a small early service on the quarterdeck for off-watch personnel. I cannot recall any different menu to celebrate the day. I do recall that the admiral's lieutenant was charged with disobeying naval standing orders in that "he did on the 24th December 1940 give alcoholic liquor to a naval rating". This probably put paid to his promotion for several years to come.

Probably for the first time we catapulted both our Walrus aircraft whilst at sea. To catapult off a Walrus (see Photo 10), which was said to be hand made and three times the cost of a Spitfire, was a dangerous and tricky business. The Walrus was craned up and fixed to the catapult sledge, which was mechanically pulled to the back of the catapult frame by wires (like a hand-held catapult). An eleven-inch-diameter charge was loaded into the catapult-release gun, whilst the pilot revved up his engine to its maximum. The catapult-releasing officer (after seeing the pilot give the 'thumbs-up' sign) would wait until the ship's movement was such that when the catapult-release end was tilted upwards so that the plane would be pointed into the sky, he would fire the eleven-inch charge. The aircraft always 'dipped' a bit before gaining altitude. The top speed of the aircraft was about 120mph and it left the catapult at about 80mph and had to climb immediately. It was important to get this right. The theory as to why so many of these sturdy Walrus survived aerial combat was that an enemy fighter, moving at 300-plus mph, took up to six miles to turn, whereas the Walrus could slow down in the air to less than 80mph and make an almost immediate right or left hand turn, making it almost impossible for an enemy fighter to hit it at that moment.

On Boxing Day we left with the 'battlewagon' (as we called HMS *Repulse*) and its destroyer screen to patrol the Denmark Straits, as Station X had signalled that two German battleships had slipped into the Atlantic to have a go at our convoys sailing to and from America. It was not long before we were picking up signs of U-boats. It was also our introduction to pack ice, which reduced our speed to 12 knots when we ran into it with our returning convoy on New Year's Eve.

'Kye' was always available on watch stored and kept piping hot in two five-foot-diameter stainless steel bowls, kept warm with a high-pressure steam pipe, next to the canteen just aft of the bridge.

Photo 10. The Supermarine Walrus coming in to land

I also learnt on this trip that boys' schooling was to continue in the schoolmaster's cabin on the ship. It was very uncomfortable for five boys and the schoolmaster all jammed together in his small cabin. We were all to be given exam after exam until we passed our ET1 and 2. It was all hard work, being on watch and being a messenger, as well as schooling. I had little sleep. I was on lookout duty (sometimes up the mast), I could be on boat's crew when we were in harbour, and sometimes a golfing caddie for the senior officer, when in Scapa – still, I used to get a cake for that chore from his wardroom galley! There was so much to do I did not have time for seasickness let alone schoolwork.

On arriving back at Scapa on 1st January we found that the six-inch main armament not only made an incredible amount of noise when it was fired but also shook an awful lot of dust onto the mess deck and into your clothes and crockery. It's a wonder how our eyes and ears survived. I suppose there was some protection from the dust in our heavy clothing, particularly our bad-weather headgear. As Tom used to say: "Hardships? You bastards, you don't know what hardships are!" Tom would often come out with a 'Confucius-type' statement when things were particularly bad. A common saying, sometimes taken up by all of the mess deck, was "roll on my twelfth", which referred to the twelve years peacetime sailors had originally signed up for. Another popular pet phrase of Tom's, which he would suddenly shout out when we were all quietly writing letters home was, following a huge sigh, "dear mum, please sell the pig and buy me out, your loving son". To which we would all reply: "Dear son, we've eaten the pig, you'd better sign on for another ten years! Your loving mum."

It was during these times in the mess that JTB and myself learnt to play Mahjong and various card games – there was always a scarcity of reading material. One of our mess mates scoured the ship's ashtrays and collected all the used matchsticks and, after cutting off the burnt end bits with the aid of an ordinary razor blade, glued these matchsticks together with a small tube of Secotine and produced the most amazing models and marquetry objects.

On Monday 20th January 1941, whilst preparing for sea to leave the Scapa anchorage in a hurry to join HMS *Arethusa*, we managed to foul our anchor and the two starboard propellers in the Scapa Flow boom defence net on the sea bed some five to seven fathoms (thirty to forty feet) down.

Our sailing orders indicated an emergency so in these circumstances the captain had no choice other than to order to slip the anchor and some five fathoms of anchor chain.

Hence the special sea duty men, of which I was one, parted a joining shackle and, after tying on a marker buoy so that it might be found at a later date, let the whole lot go (see Figure 25). The captain then ordered us to sea with only one anchor.

Our engine room artificers and stokers were at the same time in the middle of stripping and descaling our fresh-water plant evaporators. A newly-trained engine room artificer quite rightly gave orders to a brand-new stoker to lash down all the different parts of the fresh-water machinery that were being cleaned on the fo'c'sle as we put to sea in case they rolled overboard, which we watched him do as we left the fo'c'sle. I heard our L/S mutter something about 'snowball hitches'. As soon as we had cleared Nuir Skerry boom we assumed our economical steaming speed, used whenever possible to save fuel, which was 17 knots. It was not long before we were contacted by a large Sunderland flying boat, which flew overhead flashing Morse code signals with its large Aldis lamp. It appeared that we were ordered to join the cruiser HMS *Edinburgh* and the minelayer HMS *Maidstone*, which were escorting a nearby convoy. The rumour was that the German battleships *Scharnhorst* and

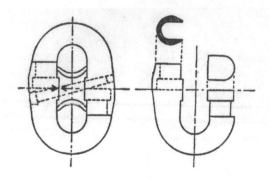

Figure 25. Joining shackle

Gneisenau could be in the vicinity. We immediately increased speed and our stoker's 'snowball hitches' melted (slipped undone) as the green seas broke across our bows and four vital parts of our fresh-water-producing plant disappeared overboard before the engine room artificer could rescue them.

Fresh water was always a problem on long trips. Whilst sailors could do without showers, personal washing and laundry, they had to drink, be it water, tea or 'kye'. The doctor and the cooks needed it too but, most of all, so did the engine room in large amounts for their boilers. The existing fresh-water tanks could not hold sufficient water for all these needs.

It was an unhappy captain who had to tender his apologies and was forced to leave the convoy and return to Scapa Flow waterless and with only one seven-ton hook (anchor). I remember this Friday as if it were yesterday. It was 'heave round the pump week'. Between 0830 hours and 1600, I and some twenty-odd other ratings became 'the diving party' (see Photo 11). We had found the marker buoy and watched as the two divers slowly got into their white rubberised heavy canvas diving suits and huge round bronze helmets, bolted on with brass nuts, enormous lead-soled boots and a large lead weight on their chests. They were connected by two three-quarter-inch-diameter flexible pipes to a four-foot-high, two-and-a-half-foot-square very heavy wooden box housing the two air pumps operated by turning two eighteen-inch-diameter cast-iron wheels.

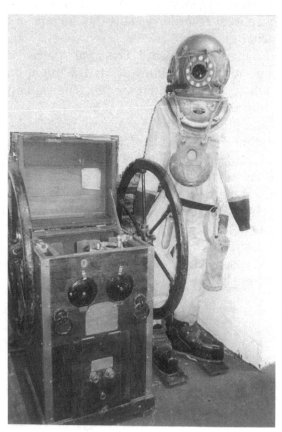

Photo 11. Diver's helmet, weights, boots and suit, showing pump, turning wheels and wooden housing

The only way to get air to these two divers was by the efforts of two very fit sailors turning the iron wheels at speed, which had to be varied from time to time to maintain the correct air pressure (shown on the gauge on the front of the box). This was continuous, monotonous, back-breaking work.

The diving operation went on from the Friday until the following Tuesday. From what I can remember these divers asked to have their tool boxes and a large jack sent down the five-odd fathoms to the sea bed. They were attached and lowered down on a three-and-a-half-inch steel wire with a heavy U-shackle (see Figure 25).

When divers were working below they were paid an hourly bonus of about double their normal wage. So far as I am aware, no other such 'overtime' was paid elsewhere in the 'Andrew'. Also if it was cold, and it was January, at the discretion of the officer of the watch they could receive an extra daily tot of rum. This officer should have made a mental note of conditions, especially as the depth of the water was less than five fathoms (thirty feet), a very comfortable diving depth. They did say that when it was cold up top it was slightly warmer below. For the next five and a half days it was 'heave round the pump' until my arms ached and with no sign of either an anchor or anchor chain rising from the deep: we saw only the two divers who surfaced like clockwork at 1600 hours to be disrobed and no doubt enjoy their extra tot. On Tuesday 28th January 1941 at approximately 1500 a message came over the Tannoy that we were to put to sea within the next two hours. The officer of the diving party gave the order to cease diving, to get the divers and their equipment aboard and to stow their equipment below decks. This was followed by an immediate order to winch up the three-and-a-half-inch wire hawser. The two confused divers arrived first and were halfway out of their suits before the labouring winch had raised the wire hawser to the surface and, surprise, surprise, attached to this wire was a seven-ton Admiralty pattern anchor! It did not take us lads long to realise that these two blokes must have found the anchor quite some time previously and had spent time securing it by the U-shackle to the three-and-three-quarter-inch wire, a fairly lengthy procedure, after which they must have been wandering about filling in time by counting the fish or, perhaps, playing underwater cards or just exercising to keep warm, all for bonus cash plus extra tots whilst all of us poor sods had been working like dogs. What a sailor would do for an extra tot!

We went to sea that day and joined the battleship *Prince of Wales* and immediately closed up for night action. I do recall how tired I was as I had been special sea duty man as well that day. Fortunately the replacement evaporator, spare parts and pipes had turned up to replace the lost parts. I suspect the captain felt he had had more than his fair share of articles lost over the side but on this ship we had all the fresh water we required and two anchors to boot, one either side. I also had to agree that an efficient ship was a happy ship.

There was a buzz about 1st March 1941, whilst we were in Scapa Flow. It was that we were to go south to Vest Fiord, Western Norway. This made us all think about Narvik, which was a haven for German pocket battleships, bigger than us! Stripey wasn't happy about this news, especially when other buzzes said we were going to do something undercover ashore.

On the way south we were told that we were going directly to the Lofoten Islands (68°N x 13°E), near the inlet Vest Fiord which was sixty miles south-west of Narvik.

We arrived there on 4th March (on what was named Operation Claymore but I didn't know it was called that until a few years ago) where we joined about 4,000 commandos who had already landed from their low-landing craft. This was a daring episode which showed the Germans that we were capable of landing on a part of Norway which they occupied. It seemed that our objective was to set fire to enormous tanks containing fish oil – we were laughing, thinking of cod liver oil!

I acted as rear seaman in the pinnace. We put ashore at a jetty at Flakstad (I think) with our special electrical AB with his tools. I had no idea what he was going to do there. Was it something top secret? I saw him leave the jetty and climb up some steps cut into the rocks, leading to a house where he was met by a young blonde lady. He told us later that he had joined her for a cup of tea.

We three sailors returned to *Nigeria* immediately. At about 1450 we returned to the jetty to pick someone up. We could see the oil tanks burning with black smoke in the distance. Eventually our special electrician returned to the concrete jetty and then we picked up one of our officers with a sixty-year-old gentleman in civvies and a bowler hat who had a wooden sea chest which we loaded aboard with the three men and returned them to *Nigeria*. The man and chest were stowed away in an officer's cabin and we did not see them again till we off-loaded them at Scapa.

When we got aboard I told Stripey what I had seen and asked him what he thought it was all about. He replied: "I think that the idea was to blow up the tanks of cod liver oil so that the German soldiers on the Russian front won't get their cod liver oil capsules to keep them fit and well!" We all speculated about what the electrician was doing with the blonde lady.

Since the war I have heard so many theories about what the operation was about. Some say that burning the oil was to stop it being used in the production of high-quality glycerine for bombs; others say that the idea was to capture the armed trawler *Krebs* which had an Enigma machine on board. Lieutenant Hans Küpfinger managed to throw his machine overboard but had insufficient time to destroy other Enigma coding documents which were eventually used at Bletchley – were they in the sea chest?

Frances Day, a West End star, turned up without any warning one chilly evening in April 1941 whilst we were swinging round the buoy at Scapa. I had already had the privilege of meeting her when as a motor cutter boat's crew member we had picked her up with her lady companion and her pianist from the jetty at Kirkwall, some hour and a half's journey in the motor pinnace to our cruiser's moorings. She had been asked by ENSA to sing the show-stopping song about losing a dog in a London fog, a song that left all the boys cold as it was not our type of music. It was chilly both ways as we had been sitting out in the wind on the flight-deck whilst the captain, officers and remainder of the off-watch crew were snugly settled down in the starboard hangar. After the show had finished, all officers that could had retired to the wardroom with the ENSA party for home-cooked goodies and very cheap gins. It was nearly 0200 before a very tired boat's crew mustered in the comfortable pinnace to taxi the party to Kirkwall. In the meantime the wind had got up and I recall delivering a very seasick companion together with a sick pianist who was the worse for drink, although Frances Day seemed to travel well. By the time we arrived back at the ship it was almost breakfast time.

We were to see, or should I say hear, Miss Day's lost dog song on three other occasions. I remember the discussions we lads had concerning Miss Day; this lady must have been at least thirty-six years old, to us this meant she had one foot in the grave! We had come to the conclusion that only amateurs and old people were sent by ENSA, although this was only our first ENSA show. In fact Miss Day's visits were to be the most exciting thing that was to happen to us for years. Her warm and pleasant personality won the hearts of everyone from the captain down, especially one twenty-three-year-old junior officer who seemed to attach himself to her either by orders or voluntarily. It became the one and only ship's scandal situation I can recall. The captain was to name our supply drifter *Frances Day* and, although we never saw her again, her name appeared on the 'daily orders' in connection with the drifter's comings and going for almost a year until we left this boat at Scapa. I suppose Miss Day became part of the ship's family.

Originally on joining the ship every crew member was allocated an 'abandon ship' station. I and forty-nine other crew members, including two officers, were allocated the starboard twenty-seven-foot whaler, with Montague sailing rig K. Although the 'abandon ship' exercise was carried out several times I never gave any thought during these drills, or afterwards, as to how on earth would all these fifty men get aboard this small whaler, particularly during cold rough weather. The whaler had five thwarts (seats) and carried a crew of five when used for sailing, or eleven when being propelled by oars (ten seamen plus coxswain). It is true to say that I only considered this very important point when putting pen to paper for this record. Obviously had we been called upon to 'abandon ship' and to take to the water in this boat (assuming we had been successful in lowering it safely onto the sea), it was possible that about twenty chaps could have got aboard, whilst the other thirty crew members would have had to jump twenty feet overboard and tread water whilst hanging onto the gunwale life-line rope hooks. It was obvious that all the chaps in the water would

Photos 12 and 13. The starboard and port whaler completely damaged by storms and the weight of the ice

not have lasted long. Fortunately 'abandon ship' never came about whilst on Russian convoys but, had it done so, who would have made the decision as to who would sit in the boat or who would be left hanging in the water? I have a sneaking feeling that no-one would have voted for a dry seat for a boy seaman second class!

It all became academic after the colossal northern gales on the top of the world had played havoc with the three-sixteenth-thick cleaver timbers of the starboard whaler.

On finding my 'abandon ship' boat a pile of matchwood I reported to the master-at-arms. "Sir," I said, "the starboard whaler is in pieces." "Yes, I know," he replied. "What shall I do Sir, if the ship is sinking?" "Your duty," he replied. "But, but, Sir . . ." I stuttered. "Well," said the jaunty with a smile, "it's easy. You just take a deep breath and walk along the bottom like me." It was also his 'abandon ship' station; I bet he would have managed to secure a dry seat if we had had to use this boat.

By April 1941 our workload had begun to increase considerably, the war in all theatres had become more involved and complicated. We were spending a lot more time at sea and I was slowly beginning to forget what it was like living in a house with loving people about. Various full-time experienced Navy members of our crew were gaining rapid promotion and taking up appointments on other ships and/or training establishments, being replaced by HO people. These 'green' recruits arrived on board mostly with only six weeks' training and little discipline, which made it hard for them as well as for us. Many of them were quickly ending up as 'Captain's Defaulters'; some kept coming back for more until they finished up with warrants, which after being read to the entire ship's company meant they were sent back ashore for more punishment or, even worse, naval prisons. During March and April 1941 there were twenty such warrants.

April Fools' Day 1941 found us in the North Atlantic with the battle cruiser HMS *Hood*. On 3rd April at midnight, travelling at 16 knots, we parted company from the *Hood* and flew off our Walrus aircraft to search for a missing convoy. At 1337 hours we sighted smoke, which turned out to be the Convoy No. OG57. We joined the convoy at 7 knots and at 1957 hours went to the head of the convoy. Communicating by loudhailer with the commodore of the convoy aboard *Ardeola*, our captain passed the usual niceties of "Good afternoon, commodore", to which he received a similar reply and a request for us to take up station three cables astern of him where our superior 'high-angle' armament would be most effective. It was in the middle of that chilly night that I first recognised the start of toothache. Although it was only mild I knew that a dentist, particularly with all these 'call ups' having their teeth checked, was a rare creature, so in order to save time I joined the 0900 sick parade, commonly known as the 'excused boots' parade. Our doctor, who was a most pleasant man, agreed to find me a dental appointment as soon as we reached a suitably equipped port. It was to be three weeks before this dental appointment became a reality, during which time we had carried out several patrols and a couple of convoy escort duties.

During the second convoy I went to see the doctor and complained about the lack of sleep due to this now bad toothache. The doctor pointed out that teeth were not his strong point and he promised me that if he took this molar out I would feel worse and would wish I had only my toothache to worry about. He suggested that I packed the cavity with aspirin before going to sleep. I followed these instructions and even before I eventually saw the dentist, my mouth, gums and side of my tongue were red raw and painful as the result of stuffing aspirins into the gap.

It was 0600 hours on 21st May when we passed Nuir Skerry Gate and finally anchored in Scapa Flow. I was informed almost immediately by the sickbay tiffy that our doctor had arranged a dental appointment for me at 1100 that morning on HMS *Hood*, moored not more than twenty minutes' journey away by motor cutter from our anchorage. I boarded the motor cutter at 1000 sharp and, being the only passenger, keen to see a dentist, the motor cutter coxswain and boy bow crew set off immediately and headed for HMS *Hood*. All three of us standing in the stern of the motor cutter could not help but be overwhelmed as we watched the huge ship grow in stature as we got nearer to its mooring. Although we had seen it before at sea this was the first time we had seen it that close. It was 857 feet long and 105 feet wide and displaced 41,150 tons; it had eight fifteen-inch guns and a crew of 1,500 and could move at 32 knots. It was one of those memorable occasions, she cut an almost pretty look and of course, importantly to me, had a dentist aboard who I was thinking about with my very aspirin-sore mouth. As the motor cutter came alongside the after prow ladder, I asked "permission to come aboard, Sir" as I was approached by the PO of the watch, "dental party from the *Nigeria*". "OK," answered the PO. "Side boy," he said to the boy seaman standing in the group, "show him to the dental officer." "Aye, aye, PO," said the very young boy seaman second or first class, and then "follow me, mate" as he led me away onto the warm wooden deck waist. The *Hood* not only looked big, it felt big. "Isn't it huge," I said to my young guide, "where's your mess?" "About half a mile down that way," he replied with a grin and I believed him. "You're aboard the biggest thing that floats in the Royal Navy. This is Britain's biggest bullshitting battleship built by Browns," he said with obvious pride as he led me through bulkhead doorways and hatch ways to a seat outside the dental surgery bay.

Waits for dentists always seem like eternity but eventually I was *in* the chair having my very sore tooth drilled by a one-ringed naval dentist. I don't remember having pain-killing injections.

The noises started after I had been sitting there for some time. The Tannoy system came alive with instructions to engine staff, the *Hood* had got up steam. Orders were arriving thick and fast to stow upper-deck gear, including booms and sea boats and the gangway. Suddenly the dental lieutenant said: "I can't finish this job, you'll have to have a temporary packing and come back later." Then as he did this I heard the bugler sound off 'special sea duty men', a call I knew so well as I was one. "You'd better be off as quickly as you can or you'll be sailing with us," he said, with a grin, as he opened the dental curtain door. I hastily heaved myself off the chair and did as instructed and ran out of the dental compartment, took a wrong turning, ended up in one of the *Hood*'s numerous compartments and realised that I was hopelessly lost just as the engines caused the ship to vibrate. The *Hood*'s shudder caused me to develop an almighty panic. I thought, what about the *Nigeria*? It was where my friends were, it was now my home. I would be letting the side down, who would be able to do my job? What sort of punishment would be handed out to me, a deserter? Fortunately I bumped into a stoker dressed in blue overalls and wearing a well-washed white cap cover over his hair like all naval stokers.

"Please," I said, "I'm lost and have got to get back to my ship, please show me to your gangway." He laughed, said "this way lad", and doubled through the compartments and up and down ladders with me hard on his heels and delivered me to the quarterdeck PO in charge of the work party about to haul up the large gangway. "You can nip down these," he said, pointing to the bottom of the gangway already rigged up with its lifting gear, "but you can't walk on water, where's your boat?" "Over there," said I, pointing to our motor cutter which was turning slow circles awaiting my return, and which I was so relieved to see. The PO waved our coxswain alongside and even before he was alongside I literally leaped into the boat before it had stopped. Our motor cutter coxswain, annoyed at my panic jump into his boat whilst it was still moving, said: "You left that a bit late, it's a good job for you I remembered you were still over here and reminded our officer of the watch, otherwise you would've sailed with the *Hood* and you would've found it a bit like living in barracks." I didn't answer; I was still trying to recover my composure after all that terrible panic. We watched this great ship slowly moving towards the 'gate'

Photo 14. The Hood

prior to leaving Scapa Flow without realising that she and all that sailed on her, bar three, were on their way to a cold, watery grave in the Arctic in an unfair contest of war. I still have terrible nightmares about missing or catching the wrong aeroplane, coach, train or ship or being left behind without clothes, money, food or friends.

The *Hood* (see Photo above) was dreamed up in 1900 and built during the Great War but she did not come into service until 1920 and despite many refits was well out-of-date by 1939. Her lightly-built ocean liner type of upper deck was completely free of armour plating, its biggest drawback. It had remarkable modern good looks as well as a speed of 32 knots. I understood that the Admiralty had recommended that it be withdrawn from service to be redecked with the modern style of armour decking; sadly this was never done. She was old and outclassed by nearly every battleship in the world's navies. The ship's major design fault was that it had one large magazine for storing all the shells and cordite charges for its many guns. It had been used successfully in gunboat diplomacy between the two wars but due to its inefficient air conditioning was known to be an unhealthy ship to serve on. I believe there were many cases of TB amongst the crews over the years.

Early on the morning of 24th May 1941 there were four salvos fired by the *Bismark* (one of the most formidable battleships ever built) but the first shell which landed on the *Hood* penetrated her by a combination of efficiency and pure luck. The communal magazine of one of the oldest serving battle cruisers known then exploded, blowing the *Hood* to pieces with its own ammunition leaving only three survivors out of the total crew of 1,400 men and boys, which included my dentist, the friendly stoker, the efficient PO and the proud boy seaman who had all been so helpful to me.

Sailing under the Forth Bridge in a large ship was awesome; I recognised even at that early age that this famous bridge was an exciting example of British engineering. Once clear of the bridge we passed, on our starboard side, what I took to be a large number of units of the Home Fleet but found out they were the 'Wooden Fleet', i.e. old merchant ships transformed with the aid of grey painted plywood to look like cruisers and battleships to fool the German airmen.

To be calling into Rosyth Dockyard held the possibility of home leave. It was over a year since I had seen Mother and Auntie, and I suppose I was getting homesick. We had been working hard and spending a lot of time at sea, I thought we deserved some leave. Unfortunately home leave did not come about except for the locals. After securing in the dockyard, I resumed my 'harbour' duties, most of which were acting as a messenger for the senior officer. This meant following him wherever he went (always keeping one pace behind) and carrying his partly canvas covered brass telescope adorned with the odd 'Turk's head' macramé knot.

Officials coming aboard, if out of uniform, invariably wore bowler hats to go with their civvies, as did the commander's first visitor that morning. This important Admiralty messenger was carrying a large rolled-up drawing. It was always understood that boy messengers 'hovered' a yard behind the commander at all times awaiting any instructions that may come from his officer, whilst at the same time pretending that he had heard nothing. "Good morning, commander," said the 'bowler hat', who had apparently come from the Admiralty. "I've brought you the diagram of the suggested camouflage, complete with its colour-coding for your vessel." The way he spoke made it difficult to know who was the senior man. He continued: "Your paint materials are already on the dockside below." As usual, my commander showed no sign of any surprise and watched as the 'bowler hat' unrolled and spread his drawing of our ship across the quarterdeck skylight. After viewing the details of the sketch for some minutes the commander looked up and said quietly to his visitor: "I see – but pink! Are you sure this is right?" "Oh yes, commander, no doubt about it," replied the Admiralty man. So far as I was concerned all of this was complete double Dutch. Red paint had sometimes been used in small doses in camouflage patterns with light and dark greys, mostly on merchantmen during the 1914–18 war, but had been discontinued in the 1940s because it showed up most of the ship's outlines rather than camouflaging them. Although I was not aware of it then, apparently Lord Mountbatten had come up with a theory that dark red paint and dark grey paint when mixed had special camouflage advantages during the dangerous periods of dawn and dusk. This paint mix was nicknamed 'Mountbatten Red'. However, a camouflage expert named Peter Scott, later to become Sir Peter Scott, had proved this red/grey colour theory to be incorrect. All this seemed to be unimportant when it was announced that one twenty-four-hour leave would be allowed to all seamen who lived within a hundred miles of Rosyth, the starboard watch first and port watch the next day. This didn't include boy seamen who lived in London, which meant that I would be given the afternoon off between 1330 hours and 1800. However, I was lucky (or thought I was) when my friendly mess mate Tom, who had only recently got married, offered to be responsible for me if I could kid the master-at-arms to provide me with a free travel warrant to Carlisle (his home town) where he would provide me with a night's lodgings in his new flat with his new wife. To my astonishment this warrant was issued to me by the jaunty.

Early the next morning Tom, a Carlisle-born marine (known as 'bootnecks' or 'Royals') and I left the ship to catch a train to Carlisle. My two companions managed to consume a considerable amount of beer before boarding the train and had managed to persuade the barman to fill some empty wine bottles with draught beer for the journey. On arrival in Carlisle, Tom insisted that the 'Royal' and myself visit his favourite pub where even I bought myself a drink, and before going home we had a group photograph taken at a nearby studio. There was no way of advising Tom's wife of our unexpected arrival as most people were not on the telephone at that time. On arrival at Tom's flat, a small two-room-and-kitchen affair in need of some decoration, his

Photo 15. Shore leave in Carlisle

wife (after sending the now drunk 'Royal' to his home) put Tommy to bed to sleep it off. Mrs 'Tom' had had no idea that we were arriving and it was left to me to explain the situation. In the circumstances she was very good-natured about it all and agreed I could sleep on their small sofa. Mrs 'Tom' made me a cup of tea, as I was the only one sober. After asking my age and apologising that she did not know any girls aged fifteen or sixteen to introduce me to, she suggested that we should go and meet her mother and father. We bought some fish and chips to eat while her husband slept it off. In the meantime, a man knocked at the door and delivered the photographs.

This lonely lady didn't seem to have much chance to talk to people and proceeded to tell me stories of the old round iron pot! I cannot remember what it was all about but I do remember one thing; I learnt that she had had awful protruding teeth. It was apparently her mother who had advised her, when she arrived at twenty-one years of age, to see a dentist. To put it in Tommy's wife's own words, "mum said if you don't have all those teeth out and get yourself some false teeth you'll never get yourself a bloke". At this stage I was given a demonstration of how easy it was to take out and replace false teeth – an experience I had never had before or, come to think about it, ever since. This small talk was not to my liking and I wished I had not embarked on this twenty-four-hour trip. I remember explaining to a night watch

Photo 16. HMS *Nigeria*

companion some weeks later about this embarrassing situation at which he laughed and said: "You missed a good opportunity there." It took me some months to fathom his meaning.

After spending an uncomfortable night on a too-small sofa, with a stomach trying to digest greasy chips, we arrived back on board to find our three grey-coloured ship had been half repainted by the port watch in four different shades of pink. The dockyard 'mateys' laughed at us as we continued to finish the job that they had started the day before with the salmon pink, light pink, medium pink and dark pink paint.

As we turned to the next day, rigged in our painting gear overalls and old cap covers to protect our hair (and I had a lot then!), we became aware of the wolf whistles and laughter, complete with ribald comments, from mateys of all ages. At 1100 hours sharp on the 30th May 1941 the First Lord of the Admiralty visited the ship to look in wonder at all our pink shades. As I stared down into my pink paint pot, I somehow knew instinctively that there must be something special going on. All that was heard on the 'grapevine' of conversations with this great man was "will it work?" Two days later, with dry paint and having ammunitioned the ship, we slipped quietly away from our moorings still feeling slightly ridiculous as we passed under the Forth Bridge, which was painted in the same shades of red oxide as our ship. We then headed for the open sea and North Pole via Scapa Flow.

Here I was, now eighteen years old, at last a fully grown man and now I was an O/S about to get a huge pay increase. My pay was now seventeen shillings a week which, when added to my one shilling, gave me a total the equivalent in the current decimal system of ninety pence a week. Remember that when I had signed up I had agreed that, whatever I earned, more than half of it would go home to Mother, so now I could spend nine shillings a week all on myself! I was looking forward to the opportunity of going ashore in the evening until midnight and of course drawing my tot, the first of which every member of 13 Mess expected to have a sip of. Most of all, I could tell all the called-up 'hostilities only' make-believe seamen to take a running jump when they started to tell me to do this or that, as they tended to do to the boy seamen.

One Friday in July 1941 at 1705 hours, for the first time since I had joined the ship nearly a year earlier, an order came over the loudspeaker system 'hands to bathe on the starboard side'. The weather had been quite good for Scapa Flow that day. I had always enjoyed a visit to the local swimming baths but Scapa was not Weymouth, so I decided to give the Friday night dip a miss.

Coming to the conclusion that watching cold, silly and reluctant sailors leaping into and out of the cooled early evening 'oggin' (sea water) would be amusing, and having made my way up to the fo'c'sle, which was some forty feet above the water-line, I had appreciated that it would take more than a bit of courage to leap over the side and this could be entertaining for the watcher.

The motor cutter had been lowered over the side and was chugging up and down just clear of the bathers, acting as a lifeboat in case someone failed to come up for the third time. I had settled down to enjoy my evening when I was verbally accosted by the duty PO. "You heard the order boy, get your clothes off and get in." "But Sir, PO, I haven't got a cozzie," was my instant excuse. "Bring me a bit of the schoolmaster's chalk," laughed the PO, "and I will draw you one. Now jump to it, off with your clothes and get in, that's an order." "Sir," I replied. I had no choice; I disrobed, rolled my gear into a heap and put it with all the other heaps of clothes on the fo'c'sle wash-deck lockers.

Being naked, it felt cold even before I got anywhere near the water. But the fear of the forty-foot jump drove all thoughts of cold water from my mind. Pausing only to pinch my nose with thumb and forefinger I shut my eyes, called out loud "stand from under" and jumped. The water was cold, cold enough to make me swim as fast as I could to the swinging rope ladder to climb back on board, only to be greeted by the duty PO once more: "This is an exercise; you have to complete three jumps." I sighed and replied: "Yes, PO." After completing my three jumps it was a real luxury to have a cold-water shower that felt warm and, once fully clothed, to get back to the mess deck for a comforting evening meal of two thick slices of bread and tinned red jam and a slice of tinned fruit cake washed down with a large mug of hot tea. So ended our first abandon ship exercise.

VIII

A Roving Commission

It was 3rd June 1941 when we left Rosyth, all painted pink (see colour photo), arriving at Scapa Flow the following day. Whatever our special 'pink' mission was it had been put on hold for one reason or another.

On entering the 'Flow' we immediately became AA Guard Ship, which meant being at third degree of readiness, even in harbour. We spent the next few days using up a lot of ammunition with our anti-aircraft fire at the occasional Jerry plane and fitting in practice bombardment in Pentland Firth. The end product of this activity was the necessary re-ammunitioning of the ship, very hard work particularly during warm June days.

On 10th June we put to sea on course for Icelandic waters. The ocean seemed to be as busy as Piccadilly Circus with almost as many free-floating mines as cars in Regent Street. It was all continuous work and little sleep.

There were the brighter moments. Trying to explode these bobbing mines from a pitching, rolling ship with .303 rifles at a range of several hundred yards was one of them. It was challenging and great fun, especially if you scored a bull's-eye with its resultant explosion.

We were constantly launching and recovering our Walrus in an attempt to identify our own fishing craft, trawlers and warships to make sure that enemy craft had not infiltrated amongst them. We also acted as 'postman' for one of our cruisers, which had been unable to collect mail from Scapa due to a plague of crabs on board (which nobody else wanted to catch!). I did not like picking up the empty sacks after they had taken out their letters, it left me with an itchy feeling. We felt they should have been flying a fever flag. Of course there were also enemy air attacks. One particularly uncomfortable moment was during such an attack whilst we were oiling at sea.

By now, I thought I had settled down to this challenging way of life but for some reason or other it never occurred to me to consider that we could be hit. Neither was I frightened by bombs or torpedoes although I had seen the damage and the casualties that such things could create. Perhaps all this was youthful stupidity but it appeared to me that there was nothing personal in it. Neither did I get excited when, using my hand-operated computer, I was told 'well done' when I had got it right and we had shot down a Jerry plane or two. It was just purely job satisfaction to us all in the HACP five decks down, with my crew of academics. On these occasions there was neither pleasure nor feelings of hatred for the enemy who made up the crews of four or six men per plane, who were killed, burnt or drowned. Being locked up in an HACP caused us to have the same feelings as a person locked in a room with a poisonous snake. Killing the snake removes the fear but there is no pleasure in the act. We would have the same feeling of relief that our actions had removed the fear of instant death for all of us shut up in the HACP. We didn't see the planes falling down on fire and ditching into the sea but the report that we had succeeded in removing the danger was heartening.

We came upon a damaged sailing boat, which had run out of petrol for its stand-by engine whilst trying to make Iceland without sails. It would have been unwise to stop because of possible U-boats, so we dropped a quarter-filled large petrol drum up-wind of them and watched through binoculars as they collected the drum as it floated down to them on the current and wind. I had a good feeling about this particular venture, especially when things worked out as they were supposed to. I always considered seamanship as a practical occupation and a trade of interest. Our Asdic operators were continually picking up 'pings', and whether they were echoes from shoals of fish, whales or U-boats did not matter, 'action stations' was always sounded off on these occasions which got everyone to their action position. Even if it was only for fifteen minutes or so it interrupted your sleep or let food and tea get cold. It meant you could not have a shower at sea because this meant opening watertight doors which had to be kept closed, and it even interrupted you in the 'heads' (toilet).

I saw my first American destroyer since joining the Navy on this patrol. It gave me the feeling that the US was on our side.

It was on 22nd June at 1823 hours that I had my first proof that (as some people had said) the Germans would flout the rules of war. We had to stop temporarily to lower our 27ft whaler (see photo 21, page 137) but immediately recommenced steaming at a reasonable speed because of the constant presence of U-boats, leaving the whaler to be rowed in choppy seas to a nearby small Faroese fishing trawler named

Visanda to pick up four badly wounded fishermen. They were wrapped into cane stretchers by our sickbay tiffy before being placed in the whaler for the uncomfortable return journey back to our ship. A cane stretcher was an ingenious device made up of bamboo strips encasing the injured person (like an Eskimo's papoose). Once strapped in, the wounded man could be hoisted by a crane or rope and carried at any angle without subjecting him to further physical damage. As soon as the ship became stationary I helped to lift the first badly wounded man up the ship's side and carried him down to our sickbay where our doctor was waiting. We hurriedly removed his patient from the crane stretcher and lifted him onto the operating table, to which he was strapped to stop him moving (ships don't stay still for medical operations!).

This Faroese man wore a white heavyweight fisherman's roll-necked jumper. When I looked at this I thought immediately of my dear aunt's wool shop, in which I had been so many times, with its Paton & Baldwins pullover pattern books. Perhaps that chap's woolly had been knitted by a loving Faroese wife during the dark evenings by a comforting fire. The woolly had two large areas of dry and wet blood where he had been hit in the abdomen and chest. The injured man looked awful. It had happened the day before we arrived when a German plane had continuously strafed them with machine-gun fire whilst they were fishing. 13 Mess was very near to the sickbay and the stink of ether hung about all that night whilst the doctor and the sickbay tiffy worked on all four of them. We got them back to the hospital ship *Amarapoora* by 1248 on the 24 June 1941, still alive. As they passed to and fro by the sickbay the whole crew had kept a strange silence – showing that they felt for these four fellow sailors and were pleased that they were still breathing. The hero of the hour was, of course, our doctor. We felt we were so lucky to have one, let alone a good one. We never had any more bulletins about them, we all hoped they survived but worse things were always happening as we moved on.

It was because of this event that I first became aware of our padre's 'action stations'. Holy men did not 'praise the Lord and pass the ammunition' as the song went, nor did they help fire the guns. We used to call him 'the Curate' because he was so young. He was not what you would call a hale and hearty sort and possibly he had never done a physically hard day's work in his life before joining the 'Andrew'. There was nothing like rushing to your action station as fast as you could to prepare your weapons to take your mind off fear; not so the padre, when he got there he had nothing to do. He was also a terribly nervous chap, which had led some hardened crew members to suggest that he was terrified, and they openly made fun of him. When you needed food and could not leave the weapons, the padre would help the cooks, however cold or rough it was, to carry and distribute hot drinks and corned dog (corned beef) sandwiches to you at your station. He would try (I must say not very well) to cheer you up with spiritual chat. His true 'action station' started when the shrapnel started flying. He would help the doctor and the sickbay tiffy; he would help the wounded and hold the hand of the dying. Over the first two and a half years he had more than his fair share of this. By his actions he forced the entire crew to the conclusion that he was probably the bravest bloke aboard and he never let down injured sailors.

The 27th June 1941 found us at Skaula Fiord in the Faroes but not to go ashore. I had the middle night watch as side boy at the gangway. Our gangway was about the size of a small three-bedroomed house's normal staircase and could be hung over either side of the quarterdeck. It had a wooden grating at its base to let unusually high waves drain through.

A side boy acted as a messenger for the gangway quartermaster (usually an L/S at night). It had been my lot to call on the duty cook to collect a billycan of 'kye' for the pair of us and, as always, being a constantly hungry lad I had begged a couple of buttered-bread slices, which the good-natured cook had supplied. This must have been about 0200 hours. On returning to the gangway post I offered the killick a slice of yesterday's buttered bread to go with his cocoa. He looked at my hands, which had not been washed since I had handled wires and ropes before we anchored, and declined. He just took his 'kye' and returned to his chair and book in the quarterdeck lobby.

My job was to keep watch and report back to him any ship's movements or the unusual. I retired back to the top step of the gangway where I sat down to drink my 'kye' and eat my bread and butter sandwich. It was whilst I was eating that I became aware of movement at the bottom of the gangway so I called the killick from his chair. We descended the gangway to investigate. It was the killick who first spotted the creature in the dim light. "It's only a harbour seal, you idiot," he laughed. "Go for a swim with it if you like, it's a bit cold in that sea," and, smiling, he returned to his book again. I had never been that close to a seal before and marvelled at its huge friendly eyes. Like any lad at that age I felt it was a kindness to give it some of my bread and butter. To my surprise it came forward and put its head underneath the morsel I had thrown in and flicked it up into the air clear of the water. I know seals are supposed to go into a torpor at night but this harbour seal kept me company for about an hour, although it never ate any of my bread.

We never had any girls to distract us from our work but I found that the seas and out-of-the-way places we visited housed an abnormally large amount of wildlife and I count this harbour seal as one of the first creatures that kindled my love for wildlife.

It was in the same week that we found ourselves close to another natural wonder, a large iceberg surrounded by a number of smaller bergs which made curious noises as they moved which, I learnt, were entered in the log as 'growlers'.

On 29th June we were engulfed by what we called a 'friendly, dense fog'. The fog seemed to emanate from the icebergs and, whilst it was a comfortable ally against U-boats, it had its problems when it came to collisions.

On the 30th, having spotted a number of mines, sometimes too close for comfort, we returned to Scapa where during the next day we touched-up our pink paintwork, a colour we had come to accept as the 'norm'.

A small cruiser, HMS *Aurora*, had arrived in Scapa earlier in the month. It was painted in four colours of pink. Whilst we still did not know what it was all about we did know with whom we were going to do it!

The occupants swinging around the buoys of Scapa, some of whom seemed never to move, had come to believe that pinks were the latest form of camouflage. They no doubt had also heard of Mountbatten red.

I was beginning to become disenchanted with my action station in the aft HACP. I suppose it was quite a thing, at my age, to be controlling eight four-inch high- and low-level guns each capable of firing up to ten rounds per minute (that was eighty half-hundredweight shells, which could mean two imperial tons of high explosive a minute). It also meant that at that tender age I was discussing air raid tactics with a full lieutenant, even if he was only 'Wavy Navy'. But I wanted to be where the action was, somewhere upstairs where it was safer and in the fresh air and where you could see the enemy.

The Royal Marine bandsmen (my HACP team) were a great bunch who happily put up with me. These six gentle ex-civilian academics and musicians had from the start accepted my authority because I was, to put it in their own words, 'proper Navy'; something they never wanted to be. I was also getting a claustrophobic feeling after climbing five decks down and shutting myself in with a three-inch-thick armour-plated hatch which might have been impossible to open if the lifting gear became damaged (see Figure 14, page 67). I decided it was alright being almost famous and talking to officers concerning the HACP but the youth in me could not help but realise the frustration of not being able to see what was going on around the upper deck. My friend John T. Box and I had often felt we had missed much of the excitement that appeared to be continuously available if your action station was topside.

On 27th June 1941, whilst off the Faroes, our escort, the Tribal class destroyer HMS *Bedouin*, had sighted a German trawler weaving in and out of the many 'growlers' and fog patches. We altered course rapidly to starboard and gave chase, trying to catch up with the enemy. I missed all this excitement by being locked up at action stations in the aft HACP. I suppose I wanted some youthful excitement, not responsibility. It seemed I had a duty to Mother and Auntie, to my country and to a large steel box full of unfriendly dials (see Figures 9 to 13, pages 63 to 66).

June and July were very busy months when everything seemed to be happening in and out of Scapa. There were two Courts Martial aboard, always serious affairs. Articles of War were always read out to the ship's company and, if the crime was treason or sedition, the accused could end up being shot after attending one of these. A Royal Marine lieutenant was admonished for discussing possible future movements of our ship with a marine of no rank from another ship whilst ashore on official orders in Kirkwall. The second Court Martial held in the starboard hangar (after removing the Walrus aircraft) concerned two ordinary seamen who had fallen foul of the Scottish police whilst on leave in Rosyth; what they had been up to I had no idea but it got them a couple of years each in HM Prison, Inverness.

I discussed this crime with Stripey and made it clear that I thought the punishment was harsh. "Ah, yes young Cutts," explained Stripey, "*we* should get those two years and be safely in prison, whilst those two lads should be made to sail this ship and perhaps end up being killed, injured, or drowned in '90 second' fuel oil or something similar." I thought Stripey had a point; it appeared that magistrates and naval captains were somehow missing the point.

On Sunday 20th July at 1345 hours, without any warning, a fleet drifter (a general supply trawler serving Royal Naval ships anchored in the 'Flow') turned up transporting some twenty-five Wrens, wearing old-fashioned Girl Guide hats. They had been invited to come aboard some weeks ago by our popular padre. There was a rush of volunteers to show them over the ship, whilst the rest of us just stood back and blinked. There had been no warning. Everyone just stood and stared as can be seen in the photograph.

At 1545 the drifter returned to take them back to Kirkwall, that is, all but the two Wren officers who were invited to dine with the officers in the wardroom.

Photo 17. The Wrens arrive

At 2000 hours the duty motor-boat crew was piped to man the pinnace which was secured to the starboard boom. The rest of the duty boat's crew, including myself, manhandled the pinnace to the port gangway just as a group of the ship's officers (buzzing like bees round a honey pot) were escorting the two Wren officers to the gangway wishing them *bon voyage*. One has to remember that other than on the twenty-four hours' leave in Rosyth, these chaps had not seen women of any sort for over twelve months and never before on board. As we two lads held the pinnace alongside the gangway our L/S, acting like a gentleman (which normally he was not!), assisted the two Wren officers aboard. Whilst this was going on someone flushed an officer's toilet, the outlet of which was within three feet of the gangplank attached to the gangway and, slowly for all to see, up floated an unwrapped thick white used condom, nearly full of air, which refused to sink. We ended up with two very red-faced lady officers and a group of confused ship's officers. I had heard jokes about 'French letters' since I was about eleven years old at school but this was the first one I had seen and my mind boggled. Did this mean that on this ship, packed with about eight hundred male occupants, during a dinner party being given by our commander, some enterprising officer or matelot had managed to smuggle away one of these two females, seduce her and then return her to the dinner table before she was missed? It took a lot of believing! The boat's crew on discussing it on our return trip came to the conclusion that this was a colossal joke operated by the officers' stewards who had been working like slaves whilst watching the ship's officers enjoying themselves with these two Wren officers. I never heard any more about the affair.

120

One of the crew, who had acted as a guide that afternoon, bragged that he had kidded a Wren to climb down to the bottom of 'B' Boiler Room after he had assured her that this was where the last rivet was fitted when the ship was built; of course it was the famous Golden Rivet. Having got this Wren all the way down to the lowest boiler room companionway, this likely lad started to undo his seven fly-buttons (or so he said), but all he got for his pains was a Scottish screech and she was gone, leaving him alone to rebutton his trousers. We all laughed but, of course, did not believe a word of it.

Rear Admiral Philip L. Vian was well known for his handling of the fleet and for his deeds in the Mediterranean. However, he was mostly known and admired for his buccaneering performance in the successful boarding of the German supply ship *Altmark*, where he had definitely shown a touch of the 'Hornblowers'. C.S. Forrester could have used him as one of his heroes. He had not only captured the imagination of the entire British Navy but of British civilians as well for his daring and brilliance in the boarding of the *Altmark* whilst he was a captain in command of the Tribal class destroyer HMS *Cossack*. Even this destroyer had the right sort of name for the occasion.

The *Altmark* was registered in what was then, early in the war, neutral Norway. The famous sea battle involving the *Graf Spee* was over. HMS *Exeter*, HMS *Achilles* and HMS *Ajax* had driven the damaged pocket battleship into a South American port and Hitler had ordered the captain to scuttle her.

Before this battle, the marauding *Graf Spee* had preyed on merchantmen using most of the southern sea routes. All the prisoners taken at these sinkings were transferred to the *Graf Spee*'s supply ship, the *Altmark*. These prisoners were only picked up after their ships had been sunk because Hans Langsdorf, the *Graf Spee*'s captain, did not want to risk them surviving and giving away his position. Some German U-boat captains overcame this problem by simply murdering the swimming survivors. Fortunately for the crews, Captain Langsdorf was a traditional seaman of the old school who obeyed international rules. Captain Philip Vian was in command of the *Cossack* when he encountered the *Altmark* on its way back to Germany via a Norwegian port. International Maritime Law made it impossible for a Royal Navy ship to attack a Norwegian-registered ship inside territorial waters, although it was known that there were British prisoners aboard the *Altmark*. On the other hand, Vian had the old-fashioned mind of a buccaneer. Whilst in Norwegian territorial waters, HMS *Cossack* rushed up to and secured alongside the still-moving *Altmark*. Immediately a couple of dozen of the *Cossack*'s crew armed only with long blue woollen seaboot socks, which held a five-inch-long by two-and-a-half-

Photo 18. Boys in the starboard waist

inch-wide and thick piece of yellow 'pusser's hard' soap held with a figure of eight knot to keep it in, swarmed over the ship's side capturing the German ship without a shot being fired, even though the officers and POs were armed with revolvers, the soap/sock weapon apparently being used freely by the 'Cossacks'. It was a great success and all the POWs were transferred to HMS *Cossack*. All of this must have delighted Winston Churchill. I cannot really say for certain when this famous man came aboard. I don't think he embarked at Rosyth, I suspect it was at Scapa Flow.

The Admiralty had dreamed up a new role for this recently promoted rear admiral called a 'roving commission' which meant, so far as we could understand, that Vian could take the war to the enemy without first asking the Admiralty's permission, or ours either! To do this he had been given, besides *Nigeria*, HMS *Aurora,* and two fast well-armed Tribal class destroyers. In July 1941, the *Nigeria* was withdrawn from the 10th Cruiser Squadron and our well liked and respected Rear Admiral Burrough transferred his flag to HMS *Kenya.*

I vividly recall my first meeting with Philip Vian. We had left Scapa and were making our way steadily northwards at 17 knots, our economical steaming and safe U-boat speed, at the third degree of readiness. I had had the middle watch (2400 to 0400) and my sleeping time between 0400 and 0600 had been interrupted with a false alarm dawn action stations at 0500. Called at 0600 for breakfast and back on watch at 0800 for the forenoon watch, the entire afternoon watch period was my free time, so after lunch I went for a walk in the starboard waist.

With the exception of the quarterdeck, definitely officers' territory, the port and starboard waists (meaning the middle part of the ship's figure) were the only part of the upper deck which were covered with wooden deck planks. All other decking consisted of steel plates with lots of welded anti-slip serrated metal strips which made it uncomfortable to lie or sit on and almost impossible to go for a relaxed walk on. Hence the waists, protected from wind (if you selected the correct side), were comfortable to lie, sit and walk on. Walking backwards and forwards for half an hour or so was an enjoyable pastime. I tried, like five hundred other users, to carry out this exercise daily if possible – looking out to sea whilst fascinated by the ship's motion through the ever-changing colours and patterns of the waves, the swooping and cries of the sea birds and the occasional unusual sights of wildlife or flotsam and jetsam (and, of course, the occasional mine!), which I found most relaxing, especially in the company of good friends.

It was sunny on this afternoon, the wooden deck was dry and warm, and I found the bulkhead smooth and comfortable as I sat down to take a rest and in no time at all I was fast asleep, helped by the gentle movement of the ship.

I don't know how long I had been there asleep when I was suddenly awakened by a naval officer's highly polished boot lightly prodding me in the ribs. My slowly awakening vision followed this leg up past its body and its heavily gold-braid covered sleeves and came to a halt on Rear Admiral Philip Vian's piercing blue eyes overhung with exceptionally bushy eyebrows. This woke me up instantly, at the same time causing me to leap to attention. "Find somewhere else to sleep," hissed the rear admiral, who was commandeering the whole of the starboard waist for a walk in the sun. "Yes, S-Sir," I stammered as I ran away.

I complained to Stripey about our new gruff rear admiral but all he did was roar with laughter, as did the rest of my messmates. "If you will sleep with such high company," he said, "you should expect to lick their boots, and you'll go a long way in the Navy." "Like to the masthead," added another mess mate.

Rear Admiral Philip Vian and his two liaison officers embarked officially on Friday 25th July 1941 and we hoisted his pennant with its small red ball onto the rear mast jib. At 2300 that same evening an Army major (Royal Engineers) seemed to sneak aboard attracting minimal attention and carrying only a small Army haversack. It was extremely unusual to have an Army man on board, let alone a Royal Engineer. He would *not* let anyone carry his light luggage for him.

At 0920 hours the following morning all our officers were introduced to the rear admiral in his cabin. At 1230 the rest of the crew were ordered to muster on the quarterdeck where Philip Vian introduced himself. He looked fierce (I have already explained this ferocity at my last encounter with the great man). This was the usual naval 'pleased to see you' speech containing the phrases "an efficient ship is a happy ship" and "I expect everyone to do his duty" and so on. To frighten the life out of us, a junior officer read out the Articles of War. Vian told us that under his command we were to become 'Force A' together with HMS *Aurora*, and the two Tribal class destroyers HMS *Tartar* and *Punjabi*, which were now also painted pink. This 'Force A' was to have a roving commission designed to take the war to the enemy at all times. Whether it was our recent swimming exercise or just the look of the man I do not know but we were all apprehensive. We had already gathered that the four pink-and-salmon-painted ships were bound together for whatever was coming and that they had possibly been picked because of their speed (all four craft were capable of 33 knots). The added presence of the Royal Engineer and the collection of special complicated portable wireless sets that had arrived at the same time from the Tyne depot ship sharpened this mystery.

Whilst all this was in progress one of our boy seamen (aged sixteen and a half) had gone sick. He had been wrapped in a cane cot and sent to the hospital ship *Amarapoora* for urgent treatment. We learnt almost immediately that he had died on the journey. It seemed awful; we were now down to fourteen boys. The boys' mess deck had another empty space. These empty spaces, sadly, always reminded you of the lad or man who used to sit there and in your mind they really never went away. The flag was at half-mast again. At 1830 hours the next day a replacement midshipman joined the ship; he looked much younger than me but they said he was almost eighteen! He arrived with four new ratings to replace our casualties and the two 'lucky devils' sent to prison in Scotland.

The next day at 0947 I joined my fellow special sea duty men on the fo'c'sle to weigh anchor and stream the PVs. We were quickly joined by our 'Pinky' friends. I recall we all had similar worried thoughts: "What was this so-called 'Force A' going to get up to?" At almost midnight we sighted the fishing trawler *Northern Reward* bearing 350º, seven miles away. This was like meeting an old acquaintance. We had come across this trawler several times before, with its men bravely fishing alone at night and minding their own business, apparently ignoring the war. On this night it was different as we quickly found out when we were forced to carry out an emergency turn due to a reported sighting of a periscope belonging to a German submarine stalking our old acquaintance. This time the *Northern Reward* was lucky. The U-boat captain picked up on his hydrophones eight incredibly fast-moving propellers dashing towards him and this persuaded him to abandon his attack and disappear. All of this of course got everyone to action stations; more broken sleep for those off watch!

On 28th July at 2326 hours we anchored in Seidis Fiord, in Iceland, keeping 'steam up' and at five minutes' notice. We had hoped to have a good night's sleep. However, at 0349 on the 29th we weighed anchor and made passage up Seidis Fiord and at 0535 secured alongside the oiler *War Sudra*. Even though it was so early in the morning I could not help but notice what a handsome vessel HMS *Tartar* was as we moored alongside her and passed the oil supply pipe across our decks from the oiler *War Sudra* to fuel HMS *Tartar*. She was the latest thing in sleek lines and gave me the impression of both power and speed.

There was a 1030 meeting aboard *Nigeria* of the four ships' captains, chaired by the rear admiral. A 'buzz' would always develop in these circumstances. They were always good for a laugh, and occasionally 'buzzes' turned out to be true. It was not surprising that after such a meeting the officers' steward, who had served them coffee, came up with the 'buzz': "We're off to Norway to sink a German battleship." When pressed, he said: "There was a chart of the Norwegian coastline on the table next to the coffee tray."

After weighing anchor at 1300 hours on 29th July, instead of plotting a course east to Norway, our navigator set our nose north towards Greenland, in company with our 'Pinky' friends who looked a splendid sight in the beautiful afternoon sunlight.

At 2000 we sighted a vast spreading dense sea fog, so thick that 'Force A' had to rig stern-towed fog buoys, slow down and form a 'line ahead fog streaming pattern'. All of this was a new experience for me.

On Wednesday 30th July 1941 at 1839, because the fog had lifted temporarily, we stopped to allow a war correspondent, his photographer and their gear to be transferred from HMS *Tartar*. As they boarded, these two people would not be rushed and took a whole eleven minutes, despite our captain's frustration. "We're sitting ducks, officer of the watch," he shouted. "Get those two to move their fat arses." "Aye, aye, Sir," roared the officer of the watch who was equally concerned. At 1850 we got underway again, speeding off at 150 revs in case the odd 'tin fish' was about. A war correspondent was a whole new 'ball game' for the 'buzz' manufacturers. The next day at 0800 hours we sighted a mountain peak on the horizon.

The AB who was the navigator's yeoman always kept us informed of our position on the planet (it made him feel important), so we knew it was Spitzbergen. It was the padre who told us that we were the first Royal Navy ship to arrive at Spitzbergen since Nelson's days. It certainly looked as if it was to be an interesting day! At 1215 we commenced spreading into a line-abreast formation with 'Force A'. This action heightened everyone's interest; we were obviously looking for something or someone. At 1300 we sighted the fleet oiler *Oligarch*, which had also been looking for us. We could now see the peak of the mountain Lexbjell. At this point, *Tartar* parted company from us to search in another direction. We launched the port Walrus aircraft to help with the search and extra lookouts were posted. The 'buzz' was that we were looking for a German merchantman that would be flying the Norwegian flag. An armed boarding party was getting ready and the motor cutter was attached to the crane ready for a speedy launch. The peaks of Mount Morace and Salfgill came into sight and not long after we arrived at Isfjoid Fiord. As a mere onlooker, I found all this exciting. It was a busy day. By 1700 hours, 'Force A' had assembled as required for the passage up into Isfjoid Fiord and at 1800 assumed course and speed for entering Advent Fiord. At 1815, we made a sudden stop to lower by crane the motor cutter and send off our boarding party. We had found our quarry, a Norwegian steamer called *Dagny*.

Photo 19. The Dagny

The Norwegian prize was taken without any blood being spilt and our successful boarding party was ordered to lock up the captain, stay aboard and guard the *Dagny,* which was to be anchored in Advent Fiord. For the Navy to capture a prize meant we all shared in the prize money but how much would this amount to for me? I had to wait some five and a half years for this six pounds and ten shillings prize money, the cheque eventually arrived with six campaign medals and ribbons, also enclosed with these two items was an Admiralty reminder explaining the contents and reminding me I could still be recalled to active service as I was automatically a member of the Royal Fleet Reserve. This arrived just before the Korean War. Regrettably, I seem to have lost this communication!

We stopped again off Longyearby to launch our second aircraft and recover the first. Intelligence reports had suggested that U-boats were landing small groups of German soldiers. (I found out after the war that there were fifty-odd Germans established some hundred miles north of this position.) The admiral was taking no chances.

At 2216 we recovered our second aircraft while hiding with *Tartar* in Advent Fiord. We left this fiord with *Tartar* in company and at 2219 stopped to hoist out our aircraft for take-off on flat calm water, and then at 2230 proceeded back to Isfjoid where we were joined by *Aurora* and *Punjabi* and set course to K Linne lighthouse. It had been a long day!

At 2230 hours, as I made my way back to the mess deck to catch up on an hour's sleep before my middle watch, I was reminded by the schoolmaster, as he passed me on his way aft to his cabin, that he had not yet received my homework for July. I was under strict instructions from the first lieutenant to keep up my schooling if I wanted to pass my ET1 and ET2, both standard Navy education tests and essential for future promotion. The schoolmaster was a really pleasant chap and I did not want to let him down either, but sleep was all I had on my mind at that moment.

After all four of 'Force A' had oiled from the *Oligarch,* which had made its way to Spitzbergen without any escort, we left Spitzbergen with our 'Pinky' friends during the middle watch and steamed for about four days due north to be enveloped, once again, in one of those amazing thick fogs that you see in the distance as an immense low black cloud hugging the surface of a usually flat calm sea. They can last for days.

Whilst enclosed in this weird environment, all the time getting nearer to the permanent summer polar pack ice, we were informed by our captain that the object of the trip was to capture (before it had the chance to scuttle) a German weather trawler which carried half-a-dozen specialist scientists aboard whom the admiral wanted to capture. We learnt that each of the four members of 'Force A' would have ready a boarding party so as not to waste valuable time. Our boarding party comprised a junior officer, a PO, three seamen, three marines, an engineer officer and two stokers. It was explained that the engineer and stokers would dash below and check the trawler's sea cocks and do all they could to keep her afloat for as long as they could. Only the junior officer and PO would carry side arms; all other chosen boarding party ratings would arm themselves with a non-lethal weapon, namely, Vian's famous six-by-six-by-two-inch bar of pusser's soap in a seaboot sock, nicknamed a 'Vian Mk II Stonickee'. The object of the exercise was to take a dry trawler with live prisoners. This boarding party was to leap aboard from our port or starboard waist, hopefully at a correct height to land safely onto a possibly moving trawler. A second boarding party of six seamen and a PO would attempt an almost suicidal leap from the fo'c'sle, if the first boarding party failed. There was a call for volunteers. All of us lads volunteered instantaneously and the PO smiled as he took our names. "I'll pick the best stonickee," he said. I immediately went below to my locker to select my best long sock and was one of the first to queue to buy a full bar of pusser's soap from the 'slops' for fivepence.

It was clear that all four ships would form a line abreast and attempt to get between the solid ice shore, from which the low sunshine would be behind us, and the moored trawler. Apparently 0500 was the best estimated time to produce these conditions. There was great excitement; it was obvious that this trawler was a complete mystery to everybody except the admiral. The thick fog clung to us for three and a half days as we steamed at a reasonable speed in 'follow my leader' formation, depending totally on radar for protection from a *Titanic*-type collision with an iceberg, during which time we hardly ever saw our 'Pinky' friends. I had, much to my disappointment, been informed that I was to act as messenger to 'Jimmy-the-One' and, therefore, could not be considered as a member of the boarding party. I kicked myself for wasting five pennies on soap that would last me for almost two years. It was during the fore watch that the fog finally came to an end. It was sudden: one moment we were in the fog and the next moment we broke free into gorgeous sunlight. We were well in the twenty-four-hour daylight latitude, as our navigator's yeoman said, "only two hundred and fifty miles from the North Pole". By brilliant naval navigation, helped by radar, we had arrived at the right place at the right time.

As the four pink-striped ships burst free from the fog they immediately formed themselves into the pre-planned line abreast formation with the *Punjabi* on our port side and the *Aurora* and *Tartar* to starboard.

We were all so positioned with the permafrost shore and sun behind us that we all immediately understood 'why pink?' The low sunshine

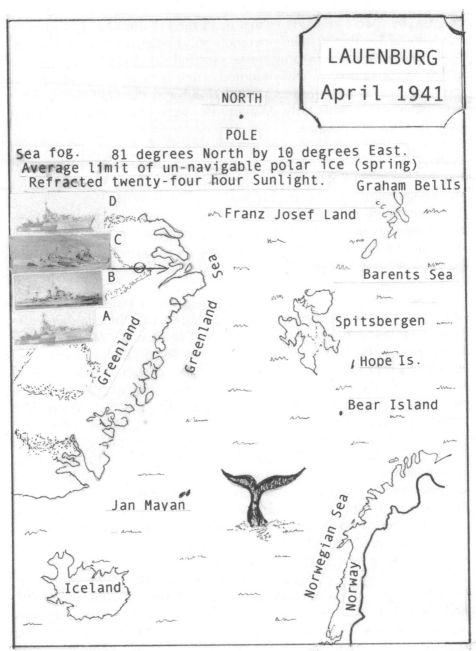

Figure 26. Capture

produced four or five different shades of pink by the refraction and reflection of the sunlight through the various prisms and reflecting ice areas, all a perfect match to our own paint job (clever Peter Scott!). Before we had arrived we had been told to ignore signalling by WT, semaphore or Morse code signal lamps. The order for full speed would be given by special signal flags that had been pre-arranged (possibly by the admiral for this specific operation only) hoisted to our masthead. As I stood waiting to take my orders behind my 'Jimmy-the-One', we all became aware of a newly-painted white trawler – at that time of day white stood out – but as we got closer and the light changed we saw that she was quite tatty. At about the same time, the pre-arranged flags flew up the halyards.

Even at 0500 hours it was exhilarating to feel a 10,000-ton ship under your feet exerting power to increase speed from 10 knots to the maximum 34 knots, and a wonderful sight to see the three other ships, especially the Tribals, on that beautiful morning.

Although we did not know it then, the German encrypted weather-reporting trawler *Lauenburg* was quietly lying at anchor some three miles ahead of us and it was not until they suddenly saw all four boats, moving at full speed toward them, that they started taking any evasive action.

Like cheetahs, the two destroyers got up speed faster than the rest of the ships and by its position alone the *Tartar* was the one that made history, by being alongside the *Lauenburg* first. It was her stokers who found that 'Jerry' had managed to slip anchor and had also managed to open one of the sea cocks. They also found some of the German scientists on the upper deck throwing documents overboard. These typewritten documents, once thrown overboard and wet, looked like blotting paper and rapidly dissolved in the sea. The *Tartar*'s boarding party quickly put a stop to this destruction. Vian ordered us to get close. Eventually the admiral got aboard the trawler and all the other officers stood back. I simply stayed on the *Nigeria* with the lieutenant commander as his messenger; some of the *Tartar*'s crew were the boarding party. It was all of a rush, everyone was picking up cases, sacks, cardboard boxes, packs of loose brown-paper wrapped around orders and, amongst all this, a polished wooden box encasing a strange-looking typewriter (see Photo 20).

All these items were quickly passed aboard the *Tartar* and some onto the *Nigeria*. I am not sure, but I think it took an hour and a half, and then there was nothing anyone could do as the *Lauenburg* was sinking. We left the scene, leaving the two destroyers to watch the *Lauenburg*'s final moments before she sank. As far as I know there was nobody hurt or killed, or any guns fired.

Whilst acting as messenger to our lieutenant commander it had been obvious that the clerical contents from the slowly sinking weather-reporting trawler were very important to our new admiral and all his hierarchy. The ship's company had been told that the *Lauenburg* had been there solely to produce weather reports for the use of the German Luftwaffe. The trawler took temperature readings and air pressure measurements, which were obtained by sending a weather balloon carrying instruments up into the heavens. This data was signalled to Germany by wireless telegraphy and enabled their High Command to pick the best weather conditions for their night and day air raids on Great Britain. This on-the-spot information gave us all a feeling of having achieved a great success, which was an added pleasure to all for a job well done. Some forty years had to pass before I found out what a fantastic

Photo 20. The 'Enigma' machine

achievement it had actually been to capture a German naval 'Enigma' machine (we had never heard of 'Ultra'), leading to the destruction of many of Hitler's U-boats and thereby saving hundreds of sailors' lives and many ships in the Atlantic and Mediterranean. I also found out that my dear wife Joyce, who had been a Wren during the war, had worked at 'most secret' establishments including Bletchley Park and had had some connection with this wooden boxed 'Enigma' machine, which has since become part of our family history. Like all the personnel working at Bletchley, Joyce was sworn to secrecy and did not inform me of these facts until her current Official Secrets Act had run out, despite writing to me for the entire six years of the war and having had three meetings with me during leave and our marriage in 1947 (even though she was aware of my Arctic trips). It made me as an ex-boy seaman feel very humble, especially as I had considered it all as a bit of a lark at the time.

We left this twenty-four-hour daylight latitude leaving the boarding party at Spitzbergen on the *Dagny* and headed straight back to Scotland. This alone should have told us how important the Arctic trip had been, leaving nine of our blokes thousands of miles from home.

I cannot recall which unit of 'Force A' took over the prisoners. When we arrived at Rosyth we were met by a 'bowler hat' who had come to collect our 'typewriter' and boxes of papers. I never pass a bloke in a bowler hat without thinking about pink and pusser's hard soap and socks. How my fellow seaman Tom laughed: "So you wanted to be a pirate and you ended up as a Chinese laundry man with too much soap. You'se loves the Navy."

It was at Rosyth that we learnt, with great joy, that each watch was to get a week's leave, and that railway warrants would be available. I could not have afforded to pay my own fare home! The last letter I had received from home had informed me that my young brother Peter had obtained a place as a boarder at Newport Grammar School on the Isle of Wight and that Mother and Auntie were moving to the Isle of Wight to be near Peter. Reading between the lines I could not help thinking that they had gone to dodge the London air raids as well but, possibly, they couldn't bring themselves to say so.

When collecting my travel warrant, which was made out to Totland Bay, Isle of Wight, the jaunty had made it quite clear that it might, if there was any enemy action, take me more than one day to get from Dunfermline to Totland Bay. He also reminded me of the consequences of turning up late after my week's leave. His warning was still ringing in my ears as I left with a bunch of fellow crew members by bus to Dunfermline railway station clutching my warrant – lose that and you were in great danger of losing everything! We arrived at Edinburgh station to find that the first train to London did not leave until 2300 hours; it was then late afternoon. Having found the already crowded platform, I sat on my greatcoat as near the front of the platform as I could get, amongst all those sailors, soldiers and some airmen, and settled down for a seven-hour wait. There were two tea trolleys being pushed round the railway station, one manned by the Salvation Army (again, these good Samaritans came to my rescue) and the other by the Women's Voluntary Services. Twice during this period of waiting they turned up on our platform. For sixpence one could get a large white vitreous enamel mug of tea and either a bun or cake. I had not eaten since midday on the ship, so these two small morsels were a godsend. The train arrived on time, as even in the war, I found out, they mostly managed to do. With luck it came to a halt with a door into the corridor section right opposite me, without any problem at all I scrambled in and bagged a corner seat.

In no time at all the train became packed, including the corridor and WC – a seat is a seat even if you have to move out occasionally! The mixed service crowd of soldiers, sailors, airmen and ATS soon settled down. The other space used in our carriage was one of the luggage racks, where the shortest soldier placed his folded greatcoat as a mattress and his backpack as a pillow and with the help of his two seated pongo (British soldier) friends heaved himself up to sleep his way to Paddington in London. Before you could say 'knife' all these wartime travellers appeared to be asleep; perhaps we had all come to realise what a luxury sleep was and therefore never wasted sleeping time. I have always found time at night to do my worrying; I wondered whether Mother and Auntie, who did not know I was on my way, would be there when I arrived? I had had no way of telling them. Telegrams were too expensive and mostly unobtainable in the war.

The train was slow and did not arrive until almost midday. I hardly had time to drink a cup of Salvation Army tea and swallow a bun (my breakfast) before negotiating the London Underground to Waterloo hoping to catch a train to the Portsmouth to Isle of Wight ferry connection. I shared the carriage to Portsmouth with a pleasant family with two children who, on hearing how hungry I was, produced an apple when we were halfway there.

I arrived at Portsmouth Ferry Terminal, a place I will never forget, with an hour to spare. I was both tired and hungry when I had what I thought was an incredible stroke of good luck. In the wooden tearoom was a pork pie residing on a large glass plate, covered with a glass lid. "May I have that pork pie and a cup of tea please?" I asked the lady, who was dressed in a green pinafore with 'Southern Railway' embroidered across the top in darker green cotton. "I don't know," she said, "it's been there since yesterday." "I've been travelling since yesterday, have you anything else?" "No," she said, "there's a war on, don't you know?" I ignored this remark. "I'll have it," I said, "how much?" as I reached in my belt wallet for the cash. She lifted the glass-domed lid and passed the round pork pie to me on a plate. "It's yours," she said with a smile, "the tea is tuppence." "Ta," I said and, without hesitation, I gobbled down the pork pie with its very dry pastry and washed it down with the hot tea. As I left to catch the ferry for Ryde I said "thanks very much" and she smiled. I found my way to the highest position on the ferry, a new-found habit – it gave you the best view and if the boat was likely to sink it was the best position for abandoning it in a hurry! Most of the passengers on the ferry were pongos, together with a few civilians, all of whom if they were so inclined, could observe my actions. We were about halfway across to the Island when I began to feel very sick, it was a nice summer day with a sea that was a standard millpond job when, without warning, I was violently sick nearly losing my hat in the effort. Having expelled my free pie into the Solent and feeling much better I was distracted from my temporary misery by the sound of loud and raucous laughter coming from some thirty-odd pongos, one of whom shouted. "If your stomach is so weak that it can't make it to the Isle of Wight on a sunny calm day, you'd better chuck the Navy and join the Army," to much more noisy laughter. Red-faced I had to hide myself from their stares and wondered whether, from the feel of my stomach, the pie might have been in that glass container since 1939!

Having found my way to their new flat in the pleasant village of Totland Bay I was very pleased to find both Mother and Auntie at home. They were both so surprised and happy to see me that I quickly forgot that I was tired and hungry. Regrettably I was unable to see my brother or sister. Peter was still at school in Newport and my sister Joan, who had joined the RAF as a nursing sister, was stationed at an airfield in Bedfordshire.

I had been on the island for two days and was realising that time was running out when my aunt introduced me to the bank manager's daughter who worked in the bank below the flat. Her name was Dulcie; she was sixteen. It was Auntie Wyn who suggested to Dulcie that she should take me to Alum Bay that afternoon and show me the coloured sand. Much to my pleasure she agreed. She was a very pretty girl. It was a beautiful summer's day as Dulcie and I made our way to Alum Bay armed with a small bottle to collect the coloured sand. Somehow or other we never achieved this and ended up sitting on a freshly cut stook at the edge of a harvested cornfield. There was a feeling of desperation in me as I was due to start back to Scotland the very next day. With determination and urgency I didn't wait to ask, nor did I pussyfoot about, I simply put my arm round her with a "do you mind?" Quite calmly she said: "It's alright", as we slid slowly down nearer to the ground. The sun was shining, the birds were singing, the distant sea was a beautiful blue-green, I started to kiss her and she reciprocated. This was my first experience of hugging and kissing a pretty girl. It had only been Postman's Knock at parties before. I felt I was sinking into some fantastic magic pool, I could smell her scent, I had switched off the world. "What's that?" she whispered. "What's what?" I asked, the spell slowly dissolving. "That drone," she answered. I could hear it now. It's a bloody Dornier, I know that throbbing drone, I thought. We sat up and looked to the heavens; I just could not believe it, there coming from the direction of Pompey, flying very low, was a German bomber being pursued by a Spitfire and apparently heading straight for us. I had been in this situation, or similar, often enough to treat it quite calmly but it was new to Dulcie and I could sense a feeling of panic building up in her. I grabbed her hand and said in her ear: "Don't worry, they'll go right over us and disappear, don't run." She stayed where she was, still holding my hand but visibly shaking. As the Dornier bomber approached the cornfield, the Spitfire opened fire with its machine-guns and almost simultaneously the German bomber opened its bomb-bay doors and discharged hundreds of small incendiary bombs, ever so low over our heads, most of which landed in our cornfield. They landed with a loud 'plop' sound before they burst into flames. Before I could even think, Dulcie tore her hand from my grasp as she took off like a gazelle for home. I watched the stacked stooks, most of which caught fire, turned round and followed Dulcie home. I was so fed up I didn't even wonder if the Spitfire had shot down the German or not, I just knew I was in love and hated all German aircrew. When I returned to the flat I found Mother and Auntie anxiously waiting for me. "Are you alright?" The whole of Totland Bay knew of it, they said. Knew what, I wondered. "Dulcie told us the both of you were nearly killed, her father has taken her home to be with her mother, you won't see her this evening or tomorrow, she is too upset." Neither Mother nor Auntie asked what we were doing in the cornfield!

As I left dear Mother and Auntie Wyn I could not help but feel that life had been a bit unkind to me but I was pleased to arrive back in Dunfermline safe and sound and on time! It was a strange feeling; I suppose the new flat at Totland Bay to me was not home, as I knew it. When I climbed up the gangway back on board the ship I had the feeling that perhaps this was home. I was pleased to see all my shipmates and tell them all about my leave. When I told JTB and old Tom about my cornfield experience and new girlfriend they laughed and laughed. Tom's remarks were: "It serves you right for trying to take advantage of an innocent young girl in a cornfield, that's why your Dulcie ran away from you – not the Hun aircraft!"

It was obvious that I was deeply in love with Dulcie and it had been my intention to write and confess these powerful feelings. However, even Dulcie and my ardour had to be put on the back burner as we were to leave the Old Country immediately. Eight months were to pass before postal services were resumed, so many other thoughts filled my mind, leaving no room for Dulcie. I was beginning to understand how the married crew members must be feeling, who had had to say goodbye to both wife and family.

It wasn't long before we were once again wending our way north to Spitzbergen with our cavalier rear admiral in company with our three 'Pinky' friends. The excitement had returned amongst us lads; buzzes were numerous by the time we had anchored in Isfjoid Fiord. The steamer *Dagny* was still moored there, our prize was safe and sound. The next day, after 'Force A' had oiled from *Oligarch* and got underway, we were informed *en route* by the captain that we were bound for Bear

Island. My memories of a pretty girl on the Isle of Wight began to dim considerably under these circumstances. Bear Island could easily be seen as a speck on the distant horizon in this Arctic twenty-four-hour daylight zone at three in the morning.

All this first-time Arctic travelling had stirred all the crew's imaginations. Capturing two enemy ships, the thought of a share of prize money – it was all a bit like a Hornblower story. Bear Island (possibly with polar bears on it) had a North Pole ring to it; things seemed to be getting more exciting, especially when 'Force A' was monitored by a German Condor reconnaissance plane that constantly circled us knowing they were just out of range of our anti-aircraft HA weapons. This Condor was finally persuaded to leave when we fired one of our six-inch low-angle guns (not designed for anti-aircraft use). We were only able to do this by raising one six-inch gun at a time to its maximum elevation of forty-five degrees, then utilising the rising effect of the roll of the ship to add extra gun elevation. It was not long before a huge bursting six-inch shot came too close to the Condor for comfort, which finally convinced the pilot to head for home (wherever that was).

This section of Bear Island turned out to be a craggy place that rose up from the sea without beaches. This area of the island did not seem to house any polar bears that we could see. The bird life was all gulls, unlike Spitzbergen which contained a rich variety of birds and gulls. At 1950 hours we anchored off Austervage where we were told about the high latticework wireless aerial, supported by wire mast stays, which was situated on the other side of the bay. I soon learnt that an armed landing party was to be put ashore in the motor cutter to destroy this radio mast. The L/S who was to be the coxswain, known to one and all as Tally-Ho, was the same killick I was detailed to serve under when we did routine harbour boat duties. Tally-Ho was famous because of his back, which displayed the most amazing artistic tattoo. It was of a hunting scene running from the hairline of his neck to his buttocks. It had been artistically designed and tattooed by a Maltese master artist for an enormous sum of money and had entailed many hours of agony for Tally-Ho. It consisted of a dozen or so fox hounds running down his back to his bum, all pursuing the fox whose large brush was all that was seen, leaving the viewer in no doubt as to where the fox had gone to ground! There were a lot of interesting tattoos about but this had got to be the Michelangelo of them all! The muscular body of Tally-Ho was certainly the most interesting naked body I have ever had the good fortune to view and would, I am sure, fill the 'highlight of the year' space in the Tate Gallery if his work was put on show there. Far more artistic than a pile of bricks!

Photo 21. Landing party

I had hoped that, as this was technically a harbour duty, I would be going on this trip ashore with Tally-Ho. Unfortunately a 'piped message' over the loudspeaker informed us all that we would be assuming action stations within fifteen minutes after the motor cutter and crew were launched. The captain's broadcast message explained that the reconnaissance Condor may have alerted both the enemy Navy and Air Force. The northern Norwegian airfields were less than one hour's flying time away and the skipper did not want to be found 'with his pants down', stationary, anchored in an open neutral harbour.

I had just enough time before action stations were sounded to witness the lowering of the motor cutter with the entire landing party wearing steel helmets and carrying .303 rifles (see Photo 21). They were joined at the last minute by our Army visitor loading small wooden boxes (the lieutenant had turned out to be an explosives expert) before I had to shut myself with my friendly bandsmen crew under the armour-plated deck-head five decks down below, from where I would only get a running commentary on any action that might occur from the AA gunnery officer above. This was not what I wanted.

It was less than two hours after we had been called to action stations that our main armament of six-inch guns began to bombard the enemy wireless encampment as soon as our landing party was clear. They returned cock-a-hoop with two Norwegian Quisling prisoners and our 'very pleased with himself' Army lieutenant having completely destroyed the wireless transmitter mast.

It was as we were patting ourselves on the back and enjoying the success of toppling down the latticework mast on Bear Island on 22nd June 1941 that the news of the German operation 'Barbarossa' (code name for the invasion of Soviet Russia) came through. The weather here at Bear Island was beautiful. At that time we had no idea that old Adolf was sending two million of his troops to invade Russia or that the German soldiers that we were going to have a tangle with would be the crack Alpine troops from Bavaria. Had we been aware of these facts I don't think we would have taken this news so casually, particularly as we didn't know that these Germans were going to be joined by a quarter of a million very well trained and disciplined Finns, who in 1938 had received arms from us. We had felt that the Finns were our friends. Neither did we know that Churchill had offered our services to smiling old Joe Stalin, who had no radar. Whether it was Vian's new role and he decided, or whether it was an Admiralty order, we did not know, but all of a sudden we were off to Russia.

Up to that moment I think that most of us felt that the Russians were a bad lot, as bad as the Germans and Italians. We had all admired the Finns who, although they had lost, had given them a bloody nose when the Russian Army invaded Finland in the winter of 1939.

During the short period of two days that it took us to get to Murmansk, we were all reminded that Russia was now our new ally who would, with their Cossacks, soon carve up the German Army. Once again there was great excitement about arriving at Murmansk on a warm sunny day. We imagined it would be full of men wearing black astrakhan hats, white silk shirts and high black boots, riding fine horses. Alas, it was a great disappointment! The port itself was suffering from a general decay, without a decent working crane in the place. The people that we did see were drably dressed and wearing practical grey felt boots.

Ours was, apparently, the first British naval unit to arrive at Murmansk. My first impression of this port and the dockside buildings was of one-storey, large, long log cabins which the 'Reds' had built some years earlier to act as shops for potential customers who might arrive by boats from foreign parts. They were full almost to the ceiling with hand-carved wooden toys and papier-mâché *objets d'art*, all painted in green, black, red and gold high-gloss paint. We were to go backwards and forwards nineteen times to this miserable place and witness at first hand its total destruction from bombing. We were going to join these poor Russians in their struggle.

It was whilst we endeavoured to moor alongside the ancient jetty on the north side of Murmansk harbour that we experienced problems of communication with the Russian jetty mooring personnel. They appeared not to understand our commander's requirements in attaching our mooring wires and cross mooring wire springs that prevent the moored ship moving forwards or backwards. Our commander, in a fit of frustration, shouted out aloud to the officer of the watch: "Can't you get those idiot Russians to understand my requirements?" At which a beautiful lady in her early thirties, dressed in a tailored, highly fashionable sable coat and beautiful boots, spoke up with perfect Oxford diction:

Photo 22. Murmansk lady

"Commander, if you would let me know your mooring requirements I will instruct our mooring team. They will be more than willing to help the British Navy." I have never heard a more sophisticated way of 'putting down' a senior naval officer. Everybody stopped what they were doing and stared at this beautiful creature. Our now red-faced commander, having been put well in his place, appeared to shrink to half his normal size, whilst meekly introducing this lady interpreter, as he thought, to the officer of the watch, followed with "carry on, cable officer", and immediately retired to the wardroom, possibly to hide himself! Our cable officer of the watch, who was also in his thirties, descended to the jetty and shook hands with the lady whilst we all watched with our mouths half open. Later the captain's messenger heard the cable officer remark: "I'm never going to wash this hand again." It was, he said, "the hand that was shaken by Olga, the beautiful Russian spy". This name stuck; later we were all going to experience what a dangerous person Olga the beautiful spy could be.

The next few days were taken up with high-level meetings between our senior officers, Foreign Office officials, several officials from the USA, and some senior officers from the Russian Army and Navy, together with Communist Party members and, of course, Olga the beautiful spy. By now we had discovered that she was pretty high up on the Communist Party list. The meetings that I attended were conducted in a depressing concrete building at the edge of the town, which was out-of-bounds to the entire ship's company, and we always had a Russian military escort as if we were under arrest. Spaced at various positions outside the hall and houses were loudspeaker systems suspended on high steel poles. We supposed, like H.G. Wells' story, that the good people of Murmansk opened their windows when they wanted to listen to the news.

There were only three messengers, the captain's, the commander's and the first lieutenant's. As the first lieutenant's messenger I did not always attend the meetings, but on this first occasion there were only two of us employed. We stood at the back of the hall and, as usual, were completely ignored by all and sundry as if we were invisible. There were lots of Russians at the meeting, all of whom seemed to speak perfect English. However, despite this advantageous position, neither I nor my fellow messenger were able to fully understand the reason for this meeting. We did find out who some of the 'higher ups' were, including Sir Stafford Cripps, our Ambassador; Averell Harriman, the USA Ambassador (I think); Lord Beaverbrook, Churchill's representative, and the Russian Admiral Golovko (see Photo 23) who was to be in charge of us. We also recognised Marshal Stalin's representative (but I forget his name) and, of course, the very important Olga.

Photo 23. The Russian Admiral

They talked of transporting 'loaned' armaments, cranes and trains, and of repairing the railway lines to Leningrad. When I told Stripey he just mumbled "it don't sound very good, could be dangerous".

I was on the bridge acting as messenger for the first lieutenant on the day when Olga forced her way onto the ship. She demanded an audience with the commander and made her way, without permission, onto the bridge – an unheard of intrusion into the officers' inner sanctum. I was standing at the required one-yard clearance from the officers when Olga made her appearance on that sunny day. "Commander," she said, without even a good morning, "how many non-officer seamen have you aboard?" We could all see that our third most senior man in authority did not like the question at all, or the way it had been asked. "Good morning madam," he answered tartly, "do you mean at this present moment or normal complement and why, may I ask, do you wish to know?" It was finally established that it was the number of men who normally lived on the mess deck (about five hundred). Olga did a quick calculation and came out with a statement: "Then you will need fifty women." This was received with a stunned silence. After a while the commander, who obviously formed a picture of some place providing lively entertainment for his lower-deck crew, asked his first question "Where?" Olga snapped back: "These women will come aboard, you will sign for them and they will be collected at an agreed time. Under no circumstances will your men or officers be allowed ashore to fraternise with the local population." The commander, who had by now formed a very clear picture of what was proposed, pulled himself upright and said in no uncertain terms: "Good God, woman, the British Navy does not conduct itself in that way." It was plain to see that this answer infuriated Olga who then turned very nasty. She made it quite clear to the commander that should any member of his ship's company be caught ashore, except on official duties, they would be arrested and tried by the Soviet Socialist Court where the penalty for such a crime would be the firing squad. Whilst this was all going on I caught the eye of the duty WT signalman who was, as usual, skulking in the corner. At the beginning of this conversation his eyes had lit up and at the end of the conversation his disappointment was obvious. Olga disappeared with a face as black as thunder. At the end of the watch I went back to the mess deck and recounted the whole scene to Stripey and my messmates, who pretended they were very disappointed with the outcome but, of course, laughed and joked about this ludicrous suggestion to use the mess deck with absolutely no privacy available. What I realise now was that the commander had made an enemy of Olga, which may have been the reason for some of her future actions.

The whole sequence must have appalled the commander, a God-fearing, upright citizen who always behaved like a gentleman. He was probably very angry that Olga thought that he would deal in such a trade.

To ensure we would have sufficient fuel oil for the journey back to Scapa Flow from Murmansk, the fleet oiler *Oligarch* had orders to rendezvous with us on 22nd August 1941. In company with *Punjabi* and *Aurora* we sighted the oiler and its escorts, the armed trawlers *Garland* and *Sealyham*, already oiling *Tartar* at 2200. All three of us having collected our oil, we parted company with *Oligarch* and its escorts and proceeded south.

At 1800 hours the following day we sighted a large iceberg accompanied by two 'growlers'. It was so big that I attempted to take a snap of it with the last available bit of film in my box camera (a present Auntie had given me for Christmas whilst I was at Pitmans).

It was to be the last picture that camera ever took, film having become unavailable to sea-going sailors. The film was finally developed in 1946 but it was not a great success. It was not long before we sighted a German Dornier18 patrol aircraft, which was becoming par for the course in these Arctic waters. An hour or so later we tried our six-inch gun trick and thought our shot had been near enough to put him off but a couple of hours later he was back on station reporting to the Luftwaffe High Command where we were. Thankfully we encountered a fog. At the speed we were doing, and despite the fog, we arrived the next afternoon and, sighting Bluebite Nair, parted company with *Aurora* and the two destroyers. This close to Scapa, Jerry aircraft were known to have a night-time habit of dropping sea mines by parachute. For our own protection we would, if we could, catapult a Walrus to look ahead and as usual we always streamed paravanes.

Photo 24. Our 'pinky friend' HMS *Aurora*

We were all surprised that on arrival in the 'Flow' we were ordered to moor ship fore and aft to two large mooring buoys.

Having moored ship, the duty boat and crew were lowered and we transferred our unhappy Norwegian prisoners ashore, and returned just as the three different types of supply ships came alongside. It was back to provisioning, ammunitioning and, of course, re-oiling which was as normal.

At 1500 hours, shore leave was given to visit one of the close-by uninhabited islands to watch a football match held between teams

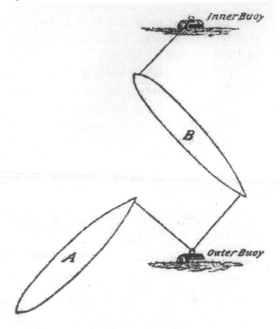

Figure 27. Two large mooring buoys

selected from the *King George V* and the *Rodney,* both battlewagons with crews of over one thousand men each. It was a good turnout.

The entire crew were bemused and pondering why we should be moored fore and aft and, what was so unusual was, no-one came up with a buzz. The next day we were all given the afternoon off; this was known as 'make and mend'. However, after a long sea trip when watertight doors had been securely shut for the ship's safety, thereby cutting off the showers and drying facilities, we were allowed to open these doors only when the ship was in a secure harbour. As a consequence, when the bugle call rang out 'hands to make and mend', the top priority on everybody's mind was showers and clean clothes, followed by sleep. At these moments I always thanked my lucky stars that I hadn't joined the Army and, up to this period, how lucky we were to be able to stand under a warm-water shower and wash everything but our feet. Some chaps even disobeyed the rules and washed their underwear whilst still wearing it under a warm shower, only taking it off to dry. On these occasions the demand was so great that the dirty water took some time to disappear down the exit scuppers to the sea. You left the totally open-plan showers, with a capacity for forty-odd matelots at a time, with greyish soapy tide marks halfway up your shins which you washed off two decks up with cold sea water. Every naval PO would always quote 'cleanliness is next to godliness'. The very first quotation in every textbook.

On Sunday 10th August 1941 we put the clocks back an hour. Somehow we knew something was about to happen, we were told to clean the ship. They got us washing paintwork, tidying every corner, scrubbing the gangways and mess decks. Down came the scruffy gale-torn and repaired flags from the mastheads and up went the posh new flags. We all knew by now that someone important was turning up and because of our mooring situation they would arrive in a large barge or something similar which would hang safely to a 'fixed' moored

ship. At 1400 it all came over the Tannoy, "Hands will muster for Divisions on the upper deck at 1730 dressed in 'number ones' (our best suits) to be inspected by His Majesty King George." This proved that secrets could be kept from us! As I stood to attention with my fellow seamen, His Majesty stopped, looked at us and smiled. I was surprised to see I was taller than the King of England! By 1840 hours he had left to board another vessel, possibly also double moored. Laughingly I asked Stripey if he thought that we had rushed back those thousand-odd miles from Russia so that the King could see him in his best suit. "No, young Cutts," he said with a smile, "he wanted to see how you were growing up in 13 Mess. But His Majesty

Photo 25. HM King George VI on board

144

only came to Scapa so that I could pull an extra tot, besides which His Majesty has asked for you two lads to do AA guard for him."

We resumed AA guard ship for the night, special watch keeping for some of us! At 1225 the following day (tot time plus splicing the main brace) a very happy bunch of sailors were ordered to clear lower decks and, with their hats on, man the guard rails on the port side to give His Majesty three hearty cheers as he sailed past at 1305 on HMS *Inglefield* on his way out of the 'Flow' and on his way to Buckingham Palace, no doubt. It must have been a bit like this at a peacetime Spithead Review.

On 16th August, Rear Admiral Vian returned aboard. The buzz was that he had been back to Murmansk to check on heavy-lifting cranes. Scapa was always a place for extra school classes as well as gunnery practice and there were exams to take. Stores and post arrived daily from our little motorised lighter barge called *Empress Snowdrop*. It was on that Saturday, accompanying Vian's staff officers, that the mail bag arrived containing a parcel which had been in transit for some three and a half months from the Isle of Wight. It was about 1500 hours when the post boy brought this parcel to 13 Mess. (The post boy was a boy seaman organised by the jaunty to deliver post when we were in harbour.) Parcels were rarer than solid gold watches! By the time I arrived back to 13 Mess, from whatever I was doing, I found my other ten mess mates sitting patiently staring at a square parcel ten by ten by eight inches high covered with brown paper and tied securely with civilian white string. The whole mess was quiet, looking at me. I was sort of embarrassed. "Open it up, Cutts," said Stripey "but do it slowly or you might break something!" They all stared as I slowly eased a round eight-inch-diameter by five-inch-deep tin from its protective box and packing. On the lid was an envelope containing a birthday card held in position by a red silk ribbon. I removed the card from the envelope and started to read Mother's and Auntie's message when JTB said: "What's it say then? Read it out loud." I read: "Happy Eighteenth Birthday, dear Jack, from your loving Mother and Auntie Wyn, hope you enjoy the cake." Judging by their faces, my mess mates felt that was the right thing to say. "Open it up and let's see," urged Tom from China, in the kindest of tones but with a look of expectation. I used my seaman's knife to prise open the lid. The inside of the tin was completely filled with a rich, brown fruit cake decorated with a marzipan anchor encrusted with half a dozen of those little coloured sugar balls. Everyone was just staring, you could have heard a pin drop. The silence was broken by JTB when he said: "Cutts, we're all going to get a piece aren't we?" Before I could reply, Stripey as usual had the matter in hand. "It's

Cutts' birthday party," he said, and detailed one of the mess to get the hot water from the galley and make the tea, another to get down the mugs and small plates and knives. The cake was sliced precisely into the required number of pieces. They devoured every crumb and passed round the birthday card, admiring the picture of a horse in a meadow of buttercups, daisies and red poppies. As the party came to an end at 1600 with everyone singing "Happy Birthday, Cutts", I and several other mess mates were aware that it was time for the first dog watch, when we were due on watch, as our ship was duty AA guard vessel. Although it was three months after my actual birthday, I shall never forget those forty-five minutes. I do not know whether it was my mother or aunt who must have shown enormous persistence to get this parcel past the regulatory authority. I do not recall whether it was the Post Office or the police that enabled the cake to arrive, even if it was three months late for my birthday party! There was never another parcel delivered to any of us from then on.

The following three days were spent in exercising in the Firth of Forth with our own two aircraft and we were surprised to receive a third brand-new Walrus flown in during this exercise. We spent the rest of the day practising ship towing ship with the *Aurora*. We returned to Scapa to ammunition ship, and then went to sea again for a night-shadowing exercise, again with the *Aurora*. On returning through the boom defence to the 'Flow' all hands were piped to clean ship during the forenoon watch. The off-watch crew were offered afternoon shore leave to an uninhabited island. I went and, after a sleepless night of exercises, lying down in the fresh grass on that sunny Sunday afternoon I found that watching the many skylarks that hovered overhead was restful, whilst my quiet Scots companion sat and used up the afternoon reading his Bible (there was little or no other reading matter on board with the exception of the standard 1936 issued *Seamanship Manual Mk II*!). I well remember that peaceful day was shattered by an air raid at 2300.

I was beginning to feel that the ship was slowly assuming the mantle of a floating prison. Scapa Flow was a bore but it was the best on offer. By this time several of our ship's company were beginning to show signs of odd behaviour. I suppose today this would be called stress. You could watch other moored naval ships performing all sorts of antics and laugh at the poor sods painting ship (see Photo 26), or swimming over the side in freezing cold water – known as 'compulsory swimming exercises' – but not much else; they were all floating prisons.

One felt sorry for the crews on the battlewagons who seemed to be moored permanently in Scapa, unlike us who were almost permanently

Photo 26. Painting Ship

at sea carrying out chore after chore. Whilst it was highly dangerous you couldn't complain of boredom.

I was lucky to be a member of the duty crew of the pinnace where, complete with large boat-hook, I acted as a stern-sheet man. There was also another young seaman who was the forward boat-hook chap, and Tally-Ho who was our L/S in charge of the boat. This fast, sleek, cabined, wooden carvel-built craft, powered by two Ford V8 water-cooled petrol engines, took us well away from the ship when carrying out journeys to different parts of Scapa Flow to deliver or collect persons or parcels. Such journeys could be interesting and would sometimes last for long periods. We could also get first-hand knowledge of what was going on in other parts of the 'Flow'. Duty pinnace crews were excused the sundry on-board maintenance jobs always necessary on a ship moored in harbour, such as washing paintwork, repainting the ship's side and mast tops, scrubbing decks, treating and wire brushing rusty equipment, and ammunitioning and stocking ship. However, cleaning the pinnace and polishing 'bright-work' were the responsibility of the pinnace crew, but that was much more fun than inboard jobs.

The black and white sixty-year-old photograph of HRH the Duke of Kent was taken whilst he was boarding our pinnace as he left the ship

Photo 27. HRH the Duke of Kent

following his official visit in August 1941. It was so sad that, shortly after take-off his plane crashed and there were no survivors. To die in a freak accident during a war when others are dying in action is awful. This photograph shows the pinnace and the decorative brass fish at the cabin entrance. These fish were later painted with a type of green varnish to stop them from shining in bright light.

Scapa was a place for training the minds of seamen which meant, amongst other things, extra school and for me extra homework. Our small motor barge named *Snowdrop* delivered hundreds of heavy waterproof sheepskin coats, sufficient for the entire crew. We ought to have realised 'Snowdrop' was an omen; snow seemed a far cry away on that warm sunny day.

On the very same morning, the 18th August, an order came over the Tannoy, 'duty boats crew man the pinnace'. I immediately ran off, as was the well-learnt habit, and clambered down the ship's side, walked along the boom steadying myself as usual by holding onto the topping lift, climbed down the Jacob's ladder and then, by hooking the lazy-painter with my foot, pulled the pinnace to the ladder and jumped aboard the fo'c'sle of the craft. Being first aboard meant that it was your responsibility to hang onto the Jacob's ladder until the other two crew members were on board. This boom and small boat mooring system was designed by old sailors when God was a boy and I enjoyed negotiating this outboard journey, a bit like all youngsters

Photo 28. Snowdrop

enjoy climbing trees, and falling off meant you would only get wet on these pleasant summer days. In a couple of months' time or so I would be negotiating this same journey to the same wooden pinnace, but weighed down with heavy Arctic clothing and heavy seaboots, balancing on the same boom which would be covered with inch-thick ice and coated by the last fall of snow, and where to fall into icy water could be your last fall. As soon as Tally-Ho had boarded the pinnace he would start up the two engines with his customary roar, order us to let go the working painter with a shout "Hold tight, you young idiots or you'll be taking a deep breath and walking along the bottom". He would then roar off as fast as he could, making to the other side of the ship to secure alongside the main gangway, much to the amusement of all the onlookers on the upper deck. As soon as we had temporarily secured our bow- and stern-rope painters to the gangway, Tally-Ho would leap onto the grating, double up the gangway's fourteen steps, salute the officer of the watch on the quarterdeck and collect the instructions for this journey and return trip.

My memory does not always serve me well with an accurate run of events – it's a long time ago – but I do know that 18th August 1941 was the day this famous man came aboard. Whether we picked him up from ashore in the pinnace or whether he embarked from the supply ship *Empress Snowdrop* I am uncertain. What is certain is that the commander's announcement over the Tannoy informed us all

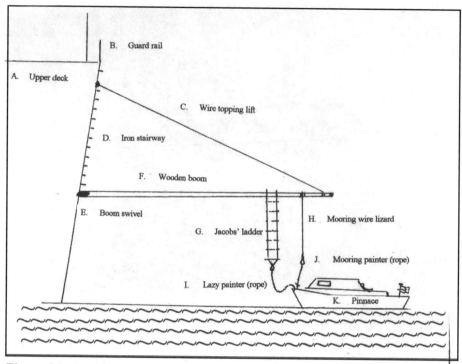

Figure 28. Jacob's Ladder and Boom

Photo 29. Noël Coward

that a certain Mr Noël Coward was aboard and that he would be sailing with us to observe the day-to-day routine of the ship's company at work during war. At this time, as Jimmy-the-One's messenger, I was instructed, along with the commander's messenger, to shadow this famous man and to inform the duty bridge officer or quarterdeck duty officer of his whereabouts.

Whilst on his excursions about the ship during the three

weeks he spent with us, he was picking up accurate images of various characters, for reasons none of us understood. I have to be honest, I had no idea who Noël Coward was when he first came aboard, and I feel that this ignorance was shared by a great many of the crew. Noël Coward was always wandering about the ship at all times of the day and night. I cannot recall ever seeing him using a camera or a notebook and pencil. He smoked a lot and, although it was never accurately measured, his cigarette holder must have been a foot long, or to put it into Tom's words, "he kept well away from smoking!" Although I can't remember seeing him, he was supposed to have wandered into the officer's wardroom fully dressed in evening dress trousers, black polished shoes and silk tie and wearing a long, dark-red and black smoking jacket. Mr Coward was obviously a good sea-traveller and so far as I could see unafraid of our routine war hazards. He didn't live up to his name! It wasn't until late 1943, when we saw the film *In Which We Serve*, that we understood what he had been doing. He had taken in every mannerism of the man and we immediately recognised our commander. (By 1943 the commander had been seriously wounded and left on a hospital ship. I never found out whether he survived or not.)

Under King's Regulations and Admiralty Instructions, a ship's postman had to be a trustworthy non-commissioned sailor, or sometimes a PO could be selected for this duty. For some reason or the other which I cannot explain the master-at-arms had decided to allocate this job to one of the boy seamen who, I think, was the oldest boy aboard. It wasn't until we arrived back into Murmansk harbour that we noticed something very strange seemed to have happened to our 'postman' boy. It all started for me when we were under seamanship instructions (not part of the education lectures) on the subject of sea rules concerning lights and international regulations for preventing collisions at sea. These classes were far more relaxed than the school classes and on this particular day were being conducted in a light-hearted fashion by a newly promoted PO, who had just introduced us to sound signals made by steam whistles and sirens used by vessels in sight of one another:

Signal	Meaning
one short blast	I am directing my course to starboard
two short blasts	I am directing my course to port
three short blasts	My engines are going full speed astern

when without any warning we were gate-crashed by the 'crusher' himself. There was an instant silence and of course we all stood to attention, including the new PO. After asking the PO about the content of the lecture, either to show off his complete grasp of coastal navigation or to put us all, including the PO, in our place, he suggested that these selections of signals were best remembered by practising the movements physically.

He formed us into two lines and produced a parade ground whistle. When he blew one short blast we all stepped sideways to our right (starboard), with two blasts we all took a step to our left (port) – it was always odd numbers to starboard, even numbers to port – and three blasts a step backwards (astern). None of us found this difficult even when he speeded up the blasts and mixed the procedure. After ten minutes or so of this, the 'crusher' withdrew and left us all in peace.

It was only after being dismissed from this class that we became aware of the 'postman' giving off a series of quiet whistles in ones, twos or threes and changing his direction accordingly. None of us was concerned and took it that he could see more in the 'crusher's joke' than we could.

We were in Murmansk for about two weeks suffering heavy air raids and beginning to feel that we would be safer at sea. It was when the second mail turned up, carried on a new Flower class corvette, that we noticed that the 'postman' was still giving soft whistles and flitting all over the place. We realised something was amiss, or was he trying to pull his ticket? His sad story began to make its way round the ship. He had done a terrible thing for those days: whilst on leave in Newcastle, he had put his seventeen-year-old girlfriend in the family way. He had received this news from her just before Christmas. He had immediately sought help from the mess deck dodger who had told him to unload his worries on to the padre. The vicar in turn suggested he applied to attend the commander's 'request men'. This took him two weeks. The commander, apparently not knowing what to do or say, suggested he apply to see the captain's 'request men' the following week. The request form he filled in was simple: "Request to be granted fourteen days leave to get married." By now he had also received a letter from her family doctor giving the true facts of the pregnancy, which the padre had asked him to obtain, and which no doubt, the captain would want to read. He had also received a further letter from the girl's father who, not understanding the circumstances (we were by now some two thousand miles away), thought this young sailor had put a bun in his daughter's oven and was leaving him, her father, to pick up the tabs whilst he, the lad, stayed at sea enjoying himself.

Our captain, on the other hand, knew that when a sailor got married 'My Lords of the Admiralty' had rightly arranged for such a sailor, or his wife, to receive marriage allowances. The captain also knew that these gentleman from the Admiralty did not consider a boy seaman, second or first class, to be a sailor, and a boy seaman still under eighteen years old was breaking the law even to have sex with a girl under the age of eighteen. As far as the Navy's rules were concerned, both youngsters had broken the law. There would be no such thing as leave for a lawbreaker and family allowance would be out of the question. Boy seamen were not allowed to be fathers. The final blow to the poor postman was a letter from the distraught prospective mother-in-law accusing him of everything under the sun. I suppose the captain, always a kind man, did the best he could for the boy, who appeared to be suffering great mental stress, when he signed all the necessary papers and documents that got the boy sent home on the first available craft. His final destination was a naval mental hospital. Perhaps he did get back to his girl, perhaps the padre did write to the girl's parents, as he promised, to explain the impossible position the lad was in. Or was this boy trying to get his 'ticket' out of the Navy forever?

We all watched our postman lash his hammock and pack his kitbag. He left the ship well wrapped up in his new sheepskin. He was transferred to a crabby-looking merchantman moored further down the wall, looking even more miserable than Murmansk itself. I know I felt it wasn't nice to see a fellow young sailor weighed down by an adult problem and being slowly driven round the bend by the worry of it. I did not think he had tried to pull his ticket, but some did and congratulated him.

The entire 13 Mess wished him and his girl good luck and happiness. The last words came from Raggie. "Let's hope," he said, "that that old rust bucket gets him home all right and isn't 'tin fished' on the way" – as approximately ten percent of all Allied shipping was at that time.

His departure meant that four boy seamen had left the ship; now our number had dropped to sixteen of the original boys.

A convoy was not a nice place to be. An average of forty to fifty ships on convoy could be sailing along zigzagging cheerfully at between 5 and 10 knots when suddenly, without any warning, a ship would be 'tin fished' by a U-boat. It made a terrible cr-u-u-mp noise, followed by a very hot bright flash. Sometimes in as little as three minutes, ship, men, everything was gone. The U-boat would have disappeared silently. On the odd occasion one would be forced to the surface and all ships would fire heavy guns and even machine-guns. Occasionally we would hit one. Sometimes Asdic would find the U-boat and we would be successful in depth-charging it.

Tammy, the Asdic man, was very depressed on these occasions; he felt it was his responsibility for missing a U-boat on his screen. We lost ships on every convoy to U-boats or air attack.

IX

We Join the Russians

On 19th August 1941 at 1400 we put to sea and joined the Canadian liner *Empress of Canada* which was already in company with the aircraft-carrier HMS *Argus* and the destroyers HMS *Intrepid, Tartar, Eclipse, Anthony* and *Antelope*. At 0400 hours just before dawn on 20th August we exercised 'action stations' and, travelling at 19 knots, passed the armed trawlers *Lord Austin* and *Northern Isle*. Having moored in Hvoolfield, Iceland on 21st August, we were immediately topped up with oil by the *Black Ranger*. We now knew we had a long journey in front of us. The other vessels already moored there beside the oiler *Black Ranger* were the cruisers HMS *Shropshire, Hector* and four of our destroyers plus the US battleship *New Mexico*, the US cruiser *Quincy* and three US destroyers. This large unit of the US Navy was in Iceland because it had just arrived with a convoy of American merchantmen loaded with armaments for Russia.

Though not at war with Germany, Roosevelt had agreed to provide a US escort for their merchantmen as far as Iceland and Churchill had agreed the British Navy would take on the task of protecting the US merchant ships from there to Russia.

Still in the company of *Empress of Canada*, and our 'Pinky' friend HMS *Aurora*, and with the destroyers HMS *Anthony, Antelope* and *Icarus* which had just arrived, we weighed anchor and left all the American and British men-o'-war in Hvoolfield, Iceland. Our captain informed us that we were making our way to Jan Mayen Island to catch up with a Russian-bound convoy.

Travelling at our economical steaming speed of 17 knots brought us within sight of this convoy at 0545 the following morning. The convoy zigzagging at 7 knots was made up of thirty, mostly large, merchantmen. Ten small naval escort vessels and two destroyers attended it. Russian convoys were coded 'PQ' plus a number when sailing to Russia and 'QP' plus a number when returning. Such convoys were often made

155

up of ships of various nationalities, Norwegian, Russian, Dutch, Free French and Belgian owned ships, which had managed to make British ports when the enemy had overrun their country. British and American shipping companies would often hire crews, with or without officers, from neutral countries such as China, Sweden, and others from North Africa and South America. Most of these crews were tempted because of the danger-money offered. The British shipping companies had a rule that covered all the seamen they employed whatever their nationality; this was that as soon as a torpedo, bomb or shell put the ship out of action or sunk it, they were no longer responsible for those crew members and their pay was stopped immediately.

During the 1930s trade recession, merchant shipping companies mothballed and laid-up their fleets of merchantmen. At the same time they paid off and dismissed their trained merchant seamen. However, in the first year of the war, a large number of merchantmen were sunk by attacks by U-boats and it became necessary to hurriedly return this mothballed fleet to sea. Some had little or no refitting and hence ended up in a convoy with valuable and urgent cargoes which were sometimes worth more than the vessel itself with its poor engine rooms and deck fittings. Some broke down and became a naval nightmare, especially if they had a cargo shift which caused steering difficulties and caused them to run amok, or if they just couldn't keep up. Remember the convoy was only as fast as the slowest vessel. British merchant seamen, as well as having the worst working conditions and contracts, suffered a higher casualty rate than any of the three armed services. A convoy of thirty large ships was capable of transferring about one hundred and fifty to two hundred tanks and the same number of planes. It would also have sufficient storage capacity to deliver some hundreds of tons of ammunition and an equal amount of high-octane aviation fuel.

I think this was the first time we had seen a convoy with a catapult aircraft merchantman (CAM). This was a vessel selected because of its high prow. A mechanical catapult had been fitted fore and aft on its prow to which a Mk I Hurricane aircraft, well past its 'sell-by date', had been attached. The catapult had been supplied with a short eleven-inch-diameter gun, which could be loaded with a brass cylinder filled with cordite. The routine for getting the plane airborne was as follows. The pilot, who like the plane was getting too old for routine work and had 'volunteered', would start the aircraft engine. As soon as the engine speed had reached the equivalent of eighty miles per hour air speed he would give the thumbs up signal. This was the signal for the mechanic to fire, when the ship's prow was rising, the eleven-inch short gun (this gun was made short especially for this job) attached to the catapult. With the CAM ship moving into the wind at 9 knots, the plane would leave this Heath Robinson contraption at approximately one hundred miles per hour. This was a highly dangerous manoeuvre and the pilot was aware that he could not land the aircraft anywhere other than in the sea. These CAM fighters were usually called into action as convoys to Russia passed northern Norway. This was where the German airfields were.

A couple of Russian convoys later I was privileged to meet such a pilot who, I think, was forty years or more of age. As he would not be required until almost North Cape, the very end of the run in to Russia, somebody (possibly the lousy desk-job officer that had cajoled him into volunteering for this suicidal mission) had felt he would be better served if he were given a comfortable bunk in our officers quarters with the use of their gin bin, or perhaps he had volunteered himself. He was to be transferred to a temporary berth, and the company of seamen who were strangers to him, on the CAM ship later. This RAF pilot was suffering from seasickness. We met one day when he was exercising in the lee waist, as did all seasick travellers looking for fresh air out of reach of sea spray. Realising his problem I offered him my seasickness cure, which was cold drinking water, dry biscuits, fresh air and lots of walking up and down. He felt lonely, why else would he have talked to me? He was old enough to be my father and had, he said, two boys about my age at a posh private school. He told me he had a nice wife at home. Despite his age he had taken part in the Battle of Britain. He asked: "What the bloody hell am I doing here?" It was about this time that doubts were beginning to creep into my, hopefully, maturing mind. As a boy I had willingly swapped my comfortable home and family for this naval family and work place. I understood and respected the loyalty we all had for fellow members of 13 Mess but he was on his own. There was a different attitude in most of the new crew members, who were mostly HOs. It was difficult to explain to these new sailors that they should consider themselves to be part of a fighting unit, albeit very reluctantly, and should be prepared to 'do their duty', as Nelson would have said. To put it in a nutshell, I was beginning to question things. This pipe-smoking RAF pilot understood the risks he was taking, or at least he said he did. I visualised a forty-five-year-old housewife with greying hair cooking and keeping house; what would she have said if she had known his circumstances?

It was essential for the captain of the CAM ship to bring his ship sharply into the wind. The Hurricane's engine must not stall. The air mechanic would have had to maintain the catapult runway and keep it well greased and hope that it wouldn't freeze or jam. The pilot had to judge the conditions correctly. Whoever fired off the catapult charge had to make sure that the CAM ship's bow was rising with the sea swell.

If the pilot was lucky – conditions could be very difficult – he got airborne! He then had decisions to make. Should he fly as fast as he could, using up fuel quickly, going for all and any of the possible forty-odd enemy planes harassing the convoy? And then, when his ammunition was used up, try to belly land this fast-moving Hurricane on the sea close to the destroyer that had been allocated to stop and pick him up? He might not find this destroyer in all the panic! He would also know that it was very unlikely that anyone else would stop for him. He further knew that, whatever the circumstances, three minutes was as long as he could survive before freezing to death in those waters. He always risked being hit by other German planes even if they were slower than him but the odds were stacked against these poor pilots. The combined box-barrage, put up by the merchantmen and us, wouldn't do him any good if he ran into it accidentally. He had another choice; he could conserve his fuel, shoot down one or two enemy planes and set course for Russia. Here he might find a flat field or frozen river. This had its drawbacks: no-one had marked these planes for the Russians to recognise. If he landed safely and Russian soldiers or civilians caught him and there were no English speakers they could mistake him for a German airman. This would result in him being brutally treated, robbed of warm clothing and left to freeze and bleed to death. I wonder whether these pilots were aware of all these dangers.

All I remember of this quiet speaking, pipe-smoking, father-figure was that no-one could tell us what had happened to him. Had he gone missing, perhaps running out of fuel before arriving on land? Perhaps bad navigation had left him flying north and resulted in him having to land on ice miles away from anywhere: such loneliness! I spent only a few moments listening to this man some sixty-odd years ago. Subsequently over the years from time to time on sleepless nights I have wondered, what was his and other such pilots' fate? Do we remember, or more to the point, were we ever told? I had lost another friend. I understand that these CAM ships were withdrawn after PQ6.

On 22nd August we joined convoy number PQ3 following its zigzag course bound for Jan Mayen Island.

We had by this time sailed to the top of the world (sometimes referred to by the crew as the edge of the world!). Here the continuous Arctic summer-time, with its twenty-four hours of daylight, left us exposed to attacks from U-boats, surface units and enemy aircraft which could find us more readily. Darkness had its uses!

Boys and young ordinary seamen were usually picked to man the masthead position. When we asked, "why us?" we were told "at your age you're nimble and sharp of eye". Climbing a swaying and moving mast to the crow's nest, some eighty feet above sea-level, was hazardous, particularly in the windy winter weather. The footholds were on the small side (see Photo 30). They were perfectly all right as handholds but allowed you to get only the toe part of your footwear home. Winter gales, snow, ice and freezing spray made it necessary to wear thirty-four bulky items of clothing and heavy footwear. This

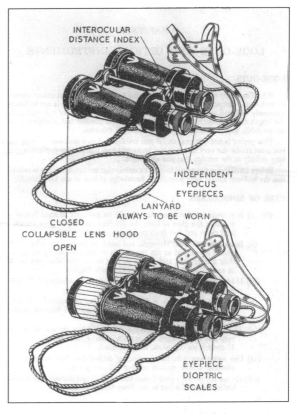

Figure 29. Binocular pattern 1900A

bulky clothing restricted the freedom of my limbs. In addition to this, the ship's movements, the intense cold, the large sixteen-inch long-distance binoculars round my neck, and the ice and hard snow that had settled in the footholds/handholds added to my natural fear of heights when ascending or descending this moving mast. It was known that a lookout's eyesight would deteriorate after an hour in these conditions.

Pairs of lookout seamen manned their four-hour watches on an 'hour on, hour off' basis. The masthead chap trusted the bridge officer of the watch to supply him with a relief within the hour as none of us had wrist or pocket watches. The officer of the watch was also responsible for recalling the masthead man if the weather deteriorated. It could put the masthead lookout at great risk if he was left up too long in intense cold or in a sudden squall. Regrettably not all officers of the watch were that efficient and sometimes forgot the lookout. There was such an occasion when a young Royal Marine was not

Photo 30. Stepladder to mast

called down from the mast for almost two hours by a forgetful officer of the watch and he had 'frozen'; the temperature was 40° below and he could not move or even shout, let alone climb down those awful, frozen steps. It took two very brave POs to climb up with ropes and tackle to rig up a lifeline on a pulley, plus help from half-a-dozen seamen on the bridge, to take the marine's dead weight and lower him down. He was immediately carried into the sickbay for medical treatment and massage. On getting him down to the bridge our rear admiral immediately offered the young marine his cup of warm cocoa, which the marine was unable to drink.

You had to climb higher up the mast than the crow's nest, wait for the occupant to climb over the top and then down before you could drop in. It was harder to get out of it than in. The lookout position was fitted with three things: a) a voice pipe connecting you to the officer of the watch on the bridge; b) a hole in the base to let the water out (I understand crows also make a hole in their nests!), unfortunately this same hole let the cold wind in; c) an electric heater, no bigger than a domestic electric iron which was fitted upside down. If on arrival you sat on the round, usually wet, wooden seat, adjusted its height so you could put a foot on either side of the small heater, and pulled your greatcoat over your knees like a tent, then sufficient heat would rise to keep your kneecaps warm.

When I climbed into the crow's nest on that sunny late August day and looked down on the forty-odd merchant and naval ships of PQ3 I could not help thinking I had joined God up there. There they all were, a breathtaking sight. The different shapes, sizes and colours in perfect lines and every ship travelling at the same speed, changing from zig to zag at the commodore's orders, spread over an area some three miles wide and five miles deep edged with eleven very much smaller,

160

Figure 30. Large locomotive

faster dark grey vessels and destroyers. There were interesting deck cargoes on some of the bigger merchantmen, such as large, brown-coal-burning steam locomotives some twenty yards long which were secured athwart ship and looking as if they were going to fall over the side as the cargo vessel rolled heavily in that northern swell. There were even half a dozen heavy lorries on one and a huge dockyard crane on another. Sometimes whales would become involved in the same area as the convoy (at great risk to their safety), and flocks of geese would pass overhead at certain times of the year. Up in the crow's nest next to God it was as if you held the most expensive box seat in a large theatre, where you were waiting for the actors after the curtain had gone up. It was a sight I will always remember.

The above locomotive was very long, about 68 feet with its packaging, weighed 120 tons empty of coal/water and was built at the Vulcan foundry, Newton-le-Willows. It was designed to run on Russian low-calorific-value brown coal, which had only 75 percent of the efficiency of Yorkshire coal. It would pull a load of 1,000 tons at 50 mph. It was going to run on a single track.

Whale and bird watching became an interest for me, after being informed by my Canadian officer of the watch of the importance of these wild creatures in relation to radar and Asdic systems. "Whales, young Edwards," explained this Canadian, "can easily be mistaken for U-boats, especially the Greenland Right Whale [Bowhead]." When it comes up for air, its head, which comprises two-fifths of its total body length (the same underwater:out of water ratio as a surfaced U-boat), would have been located by our Asdic. On the surface they look similar on a radar screen. An informed lookout knows that each species of whale has a characteristic spout which it produces on breaking the water's surface. The Right Whale has a double spout, the Rorqual a single one, while the Sperm Whale spouts at a 45° angle (see Figure 31).

"Thar' she blows!" was the whaler's cry. The lookout could tell his captain the type of whale he had seen, its length and where it would be after its next blow, all information he had gleaned from the spout. Good lookouts were paid the same wage as the harpoon

Figure 31. Whales

gunner on a whaler. This same knowledge could help the convoy. Depth-charging or firing at a whale could give the convoy away to any U-boat listening on its hydrophones up to one hundred miles away. I am afraid our particular interest was for our safety, not the whales'!

A flock of birds, particularly at night, could be mistaken for an aircraft by our radar. The resultant 'alarm to arms' destroying the off-watch crew's sleep was both bad for nerves and tiring. I think perhaps that this Canadian was an informed wildlife observer, although he was unable to identify the hundreds of little brown birds that descended quietly and covered our rigging completely for a few hours one misty day. For all the time they spent with us those birds were totally still and quiet and just watched us go about our business until they decided it was time to leave which they did as silently as when they arrived.

Bobbing along with the PQ3 convoy at its slow speed had become the usual routine which we all accepted, with day and night watches, work parties and of course school classes in the schoolmaster's crowded cabin with three or four of us using his bunk as a desk.

Suddenly the situation changed. The destroyer HMS *Icarus* had, at speed, broken through the escort's screen into the zigzag pattern of the merchant ships. Almost immediately all eyes seemed to have picked up this speed difference. It was quite exciting for all onlookers to watch this destroyer with its slim lines and high bow wave picking up speed as if it was showing off, which its captain probably was! *Icarus* bridge's Aldis lamp was flashing out a Morse code message telling our rear admiral it was closing on our port side to transfer 'most secret' correspondence. She transferred these orders as soon as she was close enough on our port quarter. It was passed to us in a large leather waterproof wallet, secured to a safety line with the aid of a heaving line with a sailor's hand-woven 'Turk's head' knot.

I remember only two occasions when secret correspondence arrived in this manner. Such messages were, to quote Stripey, 'Nelson's Navy': no telephone, no WT, on a collect, deliver, sign basis and probably 'eat after reading', but always from somebody very important. Within the hour we had left PQ3 travelling at a good safe speed in the company of the liner *Empress of Canada* heading for Spitzbergen which turned out to be a busy place. On arrival in Cronfiord we moored near our old 'Pinky' friend *Aurora* and the fleet oiler *Oligarch*. As soon as we had settled down, two trawlers moored alongside and later we were joined by a tug.

The making of a Turk's head knot was time consuming, even for a skilled worker.

The next day I was ordered to join a shore working party of some fifteen of our sailors. We transferred in our motor cutter to a substantial jetty some distance from the ship. It was a great treat to get ashore, away from the close discipline of HMS *Nigeria*. Spitzbergen was a picturesque place with magnificent mountain scenery and lots

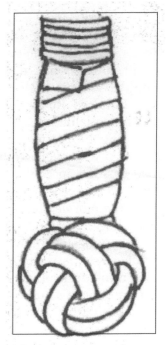

Figure 32. Turk's head knot

of streams, ponds and marshes heavily populated with restless bird life. I remember it was very muddy underfoot and we wore seaboots. There were about one hundred and twenty pongos, commanded by a lieutenant, already by the jetty when we arrived. They had dismantled the wireless mast at Bear Island. The reason for our presence was to help these pongos carry the heavy boxes of new plastic explosive up the slopes to the coalmine entrances. The object of the exercise was to sabotage and destroy the mines completely and remove the miners.

These sappers also attached, or rather stuck, a piece of this new putty-like explosive to each of the twenty-foot-high wooden poles supporting the electric cables that supplied power for the equipment in the mines. The fine fuse wire was led down the slope from the mine and each of the poles fixed to a detonator box operated by a plunger. When all the workers were safely down someone pushed the plunger and there was one big bang in the mine with individual cracks coming from all the poles as they fell, followed by a 'take off' of all the birds within hearing distance. I thought the action was very exciting.

We were informed on the Tannoy that evening that the entire population of some eight hundred people were to be evacuated and that's why the *Empress of Canada* had been brought to the island. The coalmines had been destroyed to prevent the Germans obtaining supplies of this useful high-grade bituminous coal. There were about five hundred Russian nationals and three hundred Norwegians here. It was explained that the *Empress* would be taking the Russians 'home' first but the Norwegians would be transferred to Great Britain until the war was over. Nothing was said about how long these migrants had resided in Spitzbergen or if they were recent visitors or first-, second- or even third-generation settlers. What we all knew was that both the Norwegians and Russians had, up to our arrival, been selling coal illegally to our enemy the Germans, in Norway.

To youngsters (and I was no different), everything is black and white; there is no room in their heads for grey areas. I cannot recall any mess deck opinions concerning these evacuation plans. The next day, and once again wearing my seaboots, I was part of the same jetty working party, only this time we were assisting Russian families, with their luggage, who were embarking in the *Empress of Canada*'s small boat usually used for picking up passengers.

I remarked to my mess mates that these people had a look of despair about them and that the women were doing a lot of crying. I cannot recall anyone giving an opinion as to why this should be, with the exception of Stripey, who nearly always managed a few words on these sorts of occasions: "Well, boy, they're leaving their homes." I suppose I dismissed it from my mind. There were no such depressing scenes when the Norwegians embarked.

It was some time after the war when stories began to surface concerning the horrific crimes committed in the name of 'Uncle Joe' as Stalin was known in my day. Then it became obvious to me that 'Uncle Joe' had had these people moved because he knew they had been selling coal directly or indirectly to the Germans. If he followed his usual pattern he either had them and their families murdered immediately, or sent them to a Gulag. I have never been able to find any information on this sad event or find out what orders were in the wallet. I remember quite clearly enjoying my trips ashore on this occasion, this beautiful island, the birds and above all the satisfaction I felt because I believed I had been helpful to these Russian people. I have since felt guilty for assisting Stalin's NKVD (secret police).

There was one lighter memory of this Spitzbergen story and that concerned an Arctic fox hunter. He categorically refused to go with the Russians, although he was Russian, on the grounds that he was not a coalminer. Our officer in charge ignored all this and told him he was to be packed and ready to go with the rest. During the night he did pack his gear, but took himself, his pack and rifle and disappeared into the mountains!

On 27th August at 0600 hours we launched an aircraft but couldn't find this fox hunter, and at 0930 we weighed anchor and, in the company of the *Empress of Canada*, set course for Archangel after recovering our Walrus, leaving this old hunter behind in the company of his friendly Arctic foxes!

Photo 31. Walrus on crane

X

A Twenty-Six Minute Battle

There was a change in the weather as we left Advent Fiord on that cool, misty late August morning, in company with the *Empress of Canada* and the large cruiser HMS *Devonshire*. PQ3, we hoped, had by now safely managed to zigzag its way into Murmansk, despite the German air attacks from their airfields in northern Norway and Petsamo in Finland. It took us some three days at 11 knots to escort the *Empress of Canada* with its human cargo into the White Sea to Archangel.

On our arrival we moored alongside a dockyard wall. The *Empress* was moored further up and, because of the mist, we were unable to see the Russian families disembarked. For me, always eager-eyed in a new foreign port, Archangel, at least the bit I could see through the mist, was not a place of beauty. Before we could catch our breaths a Russian admiral had come aboard. He had come personally to tell our rear admiral that he (the Russian admiral) was in charge of all Allied navies while they were operating in Russian waters. I don't think Philip Vian was very happy with this. It was a fact that some months later we did act as an escort protecting Russian mine-laying units from the Germans. This 'Red Bolshie' admiral, when invited by Vian to inspect the ship, refused to enter any of our officers' quarters and insisted on inspecting the crew's quarters only. I think he was surprised to find the mess decks, galley, showers and heads spotless, as they always were! I was surprised to hear him speaking perfect English. He left, after a forty-minute visit, in a dirty, tatty, low-lying Karl Marx class destroyer!

We left Archangel the following morning (the 30th) after being towed clear of the wall by a Russian tug. We steamed clear of the land and joined company with an 'empty' *Empress of Canada* and the destroyer HMS *Anthony*. On Monday we sighted *K. Thor* (Seahorse Line) and crossed the hundred-fathom line to enter Gron Fiord, Spitzbergen. We were joined by HMS *Icarus* and *Aurora* still 'in the pink' and took passage for Advent Fiord.

During the afternoon on 2nd September the trawler *Van Odst* came alongside with the first of the Norwegian families from Longyearby. We had already flown off our two Walrus aircraft to make room for these people and their belongings to be housed in our spacious hangars. It was 'all hands' embarking cheerful people and their luggage – including a sousaphone! Once these three hundred or so men, women and children had been settled down we got underway and secured alongside the *Empress of Canada* after the short journey down the fiord. The captain of the *Empress of Canada* had urgently requested us to supply him with some fresh water, as his tanks were almost empty. We carried an evaporating plant able to convert seawater to fresh water, but this was a heavy user of fuel oil and the plant also needed descaling after a short run, which was best carried out whilst in harbour. Fresh water was a precious commodity and was always rationed. Our engine room staff had come up with some forty tons of H_2O which our engineering officer, Lieutenant W. Chick, hoped wouldn't be lost in their huge tanks. These huge tanks were used to handle hundreds of tons of fresh water for their passengers' needs on peacetime holiday cruises on this 20,000-ton liner. Transferring these people safely, particularly the children, became difficult due to the deteriorating weather; they were obviously in for an uncomfortable voyage to Great Britain. I well recall this pleasantly spent afternoon. On returning to Advent Fiord we anchored and hoisted aboard our two amphibious aircraft, the pilots of which had anchored them upstream.

The same evening, in company with *Icarus*, *Antelope* and the *Empress*, we proceeded to sea at 10 knots in uncomfortable weather. The next morning we were joined by *Aurora* and closed up with a QP, possibly No 2. The returning Russian convoy, some ships carrying timber, others in ballast, hove into sight on that Friday morning. The convoy commodore, after passing the pleasantries of the day, suggested where he would like us and the *Empress* to take up our position in the zigzag pattern (always difficult in bad weather to find and keep without running into your neighbours, especially in the dark). We were just in time to help repel two air attacks. It was here that we received our second delivery of correspondence, sent to us in the same leather wallet as before and posted on a rope line by the destroyer *Antelope*. The Commodore had possibly sent it. We then, on that Saturday, signalled 'Good luck' to the England-bound *Empress of Canada*, now with its own destroyer screen. In the company of *Aurora* we also parted company with QP2, cutting into rough Arctic seas at high speed, a new experience for me. We kept up this 'bone-shaking' speed, when rest was impossible, for fifteen hours. The rear admiral hadn't informed the crew of his intentions on that stormy day. It was blowing extremely hard; a typical autumn gale which, when added to our speed of 30 knots, made it almost impossible to move about in a fast pitching ship. We all knew that we were steering almost due south in the Barents Sea which meant that we were heading for northern Norway. Because of our speed we were not surprised to hear the pipe that we would be oiling soon, but that it would be from a Russian oiler did come as a surprise! It was usually a fleet tanker that kept us topped up. At that moment the buzzes started. We had been told some time back that all our operations whilst on Russian soil and in Russian waters would come under the command of the Russian admiral of the north. Had he dispatched this oiler? And if so what did he want us to do? Perhaps Rear Admiral Vian had requested this fuel carrier; he seemed to have a free hand to do as he pleased.

It wasn't long after this announcement that we slowed down and entered a large sheltered bay, possibly Ozerfis Bay, where an oiler flying the 'hammer and sickle' red flag was waiting for us. It was impossible to go alongside so we tied up astern of her and passed our oil intake over our higher prow onto her quarterdeck stern. As part of my duties as a special sea duty man I was instructed to secure our three-and-three-quarter-inch special steel wire rope to the oiler's after towing bollards; then it was only necessary for me to remain on that spot in case it became necessary to cast off our steel wire in a hurry. So there I was, minding my own business, when, clad in their usual quilted bulky Arctic clothing, three of the Russian crew came up onto their quarterdeck carrying their oil pipe connection section. Realising I could be of help I lifted our matching intake joining section pipe lying on the deck and presented it in their direction for the necessary connection to be made before their oil could be pumped to us. As the first Russian approached I suddenly became aware that these three oil crew persons were middle-aged women. My amazed expression must have amused them.

The first lady, with very big breasts, gave me an ear-to-ear smile exposing a mouthful of gold-filled teeth and some broken front teeth as though she had been in a fight. She put both open hands on my two shoulders then lifted me off my feet as though I was a small child and gave me a hug, which took my breath away, as her two comrades lifted and connected the two oil pipes together, to start the pumping. The entire crew on this oiler, including their captain, appeared to be women.

On hearing this story later my mess mates pointed out that my successful love life had left them all feeling jealous: none of them had been hugged by a well-proportioned middle-aged Russian beauty wearing overalls saturated with the latest perfume of the '90 second' fuel oil. When we and the *Aurora* had finished oiling, the captain informed the ship's company: "We're going to try to get into the harbour that the *Dagny* came from, using the dark evening and this gale, which should help us pass unnoticed." It was one of the messenger boys that had told me about the Norwegian coal ship *Dagny*. "I was there," he said excitedly, "on the *Dagny* when the two 'Royals' brought in the *Dagny*'s Norwegian captain under guard. The rear admiral was sitting at a table; they told the Norwegian captain it was serious. The rear admiral looked at the prisoner with those eyes accentuated by his big bushy eyebrows," he said. (I knew about those blue eyes and had some sympathy with the Norwegian.) "The Admiral had a 'six-gun' on the table, he reached across the table and turned it slowly with his thumb and little finger until the barrel was pointing at the captain's chest, then he just looked at him, never said a word, just looked at him," said the boy. Then Vian asked: "How do I get into the sound?" "You could see," said the boy, "the Norwegian was scared stiff, then he tried to laugh it off. All of a sudden the Norwegian came out with it, without hesitation, giving details of the day signal flags, night white lights, the *Dagny*'s logged code and the boom." Then, laughing heartily, the boy said: "He gave old Vian the key to his bloody Norwegian door." Although I didn't fully understand all this at the time, it did mean that, wherever it was, there was some sort of boom defence.

A boom defence was a deep thick wire net held upright by floating buoys with the bottom of the wire barrier secured by anchors to the seabed. A small section, not secured to the bottom, called 'the gate' could be opened by a tug-type vessel with two lifting davits fixed to its bows. This allowed vessels to come and go from the guarded harbour. All shipping needing to use this entrance would carry a signal which, along with the ship's silhouette, would be recorded by the boom defence vessel. Such a signal would consist of signal flags in daylight and white, red or green lights all together or singly at night, with different time spaces between lights. Philip Vian would know he would need a pitch-black night to invalidate the use of silhouette recognition.

Even with hindsight, it appears that nobody was absolutely certain as to which part of enemy-occupied Norway we had entered from the Barents Sea just before midnight on 8th September 1941. The time and the conditions that had been picked carefully by our rear admiral was the time between midnight and 0400. The conditions expected were a northerly gale producing low clouds and poor visibility in those few hours of darkness. This also helped us to conceal our movements from enemy aircraft.

Was it Hammer Fiord or Porsangen Fiord? My copy of the ship's log for that day showed a radar navigation fix by Radar 273 taken just after the action, which would have put us at the north-western end of the Porsangen Fiord, which leads me to assume that it was Kistrand, a Norwegian township port with a harbour wall and good road connections to Kvalsund and Kolvik. It had a five- by two-mile deep-water area where the boom defence had probably been built.

It is certain that this type of action was better suited to destroyers but regrettably HMS *Punjabi* and *Tartar* had been left to guard the *Empress of Canada* from U-boat attacks, so our rear admiral had gone into battle with the two cruisers which he was going to deploy as though they were destroyers. Perhaps it took him back to the days when he was a very successful destroyer captain, but in these circumstances he appeared to ignore his best weapon, Radar 273, which was capable of giving him a clear picture of everything within these waters and the surrounding land.

When we were about a hundred miles from our destination, we steamed south at top speed in this uncertain light. If Radar 273 and old-fashioned methods had been used together on this occasion, then this should not have given us any navigation problem, and the ship's position would have been known precisely. It has always been difficult for me to understand why our captain and the rear admiral had an argument on the bridge just before going into action, especially with the enemy already very close. One thing the captain was heard to say was that "it was impossible to fix the ship's position precisely without using radar".

Captain J.S.L. Dundas was a senior captain. He was, as the crew knew, a strict but fair disciplinarian and a proper gentleman. He would always, when he could, tell us what the ship was up to by putting us in the picture, but not so on this occasion. He had said little, probably because the rear admiral decided against it, and a rear admiral was two ranks higher than a senior captain. The captain would be responsible for the well-being of the ship, its general safety and the safety of his officers, engine room staff and seamen. Navigation and seamanship were also two more of his duties but the ship's fighting efficiency was his foremost mandate. The captain must have been very worried at the thought of steaming at 'full speed ahead' through a narrow boom opening and wondering if it would stay open long enough to get out again! On this very dark misty night what would we find in this restricted space of water, and would we be in enemy-occupied Norway? Did he have charts with sufficient information of tides, depths, rocks and sandbanks positions in this almost unknown (to us) backwater? It is unlikely that he would know about mines, shore batteries or airfields. I would not like to have been in his shoes but we didn't have worries about those sorts of things. JTB and I had learnt some time previously that our captain knew as much as we did, if not more, about how radar worked and how advanced the technology was. On the other hand the rear admiral, who was 'old Navy', may not have taken on board the image advantages that this clear-seeing technology had. It should have been used on this occasion but perhaps, for some reason or other, it wasn't.

At 0037 on Monday 8th September 1941, on that very dark night with one of those famous Arctic mists, in the company of HMS *Aurora* (Captain W.G. Agnew), a depleted 'Force A' made the necessary coloured lights 'open the door' signal to enable us to commence this attack in Svaerholthavet Sound. We must have sent the correct message, as the boom vessel's skipper, despite the lack of a confirming silhouette, was moving to open the boom entrance for the supposed *Dagny* to enter. Our position was uncomfortably close to the boom, which prompted our captain to go ahead at speed as soon as the Norwegian had half opened the boom door. When we drew near enough for the armed boom vessel's skipper to realise his mistake, it was impossible for him to manoeuvre himself to stop us by closing the gate which was by now three-quarters open. We and the *Aurora* moved in, having fired a four-inch round into the armed boom vessel's bow section; it was too near for us to use our six-inch guns. In answer to our shot, this spunky Norwegian's single gun mounted on his fo'c'sle fired back at us. I believe the *Aurora* fired as well after being hit and slightly damaged by this boom vessel's shot. It was the intention of both of us to immobilise this boom vessel and therefore prevent the boom door being closed.

Once inside, the visibility improved a little, possibly because of the surrounding hills. At 0128 Vian sighted, with a great deal of help from us all, the four German merchant ships later estimated to be carrying some 1,500 German troops. These vessels were anchored in a different position (see Figure 33) from their protecting naval units which consisted of the *Bremse*, two light destroyers A03 and L30, and an armed trawler. We were also in this now crowded harbour. In these circumstances the enemy vessels, comfortably tucked up for the night in the safety of a boom-protected harbour, would not have been maintaining 'steam up' with the exception of the duty boat; our guess was that it would have been the armed trawler (the clever Vian

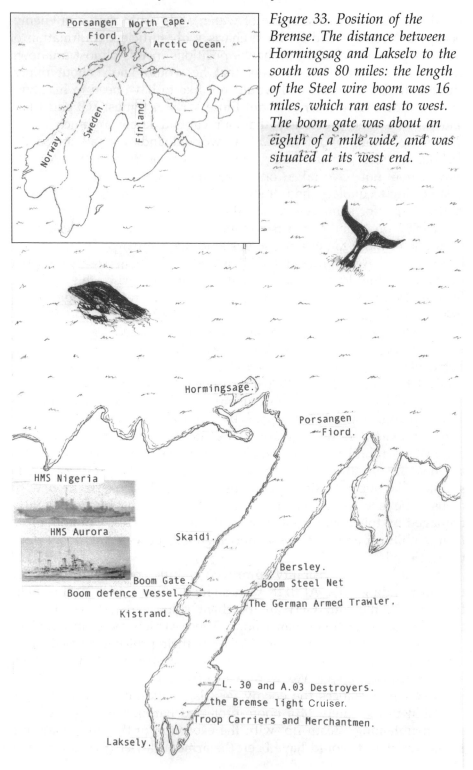

Figure 33. Position of the Bremse. The distance between Hormingsag and Lakselv to the south was 80 miles: the length of the Steel wire boom was 16 miles, which ran east to west. The boom gate was about an eighth of a mile wide, and was situated at its west end.

would have already worked this out). At 0129 hours we and the *Aurora* engaged at point-blank range the *Bremse* and the two small destroyers A03 and L30. The *Bremse* was also firing at us.

The first enemy vessel to get underway was, I think, the armed trawler, which quickly and efficiently laid a smoke screen (or had a very inefficient boiler) between both sets of the enemy and us. On completion of his first run this trawler twisted about and was reinforcing his smoke screen, with another, if that was what it was, or he may have just been returning to join his friends. At this moment hits were observed on the *Bremse*, which subsequently blew up. Before we lost vision because of this smoke, L30 was also hit and sunk, all of which showed up on our Radar 273. During the few minutes of this action I was wearing a pair of the newfangled sound-powered magnetic headphones, from which one could hear all the noises of this action and the orders that were also relayed down from the aft HACP where my Canadian spotting-officer was giving a running commentary on the important bits of this fast moving fight. This he would do routinely in the course of any action. Our two six-inch forward turrets were, by this time, firing continuously.

From this position, some thirty feet up by the rear of the mast, he obtained a bird's-eye view of events. It was at this moment, so I was informed later, that the argument started again on the bridge. I didn't hear the argument between our captain and the rear admiral – I got it second hand. My young informant was on the bridge at the time. Through perhaps not taking advantage of the technology available with Radar 279 and the more advanced 273, which was well able to 'see through' mist and gun smoke, the apparently frustrated Vian was unable to see his enemy. Our 'Guns', and indeed my messmate JTB, could have told the admiral our exact position at that moment, and Vian could have continued the action against all the enemy ships using 273, which he had, up to that moment by firing 50 six-inch shells successfully from 'A' and 'B' Turrets. At such close range a few more minutes of firing ten rounds a minute (120 six-inch shells) would have destroyed the four merchantmen, and no doubt the estimated 1,500 soldiers aboard, who were possibly destined for the Russian front near Murmansk. Why had he ordered our captain to sail into the unknown through mist and smoke cover on that dark night? At 0137, moving through smoke and mist at over 20 knots, *Nigeria* subsequently rammed a vessel, which was cut in half. The bow section of this severed craft went straight down with all enemy hands. The German sailors in the remaining part of escort vessel A03 amidships and stern section became visible for a short space of time as they calmly queued up to step out of their sinking vessel to fall the few feet into the cold water, only to be instantly sucked down by the vortex created by our razor-sharp copper–bronze propeller blades which must have cut most of them to pieces. It took me some time to take in what was happening to them. Fortunately, as I was wearing a phone headset I didn't hear their cries, which those on the upper deck did. I do not think there were many survivors, either from the trawler or escort vessel A03, or the *Bremse*. One thing I do know with certainty about this action was this special minute in my life which was spent watching the ship's white speed dial as *Nigeria's* bow rose as if to receive an extra high wave but then stayed there for a minute whilst the ship's speed dropped instantly to zero. *Nigeria* hesitated thus for this whole minute, before resuming its forward movement and reaching 6 knots on an even keel. During this special minute I cannot recollect any noise of an explosion or any evidence of a blast when the hole in the bow of the *Nigeria* was made, starting from the paint shop forward to station twenty-two (a distance of some 22 yards). I recall hearing the starboard multiple .5 machine-guns opening up when they fired at this unfortunate vessel again during this time. At 0154 the action was called off as we moved slowly forward at 6 knots with the *Aurora* following us to the boom exit position. The boom defence vessel had not been able to move, we had not sunk it. We fired at it again in case they could still use their bow gun as we crawled past. It was felt that a faster speed than six knots would produce too great a water pressure for station twenty-two bulkheads to withstand. The hole in our bows was such (see Photo 32) that the intake of seas whirling about us was causing the ship to yaw from side to side. The helmsman was unable to keep his course steady and the navigator was finding it difficult to calculate his position. Because we had lost all our PV gear we could not stream PVs and accordingly had to avoid further damage from mines by following close behind the *Aurora* and her streamed PVs.

We were fortunate that we carried a dedicated engine room officer, Lieutenant Chick, who had specialised in damage control, and who on this occasion with the help of the ship's carpenter was able satisfactorily to reinforce station twenty-two with timber beams. This work enabled the captain to increase speed from six knots up to sixteen according to the weather and differing zigzag. It was the start of a nightmare journey, limping home feeling very vulnerable, without the satisfaction of a job well done.

On that dark, misty Sunday morning, whilst the shoring was in progress, our navigator with the help of Radar 273, took a 'cocked hat' coastal fix. At 0237 our estimated position was found to be 71°10′ north by 26°56′ east, not very far from the dreaded North Cape. We were in a very tricky position with the secrecy of our whereabouts guaranteed only by the existence of dense clouds and a dark night. No doubt by now the Germans must have informed North Cape of our presence. We were all aware that, come daylight, and should the dark clouds lift, our chance of surviving the journey in our crippled state past North Cape was slim. Our first problem that Monday morning would be the airfield at Petsamo, Finland. If we survived this, round the corner past North Cape there were three German airfields, and the heavyweight German fleet including the *Tirpitz*, *Scharnhorst* and *Gneisenau*, not to mention U-boats and escorts. Then it was at least a four-day journey, at these speeds, to Iceland and fogs didn't usually last that long. There was a strange feeling of disappointment amongst the crew. So far as I was concerned it was not fear, it was an uncomfortable feeling of self-recrimination. It had been a 'cock-up', a failure. We took a ship into action that was ticking over and keeping perfect time and suddenly it had just stopped. It was a feeling of failed collective responsibility that we all felt, and we had achieved nothing because those German troops who were left in the undamaged merchant ships would still get through to Russia. We were not hurt, there were no casualties, we had been extremely lucky. The half an hour we had spent in the sound had probably caused some eight hundred German naval deaths, perhaps

Photo 32. Crunched bow

more. There were no other plus factors, except that the Spitzbergen to Svaerholthavet Sound coal run had come to an end.

Photo 32a. Damaged bow section and a broken loose paravane

With the *Aurora* in station, with us behind, always being protected by her PVs, apart from having to make a violent course alteration to avoid a free-floating mine nothing serious happened. We were joined on the third day by the two Tribal class destroyers HMS *Bedouin* and HMS *Eskimo*, a very welcome sight. We had survived these four days, always at a slow speed, mainly because of the dense clouds and sea fog (possibly caused by the cold Arctic air moving over Gulf Stream warmed seawater) we had brought with us from Svaerholthavet Sound. God too had travelled with us that week.

As we had lost our anchor and chain, we finally secured at 'J' Buoy, Long Hope, Scapa using a huge six-inch-diameter wire. The 'C-in-C' was our first visitor the next day at 1000. Had he come to look at our hole, praise our rear admiral or reprimand him? I shall never know!

We sailed later that day for South Shields to the yard where *Nigeria* had been built two years earlier. It was interesting to note the reaction of the dockyard mateys. They were amazed at the size of the hole and took pride in the fact that they had built her so well that she had been able to make the long journey home in that condition.

At 2000 on 12th September 1941 Rear Admiral Philip Vian left the ship, never to return, leaving us with many unanswered questions, one of which was, why did the ship's log state that on 8th September 1941 at 0137 the ship's stern was damaged by an explosion or collision? It is a mystery, it seems as though someone who wasn't even there at the time entered it into the log at a later date and did not know the hole was in the bow. It is curious that the fifty-odd ratings closed up at action stations in 'Y' Turret and the four sailors at the two after .5 machine-guns did not see or hear anything at this time or date!

The mood of the ship's company was curious, there was no doubt about it, we had sunk three or four units of Hitler's Navy and, despite being badly damaged, we had managed to make our way to a home port safely without casualties. I think it was the fact that the rear admiral, during the quiet dog watches, and without any fuss, had slunk off apparently not wishing to talk to us, leaving us all with a feeling of non-achievement. There was an understandable feeling of sympathy for the German crews that may have died by being cut to pieces by our razor-sharp propeller blades, which also helped to damp down feelings of having won a round. Everybody preferred to refer to the whole operation as a 'balls-up'. Here we had a rear admiral with the touch of Nelson himself, who we all admired for his reputation. Had he been bright enough to grasp the significance of the opportunity that the captain of the *Dagny* presented by giving us the 'key to the door'? He was a brilliant organiser who had worked out a way into this harbour some hundred and twenty miles behind enemy lines, who patiently waited for the correct weather conditions and time to guarantee a safe journey past two airfields, shore batteries and mine fields to end up in a harbour full of goodies. Nearly all this was wasted, as far as we saw it, because of one apparently wrong decision. In the end the entire ship's company was more than content to be safely back in South Shields waiting to go on a couple of weeks' leave. Had we returned undamaged, and had we been able to sink the merchantmen full of German soldiers *en route* to the Russian front, our rear admiral would have been more famous than he already was but, as Stripey said: "Think of it; we wouldn't have come back to Newcastle and wouldn't be going on fourteen days' leave but would be getting ready for another bit of the admiral's dangerous nonsense." As usual, our old three-badge AB was right.

As a young lad with the possibility of being granted two weeks' leave in the Isle of Wight and with a free travel warrant in his sights, I didn't lose any sleep over the rights and wrongs of our brush with the German Northern Fleet. Whilst explaining to JTB and my fellow mess mates that I hadn't written to my Isle of Wight girlfriend, it was Stripey who laughingly pointed out that, as I only had two weeks' leave and getting there and back was going to take some time, I better ask this girl Dulcie if she could learn to love me in six quick, easy lessons! They all laughed. In those days to get a girl to kiss you was a tremendous achievement. It was only a 'tart' that allowed you to get any further. On this subject they all agreed, this girl was no 'tart' and I was wasting my time going all the way to the Isle of Wight.

A couple of days before leaving for the Isle of Wight, the ship's mail, some four or five months in arrears, caught up with us. The Admiralty always tried hard to deliver post. All mail for the Home Fleet was sent to Scapa Flow first. This batch had been sent on to Iceland and then to Murmansk. The poor sods stuck in that awful port manning the RN depot had forwarded it to Newcastle, possibly not expecting us to ever receive it.

Throughout my naval career I would receive letters from only two sources regularly. One combined letter from Auntie and Mum, and one from Joyce. In those six years I did receive at least three from my brother and possibly six from my sister, which was quite good considering she was tending to wounded RAF aircrews as a nursing sister. Joyce's letters usually contained local N21 news but never anything 'lovey dovey', and I took it all for granted. On this occasion Mum's and Auntie's letter was full of news. My young brother had finished schooling in the Isle of Wight and all three of them had returned to Winchmore Hill. They had learnt that Parliament had made it possible for the local authorities to requisition all empty properties for housing bombed-out homeless people.

I was pleased with the thought of returning to N21 and possibly seeing all or some of my old school chums, especially Joyce. Dulcie, whom I loved dearly, had to be put on the back-burner and was soon forgotten; the Isle of Wight might just as well have been on the other side of the world! How lucky, I thought, to have received Mum's and Auntie's letter just in time to stop me heading for Totland Bay. How fickle young boys are!

Things were different during this fourteen-day leave. It seemed that everyone had grown up a bit, but most of all they were all war heroes; after all, they were being bombed. This young seaman no longer seemed different to them. Lots of our old neighbours were now in the forces and some already away from home. Things were definitely different. Auntie had been hospitalised to have a growth removed from her throat but I was not told and hadn't noticed anything different. I wish I had been told because perhaps I would have told her how fond of her I was and would perhaps have written to her more often. Joyce and her father were friendly as usual. He showed me his posh black car with its paint and chrome all shiny but jacked up on four jacks to keep the weight off its springs and the tyres completely clear of the ground. It was to remain like this for the next four years, due to the ban on petrol for private cars.

It was this leave that made me realise how rough and uncouth I had become over the past two years. I suppose it stemmed from "Tinkle, tinkle little spoon, knife and fork will follow soon", and the steady deterioration of table manners in an environment of constant swearing. This all came to a head at the wartime dinner party Joyce and I were invited to by the mother and father of Bill, an old close school friend. As far as I was concerned this dinner party was not a success! It was Bill and his mother who started all the small talk as we sat at the dinner table. Most of their questions were directed at me. It was Joyce who came to my rescue by asking Bill what he had been up to since recently joining the Home Guard at sixteen. He began to tell us. In the meantime Bill's father began serving the main meal. I had already scoffed the scrumptious home-made soup, tilting my soup bowl forwards instead of backwards, using bread rather than the spoon to completely dry it out. I put down the spotlessly 'bread cleaned' soup bowl and, with both elbows on the table, continued to listen to Bill twittering on about the Home Guard, occasionally absent-mindedly picking up the odd crumb or two of bread I had dropped following the mopping of my soup bowl.

Bill's mum put in front of me a large plate on which was served a piece of dark meat about as big as a child's clenched fist, a very good wartime helping, surrounded by two potatoes, cabbage and sprout. A veritable feast for a king compared with ship's grub! With my acquired bad naval table manners I asked my hostess: "What meat is this?" as I started to cut into it, even before anybody else had been served. "Snoek (the polite name for whale meat – a snoek is a large fish!)," she replied. "Is that right?" I answered with my mouth half full. It tasted very good. None of my appalling manners had any effect on Bill's story concerning the Home Guard. I don't know why I was becoming uncomfortable with Bill's story. Perhaps the recent memory of the air raid casualties both at sea and at Plymouth was more deep-rooted than I thought. At that time I hardly understood any of these feelings. It was when Bill asked me a direct question, which caught my concentration just as I was dipping a sizeable portion of a beautifully prepared potato into the tasty brown gravy. "Have you ever been bombed?" "Not f***ing much," I replied without a thought. Two things happened. It took time for my brain to realise that I was not in the company of tarry-arsed sailors, hundreds of miles out at sea, and secondly that I was in the company of two refined ladies and in a house. I stopped chewing and looked up. Everyone had been served with their food but they weren't eating and were looking directly at me. Joyce's beautiful blue eyes had grown enormous. Mrs Cope sat there with her mouth permanently half open, Bill had an expression of sheer amazement and dear old Mr Cope was hiding a grin. I did the only thing I could whilst their food was getting cold, I prayed to God that he would open up the floor and let me fall through, but he didn't! Mr Cope broke the ice by turning his grin into a laugh, which was followed by Bill. This enabled Mrs Cope to overcome her lockjaw problem and mutter "My goodness". Joyce had almost closed her eyes and wrinkled up her face showing great disapproval. I swallowed my mouthful of potato and gravy and said simply: "I'm sorry, it just slipped out." Finally Mr Cope came to my rescue with a simple: "Eat up, the food is getting cold; he's only a sailor." I carried on eating, getting two extra potatoes from a nice Mrs Cope who had always been an excellent cook, as I had learnt on two previous occasions at children's parties at that house. I saw Joyce home through the blackout at the start of an air raid warning. Her mother and father were pleased to see her safely home and hurried her down to the corrugated iron Anderson air raid shelter. At about 0300 a heavy air raid developed over Edmonton about two miles away, which amongst other things completely destroyed the Alhambra Cinema. I peacefully slept through it all; so much for a guilty conscience! Joyce chose to forget my foul-mouthing at the dinner party. While saying goodbye the next day to Joyce and her father, dressed in his new Home Guard uniform, I said I might be going back to Russia (this might have been construed as 'careless talk' and treated as a punishable offence, if overheard), but would see them at Christmas some few weeks away. I shook hands and left with a "Happy Christmas".

Christmas leave was a non-starter: on Sunday 14th December 1941 we left South Shields to carry out sea trials to confirm that everything was shipshape and watertight. We tested guns, steering and, most of all, engines, boilers and propellers. It was going to be a full two years before I was to see Joyce or her father again.

It took two months of day and night working by some forty-odd 'dockyard mateys' using welding, riveting, metal cutting and burning equipment, producing some eighty decibels of noise at times, to repair the damage to *Nigeria*. Twenty-four hours of dust, smells, din and electric arc flashes, whilst we tried to sleep and eat some twelve yards away on our mess deck.

During our working day, amongst our other duties, we managed to get ourselves covered with unpleasant red lead paint whilst brushing it onto the new metal sections being fixed, and rubbing against it when passing between these metal sections. It didn't wash off easily and gloves were not available. We and the dockyard workers were all subjected to the constant din: ear defenders hadn't been invented!

We lived and slept in the open air during part of October and the whole of a cold November (there was one wall missing from our 'house'). We were living in semi-darkness halfway down a dry dock basin with a constant smell of slow-drying red lead paint. It is on record that seven seamen were sent to hospital for ten days, lucky chaps!

Some of our lads who lived locally, and those that could afford to pay for local lodgings (mostly married men), had their wives join them in South Shields and were allowed all-night shore leave when they were not on duty watch.

To help the three local boy seamen we all readily gave up our own Saturday or Sunday afternoon and volunteered, with the master-at-arms' permission, to cover for their duty watch to enable them to stay with their parents every weekend. To be truthful, I wasn't giving much away. I usually had little or no money and, in a town that was not allowed to hold football matches (as it was almost certain that the spectators would be vulnerable if there was an air raid), and where nobody had cakes to spare in the shops for a well-fed young seaman without a ration card, this was reason enough to make me stay aboard, where at least I was in good company.

Four memories come to my mind concerning the South Shields refit. The first was a visit by six well-dressed, well-fed Members of Parliament. They apparently failed to notice us; none took the trouble to speak to any of the crew. Two officers who afterwards took them back to the wardroom to feed them showed them round. These six Parliamentary visitors, whatever party they belonged to, put me off Members of Parliament for life! A dockyard is a nasty, smelly, miserably cold place to live in during November; at least they could have said something sympathetic having walked through our open-air bedroom. Some MPs are still apparently missing the point today!

The second memory was of the forty-eight air raids that South Shields suffered whilst we were there when numerous incendiary bombs were dropped. During these raids, we landed groups of our blokes to help collect these tennis-ball-size bombs that quickly burst into flames. They had to be picked up with a small hand shovel and placed in a galvanised bucket. Using a thing called a stirrup pump they were sprayed with water and taken outside the building as soon as possible. Some of our chaps were injured doing this job and ended up in the local hospital. This was also my first unpleasant experience of acting as a member of a funeral party, when burying one of the crew; this entailed a slow march and the firing of three rifle shots at the graveside. It was always an uncomfortable feeling welcoming the casualty's new replacement. We had two of our own small fires on board, including one in the boys' mess deck that scorched the bulkhead and deck-head paintwork. More nasty smells!

The third Shields happening was a hard-drinking rating who had thumped and injured a local copper while being arrested for being drunk and disorderly after breaking up a local pub whilst on shore leave. We all watched him being escorted off by three marines on his way to Durham Prison for a two-year hard labour stay.

We felt it was probably somebody, like one of those MPs who visited us, who knew they were right when they insisted that this good seaman and fighter should be given a 'certificate of guarantee' to live for the next two years in Durham jail and not have to suffer sleepless nights in the freezing cold of Russian convoys or go without a meal because the cook happened to be fighting the enemy at that moment.

The fourth and only pleasant thing I remember whilst in South Shields was a visit to the ship by a hundred male and female Army recruits who were brought on board by a sergeant and two corporals. These raw soldiers were divided into ten groups and shown round the ship by our crew. Our sailors spared them nothing: they saw the 'open' sleeping quarters, the damage to the engine room, bath and toilet facilities, the galley and our main and high-level armament.

I managed to strike up a brief conversation with a young eighteen-year-old and asked him what he thought of it all. He told me that he was amazed when I informed him I had been on the ship for almost two years. Would he like to be in the Navy? He shook his head and said: "I'll stay with the Army please, and it's got to be warmer." A ship without its boiler room working was rather like a house in the winter without its central heating boiler turned on!

Funny how one quickly forgets yesterday's problems! It wasn't long before we were back at Scapa acting as 'AA Guard Ship'. It was just three days before Christmas when we once again found ourselves making our way slowly back to Russia with the 'PQ' convoy which had started its life in Casco Bay, New England.

The cold Christmas of 1941 went by for us as if it had never existed. The food was the same as always. There were no celebrations, presents, cards or crackers and definitely not a mince pie in sight. Christmas day for me was hardly mentioned and just disappeared: unnecessary signals between ships were taboo whatever the day. It was just another sea journey from Scapa with watch keeping, work and sleepless nights – and, of course, schoolwork. The only reference to Christmas at all was Tom's short outburst at lunchtime just after he had drunk his daily grog issue. "It was," he said at the top of his voice, "Christmas day on the mess deck and the crew had all slung

Author's medals

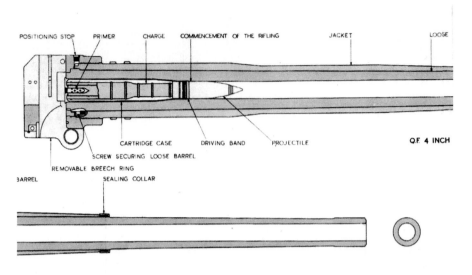

4 inch high-angle gun barrel

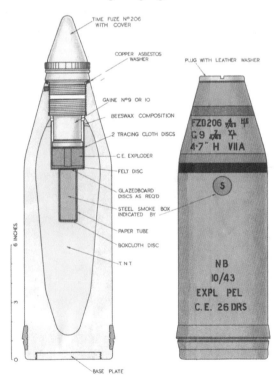

RN 4 inch shell

'Pink' HMS Nigeria - an artist's impression

Birdeating spider

Barbie Edward

Japanese money

their hammocks; because none of them had any Christmas pudding they knew the cook had done what they all asked him to do, f*** off." At this point Raggie shouted out at the top of his voice so that all 13, 15 and 17 Mess members could hear: "Who called that cook a twat?" To which the thirty-odd occupants of 13, 15 and 17 Mess shouted back: "Who called that twat a cook?" Life was hard on the ship's cooks that Christmas day.

To end the Christmas lunch, revellers sang a final chorus of: 'It was Christmas night in the workhouse / and holly adorned the walls / when up stood brave Horatio and shouted 'Balls'.' "For that you get no Christmas pudding," cried the workhouse master-at-arms, to which they, the mess deck hands, replied, "You can keep your Christmas puddings and stick them on the walls".

This was the first Arctic convoy that we had carried out during a winter and I don't think any of us were quite prepared for what came with it. We lads were not entirely wet behind the ears; we knew the everyday naval work was extra hard with long hours and we were always hungry and tired from lack of sleep.

This journey was so different from the last to Russia. The weather was bitter and it took only a couple of days after leaving Scapa Flow for the sea temperature to drop and read 32ºF. The air temperature dropped daily and by the time we had left Iceland it read 25ºF. The winds got up and I was introduced to a new noise in my life, the rattling and screeching of the rigging. You could hear these wailing banshees in your dreams. Such conditions produced black ice which resulted in a new type of job to join our workloads: 'ice chipping'. This job was continuous; everything that moved from guns to equipment had to be cleared of black ice.

In these conditions it was necessary to wear three pairs of gloves. Fingerless gloves, covered by woollen knitted gloves and a large pair of woollen sheepskin mittens. Should you touch any iron or steel object with your bare hand at these low temperatures your skin became instantly welded to the metal object so that when you pulled your hand away you left your frozen skin behind. These gloves made it both difficult and somewhat frightening when climbing especially to the masthead lookout position. Heavy sheepskin-lined waterproof coats had also been issued.

We also understood from what was said among the crew that we would have to put up with attacks from the air, U-boats and possible enemy surface vessels. Attacks from any of these three different enemy units could end up with someone dying. Below decks, if a torpedo hit, suddenly liberated super-heated high-pressure steam could strip large portions of flesh from the body leaving bones exposed. An enemy shell landing in one of the upper-deck turrets, normally full of cordite charges sewn in silk sacks, could barbecue the gun's crew in seconds; splinters from the same shell could cut you to ribbons. You could breathe in horribly choking, smelly, '90 second' oil that might catch fire on top of the water whilst you were trying to swim clear – if you weren't already frozen stiff in the sea after three minutes – 'the boiled egg syndrome'. Diving enemy aircraft firing cannons loaded with grazed-nosed shells that could take your foot, or anything else, off in one go. Added to all these known hazards, the new horror of 'black ice' simply overwhelmed me, but strangely I didn't feel afraid.

It was the commander who instructed our 'called-up civilian' schoolmaster, now a sub-lieutenant, to follow the King's Regulations and Admiralty instructions without interfering with the boys' wartime duties. These instructions were: school is compulsory for us, including preparation of class work. A minimum of four hours' schooling weekly is laid down. Voluntary school was usually held in the dog watches, and higher classes were arranged for Education Test Part I, and the higher educational test. School was compulsory for us. This meant that all in our class went on studying even when they became O/S. So, 'me and my friends' had to continue with class work to prepare for our exams.

Whilst using hammocks, which were the only comfortable way of sleeping properly in the mess deck on a tossing ship, we were subjected to a constant rain-like drip of condensation. This was due to a six-inch layer of ice on top of the half-inch-thick freezing metal deck-head meeting the slightly higher inside temperature provided by our warm breath (there was no other heating). In order to keep dry it was necessary to cover our hammocks with oilskins. These oilskins were manufactured from canvas soaked with fish oil, and stank of herrings. This smell mixed with that of tobacco was strong enough to bring on seasickness to those with weaker stomachs.

Hammocks were only seventeen inches apart. JTB was my port-side neighbour and Tom was my starboard one. My feet were between their heads; should we start chatting at night we would be reprimanded by Stripey, pointing out that watch keepers desperately required their sleep and, be it torpedo, shell or bomb, an 'alarm to arms' bugle call could come at any time. It was at times like this that I assured myself that someone was concerned about our welfare, therefore I was not being forgotten.

It was JTB who would greet me, as I would him when he was on watch, as I arrived back at the mess from an early morning watch, which had been in the snow, with "Quick Jack, here's today's bucket of warm water – it's only been used three times." Once a day whilst at sea each mess was allowed to collect, before 0800 hours, from a single hot-water tap near the galley, a galvanised one-and-a-half-gallon bucket of warm water for twelve men's early morning face wash. You might, if you wished, save your second cup of tea for a shave. Fortunately in those days whiskers had not yet appeared on my face. We were almost like a family and, like it or not, whilst it was staying afloat, *Nigeria* was our temporary home and would, we hoped, see us all safely back home some day. The sea temperature had quickly fallen to 32ºF and the air temperature was plummeting down.

The sheepskins came at the last minute; perhaps they had been held back purposely to make us appreciate them, or perhaps there was some rule that they could only be issued at a certain temperature drop, but more likely it was to keep our journey to Russia secret. The weather and that coat certainly changed the ship's fashions, which had been important to all the boys. Up till then, as with schoolboys nowadays, they all had to be dressed the same. Now we could change one uniform for another uniform of our choosing.

Those new coats from our ship's stores and the bearskin hats, called 'Ushankas', provided by the Russians, meant that we now looked like our Russian allies. These extras were warm and cosy.

Our dress up to that moment had been normal underpants and vest, blue wool socks, thick white cotton t-shirt, blue overalls, white seaboot stockings and seaboots, standard blue woollen pullover, a leather jerkin (an Army issue item if you were lucky), and a lamie coat – all held together with a knife lanyard, plus of course a round sailor's hat. I think at this point we abandoned all fashion fads; it was far too cold to think otherwise. Issued extra to the new sheepskin-lined coat and hat were three pairs of socks: ordinary blue, long blue, and extra long seaboot stockings, and three pairs of gloves, as mentioned before. In addition to all this we also had long johns knitted in three-ply grey wool, a roll-necked pullover, sailors' blue uniform trousers over the overalls, and scarves and balaclavas for face cover. You had to allow yourself time before you went to the 'heads'!

We were to need all these garments; none of us had considered that the arrival of 'black ice' would change our lifestyle and would be so dangerous and frightening. This type of ice, so far as I understood, arose only from certain weather conditions, when the air temperature was considerably lower than the sea temperature. Because of its salt content the sea did not freeze at 32ºF, but the small quantities whipped up as spray froze instantly to whatever it landed on; the harder the wind the worse the spray. Black ice was transparent and difficult to recognise, as there were no white crystals to be seen in it.

There were other strange phenomena to be experienced at these low temperatures. One was that when the sea temperature dropped considerably, the surface became covered with round ice plates resembling Amazonian water-lily leaves. If the temperature continued to drop they became bigger and thicker until they joined together and became a solid sheet, a hazard we often met when entering river mouths where the salt content was possibly less.

Black ice formed like a skating rink underfoot which made moving about on the upper deck very dangerous, so lifelines had to be rigged. As lads we soon found that there was fun to be had with lifelines, 'flying' about the ship's upper deck (see Figure 34). Normal handholds became frozen over and therefore could not be touched without gloves.

The stability and steering of the ship could be affected by the extra top-heavy weight of white or black ice building up due to extra spray generated by high-speed Arctic wind, the noise of which could change from a low moan to a shriek as it increased its speed. The 'wind-chill' factor made it seem colder than the reading recorded on the thermometer.

Figure 34. 'Flying' on lifelines

These same wind conditions aggravated the ship's rolling and pitching, which made it more dangerous to move about on the icy surfaces. These overall conditions caused many minor accidents and three deaths, which, I suppose, came under the heading of tragic accidents. The first person caught out by this severe Russian winter was our crane driver. The twenty-five-year-old fair-haired crane driver was a bright and cheerful chap who had, with practice, become a slick crane operator; to the rest of the crew he had become a first-class act. There was always an audience on the flight-deck when one of the cranes was in use, cold, wet or fine. It was, I suppose, the most interesting piece of equipment that the ship carried.

The attraction of watching him at work was in observing him co-ordinating the movement of the crane, the load, the different movements of the ship and the directions all three were going, at the same time. It was the crane driver's job to hoist stores deliveries, in or out, to an assortment of other vessels or jetties. Sometimes he would be called upon to move the ship's boats, aircraft and even stretchers with sick or wounded. To put it in a nutshell the crane operator could be called to work night or day, he was always a busy lad.

Both cranes were housed on the so-called flight-deck next to the Walrus hangars and catapult. If you heard, especially at sea, the Tannoy order for the crane driver to muster at the starboard or port crane and you were not otherwise committed, you would wander up to one of the hangar roofs to watch the crane working, which was often interesting particularly if there was a lot of rolling and pitching ship movement.

It was true that our driver showed great skill, always co-operating with the flight-deck working party handling the steadying lines. The same amount of patience and skill was also required when lifting our seaplanes onto the catapult, or bringing on board heavy items when ammunitioning ship such as twenty-one-foot torpedoes and batches of six-inch shells, which weighed half an imperial ton.

Perhaps it was to reduce the time he spent up there in the cold that persuaded this driver to take a short cut by interfering with a crane safety device; perhaps he wanted to be a star turn. He was a pleasant enough youngster and I don't think that showing off was in his make-up. I think because he always had an audience he had entered into the spirit of it, why not? It was a rotten war and we all so badly needed cheering up now and then. He gave us all the opportunity for a good laugh.

He had worked out a quick and almost automatic way to make the crane, whichever one he was using, house itself and automatically shut itself off after he had finished whatever chore he had to do. He climbed up to his crane controller's bucket seat, which was about a third of the way up the steel trellis jib construction, to do his routine. He used to lower the weighted hook onto the flight-deck as near as possible to the crane-securing, deck-fixed, steel eye. One of the flight-deck crane working party who knew his routine would place the heavy hook in the eye at the same time raising his right arm with his forefinger pointing to the heavens and then immediately move his still-raised arm from the shoulders in a slow clockwise circle. Once the driver had received this signal he set the crane in motion at a

Photo 33. Crane on ship

slow speed to wind up the slack wire with its hooked up weight, thus starting to lower the jib very slowly until it came to rest on the deck, to be held in place by the taut secured weight, hook, and purchase wire. At this moment the driver abandoned his seat and started to descend the moving jib. At about two-thirds of the way down the driver would lean forward with his head just above the gears, whilst standing on a column support to disconnect an electric switch. He would then continue his way down, step off the moving crane and take two or three steps away from the still moving crane, come to attention, look at his audience, remove his hat, bow like a King's courtier and turn round and face the crane which magically came to an immediate stop in its fully housed 'for sea' position. He would then turn once again to receive his appreciation from the crowd.

Despite the bitter cold black ice and only a handful of 'must be there' workers, our crane operator went through his usual routine. Sadly, when he leant over to throw the electric switch, he slipped on the support column and his heavy Arctic coat collar became snagged on a moving cog which pulled his head between the next set of cogs. He fell about six feet to the deck at our feet. We all just stared as the crane came to rest as usual, and looked at this huge hole amongst his fair hair. The O/S standing next to me took out a handkerchief from his pocket, rolled it up into a ball, and pushed it into the hole in his head. This scene was incredible. I don't remember having or using a handkerchief at sea. I can only remember trying to scrub one of the two issued handkerchiefs when I first joined *St Vincent* for the one and only kit inspection I attended. At sea you would grab a couple of handful of factory-floor swept-up cotton waste issued for polishing bright work in the gun turret, stuffing it into your sheepskin coat pocket, so that after wiping your nose with the back of your hand or glove you used this waste to clean your hand or glove. But here, going against all that was normal, was an O/S producing a beautifully ironed, clean white handkerchief, on a Russian convoy in the most atrocious of weather and committing a tender and compassionate act for a dead crew member. This was very moving.

I decided that I could not watch any more and deserted my working party, after watching what little blood there was instantly freezing when it contacted the black ice on the iron flight-deck. I went below to tell JTB and other mess mates what had happened: they would all want to know about this.

The mess deck took on the usual silent mood as it always did whenever there was such a tragedy. On these occasions the sailmaker would be issued with rum and would spend the night in his locker (workshop) stitching a canvas bag for the body using his 'palm and needle' and tying a fifty-pound practice shell round the poor fellow's legs to act as a sinker. The burial service was always held as soon as possible. Some unlucky sailmakers ended up alcoholics.

Photo 34. *Capstan*

We had to use a steam pipe from the boiler room rigged up by the engineer stokers, to enable us to defrost the capstan (see Photo 33) in case we needed to use an anchor when we arrived at a very cold Murmansk. The harbour had been badly bombed whilst we had been away and it showed, despite a heavy coating of snow.

The captain explained over the Tannoy that it had been our luck to be chosen to be based at this God-forsaken place for some time and that it would be our duty to shepherd PQs and QPs in and out via the North Cape, which was the biggest risk section of any Arctic convoy. "The good news," he said, "is that we're to be entertained by a Cossack singing and dancing team". As soon as we had secured alongside the jetty I was back to my duty as commander's messenger.

Photo 35. Cossack singing and dancing team

XI

Trouble with Roubles

It was on our first visit to Murmansk, about two weeks after the start of 'Barbarossa', Hitler's attack on Russian territory, that our paymaster commander broadcast over the Tannoy informing us that if we were going to take advantage of the offer of shore leave, as laid down on the daily orders, it would be impossible for us to use English currency. Whilst there was no reason why ratings should not go ashore without any local money, Russian currency could be purchased between 1400 and 1500 hours the following day.

We were pleased to hear this good news; we could go ashore and enjoy the freedom and just look. We regarded the ship as a prison to get away from if we could!

True to form, ninety per cent of the ship's company formed a queue outside the jaunty's office. Here they handed over their English money, signed their chits and collected the equivalent Russian roubles. Come Saturday, off on shore leave we all went, with or without Russian currency. JTB's and my experiences on this occasion have been described earlier. The older and more mature members of the ship's company had different experiences. Those carrying plentiful supplies of cigarettes found that the locals, who appeared to have pockets full of roubles, were more than willing to give a whole rouble for one English cigarette – whilst other Russians, including the women, were willing to pay large amounts of local currency for chocolate, tinned food of any type, or for anything useful. The end product of this run ashore was that more than half of the ship's company returned with pockets stuffed full of roubles. This turned out to be the first and the last run ashore in Russia.

Murmansk fast became a 'no-go area', for three reasons. The first, and possibly the most important reason, was the fact that there was a German/Finnish airfield less than forty miles away, from which the Luftwaffe was constantly attacking the town. This made it impossible

191

for Russians to live there, let alone for British seamen to go ashore and enjoy themselves. The other reason was because the shops and other buildings were quickly disappearing, as they were easy targets for the German ME109s and Stuka aircraft. There was another reason: the Russian authorities had also made it plain that they would not allow us to fraternise with the locals. So there was the ship's company with loads of local money burning holes in their pockets and nowhere to spend it. It was when one crew member bragged that he had won a bucketful of the stuff as a result of his success gambling at cards that the paybob decided to stifle what might have become an embarrassing situation by announcing on the ship's Tannoy that all Russian money would be changed into English at a given time. On arrival with their Russian currency, each crew member was asked his name and the paybob consulted his list of signed chits and returned to each member his original English cash outlay and took back only the number of roubles issued, leaving these sad men with pockets of roubles which were worthless. Some even passed their whole collection over to him in disgust. I remember one sailor collected about a suitcase full of the stuff convinced he would be able to change it in England. I think the mess deck dodger chucked it overboard eventually in the interest of safety. I kept only two, to stick in a book to display both sides.

Photo 36. Russian Roubles

XII

On the Russian Front

In those early winter days of 1941, at Murmansk, we had arrived as a prestige ship of the Royal Navy. We were British and proud of ourselves. Future events, however, were to raise a few doubts in our minds.

Hitler chose the code word 'Barbarossa' (after the 12th century king of the Germans, Frederick I, 'Redbeard') and had, on 22nd June 1941, a couple of weeks before we made our first visit to Murmansk, let loose on Russian soil some two million German soldiers, together with two million 'volunteers' from the peoples of Poland and the Balkans plus Hungarians, Slavs, French, Dutch, Ukrainians and some Cossacks, Bulgarians and of course the entire Finnish nation. All were heavily armed with weapons, some of which were manufactured in Germany, Switzerland, Czechoslovakia, France, Sweden and even Britain, amongst others. I once had an uncomfortable twenty minutes firing an Oerlikon gun (see Figure 35) at a German who was also firing a similar gun, the only difference being that we had been supplied with the green tracer and the German was using a white tracer which was passing over my head. It was fortunate for me that he was using his gun foresight incorrectly!

I have always found it difficult to forgive Switzerland and Sweden, the two neutrals, for making a lot of money out of the war by selling weapons to both sides.

There were only five hundred of us 'erks' and about two hundred-odd officers plus odds and sods like chippies, office types and sailmakers. At the most, seven hundred men. It was understandable that the Russian officials looked at us, then thought of the four million Axis infantry wandering over 'Mother Russia'. They probably didn't think much of Churchill's efforts and you couldn't blame them.

The Russian word 'Murmansk', when translated into English, means 'the edge of the world'. The Finns called it 'the top of the world'. Both of these were apt descriptions of the place.

193

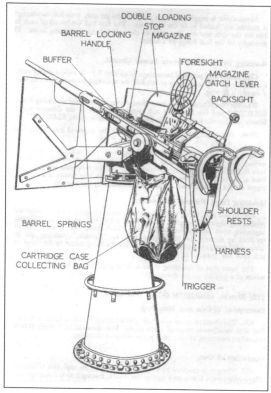

DOUBLE LOADING STOP
BARREL LOCKING HANDLE
MAGAZINE
BUFFER
FORESIGHT
MAGAZINE CATCH LEVER
BACKSIGHT
SHOULDER RESTS
BARREL SPRINGS
CARTRIDGE CASE COLLECTING BAG
HARNESS
TRIGGER

Figure 35. Oerlikon Gun

On arrival, our captain was made very unhappy when he learnt that whilst he was in the waters to the west of Murmansk down to Spitzbergen, he was under the command of the Russian Admiral of the North, Admiral A. Golovko. Whilst in the area to the east of the same division line, he came under the orders of the Admiral of the White based at Archangel, Admiral Popov. Popov probably was the chap who inspected us when we arrived at Archangel on our first visit. Popov commanded only a small bunch of lightweight craft used in the White Sea that included seventeen Russian submarines, which apparently performed well. From our crew's point of view, none of us was happy with being based on the Murmansk River permanently, only going to sea to shepherd incoming or departing convoys past the worst part of the journey. We all dreaded the North Cape where you fell prey to large numbers of German aircraft and U-boats. The enemy airfield was less than forty miles away at Petsamo and U-boats had plenty of local shore depots. Weather permitting, they could send over about twenty aircraft, subject us to a bombing raid, then fly back to their airfield which took about fifteen minutes or so, refuel, rearm, have a cup of coffee, spend a penny and in about forty-five minutes return to subject us to another twenty-aircraft raid before they returned for yet another rearming with coffee, and possibly a reindeer sandwich to keep up their spirits!

On the other hand, we were left after each raid with an upper deck to clear of our warm used empty brass four-inch and two-pounder fixed cylinder cases. We were under instructions to save and store these used brass items so that our factories could use them again. This involved collecting and carrying them some four decks below, and neatly stacking them. This was followed by bringing up fresh heavy ammunition – the four-inch shells weighed three-quarters of a hundredweight each. We were never sure whether there were hundreds of planes and pilots lined up on the nearby enemy airfields, or whether there were only twenty, who could go on all day until daylight faded. The last raid was always the most ferocious.

It was apparently on Winston Churchill's personal orders that we were stuck with this job at the 'edge of the world'. To make things more confusing, some of these merchantmen we were escorting in and out could be Free French, Dutch, Chinese, Indian, Moroccan, South African, or from the USA, Panama and Britain. All would be attacked, wherever they hailed from, but so far as I know it was only the merchant seamen from Great Britain who had their pay stopped as soon as their ship was sunk.

Murmansk's wooden-walled harbour had been built by the British in 1915 to help the Tsar import arms and could offer only a few mooring positions. This dismal place was made even more gloomy as on our very first stay there we were subjected to air attacks by several aircraft from the enemy airfield which was less than forty miles away and shielded from our Radar 279 by a three-hundred-foot-high hill. However, this left us in a vulnerable position, possibly to be attacked by the enemy's ground forces of either the Finns or the German Alpine troops who were known to be within striking distance. This meant action stations lookouts had to be posted at all times and keeping the boiler room at five minutes steam-up notice which was wasteful of fuel. But at least this was a place where I could stand and get a warm-up, sometimes for as long as fifteen minutes when temporarily relieved from this cold lookout duty. Some of our anxiety would have been relieved if we had been at sea. The captain from then on moored our ship further up the Murmansk River. This gave him extra distance from the German airfield and therefore more time both to operate Radar 279 and get fused four-inch shells loaded up the spouts before the Stukas had cleared the hill between the airfield and us.

The Russians had a team of lady soldiers hiding on the top of that same hill observing with binoculars the German airfield a few miles away. They were able to signal back – I don't know how – and inform the Russian headquarters how many planes had been wheeled out for use.

The Russian ladies passed over this information to us. We wondered why! Perhaps Olga the beautiful Russian spy told them to keep us in the picture. She seemed to have enormous influence. Perhaps it was knowing that we had lost two young boys that touched her maternal instincts; but more likely it was her interest in the women's welfare, since their women were risking their lives and more to provide this information.

This airfield was sometimes bombed at night, when the weather conditions were right, by a squadron of out-of-date and incredibly slow small Russian bombers. These slow planes could not be deployed in the daylight as the faster German Messerschmitts would have annihilated them on the spot. Young women usually piloted these Russian planes.

One of the ships we had escorted in brought with it nine Hurricanes, complete with pilots, ground crews, ammunition and spares. As soon as they became operational, the local Russian High Command ordered them aloft, facing impossible odds. Within two days all nine were either shot down or out of action. We heard that when the RAF chief in Murmansk complained to the Russian air force, they simply pointed out that the RAF pilots didn't speak Russian and therefore the two nations' air units couldn't be joined together as one force. They told us that the nine Hurricanes had shot down more Nazi planes than they had lost, and added: "Please thank Mr Churchill and ask him to send more." We were told that they had pointed out that their women pilots had to get on with the war by themselves.

There was one other occasion when Russian ladies came to the notice of the three of us, Tally-Ho and us two lads. At 0500 hours one morning on a river trip in the pinnace, we passed a group of teenage girls sitting on the frosty ground halfway up the river bank.

Photo 37. Russian lady pilots

At the top of the slope, keeping their heads below the crest, were almost the same number of armed Russian soldiers, whilst on the footpath at the base of the slope there were more Russian soldiers, also armed. Ignoring the soldiers we naturally waved at these young women who, without standing, waved back. I noticed how old and strained some of their faces were. The two vivid memories I carry from those brief meetings were the beautifully-made leather boots they were wearing and that some of these girls were smoking cigars. When we got back to the ship I told Stripey and my mess mates what we had seen. "They were, I suspect, women soldiers going over the top," Stripey said, "there's no difference between men and women here." This remark brought chuckles and saucy remarks. It was some time before I found out what was happening. We saw them on three occasions and then found out that the Russian troops at the bottom of this hill were members of the NKVD. When the order to attack was given, the soldiers at the top of the hill advanced towards the enemy. The unarmed women, only carrying a five-bullet clip, followed the men over the top to make up the numbers. On passing dead or wounded Russian comrades, they picked up the comrades' guns and bayonets and joined the fight where they would use their five bullets. The NKVD's job was simple, and that was to shoot Russian men or women soldiers who looked as if they were running away. Slowly I began to get used to, and started to understand, the fact that these adolescent girls were sacrificed for Mother Russia. What I saw years previously and thought were just youngsters having fun was mistaken; and now I have feelings of guilt that I did not regard them with the respect they deserved.

When moored on the Murmansk river it became the boat crew's job to transport the red Diplomatic Bag to a 'receiving station' some twenty to thirty miles south; the river formed a parallel line with the front line. Whilst I knew that the German Field Marshal Keitel's Alpine Division had joined the Finns on this front stretching from Leningrad to Vadso, Finland, in the north, it had never entered my tiny mind that suddenly a unit of Alpine or Finnish troops, or both, camouflaged in white and wearing skis in the winter could suddenly turn up heavily armed among the sparse pine forest which was surrounded by four feet of drifting snow on either side of the river bank. Our thinly-constructed pinewood pinnace caught on the river would end up a sitting duck. Neither did I know that Tally-Ho had pointed out to his senior officer that arming him and his crew on our trips could be a retrograde step to take. We were, he said, more likely to survive an incident without guns than with. He could quietly drop a weighted Diplomatic Bag into the drink with little chance of being seen by

Jerry and surrender immediately, to save his crew. I was beginning to find out that an awful lot of non-commissioned officers showed more 'savvy' in hazardous situations than some of their commissioned officers. I had been in situations when the officer of the day had given an order to take a certain course of action and the sailors listening had hesitated as if rooted to the spot all looking at the PO. Such a PO would say quietly "OK, carry on lads", or would tactfully discuss an alternative with the officer, who might then agree with the PO's suggestion. Such an officer was respected when he agreed. Tally-Ho was a slick diplomat. When I asked him what was in that red bag, he smiled and answered: "Probably love letters from his wife." He never locked the chain to his wrist but secured it to the pinnace. If the pinnace was going to the bottom of the river in a hurry, Tally-Ho did not want to join it on the riverbed.

As the weapons and food brought in by the convoys began to arrive in Russia, the local people at last began to smile at our efforts – especially incoming convoy work done by trawler men. Although these trawler officers and men were dressed like the rest of the Royal Navy, they were really peacetime fishermen serving on their fishing trawlers which had had a gun fixed aboard. There were about a dozen of these trawlers all carrying experienced seamen used to these waters. Everybody knew everyone and they looked after each other; their captains had always been their captains and probably owned the trawlers.

Whether at sea or up-river, there was always something going on. I had a very full diary: messenger, duty boat crew, general upper- and lower-deck work, maintenance and cleaning, schoolwork, and action stations all at different times of the day and night. One became very tired. I felt I was always hungry, perhaps young lads always feel hungry. Was it because there were insufficient calories in the wartime grub?

This business of the lack of sleep raised its head one night when I was being relieved from the middle watch (2400 hours to 0400). A lad who had not been relieved asked me if I had seen his relief. "Will you please find the lazy bastard and give him another shake." He did not want to tell on him, to which I agreed. We never took off our clothes if we could avoid it, either at sea or in harbour at the 'edge of the world', particularly at night. After a search I found this chap fast asleep sitting on a small lightweight tubular steel canvas 'stack' chair, sledging backwards and forwards with the ship's roll, on the thick brown polished lino floor in the canteen. He had apparently visited the toilet, which meant partially undressing, and had become cold, so had made his way up to the canteen because outside was the entire ship's crew's only luxury – the large, five-foot diameter, stainless steel bowl containing gallons of steaming hot, cooked delicacy known as 'kye'. Sitting down on the canteen canvas chair, being moved gently with the motion of the ship, feeling warm, drinking his 'kye', he had dozed off. I found him still fast asleep, with his empty tin mug on his forefinger. I shook him roughly and shouted at him. "You're supposed to be on watch and are adrift," a serious misdemeanour, "and your opposite number is holding down your watch for you." "Oh, bloody blimey," he said, as he leapt up. Then looking very worried he continued: "Roll on death and let's have a long lie-in." Gallows humour was beginning to take over in our communications with one another!

The hard winter of 1941 had been one of bad luck for us sailors so far away from home. The PQs and QPs had by now gone into double figures, one Arctic convoy seemed to be like any other. The only difference was in spring, summer and autumn when 'action stations' lookouts went on during the light midnight period, as well as daytime, and were more tiring. Whilst I accepted the dreaded winter and its harsher conditions of extreme cold, and the high waves and noisy screaming blizzards created by the very low temperature Arctic water colliding with the warmer northward-moving Gulf Stream, I was, nevertheless, very worried when small frost burns to the tops of my ears and left thumb tip turned up. By now we had successfully delivered to Murmansk, with PQs

Photo 38. Me with my thumb still wrapped 6, 7, and 8, I think, ten of the huge locomotives. Regrettably we lost two of these monsters on the way up from Iceland. (See Photo 38, taken with my finger still wrapped, some time later.)

The railway lines to Leningrad and Moscow had now been repaired. These heavy-duty locomotives were moving the enormous amount of war equipment that the convoys were successfully bringing into northern Russia. It was interesting to watch the Russian soldiers unloading this equipment and provisions by using the new British-built crane Rear Admiral Vian had recommended, which we had brought up on an earlier convoy. Young Russian soldiers, like any British teenager who would be delighted if given the ignition key of the latest MG sports car, were eagerly jumping onto the driving seats of unloaded tanks, lorries and, most of all, American Jeeps. They were the most sought after set of wheels in Russia in those days, for both Stalin's men and women, and a captured prize of prizes for any German lucky enough to get his hands on one. We watched in amazement at how quickly the Russians were able to start up these vehicles that had been stored for at least a month in sub-zero temperatures whilst being transported across two major oceans. The other most looked for 'goodies' from these international merchantmen were the numerous wooden packing cases marked 'Spam from the USA'. This was a processed food product, which saved many children from starvation in that bad winter of 1941.

The first time I tasted Spam was in 1947 after I arrived back in Blighty, and I realised it had a more pleasant taste than good old corned dog, which we seemed to be eating in some form or other almost daily. Some of the other wooden cases contained heavy Army hobnail boots, which, apparently, were not required at all and were therefore a complete waste of shipping space. The severe Russian frost froze the hobnail metal bits, which, apart from lowering the wearer's foot temperature, caused the nails to shrink and fall out. This allowed the leathers to come apart, as had happened to the German Army's jackboots; the end product for the user was frostbite. These boots were not popular for use in the Russian spring mud either!

About this time whilst we were unloading I learnt, somewhere in my duties as a messenger, that both Stalin and Churchill were concerned that if the Japanese came into the war they might link up with the Germans on the river Don. The war was bad enough without this possibility.

Just when we were all fed up to the teeth with badly-bombed Murmansk, and the in and out journeys of PQs and QPs, we had a pleasant change of scenery. Under the command of the Russian Admiral of the North we went to sea, I think with our friend *Aurora*, to cover a Russian mine-laying operation, something we had never done before. The Soviet *Karl Marx* (Ukraine class) destroyer with a low freeboard (the distance between the water line and the upper deck) joined us in company with a large mine-laying vessel loaded to the gunwales with large, vicious-looking underwater Russian mines. Sailors were always uncomfortable in the presence of any sort of underwater mine. Mines had a habit of breaking free from their mooring tackle, perhaps due to a bad storm or to being laid in the wrong position due to a navigational error, nevertheless our skipper knew what he was about and had instructed the officer of the watch on the bridge to stay upwind as the mines came rolling slowly off the stern of the Russian minelayer. "After all," said the officer of the watch to his associates on the bridge, "we're here to protect these Russians from air attacks and surface raiders, it's up to that *Karl Marx* boat (all destroyers were called boats; the RN 'Tribal' destroyers were always referred to as 'the boats') to chase after any of their mines that break loose from their mooring tackles." It was surprising how much information came down to the mess deck via the big ears of messengers doing a turn with their senior officers who had called in on the bridge to pass the time of the day. We were well north of Murmansk at this time.

Whether it was Admiralty instructions, or our captain's on-the-spot decision to give himself a break from taking orders from our class-conscious Russian admiral, or because this mine-laying chore was completed quicker than expected, or perhaps because we were somewhere near to a place he wanted to see or had been told to investigate, or perhaps realising he had almost full tanks of both water and fuel oil – whatever the reason, there were no buzzes, neither did we get the Tannoy's normal bulletin – having said our formal farewells we parted from the *Karl Marx* and the now empty minelayer and sailed north for a day at our normal economic steaming speed.

After eighteen hours' overnight steaming and approximately five hundred land miles further north from our mine-laying operation, at the beginning of the forenoon watch on the next day, to the complete amazement of the entire ship's company the following piped message came over the Tannoy: "Stand down all third degree watch keepers. Assume fifth degree of readiness."

I think it fair to say that all of us, with the exception of the captain, misunderstood this order. It had to be a mistake, up here next to the edge of the northern ice cap. Instinct and a considerable period of fighting without a break told us that this was a mistake and it really meant 'action stations'. In all this confusion came the shrill bosun's pipe followed by "Do you hear there?" This stopped us all in our tracks; we thought that an updated instruction was imminent. To say that what came next was a surprise is to put it mildly. "This is the captain speaking; we and our companion cruiser are so far north as to be off the beaten track of U-boats, enemy aircraft, or surface warships. This means that, except for radar operators, the Asdic section, special sea duty men, and lookouts, the rest of the crew can revert to the fifth degree of readiness and have a 'make and mend'. However, watertight doors will remain closed."

Everybody was smiling, JTB and I asked our mess leader, Stripey. "Have we got it right, we don't have to do anything?" "That's right you young lads," said Stripey, "we all have a day off from the war, a real bank holiday." I have long thought about this day and our captain's part in it. Was it his idea, or part of Admiralty rules and regulations?

The funny part of it all was that having been given a day off nobody seemed to know what to do with it. As it was an extra-nice sunny day, JTB and I went for a stroll in the starboard waist to start enjoying our very first freedom. Standing there enjoying the northern sunlight looking out to the *Aurora* sailing some half a mile away on a parallel course and at the same speed as us, as both ships followed the picturesque colourful permafrost shoreline, JTB and I became aware that there were some half-a-dozen stokers standing round the starboard twenty-one-foot three-torpedo tube launcher mounted in the starboard waist. All were carefully watching the torpedo gunner. Having no set freedom programme in mind, we simply joined these stokers to see what it was all about. It was unusual to see stokers in their lightweight blue overalls and white cap covers (provided to protect their heads from '90 second' oil drips sometimes found in their engine rooms) on the cold upper deck whilst at sea, but anything could happen when you had a day off from the war! We found that the torpedo rating whose action station was these very tubes, and who had serviced and cleaned them twice a week for years, had decided to use his free day to pick the grey paint from the three-inch brass casting bearing the legend 'Manufactured by Thornycroft'. It was his intention to scrape off the grey paint with his seaman's knife and then polish this plaque with Bluebell metal polish, after which he would have to paint it with blue see-through paint, which would stop the sun's reflection flashing on his new shiny plaque whilst we were at sea and giving away our position. Whilst we were all staring, and I suppose wondering why this chap needed to do this on his bank holiday at about 1030 hours on that sunny morning, a stoker, asked this serious 'polisher': "How do you fire these torpedoes?" "We don't," was the polisher's immediate reply, "they're fired by the bridge." "Well," said another spectator, "say the bridge is hit and they're all wiped out up there, what happens then?" "Well," said the 'polisher', "you switch to local like this," and he demonstrated by moving a highly-polished brass handle at the rear of the tube casing. It was coming up to 1100 hours when an inquisitive friend of the first stoker asked without warning, "what next?" "That's easy," replied the 'polisher', now warming to his subject, "all you do is check that the tube is armed, take off the safety catch and switch to local." His speech had got faster as his fingers flew to the two red and green electric switch buttons, to which he applied pressure. All of the onlookers watched with amazement as a silver twenty-one-inch-diameter, twenty-foot-long 'tin fish' whooshed out of the tube on its way towards the *Aurora*. The group of stokers suddenly felt very cold and retired to the boiler room for a convenient warm up, leaving JTB and myself to watch the 'tin fish's' progress. Our thoughts were jumbled; we felt we should be doing something. JTB was quickest: "We must tell the bridge," he said. We needn't have worried; by the time we had arrived at the bridge, which was very near to the starboard waist, it was swarming with off-watch officers enjoying their own day off from the war. All of them therefore must have had a ringside view of the events. We could see the duty signaller frantically sending Morse code messages to the *Aurora*, which seemed to be awfully slow in increasing its speed and taking avoiding action, which it finally did without harm befalling them. I wonder what her captain's Morse answer was. I would have loved to know, and what they had been up to on their bank holiday. The 'tin fish' missed our cruiser friend by miles and when last seen was heading for the shore ice where, because it had not been correctly fused, it did not explode on contact with the ice. In these days of global warming, if the ice has melted, perhaps the finder will return it to our torpedo gunner who, at the Captain's Defaulters, was threatened with stoppage of pay until he had paid the two thousand pounds cost of this 'tin fish'! (The equivalent price of at least four average houses in those days.) At noon, the day off from the war was cancelled and we all sadly resumed third degree of readiness as ordered by a disillusioned captain.

In works of labour, or of skill,
I would be busy too;
For Satan finds some mischief
For idle hands to do.

Isaac Watts, 1674–1748, 'Against Evil Company'

We didn't know the particulars of how we almost got a day off from the war but we were very sorry for our captain because it had gone so wrong. However, if you took the average prison today with an exercise yard and gave the prisoners a day off but told them they couldn't use the exercise yard, they would probably riot! Our prison was far harsher; we worked harder and longer hours and it was terribly dangerous. We were enduring a six-year sentence with no remission for good conduct. A day off with watertight doors shut meant no showers, no clothes washing, no clothes drying (our major comfort) and therefore all we could do was just wander on the cold upper deck.

Our ship boasted a music section; it was roughly the size of small garden shed, and housed thirty-six '78' records. These had been played over and over again, usually between the early dog watches by someone from the wireless department. This happened mostly in harbour, and only very occasionally at sea. Sometimes the padre would act as the master of ceremonies. Whilst BBC programmes or news bulletins could be transferred via this music section to the ship's Tannoy speakers, this was seldom allowed and was unusual at sea. That's possibly why I remember the following. The padre was the disc jockey who one day proclaimed that by special request he was going to play the recording 'McNamara's Band', which was the most popular record on the ship (our Top of the Pops). It was known that the entire crew was word perfect and at least seven hundred of us would sing along with this record as soon as it was switched on. These singing voices vibrated throughout the ship and could be heard from every porthole. One of my pleasant memories of that time was conversing with an Irish merchant seaman at the end of a summer PQ (incoming) convoy who, when he found out what ship I was on, laughingly slapped me on the back and said: "Seeing your ship proudly sailing down the centre of the convoy and, instead of all your guns firing as they usually did, having every silly bastard you'd got aboard there singing their bloody heads off to 'McNamara's Band' did us all a lot of good."

On the first trip we took in the pinnace with the red Diplomatic Bag to the so-called 'reception section', we were surprised to find that it turned out to be a small log cabin close to a rather flimsy small jetty on the river bank similar to other jetties fixed up and down the river. The cabin was apparently the home of a fifty-year-old man and his wife of a similar age. It contained two rooms: one was a sleeping area, which was possibly used for other purposes, the other a living room. During our visits we never left the main living room, which had a dry dirt floor. How it stayed dry with snow right up to its doorway I do not know. This room contained a cast-iron stove with a five- to six-inch metal flue that burnt nothing but wood. The stovetop supported a large iron saucepan with curved sides, which on that very cold day gave off delicious home-cooking smells. Below and to the left was an oven, which had a large lever handle. Whilst Tally-Ho was handing over his precious documents, the lady of the house offered us two lads a bowl of the tasty-smelling soup (possibly reindeer soup). We thought she had been ordered to supply us with victuals, we did not think she was doing this out of her own good nature. We did not know how short food was; her offer was accompanied by a smile, which showed a flash of gold-filled teeth. To show our appreciation for the soup, the warm-up and hospitality, we went through our pockets to see what we could find, and I left her with a half-opened 1oz bar of plain Nestlé chocolate in a red packet. None of us was aware that there was a serious shortage of food and that this part of Russia was facing starvation. As we left, the old man made signs imitating someone smoking a cigarette. All I could do was shrug my shoulders; how could I tell him in sign language that I didn't smoke. Back at the ship, I told the mess about the old lady and her husband and their gifts. "That's alright," they said, "we can ask for an extra tin of herrings in tomato sauce." "Nobody likes them at any rate," said JTB. "I reckon we can drum up a tin of 'Ticklers' cigarette tobacco and a couple of packets of Rizla cigarette papers," said Tom.

On the next trip we took up-river with the Diplomatic Bag, I handed over to the old lady two oval tins of herrings in tomato sauce, two long loaves freshly baked by Joe, our PO cook, who made beautiful bread, which he had baked specially for them the day before, a full 8oz tin of 'Ticklers' tobacco, sufficient to roll some 150 to 200 cigarettes, complete with a couple of packets of Rizla cigarette paper, a gift from 13 Mess. "Enough," as Tom said, "to learn how to roll your own" – it was Tom who had found the 1/6d to pay for the tobacco. I had sported the penny for another 1oz Nestlé chocolate bar, purchased with some difficulty the night before from the NAAFI canteen manager (known as the No Ambition And F-all Interest rating). "I've none left," he said, but then changed his mind when I told him about the hungry old couple living in a dirt-floored wooden hut up-river, and found me the last Nestlé bar on the ship! The paymaster commander unknowingly supplied the bread and the tinned fish.

The engine room engineer officers had designed a type of electric immersion heater to put into the pinnace's two engines at night which stopped any water left in the cooling system from freezing. This helped Tally-Ho to get the pinnace started and warmed up before we left. During the hours of darkness, so that I could not be seen loading these goodies, I had smuggled and hidden them in the motorboat's lockers and as a result of the cold night we were delivering frozen food to the lady with the shiny gold teeth. Frozen or not, both the old girl and her gent were obviously delighted with our meagre gifts. It was great fun watching Tally-Ho trying to teach the old boy and us two eighteen-year-old non-smokers to roll fags. "It was well known," said Tally-Ho, "that American cowboys could ride a horse whilst they rolled a fag with one hand and used their six-gun with the other." I don't think these two Russian citizens understood any of that, even if they did join in with our laughter!

It had become a lot colder the next time we went up-river. This river was beginning to get coated with thin, eight-inch-diameter ice pancakes. This slowed us down considerably and, by the extra blaspheming coming from Tally-Ho, we two lads knew he was not happy. We were about two hours late by the time we arrived at the log cabin. The old pair seemed surprised to see us and looked uncomfortable. There was no saucepan on the hotplate. Whilst warming my back almost sitting on their stove I passed over the two full-sized white loaves that PO Joe had given me when I told him we were off up-river again. We had also managed to get some more tins of herring in tomato sauce and some 'Ticklers'. We knew they were delighted with their presents, particularly the bread, but they appeared uncomfortable, possibly because the borsch soup saucepan was empty, or perhaps they had eaten the contents, perhaps they had not wanted visitors. It was a nasty day and we were behind schedule, so Tally-Ho indicated that we must leave. As we were leaving, the old man thrust into my hands a small brown paper packet of Russian pipe tobacco, possibly thinking that because we didn't smoke cigarettes we must smoke pipes, then he went over to the mantelpiece, which was above the cast-iron stove opening, and grabbed the only object on it. He gave me a six-by-four-inch photograph frame made of tin and pinewood surrounding a poor photograph of Lenin. This being the only personal object in the room I tried to give it back to him. He stepped back a pace, shook his head and looked at his wife who was smiling. I had no other choice than to take it. I reached across and shook her hand and gave it a squeeze, we smiled at one another and I stepped out onto the snow. It felt very cold after the warm cosy cabin. Once the three of us had climbed aboard the pinnace, and after he had got the engines going, Tally-Ho said: "OK boy, give me that frame," which I did. One didn't argue with a killick.

It had got much colder and we were late and hungry. On the way back to the cruiser the engine began to cut out, as it did when slush blocked the cooling system's two-inch-diameter port and starboard outlet pipes. To keep us going, Tally-Ho got us two lads to hang over each side to keep prodding this slush build-up, which we did by using a couple of foot-long, eighth-inch-thick welding rods.

The outlet pipes were fitted four inches above the waterline and quite often became submerged due to waves, however small, and the pinnace's movements. To use the welding rods meant kneeling on the ten-inch-wide walkway, hanging on with one's left hand to the low cabin top hand rail, then hanging down and taking one's bodyweight, some two feet lower down, just above the water line, and constantly prodding at the slush build-up with this welding rod. Besides being a tiring chore it was also very cold and dangerous if you fell in the water from the moving boat.

With one engine spluttering and the other stopped, Tally-Ho pulled in alongside one of the many riverside jetties. Although the incredibly fine snow came up to our bums, it was much easier to clear the outlets whilst standing on the jetty. We had just turned the pinnace round and completed clearing the outlets on the other side when all three of us became aware of a Finnish soldier. There was no doubt that he was a Finn; he looked smart in his almost navy blue uniform, with his peaked cap, so unlike a scruffy Russian, and the uniform was of the wrong colour for him to be a German. The Finn was standing some ten feet higher than us and no further than fifteen feet away. He was wearing a white camouflage cape and ski shoes. What really worried me about him was that he had a rifle to his shoulder and it was pointing straight at me. I was terrified; I thought I was about to die. This was the first time I had experienced the terror of imminent death. He didn't fire. I looked at my companions; they both had their hands up and I joined them instantly. I and the other lad stood still with our hands still above our head, we just looked at Tally-Ho. We had not even started to get our brains going again. As we watched Tally-Ho he produced a pleasant smile but stood still with his arms aloft and watched the Finn. Although it was difficult to do, we tried to follow his example. The Finn, with his rifle still pointed at me, moved his head slowly and stared at the pinnace's stem flagpole supporting

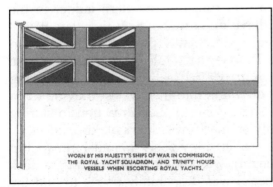

a two-foot-long naval ensign with its small Union Jack. Then, after what seemed ages, he slung his rifle over his shoulder and without a word skied off with great skill. "Quick," roared Tally-Ho, as he started the engines, "let's shove off", which we did without any hesitation, all three of us praying that the engines would not

Figure 36. Miniature Union Jack

207

stall. After a while, when it became obvious that we were not being followed or fired at, Tally-Ho slowed down and we got back to the job of hand-clearing the outlet pipes with the welding rods.

"I wonder," said Tally-Ho, "if he's gone for help, although he doesn't need to with us being unarmed! It's a cert he knew that we weren't Ruskies; perhaps he thought we were Jerries." I wonder if he knew we were British and if he was educated enough to be able to read our flag? I think, if he had decided to make a name for himself by capturing our pinnace as well as us, he could have only carried it out by shooting two of us and taking the third as a prisoner together with the pinnace. On the other hand he could have shot all three of us and had the pinnace without any trouble at all. Whilst all this was happening it began to snow.

I had been terrified when this Finnish soldier had aimed his rifle in my direction; now, after listening to our L/S's interpretation of the event, this terror had returned. I was still worrying in case this Finn reappeared. Until that moment I had not really thought about the possibility of being shot or injured but this incident brought home to me that I was just as vulnerable as anyone else.

We had more trouble with the V8 engines slushing up and by the time we arrived back at the ship we were listed as overdue or, as the Navy said, 'adrift', and the quarterdeck gangway and the boom had been hoisted inboard for the night. This meant that we would have to be hoisted in by the crane. Tally-Ho explained to the officer of the watch that he and his crew had been in a cold boat, on a river fast freezing up, since early that morning, and his crew had been working all day on the two V8s without any food or grog ration and were so cold that they could hardly move. He also pointed out that he had an urgent report for the commander, which caused the two-ringer to relent. "Moor your pinnace astern, leading seaman, and get your crew aboard for a warm up and food." "Thank you sir," replied Tally-Ho.

Climbing the slippery frozen iron rungs of the stern ladder in the dark was a nightmare I could have done without on that day. It was both dangerous and frightening. With hands painfully stinging and every joint feeling immovable I made the unpleasant journey up the flat stern section to the top. On arriving I realised that I was crying with cold, exhaustion and fear of falling into the icy, fast-moving river. I suppose, too, that there was some delayed shock reaction to staring down a rifle barrel on an empty stomach, which was taking effect.

The assistant officer of the watch, previously a midshipman but now a one-ringer (a sub-lieutenant), was standing on the quarterdeck not more than a yard from where I was desperately trying to find the courage to change my handhold from the lower iron rungs up to the iced-up wire guard rails, which I still had to climb over. A fall could have killed me. "For God's sake man, help me over. I can't manage it by myself," I said between my tears. He dropped his telescope and helped all three of us aboard.

As soon as I put my feet on the quarterdeck I felt ashamed of my tears. I heard the officer of the watch ask "why're you so late?". I didn't answer but went straight below to 13 Mess. They were all there from JTB to Stripey. On the mess table were two pieces of buttered bread and a generous slice of 'pusser's' tinned cake. "Come on lads, make him a cup of Rosie Lee and someone get his kept warm meal from Joe in the galley," called out Stripey. "Are you alright lad?" "Yes, thank you, Stripey," I replied. "Then sit yourself down, you look cold, and get a hot drink into yourself, then tell us all about it," he said with one of his nicer grins. It was great to be back aboard, and amongst mess mates, I thought as I tucked into the very hot plate of a dried-up midday meal that had been residing in the galley hot cupboard for the last eight hours. Never mind, I thought, as I covered the well-buttered bread with a generous spreading of jam taken from a tin marked 'Red Jam'. After all this I went to sleep worrying about what action the one-ringer duty officer of the watch might take the next day.

At 0900 hours on an incredibly bitter cold forenoon in late January 1942, whilst we were inland, up-river near Murmansk under the command of the Admiral of the North, a particularly heavy air raid occurred. The result of this was, for me, both savage and tragic, and

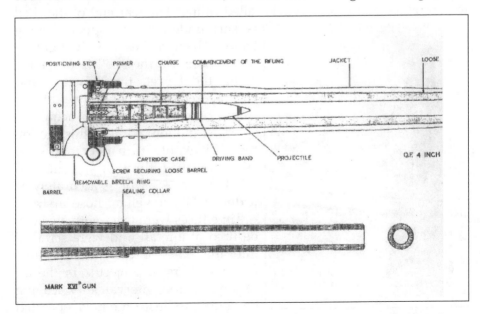

Figure 37. 4 inch high-angle gun barrel

in the circumstances it was so shattering. To explain what happened I am afraid I shall have to give my reader a naval gunnery lecture on how a high-angle gun fires a fused anti-aircraft shell. (see Figure 38, also in colour, showing a four-inch high-angle gun barrel.)

All naval guns are loaded at the breech end (coloured blue), in this case the projectile and the firing charge had been inserted and, of course, the breech closed. The charge or propellant is cordite, a mixture of nitro-glycerine and gun cotton, dissolved in acetone and stabilised with a small amount of gunpowder. As the cordite burns, it becomes a mass of burning gas (a great amount of this gas is produced, at a very high temperature). This gas is confined in the small space surrounded by the barrel of the gun, the closed breechblock and the base of the projectile and exerts an enormous pressure on all three. This pressure increases as the temperature rises. The barrel that is being pushed outwards in all directions cannot move outwards without bursting, therefore the projectile is being pushed forward by the gas at its base, and moves forward up the barrel at an ever-increasing speed, whilst the breechblock is able to withstand this gas pressure. Cordite is used because it takes a relatively long time to burn, about a fraction of a second. Because the projectile is moving along the gun barrel the total amount of gas produced is never all compressed in the original space and in fact is at its greatest just when the projectile begins to move, that is why the gun barrel is made thickest at the breech, and tapers gradually towards the muzzle. A spiral groove is cut on the inside of the barrel (coloured red); this is called rifling. The rear end of the shell

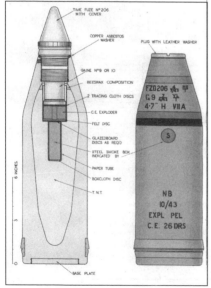

is surrounded by a copper driving band, which makes a very tight fit to the bore. As the shell is propelled along the barrel, the driving band is squeezed into the groove of the rifling causing the shell to acquire a spinning motion; without this motion the shell would turn over and over as it travelled through the air and wouldn't go as far or as accurately as it does when travelling nose first.

Time fuses were used with shells to be fired at aircraft and were screwed into the nose of the shell. A time fuse will burst a projectile in the air at any desired interval after leaving the gun. An instrument is operated

Figure 38. RN 4″ shell   by the gunnery control to set this delayed time setting before the shell is loaded. When firing the gun it is the twisting motion created by the barrel-rifling groove that starts the time clock ticking as the shell leaves the barrel. There was a safety device that never allowed you to load a shell with its fuse set on zero, or almost zero, as the gun's crew could be within the blast capabilities danger zone.

It was an extremely cold forenoon and the quick-firing four-inch Mark XVI round gun barrel housed on the upper gun deck without any covering had been exposed to the even colder night's frost and had 'shrunk'. The four-inch shell fused with a 206 time fuse had also been stored on this same deck but in a 'ready use' locker not far from an engine room exhaust ventilator, so it was just a teeny bit warmer. The theory was that this shell (which weighed almost a hundredweight with its driving band), because it was made like a solid metal casting, was possibly at a slightly higher temperature when it was rammed home by closing the breech into this much colder 'shrunk' barrel. The gun was fired and, because of the shell's reduced speed through this tighter fitting rifling, it was slightly late leaving the barrel. This led to a very unusual Arctic accident. The other necessary requirement was the low fuse setting, needed because of the close vicinity of the enemy airfield. The approaching German planes were flying low over the nearby hill, as they always did, and as usual we had used a low fuse setting which, on this occasion, caused the shell to burst as it passed over our ice-covered quarterdeck. There were only three crew members whose action stations were in this area; one was a senior officer who, when hit by our own shell fragment, had both cheeks

Photo 39. Funeral of two boy seamen

of his buttocks cut off. When I arrived he was lying there, still alive, I don't know if he survived. The others were two of our boys, aged between seventeen and eighteen, who had been cut to pieces; their blood had stained the ice and tragically they were dead. This had a serious effect on my morale: firstly they were my friends; secondly twenty of us had started out on this ship when it was commissioned in 1940 and now there were only nine of the original boys left; and thirdly, I had to walk round that dreadful bloodstained ice which, because of the weather, we couldn't get rid of for several weeks. (See Photo 39 of their funeral.) The ceremony for these two boys took place within a few feet of the bloodstained ice where they were killed. The two Oerlikon gun mountings are clearly visible in the photograph.

There was no inquest, since the second and subsequent shots worked exactly as they should. Neither was there an enquiry into the fuse side, other than the gun crew making sure that all was working correctly. Like our poor crane driver, it was one of those unfortunate accidents that occurred when the temperature was so low. Every crew member felt very sad and the mess decks were devoid of laughter for several days. It was some time before these two deaths occurred that the ritual of auctioning a sailor's non-personal kit from his locker was suspended, a ritual I was pleased I didn't have to take part in any more. The routine was bad enough for the poor old sailmaker, who had his all-night sewing job to do to get everything ready for the next morning, to enable us to cast my two friends into that very cold 'deep'.

The schoolmaster, who was proud of his pupils' progress, was devastated watching his class dwindle, and he was probably hit harder than any other person on the ship. He was about twenty-six years of age and he was losing boys of an average age of seventeen. To add to the misery, we could all see the bloodstains in the ice on the stern deck whilst we were burying these two boys. These stains remained for several weeks as we sailed in the next QP. Anybody using the quarterdeck stepped around these stains out of respect.

The cold Arctic weather had set in and made it impossible for us to launch the pinnace onto a river recently frozen solid. Small-boat movements up and down this river could only be attempted by following an icebreaker. Even this was denied to our carvel-designed pinnace, constructed as it was of three-ply wood. It was hardly a material that would stand the strain of colliding with the large slabs of ice left behind by the Russian icebreaker – the pinnace and its engines had been designed for use in mild Mediterranean seas.

The food and tobacco goodies we had collected for the old Russian man and his lady would now have to wait for delivery until the spring thaw. How would the red Diplomatic Bag be delivered? This slipped from my mind when I learnt, whilst acting as the senior officer's messenger, of the dreadful chain of events which were being put into motion by two of our young inexperienced officers who, without consulting with the commander, had made a direct complaint to Olga 'the beautiful spy'.

They had, apparently, been subjected to the same rough-and-ready treatment that we all had by the Russian sentry with the tall pointed hat, stationed on our lower gangway grating. We all had to put up with him when we used the ship's gangway to go ashore or return to the ship. This Siberian soldier appeared to suffer from acute short sight and was badly in need of a pair of glasses. The brief he had received from his senior officer had been simple: he was only to give these foreign sailors permission to go ashore or come back on board when he had made certain that their faces matched their paybook photos. My paybook with its photo of me also acted as a passport.

To carry out his simple task, this unfortunate 'spectacles candidate' developed a routine. Snatching the paybook from your hands, he peered at it long and hard and then to assure himself that it was the same person he grabbed a handful of your clothes at chest level and pulled your face close to his as he scanned your features. This procedure took long enough for you to realise that Red Army soldiers were not issued with toothpaste or soap, and because of movements on his face you felt that this poor chap was suffering from lice. This performance was irritating and a little humiliating to all, especially our two junior officers. This resulted in the complaint to Olga. It was then that Olga did the 'Communist' thing. "Which soldier are you talking about?" she asked. Even though it was obvious that we had only one Russian soldier on the ship, Olga insisted that these officers should point him out. Neither of these two was happy about this. Reluctantly they pointed out the poor devil. "Leave it with me," Olga said with a smile. It was some hour or so after this conversation that ten Soviet NKVD troops were seen approaching the ship; despite the snow smartly using the 'goose step' used by the Russian Army. Holding their position of two abreast they came to a halt at the bottom of our gangway. We heard some shouting and the poor short-sighted Siberian left the gangway platform and took up the position vacated by one of the last two marchers.

This Russian soldier then climbed aboard the gangway platform and it became immediately obvious that he was to be our new gangway sentry. At this stage the nine NKVD and our old sentry marched back the way they had come and, as if to ensure we had a good clear view, halted by a nearby wall, and formed into a single line facing the wall some twelve feet away. Our poor short-sighted sentry, the only soldier wearing a tall pointed hat, was ordered to step forward and stand with his back to the wall. I think it was only then that he realised what was going to happen to him. To our horror, the rest were then ordered to shoot him. This they did, and then made an immediate about turn, formed up two deep and marched off leaving him in a heap in the snow. Olga, with an ear-to-ear smile, asked the young officers if they had any further complaints. On receiving no answer, Olga calmly left the ship, pausing only to pass the time of day with the new Russian sentry who looked terrified.

After a long time, two workers turned up and took away the Siberian's body. The aftermath of this affair was that these two now horrified and very worried young officers were obviously due for the high jump. They were going to have to face the captain at the captain's disciplinary inquiry, where no doubt they would be asked why they had made a complaint to Olga without first bringing it to the commander's notice. The upshot of this affair was that the captain instructed the padre to contact each and every one of the ship's company and inform them never to talk directly or indirectly with Russian officials or become involved in requesting any assistance from the Russians whatsoever, without first contacting our commander. Neither should we speak to any Russian even to say 'Good morning'. "It was a miserable situation," said Stripey, "these guys should be friends with us."

The routine daily grog issue, whether in harbour or at sea, started sharp at 1100 hours. This was a special time for all grog drinkers and their only daily relaxation. There would be a bosun's whistle call on the ship's Tannoy by the duty PO of the watch, who would follow his whistle with a shout at the top of his voice "Up spirits," knowing that the entire ship's company in all parts of the vessel would answer his call with "Stand fast the Holy Ghost". It wasn't that the crew was being irreligious, it was all part of the game.

If a member of the crew didn't want to draw his grog for any reason then he was entitled to receive threepence a day extra pay. These non-drinkers could be counted on one hand. Any crewman who had a tot of rum to sell to his mess mates, even if it was diluted with two parts water and had to be drunk the same day, was going to make a lot more than threepence. To just cancel his tot and collect his three pennies seemed to be a retrograde step. Boy seamen on the other hand were not allowed to drink alcohol. However, there was a rule, so we understood, that boy seamen could be issued with a cup of lime juice; wasn't that why the Americans called us Limeys? It is true that I rarely saw or tasted lime juice in my six years in the 'Andrew'.

214

The West Indian grog was specially made for the Navy and was known as pusser's rum. Officers did not receive a daily tot of rum; however, they could buy spirits from the wardroom bar when it was open. Neat rum was kept in oval wooden barricos and securely locked in a special store below decks. Each barrico housed enough neat rum for the lower decks ship's company's daily issue, with sufficient extra rum to account for spillage – and thereby hangs a tale.

The canteen flat, a spacious open area on the top deck above the mess decks, situated between the canteen and the junior POs' mess, was where the rum was issued. Unless we were at action stations, the following officials would muster for this most important ritual! The first to arrive was the one-ring commissioned gunner followed by the marine colour sergeant, the master-at-arms, and the supply PO with the book with records of each mess' rum entitlements. At the same time, a junior supply rating and an AB would take up their position in front of this half barrel and finally the duty officer of the watch would turn up to see that all the rules of accurate grog measuring were obeyed. These four formed a line two feet behind this wooden half-barrel bound with three well-polished brass hoops and marked in four-inch high bold brass letters, 'The King, God Bless Him'.

At 1130 sharp under all these watchful eyes, the supply PO, the supply rating and the AB would remove the bung from the barrico they had just brought up from its special store. They would then pour

Figure 39.

sufficient carefully measured neat rum with the extra for spillage into the half-barrel, to supply all the tots required on that day according to the jaunty's book of crew numbers entitled to rum. On completion of this, the supply assistant and the AB working as a team (it was a four-handed job), using the brass imperial measures would, under the supply PO's instructions, start serving the queue. The first to be served would always be the PO mess men, who would collect their PO's neat rum issue.

Now we come to the procedure where twice the volume of water had to be measured to add to the neat grog after the PO's tots had been removed, and it wasn't only the officer of the watch who was interested in watching this clean water being added. Between 1130 hours and 1200, a seaman from each mess had arrived with special clean rum-collecting containers to collect their tots, the flat area was jammed tight with them. All eyes were fixed on the incredibly fast-moving brass imperial measures (as they had done since Nelson's days) to make sure that the water collected from the PO's mess sink was the correct amount and not one drop too much.

After the last seaman with his container filled with his mess' rum entitlement had left the 'flat', the officials emptied the residue rum mixture (if the measuring had been really accurate then this would be what had been allowed for as spillage) from the half-barrel to a large container which was then taken to the PO's mess stainless steel sink and watched by all as its contents were poured away.

Once the officer of the watch had witnessed the last of the left-over rum disappearing down the PO's mess sink drain, he would have felt that his duty as a rum observer was well and truly finished. Thereupon he retired to his bridge duties if at sea, or his quarterdeck duties when in harbour – a routine that was apparently happening on every warship, small and large, in His Majesty's Navy.

It was during a cold night whilst on the river near Murmansk, that we were sitting fully dressed in our outdoor Arctic gear in the starboard hangar watching the film of Laurence Olivier acting in the role of Henry the Fifth, when a newcomer, a junior PO engine room artificer who had joined the ship as a replacement, arrived on board. He was told where we all were and he was shown to the PO's mess where, espying a nice clean stainless steel sink, he proceeded to wash a couple of pairs of blue woolly socks, in the peace and quiet. Having finished his hand washing job he pulled out the plug to get rid of the dirty water, intending to replace it with fresh water for rinsing. Away went the soapy water down the waste pipe; that is, an amount of water equal to the volume of the rum spillage amount, but he couldn't get rid of the rest of the dirty water, and was unable to unlock the cupboard underneath so that he could investigate the cause of the blockage. He became uneasy. All he could do was sit down in the empty mess and await the return of the cinema-goers as he watched his dirty water very, very slowly draining away.

It was only when the mess residents returned from watching 'England and St George', and he saw the looks on their faces, that he realised that he had done something really awful, but he didn't know what. He tried to explain who he was and how he had been allocated to the PO's mess to relieve one of their mess mates for other duties elsewhere. They didn't care who he was and why he had come.

They just wouldn't talk to him at all. He watched as they unlocked the cupboard door under the sink and just stared in utter amazement and disbelief at what he saw.

The open cupboard door revealed an incredible piece of automatic stainless steel plumbing; a mass of different-sized shiny steel pipes, with glass and stainless steel containers, a creation of sheer genius, manufactured on board by the brightest stoker afloat. The object of this spotless distillery was to provide by gravity an equal amount of two and one rum spillage to each of the six, equally-sized, empty gin bottles secured to the levelled support tray. All this equipment was securely screwed and bolted inside this cupboard, allowing for every contingency, such as rough seas and firing broadsides – but obviously not for smelly, soapy water and wet socks!

Five of these six empty gin bottles were labelled showing a coded owner. Only the sixth was marked 'Mess' and was obviously the PO mess perks. It was anybody's guess who the other five daily collectors were!

One day whilst we were still in Murmansk, the sickbay tiffy informed me that I had been put on a list to go ashore to see a dentist. When I arrived I was amazed to see this Russian wearing the tallest chef's hat I had ever seen. I wasn't sure whether he was going to invite me to join him baking a cake or if he really was going to remove my temporary *Hood* filling, which had kept me free from pain, and put in a permanent one.

He sat me down and sat behind me and began to pedal a generator furiously with one foot. This I discovered was the way the drill was powered; the harder he pedalled the faster it went. There was no offer of any painkilling injection (I suppose they were in short supply).

Having cleaned the tooth out he produced a small lump of gold which he put into my cavity and, using a small hammer, he tapped it into the tooth. Despite this old-fashioned treatment, that filling served me well for over forty years!

XIII

'X' Turret

By May 1942 any journey that was attempted in or out of the Kola Inlet was, according to our crew, 'a journey through hell'. Merchant ships were no longer attempting to navigate this impassable stretch of water into Murmansk, and were seeking a berth elsewhere in Russia. Ships, naval and merchantmen, that could move had sailed out, either independently or were lucky enough to be escorted out by the last remaining intrepid armed trawlers manned by ex-fishermen from the north-east coast of England and Scotland.

The German High Command had been counting the number of British and American aircraft (bombers and fighters, including Spitfires and Hurricanes), tanks and field guns, but most of all the large numbers of American Jeeps that had turned up on the battlefields, particularly on the Stalingrad front.

In an effort to stem this inflow of military hardware, especially the Jeeps which did so well on the flat Russian Steppes, the German High Command had reinforced their northern Norwegian airfield with extra dive bombers and fighter aircraft. They had also enlarged the northern U-boat fleet.

The entire Russian civilian and military population, and ourselves when at sea or ashore, had felt the brunt of these extra planes, especially as we were without any form of air cover once we had sailed. This newly reinforced enemy in all its forms was waiting for us to move where, even in May, these Arctic waters could be merciless. What we needed up there 'at the edge of the world' was an aircraft-carrier. When the alarm to arms sounded off several times a night, and tired sailors had to force themselves to wake up, it was common to hear that gallows humour of 'roll on death and let's have a long lie-in'. There was no way we could hit the enemy airfields, not with our 80mph Walrus with its .303 Browning machine-gun and one 250-pound bomb.

Photo 40. Lifebelts

I was invited aboard one of the American 'Liberty ships' as they were called. The great American Henry Kaiser had set up a Liberty ship production line and had created a miracle for those days; namely one completed Liberty ship every four days, using quickly-trained welders who were mostly women. These Liberty ships were built as well as anything that sailed in those days; some survived the war and gave years of service to private merchant steamship companies and lasted as long as ships built in the traditional way. The one I visited was packed tight with drums of aviation fuel and explosives, even in the living quarters, as well as the normal cargo of planes, tanks and other cargo. I can recall the large notices in their mess deck and sleeping quarters, which read 'Definitely No Smoking'. It was a terrible experience when one of these new ships suddenly blew up and left these fine fellows swimming in freezing oil-coated water ablaze with yard-high flames of burning aviation spirit and fuel oil that could get into their lungs. You could sometimes hear these poor devils calling for help, which you could not stop to give without putting the whole convoy at risk.

It was only about two years since we had arrived in this terrible war zone but it seemed to me as though I had spent my whole life there, living like this in a country where none of its inhabitants owned a bath or shower. We never ever saw a public toilet. A country where you didn't rub shoulders with its sailors or soldiers in case you picked up fleas, lice or some skin complaint. A country whose climate could kill or wound you more quickly than your enemies, a country full of generous Russian heroes. For us afloat, all the time it was rules, rules, and more rules. DON'T waste fresh water. DON'T relax on watch. Each ship keep in its place. DON'T show a light. DON'T put yourself at risk from frostbite. DON'T be untidy and leave things about in case water gets into compartments (clothes that had been left about could block the pumps). DON'T ever be late at your action station (someone, or all, could die). DON'T ever answer back. Always keep your mechanical equipment clear of ice. DON'T forget a happy ship is an efficient ship. DON'T forget to do your duty. DON'T forget to fit in your homework. DON'T forget to clear up gunfire dust. DON'T forget it's your turn to climb up the moving swaying eighty-foot mast. DON'T forget to put your heavy clothing on, it's usually cold, windy and wet up there. DON'T forget to check that your personal lifebelt air-pressure, red light bulb and battery are working otherwise you will never be seen if you fall overboard or have to abandon ship (see Photo 40 – Lifebelts). This lifebelt is subjected to very hard wear; one lives and sleeps in it. DON'T ever put cotton wool into your ear to damp down the noise from gunfire; a near-miss bomb when exploding can create sufficient pressure to drive this cotton wool through your eardrum causing deafness. DON'T forget to have a completed letter ready written and in its addressed envelope for Mum and Auntie in case you fall overboard or something similar so that the padre can post it, or in case some lucky ship is going home and will act as postman. Fear had become everyone's companion.

'The powers that be' had finally found a junior officer to take charge of the HACP and I had got the sack. I wasn't sorry; after all it had been JTB's and my ambition to rise up four decks to the upper deck, where everything important happened and where it was safer. Poor old JTB had to stay in his TS because the TS was where the warrant gunnery officer, Mickey Fullerton, had his action station and he wanted to keep JTB as the second-in-command. This trip was the first time I had experienced what it was like living for a week and a half, night and day, enclosed in a two-inch steel armour plated turret. Even in June, such a place is like a refrigerator with guns; we were less than eighty miles from the permafrost. The turret was all steel. There was nothing warm to sit on and you couldn't lie down. At least it had been warm in the HACP. When closed up at first degree of readiness, the thing I could never cope with was the lack of privacy when using the galvanised toilet bucket in the gun house where there was nowhere to hide. I found using it embarrassing. I overcame this problem by not going at all or by using it only at night when most were asleep, although this was not popular for obvious reasons. Anyway, it was always smelly in the turret. Emptying the bucket was a greater problem, because the turret had to be rotated to avoid someone stepping out into the oggin. When the door had to be opened, and when the turret was on an outboard bearing, the cold came in and the lights had to be turned off. As one of the gun's crew put it to me as a newcomer: "You may die in here, but if you don't and have to sit in here long enough you're sure to develop piles." The turret was a noisy and dangerous place, different motors drove various parts. The occupants had to shout their commands. As soon as the crews turned up to man the three guns, they had to report their readiness by shouting as loud as they could "left (centre or right) gun closed up, cleared away for action, breech air blast and interceptor correct, bore cleared, hang-fire latch switched to action, recoil cylinder full, intensifier full, run-out pressure showing a thousand pounds, tompion cleared, left gun closed up ready for action". It could be fired at this stage. During quiet moments in this steel box conversations were coarse, as if we were in a back street bar, but without the beer! This was a culture shock after the HACP where I had had gentle Oxford common-room type conversations with my academics. The other problem with my new location was the turret PO. He was a dyed-in-the-wool disciplinarian. Whilst he knew his job well enough, he was not able to distinguish between a Royal Navy fighting ship trying to survive a war in the Arctic and the same ship on peacetime duty. Although this guy could be a pain in the butt, he had worked hard in his spare time crocheting seventeen blue woollen jerseys with grey motifs on the front, one for each member of the turret, using wool which he got us to spend ages unravelling from woollies that the ladies at home had knitted for the forces. About this time the Government in Britain had introduce a campaign called 'Knitting comfort for the Navy'. We had received a delivery of five hundred or so of these garments, a few had notes attached, held by sickbay shackles (safety pins). Apparently the censorship people frowned on this practice. I saw three such notes: one said "Look after yourself, Jack". Another said "Hope this keeps you warm sailor-boy" and a third, which had been saturated with scent, said "Good luck from Beryl".

The padre would turn up with the food and try to cheer us up without giving a sermon. Most of us had seen him in action, doing his best for the wounded, and we all grew to respect him. At any rate whilst you were listening to him you weren't noticing that it was corned dog sandwiches again!

Murmansk was burning as we left. The recent hourly air raids had done their work well. It would be more accurate to state that Murmansk was burnt and had almost successfully been put out of action by the German Luftwaffe (see Photo 41 – burnt Murmansk). There wasn't anywhere that could be used to moor and unload a merchantman and cart its cargo to a safe area. Because of these circumstances we were made aware that our old Kola Inlet routine had to be altered for this trip. We had to catch up and find a redirected PQ17, which we did, just a short distance from Jan Mayen Island. It appeared that it would be heading for Archangel. PQ17 was no different from the usual convoys. It had started its life in New England, USA and, by the time we had found it, it had already overcome and survived the

'Battle of the Atlantic' and therefore had completed some 90 percent of its journey to Russia. There was, however, one difference with this PQ17 and that was that the German High Command would have, no doubt, found out our movements when they checked the aerial photographs that their Blohm Voss 138 reconnaissance aircraft (easily recognised by its low-slung nose) took when the pilot first found this convoy on its way up from Iceland. It was a group of some fifty ships comprising seven small escort vessels, three tankers and forty Liberty merchantmen, all of the same pattern. The Germans must have wondered how the Americans were achieving these remarkable replacements for their losses. Having hitched ourselves to PQ17 we finally passed Jan Mayen Island on our port side. We then knew from experience that after half a day's steaming at the average speed of the convoy on an almost straight line course, we would see Bear Island on our starboard side that evening. By altering course to green 090° we would eventually end up in the White Sea.

Photo 41. Burnt Murmansk

It was early July 1942, during the first dog watch, that we suddenly found ourselves to be in really illustrious company, with big boys as well as smaller ones. There was the cruiser HMS *Norfolk,* the American cruiser USS *Tuscaloosa,* then on the other side of the convoy were the battleships HMS *Duke of York,* USS *Washington,* the aircraft-carrier HMS *Victorious* and the heavy cruiser HMS *Cumberland,* as well as sixteen British, Russian and Yankee destroyers. There was a lot of fog about and all these ships looked unreal in this cold mist. The poor old merchantmen, trying to keep in their zigzag positions together without colliding with one another, could have done without it. The Admiralty sent one of their 'obey us at once' messages, instructing the convoy not to go to Murmansk as it had finally gone up in flames and was totally destroyed. The message was probably sent after they had received our captain's report as we had left Kola Inlet. A second Admiralty report came after we had settled down to our allocated position amongst all these important international ships. We were told that it had been reported that the German battleship *Tirpitz,* the heavy cruiser *Hipper,* and four destroyers had left Trondhjem, Norway, and had disappeared in the fog. In answer to "what do you think Stripey?" I got the response "they're not very far away, young Cutts, but look what we've got around us". As usual I stopped worrying. PQ17 continued and it wasn't long before Bear Island showed up on our starboard side. Not long after, QP16 and its escorts hove into sight with its empties on their way home back to Lock Ewe in Scotland, via Reykjavik. They reported that enemy aircraft had attacked them hour after hour since leaving Russia. Stripey made it clear he would rather be where he was than with QP16. I think that this was the first time I had noticed that one of our own submarines was being used as part of an escort. This sub was trailing well astern of this convoy. How anyone could volunteer to man a sub in the Arctic beggars belief. We all knew that the *Scheer, Lutzow, Hipper* and a number of units of the German northern fleet were anchored no further than five hundred miles away at Altenfiord, Norway. I think everyone had got a bit uptight. The unexpected cold summer without any let-up had been exhausting, not surprising since we were near the permafrost. It was on the 6th, 7th or 8th of July 1942, during the middle watch, whilst we were at the third degree of readiness, that we were ordered by our Lords and Masters to leave PQ17 and proceed alone in the direction of QP16. At this time nobody mentioned the possibility of us bumping into German naval units. What we didn't know was that the Admiralty had signalled the following messages to the admirals in charge of this large fleet of American, Russian and British warships and merchantmen. The first message was: "German naval units believed to have put to sea, including the *Scheer, Lutzow, Tirpitz, Hipper,* accompanied by cruisers and destroyers." The second Admiralty signal said: "Movements by enemy naval units to the north. (I was later told that this was received as a result of a report from a Russian submarine which had been patrolling the coast.) This of course threatened PQ17 and QP16, but how far off were these heavy units? This Admiralty signal was possibly the reason we had been directed westward at full speed and, as Stripey said, "Full speed means trouble". The third Admiralty signal that came said: "Convoy is to disperse and proceed to Russian ports." It looked as if the heavy German units were just over the horizon. The fourth Admiralty signal came during a heavy air attack and was blunt and ordered: "Convoy is to scatter." Who were these so-called Admiralty experts and were they only talking about PQ17 and its forty merchantmen, travelling at an average speed of six to eight knots? To scatter without escorts and separate themselves from one another was going to take days at this fast walking pace. The only Russian port available to PQ17 was Archangel and that was nearly eight hundred miles away. If PQ17 turned back they would be in deep trouble and muddled up with QP16. If they went north they would hit the ice and if they went south they would meet the oncoming enemy subs and aircraft. We wondered why the Admiralty didn't see this. Out of the original 49 ships in the PQ17 convoy, despite each individual skipper's effort, only 15 ships made it to Archangel. That meant the loss of 34 captains and 1,000 crew members, mostly Americans. One can imagine a ship's crew alone in the Arctic, despite it being summer, some eighty-odd miles from the permafrost on life-rafts and open boats, perhaps some already injured, and the nearest safe land some seven hundred miles away.

It was some time after this event that we learnt that our ship, as well as the British Home Fleet, had been accused of cowardice by the American media. They suggested that we ran away. However, had we met with the Germans heavy units, as we had expected, we would have had to be braver than we had ever been before. I suppose the US media couldn't say that the British Admiralty in London had seriously misjudged the situation. Historians, who tell you they are always right with their guesses, will no doubt say what they like, so why shouldn't I? We did not run from danger. I never did learn what happened to QP16 with its empties. The Admiralty signal that had directed us westward, before all this sad nonsense started, had sent us at high speed on a wild goose chase.

This trip, looking for these 'German heavy naval units' which we were expecting to bump into without any warning at all, was another exercise that kept us locked up like prisoners in the turret day and night. It was nerve-racking, cold and unpleasant.

We were locked up in the turret, in stages of first or second degree of readiness, for ten days whilst we hunted high and low for the mighty German ships. My Lords of the Admiralty only called it off when our air reconnaissance reported that they were all comfortably anchored back in their harbours. We were also told the *Hipper* and the *Lutzow* had run aground. When this sad episode finished, we were ordered to proceed to Iceland and wait to escort PQ18 to Russia.

It seemed so warm in Reykjavik that we were all pleased when the Tannoy piped 'Hands to bathe' and we all jumped naked into the sea and enjoyed a swim in the harbour. After the excitement of our swim, in the reasonably warmish seawater, the buzz was that we were to go to Scotland which, of course, might mean at least fourteen days' home leave for both watches, no matter what part of Scotland we were anchored in. There was no sailing of any sort the next day; instead it was all hands to paint ship with dove grey and dark grey camouflage. The buzz increased; our ship was looking crabby and needed to be smartened up before we could go on leave in Scotland. What the buzz really meant was the entire ship's crew was homesick and needed a well-earned rest away from the war, but that was wishful thinking. The very next day, 21st June, we lost one of our Walrus aircraft, complete with its pilot and air gunner. It was a very sad accident that occurred when the plane was being catapulted off the flight-deck. One minute it was

Photo 42. Frozen 'Charlie floats'.

leaving the catapult rising at 80mph and the next it had dived and had completely disappeared under the water with its two crew members. The plane must have lost take-off speed and dived instead of rising; hence the ship ran over it as it hit the water. As always the entire crew acted as though they had lost some close relations, even though they hadn't been in close contact with these fellow crew members. They were after all *Nigerians*. If anything it made us all think more about home leave, which was what the whole crew needed. However, we put to sea on 23rd July to join a heavily guarded convoy code-named ONSUT until 28th July, when we left to keep an appointment with some specialist divers at Scapa Flow. It dawned on us that, having run over our Walrus and torn it to pieces, we might have damaged our propellers. On inspection there was found to be nothing wrong with them. It had never been known for watch leave to be given in Scapa, so it didn't come as a surprise to me when I was told by the schoolteacher that now I was nineteen years of age, I would have to take my Education Test Part 1 Paper A English, and Paper B Arithmetic examinations again because I had failed the English Paper A. This would all take place aboard HMS *King George V*, a battleship moored in the 'Flow'. This exam had to be passed before I could be considered for any form of promotion. It was spelling on both of these papers that had let me down. I thanked the teacher for his interest, nice bloke!

We were all amused and interested to watch a lighter arrive alongside carrying an upright piano lashed to its derrick

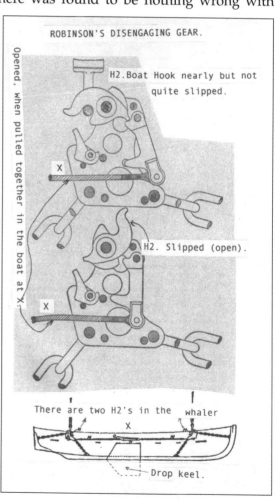

Figure 40. Disconnecting gear.

supports. Our old 'Joanna' had many faulty parts, mostly the results of Arctic storms, and it was out of tune. Many willing volunteers from the ship's company carried this precious instrument to our canteen. "Music with Gofers," laughed JTB.

The afternoon weather was good and the officer of the watch instructed me to take out eight recently enlisted ordinary seamen pulling in the starboard twenty-seven-foot whaler. I had often lowered and hoisted this whaler and it was my 'abandon ship' position, but this was the first time I was to be in charge. At nineteen years of age I could see no difficulty. It was the first time these new chaps had been lowered over the side in a juddering sea boat with its final noisy bump caused by meeting a moving sea, all of which was normal. I was left with eight very nervous young men. We disconnected without a hitch, not an easy thing to do. The man in charge of the boat had in hand the central control to the fore and aft chains which held the boat. If he pulled too early the boat would fall down into the sea and the jolt might break his comrades' backs. If he pulled too late the boat would be dragged along the surface of the sea, and if it tipped like a bucket the crew could be drowned. We pushed off with some difficulty whilst these weak-armed rowers found their respective rowlocks, and got used to their fifteen-foot-long oars. It was all a great success and we were moving quite well, until the officer of the watch, using a loudhailer, ordered me to hoist sails and make use of the available breeze. I replied to the officer of the watch at the top of my voice, "Sir, these ratings have never been sailing before". I had decided that I was not going to explain to that duty officer and anyone listening on the upper deck, plus these eight greenhorns that, despite the one classroom theoretical lesson I had received on sailing during my lessons as a boy seaman on the Isle of Man (and the only thing I remember from that lesson was that it was only a well-designed sailing boat that could sail to within six points off the wind – a pusser's whaler was such a boat), I had never sailed anything except a toy sailing boat I had been given as a Christmas present, which I sailed on Grovelands Park's toy boat lake in Palmers Green! The officer of the watch, who had been talking to someone in authority, called out: "Starboard whaler, the captain wishes you to commence sailing exercises." All I could say to this was "Aye, aye, Sir!" So then I ordered my eight to ship their oars. They looked terrified as they obeyed (Scapa Flow isn't Grovelands Park). The water, and there was a lot of it, looked cold and the breeze looked healthy, but after a lot of fuss I finally rigged the three sails, reefed as close back as possible. I knew that we were being watched by the entire Home Fleet including the *Nigerians*. In all the places we had been lately it had not been open-boat sailing conditions

227

and I could well imagine they were looking forward to watching this brand-new O/S's skill or otherwise. We were quickly 'in irons' and just drifting aimlessly. I hadn't a clue what to do. There was just one hope that perhaps one of the eight knew how to sail. I got no takers; I knew that I had dropped a clanger and they were now losing confidence in me. In desperation, I unfurled the reefs to the mainsail and pushed the rudder hard over. For a couple of minutes or so we moved, only to stop and then, slowly and gently, capsize until the mainsail lay flat on the ocean and all nine of us were in the drink. It was at that moment that I was so pleased that I had established that all eight of them could swim and had ensured they were wearing their lifebelts. I now knew without any hesitation what to do. We quickly disconnected the two masts and three sails and all re-entered the capsized boat from one side, righted it, and bailed it out.

The ship's log states for 28th June 1942: "Position Scapa Flow. Time 1750 first whaler capsized. 1830 first whaler salvaged and hoisted on board." It does not say that this debacle was watched by the crews of some three dozen ships of the Home Fleet, a possible total of two thousand laughing seamen and officers of all ranks! Scapa was normally a boring place, but not on this occasion. It wasn't until I came aboard, wet through, and reported to the captain, who seemed to be sympathetic and reminded me that I hadn't lowered the centre-plate, that I relaxed. He quickly realised I hadn't had any sailing instruction and said: "That was a hard way to learn. Get out of those wet clothes." He was always a good captain was Captain J.S.L. Dundas, RN. On this same evening he left the ship, bound for I know not where, and was replaced by Captain S.H. Paton, RN. Stripey's remarks were, as always, friendly: "You do seem to enjoy your swimming, Cutts." Ordinary Seaman Edwards was the idiot of the week but it was a way of getting oneself known! On 1st July we sailed to join a convoy code-named 'Force Q'. The weather was good but the U-boats and air attacks were becoming more numerous. Also, enemy planes and subs were laying more mines these days and so everyone had to keep their eyes open. There was not much sleep for us but everyone was happy because the buzz had it that we would be in Greenock soon and that could only mean fourteen days' leave. The buzz was right, or partly right, and within three days we had arrived in Greenock and were booked into Princes Dock in a couple of days' time to fit a new high-angle director tower. There was no mention whatsoever about leave except runs ashore to Glasgow in the evenings. All the operators were going to attend a crash course on this piece of radar high-angle equipment and thus, poor devils, they would lose their evenings in Glasgow.

It was about that time that we learnt that our respected doctor, Mr Marks, whom we all liked and felt comfortable with, but above all trusted because of his advanced skills, had been promoted to surgeon commander and had been posted to serve elsewhere. We were losing a lot of these good people from our 'team'. It was only a couple of weeks before that we had buried our pilot and gunner, and just a few days later our respected captain had left without a 'goodbye'. Admiral Burrough had been given promotion; he had gained a bigger workload and was now responsible for a larger number of vessels, including us.

Personally I was sorry to lose a kind and considerate captain, and Mr Marks who had treated both my ears and left thumb for early frostbite when I was very frightened that I could lose some parts of my body. Of course we would still carry our sickbay tiffy who carried out all the treatments on my ears with great skill, but if you lost a leg or something similar you, the patient, would always feel more confident if there was a doctor about.

It was whilst we were having our HA director tower changed in Princes Dock that a dockyard technician working on our secret radar tower drew my attention to some large packages clearly marked 'Malta' for everybody to see. There were notices posted everywhere on those dockyard walls. I remember one that stated 'Careless Talk Costs Lives' under a picture of someone with a hand over his mouth. I told Stripey what the technician had said, to which he replied: "It's too late to say anything now, perhaps it's been done purposely to mislead, we might be taking them back to Russia. I think I'd prefer the Malta sunshine." We were all hoping for home leave. It would give me the opportunity to see Mum, Auntie and Joyce Dyster who were only three hundred and fifty miles away. The mess deck dodger must too have known something was up when he ordered us (now we were in Scotland in the summer, in our normal uniform, almost sweating), in the interests of safety, to stow our heavy sheepskin waterproof coats, seaboots, Russian bearskin hats and the three pairs of heavy gloves in our hammock netting to keep the mess deck clear.

We had three ratings able to play the new piano, two who could read music and the third, a six-foot-tall marine with hair sticking up in the air like Mozart, who played with both hands together using only his little fingers and his thumbs, oscillating his hands the whole time. His type of rapid hand movements drew a large crowd of onlookers when he took his turn at the piano.

XIV

Operation 'Pedestal'

This chapter is presented in a different way to preceding chapters because events happened so quickly and I feel the ship's log may be needed for the reader's reference to help understand my daily observations and to get a clear picture of my reactions to the situations I found myself in until I arrived in the USA. (See Ship's Log at the end of the book.)

Saturday 1st August 1942. In Greenock I was dreaming of going home on leave. I had washed my one and only spare pair of underpants and spare blue socks, pressed my Number One trousers and top and brushed the dust from my posh blue canvas service holdall. I was ready to collect a travel warrant, go home and say "Hello Mum, Auntie, and Joyce, I've just spent two years in Russia having a good time". I didn't want to worry them with the truth. Sadly I knew I had wasted my time dreaming about this when a large oiler came alongside, followed by stores and petrol top-ups. This was the same day that a very pregnant cat was calmly walking past the ship, minding its own business, when it was 'pressed' and brought aboard by an animal lover from 7 Mess, wearing a sailor's cap marked HMS. Only two of the ship's company had actually managed to take unofficial leave and see their wives, who resided in Scotland.

Sunday 2nd August. At 1600 hours the starboard hangar was filled to the brim with merchant seaman captains, all behind locked doors guarded by the master-at-arms and the chief gunner's mate. Their own boats picked up all these gentlemen at 1800. This was all so sudden and for once there were no buzzes, we still had no idea what was happening (see Photo 43).

Monday 3rd August. On convoy again. Three things were new to me on that day. In all the twenty-three convoys I had attended none had been as fast as 13 knots and never before had we practised as a group, all together, so many emergency turns (ETs). All the previous

Photo 43. Merchant Captains

convoys had consisted of approximately two-thirds merchant vessels and one-third Navy, if they were lucky. This convoy was the reverse. It was unheard of before to accompany a convoy with two battleships and three aircraft-carriers. It was not until the first watch, just as it was beginning to get dark, that I viewed this immense fleet of fast-moving naval heavyweights. The whole of 13 Mess shared my excitement and amazement. "Have you seen that oiler?" said JTB, as he disappeared down to the locked TS. "It's got more Oerlikons on its upper deck than a hedgehog's got prickles on its back." I came off watch at midnight and knew by the night sky that we were all heading south and I thought "Thank God, not Russia", and enjoyed my four-hour middle watch sleep, without a blanket as it was so warm.

Tuesday 4th August. As one of the special sea duty men, I had to assemble the necessary wires and shackles to top up the destroyer *Wolverine* (see Photo 44). I knew she was one of our older destroyers but why she had to be topped up when she had been at sea for only three days all added to the mystery as to where we were all off to. The Tribal destroyer *Amazon* wasn't in any way ancient but we did the same for her that evening.

Wednesday 5th August. All was pleasant, it was a good sea, and the temperature was approaching 70°F. The RDF (radio direction finder) came up with enemy planes to port, but nothing came of it. Stripey pointed out: "We've never had it so good, look at all this Navy looking after us, especially three carriers with dozens of Hurricanes and Spits. You'll be alright Cutts." The cat gave birth to three kittens: now we had four stowaways locked up in the paint shop forward.

Photo 44. Wolverine

Thursday 6th August. We had to start and retrieve the 'log' (see Figure 41). If during action there was damage to the steering, its navigation, and if its electricity supply was cut off, then the secondary steering (which was always provided on a ship) had to be used in conjunction with the 'log'.

The housing for the 'log' was located on the deck just above the top of the rudder, about two feet in, so that the PO or L/S whose action station it was could set the 'log' into the slot on the deck and plug the electricity supply into the

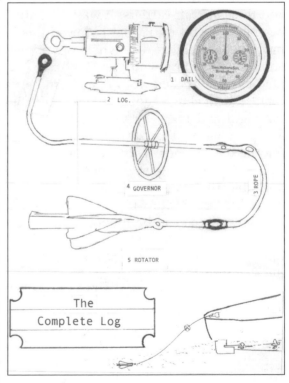

Figure 41. A 'log'.

waterproof connection. Close by was a hatch which could be raised so that he could call down to the four seamen two decks below where the rudder gears were. There were special tackles fitted for emergency use if the machine-driven chains were out of action. These tackles could be attached to the rudder gearing so that it could be moved manually from port to starboard. It took four strong sailors (two each side) to pull on their chains to swing the rudder.

In these emergency conditions, a navigator would have to calculate the necessary course. First he had to know accurately the speed of the ship. A 'log' was used to do this. Our 'log' was (I think) called a 'Cherub Mark II' and was about eighteen inches long. Having slotted it home and connected the electricity, the rest of the apparatus was fed down to the sea. This consisted of about ten feet of strong rope around a wire (attached to the end of the 'log'). The other end ran down to a wheel (governor) and continued for another twenty feet at the end of which was a rotator which would be in the sea. The governor prevented vibrations or jerky movement being conducted back to the 'Cherub'.

Knowing the speed, the navigator on the bridge could calculate the position of the rudder to keep to a given course. He then sent instructions to the sailors below to pull on the gears to hold the course. These instructions were sent by telephone – assuming that was still operational. This procedure was practised regularly by the team responsible and was to come to our rescue later.

Spent the forenoon in 'X' Turret assembling the calibration unit. This was used for a high-angle practice shoot at our Walrus aircraft towing a two-yard drogue, one of the gunner's new ideas, we had never tried this before. This brought the usual Morse answer from our pilot: "I'm towing this drogue not pushing the bastard." We had probably been a bit closer to him than the drogue!

Friday 7th August. Callout for special sea duty men at 2350. RDF had picked up a line of small boats. It was dark but as we got closer we could see that there were some thirty to forty Spanish fishing trawlers, using surface nets and very bright lights. After some discussion with the commander concerning our safety from enemy mines, the officer of the watch ordered us to recover our PVs so that they did not become entangled in the fishing nets. Two things had now become obvious to us: the first was that we were smack bang in the middle of the Straits of Gibraltar, the second was that every German agent residing nearby and enjoying his late night noggin must have seen this British convoy illuminated by the fishermen's lights.

Saturday 8th August. Cable party was part and parcel of the special sea duty men's duty, so at 0035, when we had finally anchored in

Gibraltar Bay on a very warm night, I and the rest of the cable party were still on our feet at 0300 and feeling tired. By the time we had reeved up our wires and prepared the PVs for launching, it was almost time to weigh and proceed on our way, which we did by 0445. We hadn't yet been told where we were off to, but had guessed it must be Malta. There must have been a mistake when we were topped up with ordinary petrol as we spent all day and half the night pumping the stuff over the side. Pollution was considerably added to in the Mediterranean!

Sunday 9th August. Stripey looked at the host of RN ships and remarked: "There can't be anyone left at Scapa or Russia, the padre must think he's dealing with the five loaves and fishes for the five thousand by the water's edge." (The padre was assisting the cooks with the distribution of the sandwiches and drink.) When there was a quiet moment, one member from each mess was allowed to collect the rum issued for his mess mates. A hundred and fifty Italian high-level bombers, too high to shoot at, passed over the convoy and dropped a number of newly-invented 'tin fish' by parachute in front of the moving convoy, the idea being that as soon as the convoy was all muddled up with these circling torpedoes their bombers would turn about and drop oil bombs that ignited as soon as they hit something, sometimes even hitting the sea was enough to set them off. Our emergency turn practices had been carried out to enable the entire convoy to change direction rapidly whilst keeping station to avoid these small parachute torpedoes, which we did on this occasion, but this was no answer to avoiding these oil bombs. We were lucky to have carrier-launched Spitfires already in the air which soon disrupted the Italians.

Monday 10th August. Everybody was at action stations. It was over 80°F inside our uncomfortable turret; we wished we were back to freezing point. We were wearing anti-flash gear which made us sweat and I was suffering from 'dhobi itch', which had kept me awake the previous night. I had not had any sleep for two days. I was wearing my overalls so I cut the sleeves off with my seaman's knife to make me feel cooler. I was finding the firing and the diving enemy aircraft very noisy. There were more planes here than we had been used to, they were to be counted in hundreds rather than tens.

Tuesday 11th August. Actions with the enemy went on throughout Monday night; there was no chance of any sleep. One rating at a time was allowed out of the turret to collect a breakfast from the galley, eat and visit the heads, with strict instructions to return to his action station within ten minutes. The first chap was allowed to leave at 0600; my turn arrived at 1315. I collected a six-by-six-inch shallow baking tin loaded with two bacon rashers, a tinned sausage, and a slice of well-fried bread, covered by tinned tomatoes. I quickly ran to 13 Mess, which wasn't far from the galley, grasping my tin of food. On arrival at the deserted mess deck I put my 'train smash' on the table, sorted out our galvanised deck-scrubbing pail and immediately relieved myself by having a large pee. Having opened our porthole cover to transfer my urine to the Mediterranean, I suddenly became aware that we were sailing on a parallel course to our aircraft-carrier HMS *Eagle*, which had turned into the wind to fly off Spitfires destined for Malta. Thinking about my allocated time I grabbed up my tin of food and, using my dirty fingers, proceeded to gobble it down. As I watched with interest these planes leaving the *Eagle's* flight-deck, she was hit by two or more torpedoes. Almost at the same time a Spitfire raced across the flight-deck of this sinking carrier, and successfully took off. Although the *Eagle* had developed a considerable list, a second plane moving at great speed also managed to clutch at the air and fly off. I wanted to cheer but had a mouthful of food. The *Eagle's* flight-deck crew pushed another Spitfire ready, despite the fact that there was now a considerable list to starboard and she was sinking and well down by the bows. This third aircraft gathered speed on a now moving flight-deck but, due to the dip forward, was unable to gain sufficient height and crashed into the sea. Having watched this pilot's sad act of heroism and the sinking of this large aircraft-carrier, with all those lads leaping over the side and wondering how many poor sods were trapped or wounded below, I suddenly remembered my ten minutes – there were no clocks or wrist watches to check with. I picked up my half-finished meal and rushed back to 'X' Turret, put the tin with a half-eaten sausage and piece of fried bread by my feet and took up my action station just in time to hear the captain of the turret order us to open fire. It was some time before I had a chance to finish off my meal. This was to be my last food for the next forty-eight hours. No-one accused me of being late. That carrier must have disappeared in ten minutes or so. So much seemed to have happened in such a short space of time. This left me with a feeling of great loss. All those planes gone, and all those lives. This carrier had been there to protect us; it was no longer there. The Italians and the Germans must have been cheering and the buzz was that they had at least a thousand planes left with which to continuously attack us. As the day wore on and the attacks continued I forgot about food, and without any sleep I was becoming so tired I could hardly work the six-inch breech (see Figure 42). Because the turret doors had to be closed the whole time, the temperature inside was in the eighties. We were not used to being so warm and, like me, lots of the crew were suffering with 'dhobi itch'. We now couldn't leave the turret and the toilet pails had come out; with the smell of sweat and the pails it stank. It was such a relief when the padre turned up with a drink of water and we were allowed to open the door because it had got dark at last. We settled back into the same routine for the night and we would have to shut the door again as soon as the E-boats and U-boats turned up.

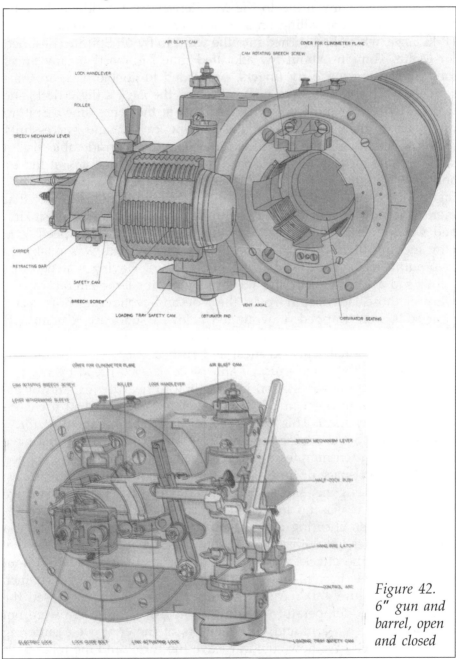

Figure 42. 6" gun and barrel, open and closed

Wednesday 12th August. After a bad night everything became a blur of unbelievable noise and mind-numbing tiredness. I didn't know what time of the day it was. This was the day we had got as far as the Skerki Bank, less than eighty miles from the Axis airfields at Trapani (see Figure 43), and getting closer all the time. This position was where our carrier air cover would have been needed most of all. The buzz was that not only had the *Eagle* been sunk but also the carrier *Indomitable* had been damaged and couldn't use its flight-deck, so had returned Gibraltar. Fortunately, as planned, all the Spitfires and their pilots had left for Malta and this was a great achievement; this had been our first objective. This left only the carrier *Furious* with a limited number of pilots and planes to protect us all, and they couldn't continue to fly without sleep. Although I felt lethargic, I had forgotten I had not eaten and didn't feel hungry anyway. With the lack of adequate air cover we and HMS *Cairo* joined the escorts protecting the American oil tanker *Ohio*.

The *Ohio* was a special oil tanker. It was one of the first all-welded ships constructed and it was twice as fast as the normal all-riveted fuel tankers. Winston Churchill had requested it personally from President Roosevelt because of its speed and the fact that all-welded ships didn't seem to suffer with leaks as riveted vessels did when subjected to near-miss bombs. It was constructed in North America. Greenock dockyard had fitted six Oerlikons, two of which were on the bridge top and were manned by young apprentices. A 40mm Bofors was fitted aft of the funnel, these were extra to the three-inch bow and after-deck five-inch anti-aircraft guns already fitted. If we were unable to get *Ohio*'s cargo of fuel oil and aviation spirit into Malta we all knew 'Operation Pedestal' would be a complete failure. Judging by

Photo 45. The Ohio

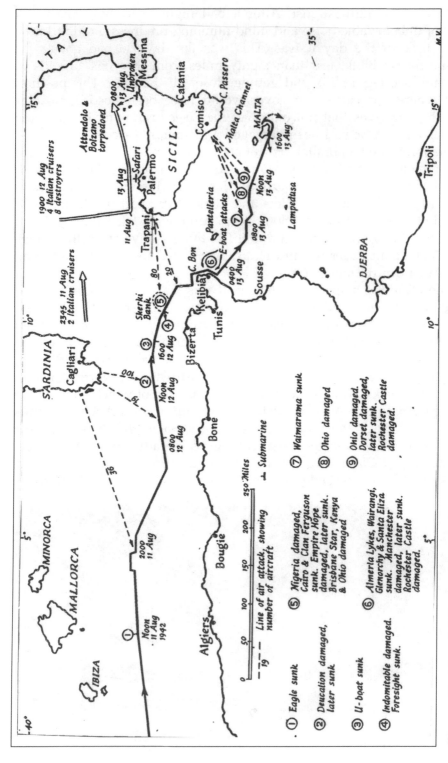

Figure 43. Nigeria hit.

*Photo 46.
Bomb blast
near miss*

*Photo 47. Near
miss bomb,
taken from
Nigeria*

*Photo 48.
Another near
miss taken from
Nigeria*

Photo 49. Nigeria at front, Cairo at rear

Photo 50. Nigeria listing heavily

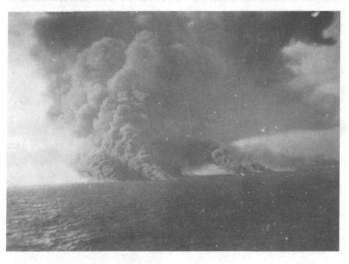

Photo 51. Ohio burning

the way the Axis aircraft, U-boats and E-boats were trying to sink the *Ohio*, they knew this too.

At 1850 hours as it had all become quiet, I was with the next three guns crew members who were allowed out to get a breath of fresh air. It was at the beginning of a cool, lovely Mediterranean evening. There was no gunfire at that moment; the whole convoy was proceeding as if nothing had ever happened. The *Ohio* was steaming on a parallel course to us on our port side, as was HMS *Cairo* to the port side of the *Ohio*. It was a very peaceful moment. Free from the turret I was leaning over the guard-rails, looking at the nearest ships and staring vacantly at the sea and sky, taking great gollops of fresh air down into my lungs, when at 1956, a torpedo struck some eight yards forward of where I was standing. I felt the heat of it on my face and bare arms. It was the roar of 'B' boiler exploding in the engine room below where I was standing, and releasing its super-heated steam at a pressure of several atmospheres, that made me turn around and look at the after funnel where this noise came from. Out of this funnel, like a colossal geyser, super-heated steam rose to the sky. Still fresh in my memory was our medical officer's talk on the dangers of tangling with pressurised steam, particularly his example of the guy not wearing protective clothing, who had his flesh stripped off, so one could see his heart intact and still working. Whilst I was thinking of this the column of escaping steam began to descend. I made no effort to move, I was terrified and rooted to the spot and braced myself for this boiling hot liquid to fall on me. When it finally hit me it felt freezing cold, the shock was tremendous and I called out at the top of my voice "Oh Mum!" and it took some time for my thoughts to return to reality. In the meantime the *Nigeria* had stopped, it was listing to port very rapidly to about eighteen degrees. At that angle of list I was sure we were going to sink (see Photo 50).

Never mind, I thought. I had quickly convinced myself that the entire crew and I could easily swim to the *Ohio*, when there was a tremendous explosion and a great cloud of black smoke went up from the *Ohio*, she had been hit by a torpedo too (see Photo 51). Then I thought we should have to swim to the *Cairo* instead, which was almost instantaneously hit by the third torpedo as I was thinking about it! Always being an optimist I decided I might as well stay where I was. All this happened in less than the five minutes since I had my lukewarm drenching, which had seemed so cold. Standing there soaked to the skin I suddenly began to feel cold, when I noticed a stoker, with whom I had occasionally passed the time of day, wearing a well-washed cap cover sitting on the deck. This was the same stoker who used to give me permission to open the twin pressurised boiler room doors to hang up my dhobi to dry. He was looking at his right leg; I then noticed that the bottom part of his leg was missing. I put my hand on his shoulder; he looked up, I think I was going to say something to him when we both became aware that our port and starboard pom-poms had opened fire on a low-flying twin-engine aircraft approaching our stern. Without saying a word I rushed back to the turret, but by the time I got there all the firing had stopped. Everybody was getting nervous because our newly provided mobile phones which were supposed to enable us to control the Spitfires (now in Malta) could not be used because the torpedo had damaged the electrical phone control equipment which had been fitted in the *Nigeria.* As a back-up, a spare control had been fitted in the cruiser HMS *Cardiff* which was torpedoed the same day as us, but the *Cardiff* sank. I looked out of the turret and saw the padre and the sickbay tiffy were with the stoker. (He survived his wounds eventually.)

At 2010 the *Nigeria* had stopped aimlessly turning circles. As ordered by Rear Admiral Burrough, the Tribal destroyer HMS *Ashanti* came alongside to take off him and his staff. This was an amazing sight. As the *Ashanti* closed to our port side it passed over the heavy fore and aft rope lines; it was plain to see that she had been subjected to several near misses by bombs and had received a number of aircraft cannon hits, she was full of holes. These had been stuffed up with the crew's lashed-up hammocks. The *Ashanti* looked like a cactus plant with a lot of new side shoots that had fallen out of its pot. It took no longer than fifteen minutes for the admiral and his six staff to get aboard with their luggage and for the admiral to wish us all good luck. As we were casting off their ropes, one of our ABs, to everyone's amazement, deserted ship and jumped aboard the now fast moving destroyer, had he not made it and fallen between the two vessels he would have ended up as mincemeat.

HMS ASHANTI G51; with green hammocks stuffed into the shrapnel holes.

Figure 44. The Ashanti stuffed with hammocks

It was our engineering officer William Elijah Chick, who had performed a small miracle at our North Cape battle with his temporary repairs to our bows which saved the day and got us all home to South Shields, who once again came to our rescue. A working party of twelve seamen was organised to disconnect the rudder from its power steering and, by using purchases, move the heavy rudder by hand. Because the phones were damaged, another twelve seamen were required to form a voice chain to pass the navigation orders from the bridge to the rudder movers. In what seemed to be a very short space of time 'A' engine room had started up, very slowly at first, but this improved once the flood water was evened off by pumping some of it to the starboard side, thus levelling the vessel. Just before midnight on this dreadful day we began to realise how many of our mess mates were missing. We turned our sharp end and sailed towards Gibraltar.

Thursday 13th August. Still in the turret, still no sleep, still no fresh water for drinking or washing. The engineering section started up the two sets of evaporators making good the shortage of water by converting sea water into fresh water. I managed to collect a lukewarm drink during the middle watch. These same evaporators, some hours later, supplied sufficient fresh water to hose down stinking seamen whilst they stood naked in small groups on the quarterdeck; this was called a 'hose shower'. I started to think seriously about JTB and my old sophisticated musician friends in the after HACP. The crew were discussing the possibility of these chaps being trapped alive in their compartments because of the watertight doors that would have been closed during action stations. Apparently two POs had volunteered to swim down with lifelines and hammer on the bulkhead doors to see if they got any response. This would have meant stopping, and would have been risky for the two POs as well as the ship, and was turned down flat by our new captain, so the buzz went. I was beginning to take on board that there was every possibility that I had lost all my friends. To add to this nightmare were these thoughts: but for a few officers worried about class distinction, there I would be, in the same horror that the marine bandsmen and JTB were in now. Mickey Fullerton, the gunner, who had trained JTB and me when we first came aboard, had sent, one at a time, every member of the TS to the upper deck for a breath of fresh air, before at their insistence he took his break. At the moment he reached the upper deck the torpedo struck. He was inconsolable and had to be given a morphine injection by the sickbay tiffy.

Now that Rear Admiral Burrough had left the ship, we were no longer the flagship; neither were we hell-bent on trying to get to Malta but going the other way towards Gibraltar. A certain amount of the tension seemed to have disappeared. There was a lot of sadness about, it was estimated that we had lost at least fifty-two members of our crew; we had never lost that sort of number in one go before.

My turn for a 'hose shower' came at 1020 hours and I was back in the turret by 1030 still drying myself off but feeling more comfortable. This was the first time anybody had commented on my hair, or really the loss of the front of it. I was aware at the time of the torpedo that my eyebrows had disappeared, along with some of my eyelashes, but my hair was another thing. It all added to my feeling of insecurity. At 1108 a bugle call of 'bomber overhead' took my mind off it, to concentrate on three enemy aircraft. For the *Nigeria* to make a rapid change of direction, in our condition with a broken rudder, was not on the cards. Fortunately at 1110 a Malta-based Beaufighter turned up and the enemy aircraft left. Later, our escorting destroyers opened fired on a shadowing aircraft. About then corned beef sandwiches were dished out; this meant the cooks had been able to make some bread. At 1512 we were attacked by what we took to be three Vichy French torpedo planes and, despite the fact that we all opened fire on them, they came at us in arrowhead formation. The first plane apparently dropped its torpedo a long way from us and then disappeared towards North Africa. We wondered if they were going through the motions, or just not very good at their job. We ceased fire at 1528 when they seemed to be going home. Whether it was because of the lack of sleep, or that I had lifted too many one hundredweight six-inch shells in the last three days, the result was that I ended up with a very bad back!

Friday 14th August. At 0325 we sighted searchlights some three or four miles away bearing 160°. At 0725 we were forced to make an emergency turn; swerving quickly with our damage was not popular. To correct and return to normal stability seemed to take hours. The junior cook who delivered the breakfast – gourmet corned beef sandwiches – told us that on his way across the upper deck he had had one foot on the undamaged bow section and the other foot on the damaged amidships section, which he said moved separately, it made him feel they were going to part from one another, with only the bow section moving forward. By 1054 we were back to 11 knots (see diagram 'damaged section', and Photos 52, 53 and 54).

During that afternoon watch the destroyers *Wrestler*, *Keppel*, *Vidette*, *Tartar*, *Malcolm*, *Bicester*, and *Ithuriel* with a smashed bow (she had rammed an Italian submarine), joined company. We made two more emergency turns during that watch, one of which was to dodge a 'tin fish', but with all these destroyers around us who cared! It was during this same watch that we all learnt that two of the kittens had died. They had been shut up in the paint shop forward to minimise the noise and

keep them safe, but sadly they were found to be badly contaminated with red lead paint, which possibly they had tried to remove by licking it off. If my memory serves me correctly, their mother died later, possibly she had tried to help them by licking too. We were all so sad to learn the news of the cats; there was enough death about, but to die like that of red lead poisoning was really nasty. We badly wanted something to cheer us up. At 1730 hours we sighted a fishing vessel and altered course to keep well away from it. We hoped that we were nearing Gibraltar and sleep – it must have been five days and nights since I had had some! 2338, clocks put back half an hour.

Saturday 15th August. At 0200 we tied up at Port Light at 43 berth in Gibraltar at last. "We'll be as safe as houses here," remarked a weary Stripey as we both made our way down to our mess deck (which stank of fuel oil) for a much-needed breakfast. "We're nearly home and dry," he said, before I could reply. At 0750 that morning the bugle sounded off the call for an air attack and the pair of us rushed back to our action stations. After this deferred breakfast at 0920, and as tired as we were, we started to unload our unused shells into an ammunition-lighter secured on the starboard side. This hard work was only stopped at 1130 hours so that we could be paid but resumed until 1250 when we cast off the full ammunition-lighter.

Photos 52, 53, 54. Torpedo damage

Despite the fact that we were almost asleep on our feet, all the lower-deck personnel wanted to know what had become of their mess mates trapped below. Finally the buzz went round that the compartments below were so damaged that the occupants in both the TS and the after HACP must have perished. This news had a terrible effect on me; not only had I lost JTB, my close friend of the last two years, but also the seven gentle, genial old men who had shown me such kindness in my early years at trying to be their very young boss. I was also aware that, but for the fact that I was moved out of the HACP and transferred to 'X' Turret, I too would be lying dead with them on that day.

At 1535, HMS *Ithuriel* came alongside to put aboard the body of one of their officers, recently killed in the convoy, for us to transfer to the Gibraltar harbour boat RN *Minkway* to be taken to sea for a Christian burial, with a firing party guard of honour supplied by the *Ithuriel*.

The *Ithuriel*, whose bows had been squashed when she rammed the Italian submarine, was in no shape to host this funeral. Three destroyers left harbour, presumably to make room for other returning ships, possibly also damaged. We had no idea how many casualties the fleet had suffered. I remember feeling very tired and depressed. I had lost special friends and, so far as our crew understood, the convoy had been a complete failure. We cheered up a bit when, at 1745, the rest of the task force entered the harbour, at least they were still afloat. At the same time, the undamaged destroyer *Derwent* secured alongside in the space just vacated by the *Ithuriel*. At 1845 hours, five absentee seamen were escorted back to us. It was Stripey who drew my attention to them. "Have you seen who's just turned up? They're for the high jump!" I wasn't in the mood to worry about them; they had left us to do it all on our own and good crewmen had died doing it. Third degree of readiness was piped. I had the middle watch off and fell into such a deep sleep that it took my mess mates some time to wake me. Rear Admiral Burrough returned on board. At 1932, *Kenya* entered harbour.

Sunday 16th August. Before 0900, a number of the 'Pedestal' task force ships had left harbour which made it less crowded. At 0905 the rear admiral and our captain visited *Nelson*. At 0955, *Indomitable*, having completed its temporary repairs, undocked. It was great to see that she would live to fight another day. At 1210 the rear admiral returned for his personal gear and at 1315 he transferred his flag to the *Kenya*. He returned to the *Nigeria*, if I remember correctly, to inform us that he had received a signal that read: "Well done all, you have achieved the impossible, three merchantmen including *Ohio* with 10,000 tons of fuel oil and an equal amount of aviation fuel, arrived in the Grand Harbour today. Well done 'Pedestal'."

246

Monday 17th August. At 0950 hours the ammunition lighter secured alongside; it was back to unloading all our ammunition again. This hard work went on till 1730 when the ensign was lowered to half-mast. One of our lads had died in the hospital; this made me forget that I had a very painful back and that my eyes were very sore. The rear admiral's 10th CS Flag was lowered (the admiral had forgotten to take it with him). *Westcott* left harbour.

Tuesday 18th August. At 0900 I was seen by what I thought was a local Army doctor. He looked at my eyes, red skin, and my back, and he was very pleasant. "You'll be back in England in a few days so I'll give your master-at-arms a note for the hospital. Don't go on any more convoys in the meantime," he said with a smile. HMS *Furious* and twelve destroyers entered harbour.

Wednesday 19th August. At 0800 we were issued with dockyard-type shovels with turned-up side and back edges. These enabled us to scoop up fuel oil and bits of blown-up meat from the destroyed cold store into large galvanised buckets, the larger pieces of meat carcasses had to be manhandled. The problem with trying to lift the bigger sections of meat, without gloves of any sort, was that our hands and overalls became covered in oil and we couldn't always be sure that it was meat and not part of someone's body. The smell was awful. It was a particularly bad day for me because the first six bodies that we brought up for burial were my six marine gentlemen friends. The only consolation I had, when I looked about me down there, was that they could not have known a thing, as the end would have been so sudden (see three photos taken after the clean-up). I told Stripey what I had seen. "Have you seen the sailmaker?" he said. "He's got to stitch them all up in canvas shrouds and he's as pissed as a newt already, that's the only way he can cope with his task."

Thursday 20th August. At 0100, three of our lieutenants left the ship to replace casualties on other ships. 0212 *Argus, Furious, Nelson*, and *Kenya* left harbour. 0930 tugs secured alongside. 1030 secured *Nigeria* in No. 2 Dock. Dock gate shut to start pumping water out of the dock. 1545 engine room ratings mustered to shore up our damaged section, before all the water disappeared from the dock. 1730 the *Nigeria* settled in dock. 1945 twenty-one of our lads left for Blighty. Our ship's fifty-odd heads were closed and we now had to walk some distance to the hundred-year-old brick-built toilets ashore. Now that our boilers had been quenched, our engineers could not manufacture fresh water using our evaporators so all our fresh water had to come from shore sources through a four-inch canvas fire hose, which immediately meant water rationing.

Friday 21st August. At 0801 started to pump out dock. 1035 dock dry. 1100, landed as burial firing party for my 'old gentlemen' friends (they must have been well into their thirties!). There was an air attack on the way back to the ship. Colours were at half-mast for the funeral. The digging of rubbish continued according to one's watch, in this way everybody shared the misery of digging, funeral party and dockyard work (where the oil and general muck was spilling out of the damaged section). It meant both hard work and long hours. 1745 funeral party for the burial of four lads placed aboard HMT *Laurel* (small dockyard transport). 2030 landed shore party to work clearing the dockyard. This was work that the local dockyard mateys would not do. 2303 dockyard party returned. All of us had been sweating in the 80°F temperature, especially those of us working near the bodies and rotting food; our hands and overalls had become soiled by this mixture. With only a limited amount of cold water and nothing available to remove this oil we remained filthy and had to eat and sleep like this.

Saturday 22nd August. The fact that all the water had been drained from the dry dock had allowed air to enter through the hole in the side, this had percolated into almost all of the ship's compartments, including our mess deck, bringing with it more of the awful smell. When it was my turn to dig in the damaged section, I could not help thinking of JTB. Would we find him this watch, or had he already been found and buried? At 0900, four seamen were found, I tried not to look. 1145 one offender (our *Ashanti* jumper) left the ship under escort. It was a source of great speculation amongst us, it exercised our minds for some time, as to what his punishment would be. Would he only go to prison? He deserved something worse. All of this helped to take our minds off the gruesome task in hand. At 1800, three of our deceased seamen were transferred to HMT *Laurel* for burial.

Sunday 23rd, Monday 24th and Tuesday 25th August. The same grim routine continued, and in all a further sixteen bodies were recovered. Welcome help was given by two doctors who were sent to assist us. I hoped by now that poor old JTB had been laid to rest. Our living conditions had not improved, although we had been told that the engine room artificers were endeavouring to improve the fresh water situation, but the smell had got worse. Because the 'bootneck' mess deck was completely contaminated with fuel oil spillage and could not be used, the whole Royal Marine section had been sent ashore to a 'rest camp', or at least that's what was entered in the ship's log. The fact was that they had been billeted in the Durham Light Infantry Barracks, where the drill sergeant found out that they had been sitting on their fat arses swanning around the Russian coast, therefore these out-of-condition marines should be exercised. Like the grand old Duke of York, he marched them up to the top of the hill and marched them down again – but the hill was the Rock! Not content with that he introduced them to the DLI marching pace, which was 140 paces a minute whereas Royal Marines march at 120. Some rest camp!

Wednesday 26th August. By 0900 the diggers and the doctors had produced the body of an unknown person, which suggested to some of us that it was made up of some of the parts found. I think that this possibility made us all try to treat what was found with even more respect, if that was possible. The firing party and our kind-hearted padre buried him with great respect and consideration at 1100. Shore leave was to be allowed from 1800 hours to 2200 and I decided to go with the other four off-watch members from 13 Mess. We felt scruffy even after getting into what were our best suits. "Never mind," said Tom, "we'll all feel better when we get a pint." Getting a pint was not easy; we passed a queue of about two hundred matelots outside a grim-looking building, all apparently with the same beer idea in their heads, and so we went on until we came to a building with a sign that read 'nightclub'. "This looks like it," said Tom, "they're bound to sell bottled beer in here." So in we went. We were shown to a table and a tiny, very young girl came up and asked us what we wanted. "Five beers, please," said Tom. "We only serve cocktails," she said. Tom looked at her list. "Let's have five green ones," he said, as if he had been doing this sort thing all his life, and sat down. The girl brought the five small glasses full to the brim with clear green spirit and promptly sat down with us. We all just looked at her until finally Smithie asked: "Are you waiting for the money?" "No," said this under-age child, "I'm your hostess." We all looked at one another in amazement. It was Tom who 'came to' first. He said: "And I've never seen a prettier one." We all laughed our heads off and she laughed with us. Looking into the child's face all smothered in make-up made me feel like crying for some reason. We downed our liqueurs in one gulp (and later wished we hadn't!).

Having declined the little girl's offer to fetch five more Green Goddess drinks for us, we left the nightclub feeling slightly dizzy and giggly and made our way down the hill towards a crowd of some three to four hundred sailors playing housey-housey in the street. We joined them by buying tickets at one shilling each. Because of the size of the crowd the prizes were gi-normous, a line could win anything up to a fiver and the 'house' perhaps a hundred pounds or so. Of course we didn't win. Time was getting on so we returned to the ship. It was still a depressing scene; the smell was still there, and the drink was getting to me. I had a feeling of deep depression, so many of my important and close friends had gone, especially my mess mate JTB. Other mess mates enquired after our run ashore. Raggie was upset to learn that beer was unobtainable. It was Raggie who started me off, when he said how quiet the mess deck had been all that evening and how they had all missed Tug, an extra-merry member of 15 Mess who used to cheer up everybody with his idle chatter. I thought of everybody who had been lost and with the help of my green drink I sat and sobbed my heart out like a two-year-old with everybody quietly watching me and Raggie patting me on the back saying "Let it all out laddie".

Thursday 27th August. At 0700, woke up with diarrhoea, dashed to the old shore toilet, lucky to find one with paper, told Stripey about this shortage in case anyone got caught short. "We've got some here," he said, "in JTB's old locker (that had been cleared by Stripey and the mess deck dodger)." "Watch out you don't end up with a burnt bum," said the 'three badger'. The dozen outside WCs were constructed of twelve separate compartments, each with its own lockable door, and with a fixed wooden seat. Underneath was a twelve-inch-wide half-section of cast-iron pipe about twelve yards long, with a drainaway at one end and a flush at the other. It was designed to flush automatically with a pre-set time lag, when flushed water moving at great speed ran along under the seats. Our 'three badger' explained with a smile that some idiot had waited for a full house then, taking yesterday's Gibraltar local newspaper lightly squeezed up into a ball, he ignited it so it would float down this section of half-round pipe with the flush. It would automatically follow a straight line allowing it to pass unhindered under each of the eleven seats whilst it emitted a short blast of uncomfortable heat to the suspended private parts of concentrating unfortunate sailors. Any passer-by would hear a sequence of Ow! Ow! Ow! Ouch! up to eleven times.

I had been blaming my diarrhoea on the green drink but everybody seemed to have become affected. I pitied the newspaper joker if he got caught.

The stokers had rigged up a method of pumping in sea water through the dockyard gate, using a portable pump. This water travelled by canvas and bronze hoses to the ship's bottom for connection to an evaporator which, when used with a Donkey boiler on the jetty, gave us an extra forty tons of water a day. We could now have a shower, even if we had to queue; there was better drinking water and no water rationing. It felt so good to be clean again but there was still no answer to the oil stains.

Friday 28th August. 0957, fire in 'A' boiler room. We couldn't control it. 1017 commenced flooding dock to help control fire. 1045 fire under control. 1101 stopped flooding. It all smelt worse after the fire went out, but was still smoking. 1115 one of our ratings, badly hurt, was sent to the local military hospital, and our last midshipman left for a better life at home. Lucky devil! 1800 other watch given leave to hunt for beer. 1930 dry dock emptied.

Saturday 29th August. The battleships HMS *Ramillies* and *Malaya* entered harbour; we wondered where these very old battlewagons had come from. Everyone was still trying to clear up this smelly mess. I was employed with the stores PO going through the new clothes stores, which consisted mostly of underpants, vests and socks. Despite the PO's efforts, all these items were in some way spotted, if not soaked, with fuel oil and were ruined and unusable. We did manage to save about three dozen pairs of tropical shorts that had only been affected by very small spots of fuel, which he felt might wash out eventually. He gave me the job of carefully unpacking these and dabbing each spot of oil with clean cotton waste. When I explained what I had been doing to my messmates, I was greeted with "You've got yourself a quiet number you lucky devil!"

Sunday 30th August. At 0900 hours prayers were held on the quarterdeck, everyone was sad, there was no service or normal Sunday church parade. The chapel below had suffered damage so there was no 'Holy Commotion' either. We had to man the small-boat harbour patrol that night, looking for saboteurs.

Monday 31st August. At 1115 a pay parade was held on the quarterdeck. At 1440 soap and tobacco were delivered to the ship. Whilst we had to pay for the tobacco, the soap was issued free. Soap was in short supply and the stores' officer must have been aware of our cleaning problems. All the forward crew were suffering with stomach problems, which some said was due to the Levant wind which blows off the Rock; others blamed them on the smell. There was nothing available that would remove the oil fuel from our hands or clothes. We could only try soap and constant hard scrubbing. At 2045 I joined the dockyard patrol looking for possible saboteurs. Clocks were put back half an hour at midnight.

Tuesday 1st September. It was the same old dry dock routine aboard until a 1330 air attack. There was nothing we could do about that except take cover; we had no ammunition aboard. Fortunately our Spitfires discouraged them. 1440 a good friend from 15 Mess, who as a married man had expected to get home on leave soon (he had more than done his time away from home during his long Russian stint), had just learnt that he had to pack up his kit and report to the *Malaya* to relieve one of their sick crew. This meant he could be left stationed in the Mediterranean for years. This seemed so unfair and we all sympathised with him. We helped him with his gear and wished him good luck but we hoped that *we* would get home leave. At 1600 there was a high-level officers' meeting to discuss Warrant No. 95, which we thought concerned our *Ashanti* jumper, although he was no longer aboard. A charge of desertion against him was very serious. We were unlikely to know the outcome of this warrant. Neither was it likely that these top brass individuals would ask our opinions. We could have told them that we had noticed, a long time previously, the strange behaviour that this young sailor had shown in times of stress. To be fair, none of us would have stood up for him because he would have been a liability to us all. At 1700 hours, Gibraltar councillors came to complain about the awful smell and the fire hazards. With all the leaked fuel oil about there certainly were fire hazards. The dockyard mateys had to use a lot of oxy-acetylene cutting equipment to remove the wreckage of twisted plates and bent six-inch ribs. It was necessary to make room to renew the damaged square, with a two-foot-thick reinforced concrete patch of some two thousand square feet set on new six-inch ribs and to be six inches proud of the normal line of the ship's side.

Wednesday 2nd September. Warrant No. 95 officers still in serious session.

Thursday 3rd September. Spent clearing up damage in stokers' and bootnecks' mess decks, a messy job.

Friday 4th September. At 0020 three ratings were attacked in their hammocks. I had the middle watch that night and my duty was acting as the quartermaster's messenger. The quartermaster, an L/S and myself were standing in the quartermaster's lobby, just opposite the incoming gangway erected between the dry dock's wall and our quarterdeck entrance, when one of our ABs came onto the quarterdeck holding his forehead which was covered in blood and stating that he had been hit on the head by a pusser's mess brush. (A pusser's mess brush was well made! It was a square-backed hardwood hand brush with two-inch bristles, fitted into a sturdy thirty-inch turned handle. This general purpose cleaning brush was supplied to each mess deck, i.e. one to share between three messes.) If the chap's head had not been covered with blood I think we would all have burst out laughing. "Sit down lad," said the killick to the bleeding AB. "Get hold of the sickbay tiffy and show him his head," he said to me, "I'm going to find the officer of the watch." By the time I returned with the tiffy, who inspected the poor chap's split head, the officer of the watch had arrived. I heard the sickbay tiffy mumble "it needs at least six stitches". "We'll go below and look at the other two casualties and investigate this mystery," said the officer of the watch. "Edwards, you hold the fort up here." "Aye, aye, Sir," I replied, and the entire quartermaster's crew disappeared below with the officer of the watch, whilst the male nurse took his patient to the forward sickbay. At 0050 all the duty watch hands were called and the whole ship was searched, which must have woken the entire ship's company. At 0400 I came off watch and returned to my hammock and fell asleep immediately until a bugle woke me at 0630.

Saturday 5th September. At 0130 first starboard watch fell in and searched the ship for anyone who might have been attacking sleeping sailors by hitting them on the head. The sickbay by now had about a dozen casualties caused by this maniac. Our captain was taking this weird situation seriously. He had added a note to the daily orders, pointing out that he and the commander would be patrolling the ship during the first, middle and morning watches armed with their service revolvers and assuring all the crew that they would shoot anyone found suspiciously skulking about.

As I woke up that morning, everybody was talking about this violent madman roaming about the mess deck at night. I reached inside my locker for my towel and soap and there it was, a sheet of typewriter paper with the following hand-printed message in inch-high writing: "You're next. Bert the Basher." Some idiot had done it for a laugh. We wanted to laugh but we couldn't. I suppose we all knew somebody had gone off his rocker and it was no laughing matter. Two warrants, Nos. 96 and 97, were to be read this day for the two blokes late back from leave at Greenock, who had therefore missed sailing with us on 'Pedestal'. They were in serious trouble. 1200 hands to 'make and mend', or go on the swimming outing to La Linea Bay, where an engine room artificer accidentally drowned.

With Bert the Basher in mind, I decide to sleep that night in the starboard or port lookout position. Both these six-by-four by five-foot-high steel sheds would keep any rain out, and had doors that could be shut from the inside and kept shut with a two-foot length of hammock lashing. Having climbed to the port lookout position at 2100 hours with my hammock over my shoulder I found I was staring at another rating who had had the same idea. "The other lookout is taken," said this chap, "I'm not going to share with you, let's toss for it." I agreed and lost, still I didn't want to share. I didn't trust him either; we were all suspicious of one another.

Sunday 6th September. 0710, 'Holy Commotion' in the chapel. 1055, prayers and divine service on the quarterdeck. 1320 Commander Perry arrived on board. 1615 funeral for engineer artificer, buried with firing party at La Linea, Spain, for which I was part of the firing party.

Monday 7th September. 0950, small fire in the damaged compartments, 1003 fire under control. 1130 captain of the *Malaya* arrived on board. 1150 captain of the *Malaya* left ship. 1430 air attack.

Tuesday 8th September. 0900 two of our 'bootnecks' left for the so-called rest camp!

Wednesday 9th September. 1330 two of our wounded returned from hospital. 1630 the same two ratings left for the rest camp!

Thursday 10th September. 1745, air attacks, mines dropped.

Friday 11th September. 1720 air attack. 2345, Army escort for one other rank. We wondered what he had been up to.

Saturday 12th September. Order, 'nil work', because there was too much tummy trouble, blamed on the Levant by the local doctor.

Sunday 13th September. 0930 L/S Coppelman and O/S Edwards transfer to HMS *Tynecastle* as ranging party. "Lucky devils", everybody remarked. 1030 for church parties in starboard hangar and ashore. 1610, ratings for rest camp fall in. Bugler admitted to hospital.

Monday 14th September. A jolly Coppelman and I had yesterday looked up and down the harbour wall for this ocean liner called *Tynecastle*, which would no doubt carry a bar and posh toilets and would not stink, but we couldn't find it. Finally, at about 1100, we came upon a very smelly Newfoundland-built converted wooden fishing trawler, called *Tynecastle*! Wherever we went on it we could not escape the strong smell of Newfoundland Bank cod. Even the crew peed over the side rather than use their own heads.

Tuesday 15th September. At 0800 a bright morning saw us putting to sea towing an Admiralty pattern target for the *Malaya* to use for target practice later that afternoon. Before any lunch had been offered,

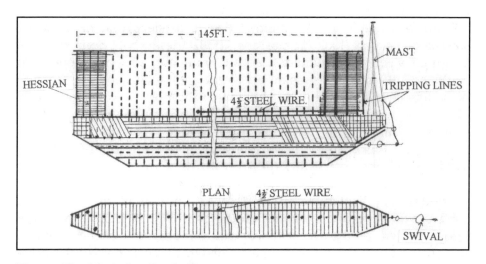

Figure 45. Admiralty Battle Target

I had unbuttoned my overalls all the way down (see photograph of myself in this attire showing my bandaged left thumb still recovering from frostbite) and was enjoying a pee over the side in fresh air.

Whilst watching the curve of my water splashing into the blue Mediterranean, I became aware of a splish-splosh noise as if someone was throwing stones, and six-inch columns of water were being thrown up by the stones landing into the water. It was the killick who reacted first. "It's a bloody Heinkel 111," he roared, "put your weapon away and come and fire this twin Lewis gun while I load it." I did as he said but I didn't stop to do up my overall buttons. The German plane had completed its first run and all those cannon shells must have passed no more than a couple of feet over our heads. None of the trawler's crew had appeared on deck; perhaps they were all busy eating their midday meal. There was no time to do anything, the green Heinkel 111 was fast and was on it way back. I was about to open fire with the twin Lewis that had two pans that Coppelman had loaded, when I felt a tap on my shoulder. The killick called out "wait, he's too far away, I'll hit your shoulder when it's right". I concentrated on the spider open sight, felt the tap and gently pulled both right- and left-hand triggers. The left-hand barrel had jammed. "Cock it," called out the calm killick, which I did, by which time the Heinkel had started its turn to start its third attack. There were cannon and bullet holes all over the place by now, we still couldn't see any of the crew on deck, everything was moving so fast. The Heinkel 111 was coming in very low on this run and the pilot must have made his mind up that we couldn't put up much of a fight and he must have felt safe. We had reloaded with two new pans of ammunition. I remembered that the .5 machine-guns had been removed from the *Nigeria* because the bullets moved too slowly to catch up if fired at a retreating aircraft and if they did, caused it little harm. This chap was going to be extremely close. The killick and I had our chests protected by a 'v' section of armour plating fitted to the Lewis mounting that gave us some protection and made us feel more secure.

It seemed to take a long time for the approaching plane to arrive and I could clearly see the Perspex-covered nose cone with a cannon firing as it came even lower on its approach, when I felt the killick's hand on my shoulder. I opened fire and aimed at the Perspex. Fortunately neither gun jammed and I was able to empty both pans before the plane was out of range. It seemed so big I couldn't see how these little Lewis guns could do it much harm and I was sure it would be back. I wondered why it had not dropped a bomb or two and I scrambled to remove the empty pans. I didn't have to worry; our 'friend' was heading for the horizon.

I was distracted from all this by the killick hopping about and telling the suddenly arrived crew that he had been hit in his left foot, but they were not taking any notice as they were all excitedly pointing to the Heinkel 111, which was getting lower and lower in the sky whilst trailing smoke from the front end. I had moved from my firing position to get a better look at the German plane, which was steadily losing altitude, when I felt the most incredible pain in my lower stomach. I shouted at the top of my voice: "Medics, I've been shot in the crotch." All I got was a lot of laughter. "Seriously," I said, "I've been shot," and to make them believe it I said: "Look at this deck." The wooden deck around the mounting was in a terrible state and had been very badly damaged. The deck damage was later found to be so bad that it could not be repaired in Gibraltar and the lucky devils were ordered to take her back to Newfoundland.

The Heinkel 111 must have been very surprised to find us in the first place, towing a target and all by ourselves. After the pilot's first attack the fact that we didn't slip our tow, increase our speed, alter course or open fire with our three-inch gun, must have made him think he was onto easy prey. Perhaps this was the reason he didn't waste a bomb on us. Whatever, the trawler's deck had been well and truly shot up. Wood splinters must have been flying everywhere; the killick and I had been very lucky not to be killed by splinters or cannon shells. Had the crew manned the open three-inch mounting, as they should have done, they could have been killed. The entire wooden deck would have to be renewed.

The killick hobbled over to me and asked "Where've you been hit Jack?" "Here," I said and pulled open my unbuttoned overalls which exposed my singlet and pants. There was a smell of burning and four or five hot expelled cartridges fell out. Two other red-hot brass shell cases had made their way through my underpants and were lying neatly across my penis, as if stuck by glue to the two nasty burns they had created. It became obvious that the open-fronted overalls had collected the very hot used brass cartridge ends as they flew out of the Lewis guns, acting as a funnel to direct them onto my private parts and down my legs. I felt like an idiot. These 'non-doers' were laughing at me, when somewhere among them were two layabouts who

Photo 55. Heinkel

should have been putting themselves at risk instead of the killick and me. The Heinkel 111 had disappeared, nobody had taken the trouble to pick up a pair of binoculars and follow it to the bitter end. The skipper of this now damaged and unseaworthy vessel that had just arrived in the Mediterranean with his novice crew told us he was going to claim that his trawler's crew had shot down this enemy plane he couldn't name. The killick and I would have given a week's pay to find out if we really had shot it down.

The afternoon shooting appointment with the *Malaya* was cancelled and we headed back to Gibraltar. The trawler's skipper was obviously a 'called-up' volunteer Newfoundland fisherman. He decided on the way back to 'Gib' to exercise his three-inch gun's crew, something he should have done earlier.

I felt very disgruntled; there I was just nineteen years old, I had an upset stomach, I had lost almost half my hair together with my eyebrows and some of my eyelashes, my skin was red and sore from the flash and 'dhobi itch' and I had lost all my pubic hair, now I had added a burnt dick to the collection, it was painful to walk and I felt miserable.

We arrived back on *Nigeria* where the killick and I received medical attention. The doctor made light of our injuries; the sickbay tiffy had a job to stop himself from laughing. "You'd best keep away from your girl-friends with this lot, you'll frighten them to death if you show them this," he said as he smothered me with a thick yellow ointment and wrapped it in heavy gauze bandage, "and keep it clean or you'll go rotten." The doctor and the tiffy had removed the bits of metal and wood from the poor old killick's boot and foot and had stitched up his foot "but not my boot!" grumbled my new friend. Bert the Basher still had not been caught.

Back on *Nigeria*, at 0800 five hundred fifty-gallon drums arrived for the stokers to stow in the damaged area for ballast. They were to be filled with seawater as they were lashed into position. 1130, payment on the quarterdeck.

Wednesday 16th September. 0915 air attack.

Thursday 17th September. 1345, the killick went to hospital for X-ray.

Friday 18th September. 0800 the first load of concrete arrived.

Saturday 19th September. 1200 *Lowestoft* arrived in dock.

Sunday 20th September. 1100 church service on board and ashore. All spare hands to assist with fifty-gallon drums that must be in position and full of seawater by 2300 today.

Monday 21st September. Nil.

Tuesday 22nd September. 1730 one rating back from hospital

Wednesday 23rd September. 0530 air attack. One rating injured by falling off a moving lorry.

Thursday 24th September. 0800 more concrete pouring. Engineer returned from hospital.

Friday 25th September. 1045 one rating to hospital with head injury. Two ratings to shore signal station.

Saturday 26th September. At 2125 a commander (engineering) joined the ship. He was going to be responsible for getting it to America.

Sunday 27th September. 1100 church services.

Monday 28th September. 0930 Board of Inquiry for rating who deserted ship on 12th August. 1800 band of the Second Battalion Gibraltar Light Infantry played on the flight-deck.

Tuesday 29th September. 0145 unberthing party for the *Penn* fell in. 0230 Party returned. 1800 embarked 2,400 gallons of lubricating oil. 1809 air attack.

Wednesday 30th September. 0800 *Maidstone* left harbour. 1215 *Maidstone* returned. 1245 air attack. 1845 nine ratings left for the UK. 1920 five officers left the ship.

Thursday 1st October. 0800 Colours. 1427 air attack.

Friday 2nd October. 0800 Colours. 1435 air attack.

Saturday 3rd October. 0800 Colours. 1200 'make and mend'. The start of concrete shuttering to contain the temporary concrete ship's side (see Figure 44).

Sunday 4th October. 0700 erecting more concrete shuttering. 1200 'make and mend'.

Monday 5th October. 1100 *Sundra, Partridge* and *Quiberon* entered harbour. 1545 air attack by French Vichy planes.

Tuesday 6th October. 0800 Colours. 1100 air attack.

Wednesday 7th October. 0930 Board of Inquiry in captain's cabin. 1430 Colours half-mast for the last unknown body found. 1500 Colours hoisted. 1859 docks flooded. 1930 ship entered No. 1 Dock.

Thursday 8th October. At 1442 we were supplied with two new whalers.

Friday 9th October. 0810 *Wishard* entered harbour. 0925 our pinnace was hoisted aboard. 0941 *Nigeria* launched from dock. Everyone was pleased to see that the scrap iron placed in the damaged compartment with the five hundred fifty-gallon water-filled drums and the concrete weight had overcome the 18 degree list. 70 percent of the leaking fuel tanks had been repaired.

Saturday 10th October. 0800 Colours. First port watch secured barrels.

Sunday 11th October. 0800 Colours. 0925 Divisions and church. (The buzz was that it would not be long before we would be

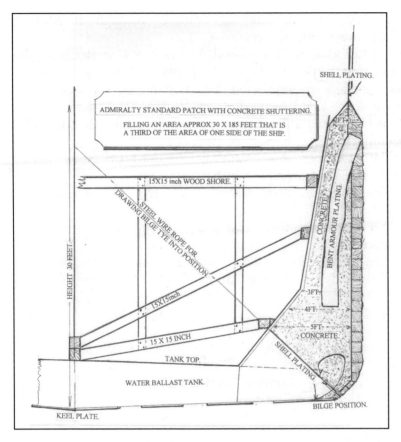

Figure 46.

back in South Shields with months and months of leave!)

Monday 12th October. 0800 ships undocked. 1845 berthed in section 47.

Tuesday 13th October. 0830 both watches prepared to ammunition ship. 1800 ammunition completed.

Wednesday 14th October. 0700 petrol lighter came alongside. 1130 petrol lighter cast off. 1430 both watches prepared for sea. 1445 Walrus returned to ship. 1530 tug secured alongside for after-slip procedure. 1950 set course 267° 20' minutes, 176 revolutions, No. 16 Z/Z.

Thursday 15th October. 1750 darken ship. Lots of starboard porthole covers would not close.

Friday 16th October. 1908 star fix 35° 01' north and 25° 33' west.

Saturday 17th October. 0600 stellar observation unobtainable. 1045 low-angle armament assumed third degree of readiness.

Sunday 18th October. 0800 L/A third degree of readiness.

Monday 19th October. 0800 assumed Z/Z No. 10 throughout. Fourth degree of readiness.

Tuesday 20th October. As Monday 19th.

Wednesday 21st October. 0800 Z/Z No. 10 throughout. Midday sighting 33° 01' north, 68° 34' west.

Thursday 22nd October. 1104 passed A2 buoy. 1145 embarked pilot off Charleston breakwater, USA. I was so disappointed and fed up, and the place looked so depressing, I had so hoped we were going home for some leave. 1415 secured alongside No. 317 Wharf.

Friday 23rd October. 0740 removed ammunition from the ship. 1040 X-petrol disembarked.

Saturday 24th October. Rear Admiral Glassford US Navy visited our captain. 1400 *Churchill* arrived in harbour.

Sunday 25th October. 0800 Colours. Church in the starboard hangar.

Monday 26th October. 1020, disembarked Walrus, proceeded to naval air station.

Tuesday 27th October. 0540 one rating rushed to naval hospital. 1510 seamen's guard and marine band fell in on jetty for US Navy Day ceremony.

Wednesday 28th October. 0830 conference in Navy yard new building.

Thursday 29th October. Crew shortage, both watches employed working ship.

Friday 30th October. Committee meeting.

Saturday 31st October. No orders.

XV

Charleston, South Carolina

By the time we had arrived and passed A2 Buoy, our oil tanks were empty and our new commander was considering requesting a tug. I was one of the ratings picked for my height to march with twenty-two other matelots to act as a seamen's guard in the US Naval Day Ceremony on 27th October. I remember being ashamed of myself on the day. This event was held in a place called the Citadel, where the US students were dressed in spotless white uniforms with foot-high white and gold hats and their parade rifles were chromium-plated. We on the other hand were scruffy. Our shorts and short-sleeved shirts, which we had worn and slept in whilst on our Russian convoys for the past two years, could only have been described as grey with occasional spots of fuel oil. Added to this there was my personal embarrassment of a red skin with a rash still behind my knees, and the occasional blot of yellow ointment on the odd mild burns, which could not be hidden by my socks and made me look as though I had caught the pox! All those Americans living in Charleston, although at war, were not being rationed on anything, they were still running cars and not even observing blackout. How could you explain seventeen Russian convoys, or living in starving Russia? I also felt tired and ill, a lot of us did. These well-dressed people seemed to be staring at me; I felt awful and just wanted to be home with Mum and Auntie.

Two days after this event I joined the sickbay parade but instead of seeing our sickbay tiffy I was sent to the US hospital were I stayed for a bit. I can't remember for how long, but I do remember the food was good and the showers had really hot water. The young doctor didn't laugh but suggested that it would be some months before my penis would be well enough to have more sex. I thanked him but was too embarrassed to tell him that I had not as yet had a chance to indulge. I also remember that he was concerned about my weight. My service certificate, I think, gave ten stone and a few pounds but after he had worked out the difference between his reading and what he saw on my records he concluded that I had lost well over a stone. Whilst I was in this US naval sickbay, the *Nigeria*'s crew were being drafted to other ships and establishments, but most to Blighty. Sadly, when I arrived back at the ship all my mess mates had gone. There was no reason, as far as I could see, why I should have been left with the ship; I was more than keen to get myself home. It seemed that the American doctor wanted me to stay whilst I put on a bit of weight; perhaps he was just short of patients.

There was a newly-formed group of local volunteers, mostly ladies, who liaised with the US armed forces to provide support to wounded servicemen. They had apparently been given my name. The first I knew about it was when I received an invitation to spend a weekend with a Mr and Mrs Russell Mallard and their young son Jimmy, who lived at Box 224 Summerville, South Carolina. I looked at my hair, eyes, and yellow spots and the state of my whites, thanked them and turned down the invitation.
The next thing that happened, was someone in the sickbay presented me with a set of car keys, and said: "A guy has left a huge blue 1941 Plymouth automobile in the sickbay lot for you with sufficient gas to get to Summerville (a distance of some twenty miles), and a telephone number, 5171." I felt I should go. I couldn't drive but we had a stoker still aboard who was a London fireman before joining the 'Andrew'; he was delighted to drive me up to Summerville as long as I paid his bus fare back and gave him my tot. Having obtained permission from the doctor to take the time off, and with one month's O/S's pay in my pocket, I arrived in style at the Mallards' bungalow (see Photos 56 and 57) without any luggage. The Mallards welcomed me with open arms, as did their dog. I immediately felt comfortable with them all. I didn't have to explain why I looked as scruffy as

Photo 56. The Mallards at their bungalow

Photo 57. The Mallard bungalow that winter

Photo 58. Jimmy, me and Trixy the dog

I did, because they didn't ask. I never brought up the subject. Neither did they. I gathered some weeks later that someone had spoken to the doctor. He had probably told them how touchy I was about my looks, especially about the loss of hair. I hoped he had not mentioned my private parts, which in those early days were both painful and embarrassing, especially when I woke up at night from a romantic dream.

I quickly got used to a way of life which included being introduced, by one of the Mallards, to a new pretty girl almost daily, this I found difficult to cope with. It seemed somewhat unfair. Still, I told myself, it was better than Arctic convoys. That first weekend I spent with the Mallards I was shown to my bedroom (complete with pyjamas) and the bathroom, which had a bath and shower – neither of which I ever used because of the bandages and ointment

Photo 59. Mallard family on bungalow steps

263

problem. I was introduced to their friendly black maid, it seemed exactly like a Judge Hardy/Mickey Rooney Hollywood family. I carefully folded up my smart borrowed pyjamas without thinking about the yellow ointment that might have been left on the inside. I had apologised for the grey colours of the tropical kit I was wearing, but pointed out that replacements were not available.

After a smashing short weekend, with good food and a good night's sleep, the entire family accompanied me back to the Navy yard in their posh Plymouth. They showed me where the bus stops were, both in Summerville and just outside the Navy yard. I was invited to come and stay for the whole of the next weekend, and I accepted. We were all instructed that under no circumstances were we to talk about 'Pedestal' to the locals and there would be strict censorship, so I couldn't write anything about the USA to Mum and Auntie. A couple of weeks after these stern instructions 'Pedestal' was shown in all the American cinemas. During my next visit to the Mallards young Jimmy told me that he had seen my ship at the movies.

We had crossed the Atlantic at 20 knots using the two inner propellers and trailing the outer propellers with their turbines under vacuum. Steam was kept in 'A' boiler room by using the lighting-up fuel pump. The 'tin fish' had blown up the main pumps. It was hoped that the 20 knots would be sufficient speed with zigzags to outpace U-boats should we accidentally encounter one carrying a spare torpedo. Despite our inefficient outer trailing propellers, the fuel had *just* lasted. The seawater in the five hundred ballast drums was drained into the bilges; the small amount of fuel oil left in the repaired tanks was used to pump this seawater, all the gash from the wreckage, and the bilges.

Charleston was a small peacetime yard, which had been expanded to assemble tank landing craft which came down the Cooper River in pieces on barges. The *Nigeria* was coded S182 and was the biggest ship and job they had ever handled. It took a long time for the yard to repair S182, about seven months. It would have been completed much quicker in a British naval yard, where they would have had all the necessary spare parts, but I felt this time lapse and Mrs Mallard saved my sanity and repaired my health. I was really pleased one day when she remarked: "Oh! Your front hair is growing again."

As all these repairs were going on and my personal health was improving steadily, I was bowled over at being promoted to L/S, at almost double my salary. At four dollars to the pound this was gratefully received. How I went from O/S to L/S without going through AB I don't know, although I had been recommended whilst I was a boy, a long time previously.

Photo 60. Anna Lula Meyers and me

The next time I visited the Mallards they had found me a pair of American 'bags', a sports jacket and a shirt and classy tie. I was introduced to Anna Lula Myers (see Photo 60) who became a firm friend. They took me everywhere and even taught me how to drive so that I could take a driving test for a temporary licence with the local police patrolman in the city square.

Although the ship was deserted of crew there were a considerable number of dockworkers aboard so we got used to going about our business and ignoring them, as we would have done in Blighty. Hot water was back in the showers, so I took myself along complete with soap and towel, waved my hand to the helmeted electric welder in the corner, stripped off my clothes, undid the gauze and bandage round my private parts, and showered – taking care not to look at the blue arc. Having finished I replaced my bandage and glanced across to the welder standing with her helmet off in the corner. "I'm sorry," I said, "I thought you were a man, welders are in Great Britain." "That's alright," she said, "that looks very painful, how did you do that?" "I didn't," I said, "a Jerry plane did." Then I ran away with a very red face.

Although *Nigeria* had shared about half-a-dozen operations in the Arctic with US naval units, which were definitely in the war, mainland America at that time did not appear to be at war. There were no shortages in the shops, and food and petrol were plentiful. Towns were not blacked out. However, it was obvious that the whole nation had the feeling that the Japanese had stabbed them in the back, because they had been attacked without the formalities of war being declared. What impressed me most of all about the Americans in those days was the speed with which the entire American nation came together in everything they did. It was obvious even in little Summerville that all the different women's organisations had come together and were working as one unit. This unit organised a trip for a friend and myself to Stone Mountain and Atlanta, Georgia.

I suppose it was very unfair of me but I always looked upon Mrs Mallard as a mother figure and therefore old, but she could not have been any more than about forty-four and she was always bright and jolly and incredibly kind. The Mallards kindly organised a trip for us all to go to the Everglades in Florida, where young Jimmy and I saw, while swimming, our first Copperhead snake. I also enjoyed a turkey and pumpkin pie party with the Mallards on Thanksgiving Day, even though I had helped to catch and kill the family turkey, following the instructions of their black maid. It was about this time my hair had grown and the yellow ointment had disappeared. We had not received any mail from England, and although I was having the time of my life, it was now about two and a half years since I had had home leave and I supposed I was suffering with homesickness. I enjoyed an evening meal with a lot of American service personnel given by the Robert Burns Club on Burns Night and it was there that I gave my very first after dinner speech of thanks, which I am sorry to say wasn't done very well.

More and more seamen were turning up to join the *Nigeria* from all sorts of places. It wasn't long before I lost my five-day week and we went back to watch keeping, which meant I had to do my share of shore patrol among the pubs, dance halls and nightclubs in Charleston, all so different from pleasant Summerville with its old plantation houses covered with wisteria and lichen and its modern bungalows like the Mallards'.

Just before we left South Carolina, Jimmy held a party for me, which was reported in the local press, in which it said: "In honour of L/S Jack Edwards etc. … with refreshment served buffet style … with Miss Anna Lula Myers presiding at the punch bowl." There were twenty-five guests present and twenty-five presents. The Americans were a really nice kind bunch, especially the Mallard family and Anna Lula.

The welding lady and I had got to know one another quite well; I think that, as she had seen a lot of me and knew more about my private life than I did of hers, she took the trouble to teach me to how to weld. She had only just completed a six-week electric arc-welding course, which had 'promoted' her from housewife to a dockyard welder!

My time in the US Navy yard in Charleston, South Carolina was coming to an end. As we were about to leave, our old friends arrived on the badly damaged *Aurora*, having suffered terrible casualties from fire in the forward part of the ship. Sailors had been unable to escape because extra clips secured the watertight doors to the upper deck against gun blast, and these clips could only be operated from the outside and there was no-one outside. This incident made me feel ashamed because of the fuss I had been making about a scorched dick. This reminded us that we would all soon be heading back to the horrors and deprivations of war.

I sadly said my last goodbyes to Russell Mallard, his wife and their son Jimmy, and of course Anna Lula and many others. I promised to write as soon as I got home, but sadly censorship did not allow this for another two and a half years, although they wrote to my mum. I had arrived in the USA dirty, hurt, and miserable, and left at the end

Photo 61. The Cooper River Bridge

of May 1943 clean, mended and with twenty-five presents. I had also been taught to drive and weld. I also took with me a great respect for the American people and a fondness for all the friends I made in Summerville, SC.

The sadness I felt because I was leaving this pleasant place was softened when I finally realised I was going home after being away for just on three years. Although she was not fully repaired it was good to feel the *Nigeria* picking up speed to 300 revolutions – about 30 miles an hour – off down the Cooper River bound for Norfolk, Virginia. (See Photo – Cooper River Bridge.)

After anchoring at Norfolk, Virginia, in June 1943, we spent almost a month practising our seamanship and gunnery. The whole of our below deck gunnery control system had been replaced and rewired by the Americans at Charleston, SC, following instructions and plans sent by the Admiralty. There were a huge number of mistakes on these Admiralty plans and we were constantly sailing from Norfolk to the nearby Fort Wool to test the corrections when we had made them. These mistakes had to be corrected before we attempted the Atlantic. As one of our temporary officers put it to me: "What with this muddled-up crew and this US electric wiring, if I pull the trigger for broadsides I'm more likely to flush the officers' toilets than hit the enemy." All this was delaying my home leave.

Eventually we risked the Atlantic but went to Greenock instead of Chatham. From Greenock we sailed to Sheerness and finally landed up in Chatham Dockyard on 23rd July 1943. Almost immediately most

of us were 'paid off' (a saying which has nothing to do with money!), packed our kitbags and hammocks, left the ship and boarded a blue lorry which ended up in the Chatham Barracks *Pembroke V*. I was so pleased to have left the *Nigeria* and all its bad memories.

Within a few days I was enjoying fourteen days' leave with Mum and Auntie but I was sorry to hear that Auntie had been in hospital to have an operation on her throat for cancer, a disease I had not heard of. I didn't tell my dear ladies about my burns but there was plenty of the Arctic to tell about. My brother was home at Winchmore Hill but my sister was

Photo 62. Mum and Me

away nursing at the RAF Emergency Hospital, Arlesey, Beds. I was very disappointed that I hadn't seen Joyce (although I didn't know it, she was locked up working on a top-secret assignment at Bletchley Park). Fourteen days soon disappeared and I was back at *Pembroke V* awaiting a draft to a new ship. It came: it was the *Nigeria* again with a brand-new captain and crew and we were going back to Russia. I just didn't believe it.

Rear Admiral Burrough who was on our ship on many of our engagements

XVI

Eastern Fleet

I was so unhappy; sadly here I was on the *Nigeria* again with seven hundred new shipmates, a *Nigeria* that held so many sad and terrible memories for me. I felt as if I had travelled over a million nautical miles aboard her since I first joined, when she was brand new, in 1940. In those three years with twenty other fifteen- to seventeen-year-old boy seamen, and after fighting nearly every one of those 1,095 days (mostly in Russia), thirteen of my friends had died before they had arrived at their eighteenth birthdays and I had witnessed most of them losing their last drop of blood. We had suffered losses of over ten percent of our main crew as well.

Most of the new crew had not experienced my sadness and were unable to understand the loneliness and my hidden terror. I felt utterly alone; there was no fifty-year-old Stripey or forty-year-old Tom to 'hold my hand'. Although I had had fourteen days' leave, I was not fully recovered from the ordeal I had been through.

Here I was again on my way to Archangel but this time being escorted by the aircraft-carrier HMS *Furious*. Her planes were protecting us whilst we were shelling the airstrip at Bergen, Norway. It was good to be doing well against the German aircraft for a change. This was the first time I had experienced carrier cover for an Arctic convoy; it helped a lot. The new crew were doing quite well but they would have to improve if we were to get home again. It reminded me of our first convoy to Nova Scotia back in 1940 when we were lucky to stay afloat. By the time my old crew had completed more than twenty convoys, mostly Arctic, we had achieved lightning reaction to crisis situations but still someone always died on these trips and sixty-eight unlucky lads had died on the 'Pedestal' convoy.

Now Germany had had to move most of its air force over towards Stalingrad, which left fewer planes in Norway. Malta and Gibraltar were now able to provide complete air cover to protect the Mediterranean, thanks to the success of 'Pedestal'. Rommel was in a tough position because he was tied down and not getting supplies through.

We were called off action stations after the shelling of the airstrip at Bergen and proceeded north until we had sighted our PQ Russian convoy. We were instructed by the convoy commodore to take up our position. I expected it to be the usual old routine but it didn't come because there were no air attacks. It was back to very cold weather on 19th February 1944, the usual harsh, nasty, cold Russian winter. The Germans were facing their third winter there and I began to realise that they were having a bad time of it and now they were much worse off than we were. Their supplies of food, medicine, cold-weather clothing and ammunition weren't getting through and they had little or no air backup. I believe the following day, 20th February, was the last day that the RN used the PQ number for a convoy up to Russia. HMS *Jamaica* joined our PQ and relieved us of convoy responsibility. Hip, hip, hooray and off we went to Greenock with promises of fourteen days' leave.

Within a couple of days we were back in Greenock happily moored alongside the wall. No-one mentioned anything about leave, fourteen days or even one single day, or an evening off.

Arriving back in a home port we would be expecting to receive our mail. These new members of the Navy had great hopes of this event; they would learn that mail was a rarity. I was still waiting for my nineteenth birthday congratulations from the previous May. I was certain that Mum, Auntie and family would not forget.

All mail (incoming and outgoing) could just disappear. (I had not been allowed to post anything from America to England.) Mail which did catch up with us was subject to heavy censorship and was usually very late. Some mail was seven fathoms down below! Letters which came from my sister and brother seemed to be a repeat of earlier ones as they were aware that they couldn't tell me where they were and what they were doing. This censorship was particularly tough on fathers. Some pages were smeared with black ink and sometimes pages had been removed, which made their letters confusing, and difficult to read.

I was requested to report to the commander's cabin. I suppose he was one of the few people who knew me and was aware that I had joined the ship as a boy.

"Well, Edwards," he said, "you're no longer an acting leading seaman. The Admiralty has confirmed the removal of 'acting' from your rank, you're now a fully blown killick. Our leading seaman, who is the ship's chief quartermaster at present, is leaving us for training purposes in the next few days and I'd like to offer you the job of CQM which would give you acting petty officer's pay. Are you interested?" I did not hesitate at all but before I could say anything he continued: "As an acting petty officer and CQM, you'd finally be able to become a fully qualified petty officer and of course there would be another pay increase." It was big money and an easy job for me. Before I could say anything, he continued, as if he wanted to get the matter finalised: "It's a straightforward job."

The CQM's action station position was at the wheel and I would have to steer the ship at the captain's commands, which was a straightforward and safe job. This was my birthday present! "I'll take it, Sir." "Good," said the commander, "you'll have time to run through the job with our CQM before he leaves the ship, and he'll explain the system."

Although I wasn't overcome with joy at the prospect of the job, the money was very good and the great advantage was that I would be using the POs' mess which had lockable toilets for privacy and also private showers where I could wash my feet, no more tide marks on my legs. That had to be good! All I had to do was to provide packaged food for the cooks to prepare for seven hundred ravenous, inexperienced sailors.

The commander's last words were: "Call in to see me this evening and pick up the keys." I met the departing L/S CQM and he took me on an inspection of the first store, which was full of heavy cardboard boxes, each containing twenty-four tins of Carnation milk. These were stacked from floor to deck-head in rows with just a few in a small heap and he opened one box to prove that it was full of tins. On one wall was a notice-board recording the number of cartons coming in and going out. The figure on the board also showed what was available after cartons had been removed; these figures were given to the paybob every day or so. The paybob was a commissioned officer, in our case a lieutenant commander. Apart from the stores he was responsible for money for our pay and so he was also called 'paymaster'.

There were six storerooms in all, five contained food, and one was full of engineering items such as clips, special cordage, skeins of rope and steel wires. The other contained Tate and Lyle golden syrup (in exactly the same tins as you see today), Fray Bentos corned beef, tins of jam (marked red or black), instant potato, powdered egg, custard powder and dried fruit and so on; in fact all the provisions that didn't need refrigeration.

We toured all the stores and the CQM explained how I could easily consult each notice-board for my report to the paymaster commander. He also advised me to remove the cases one by one starting on the top row, rather than stack by stack.

On completing our tour of the stores he left the ship. We raised steam and moved out into the sound and anchored where we were oiled by a fleet oiler and took on fresh water from a barge. We took on Arctic clothing for everyone to see in see-through cases from a large wooden drifter.

We finally weighed anchor and set sail for what we thought was to be Russia, bearing east into the Atlantic. It was on the first day out that I discovered to my horror that the cases below those I had been told to use first, which should have contained evaporated milk, were in fact empty. I informed the master-at-arms, who accompanied me on an inspection of the other food stores. We were amazed to discover that they too were full of empty cartons. Just as we were going to inform the commander, there was a 'Do you hear there, this is the captain'. He informed us that we were actually off to Ceylon and the cold weather clothing was just to deceive spies. Obviously we were, in contrast, going to be very warm. The crew were overjoyed at this news.

The master-at-arms said: "Oh my God, I hope they've got some Carnation milk in Colombo!" I thought originally that we would have a problem feeding seven hundred cold chaps short-term but now I realised that we had a greater problem feeding seven hundred warm chaps for a long journey.

The paybob immediately reacted by accusing me of appropriating the stores; that was silly and it didn't bother me: I knew that I hadn't had the time to organise a buyer with several heavy large lorries (which couldn't have been got alongside the wall), and there were no cranes. In fact I hadn't even had time to think about getting ashore to meet up with a girl (which would have been more important to this nearly twenty-year-old), let alone give her some several thousand stolen tins of evaporated milk.

The captain must have realised I couldn't be responsible for the losses and instructed the paymaster commander (who obviously hadn't been doing his job properly) to give him the files immediately and asked him why was he (the paymaster commander) not fully aware of the facts? There could only be one explanation: the departed killick must have sold off the stores over a period of time but he couldn't have done it all alone. How many of the crew had been taking tins of milk home when they went on leave?

If the killick had stolen the provisions then he had endangered a fighting ship; this was serious. This offence would have carried a severe penalty as it put the ship and crew at risk. He was sabotaging an HM ship whilst at war. The problem this presented was that others would be held to have neglected their duties as well, moving upwards to the paybob and even the captain, so everybody concerned was looking at one another. This was the moment that I became aware that I was in the middle of it. There was no easy scapegoat, so a conspiracy of silence was settled upon. The other ranks meanwhile were happy enough sailing into warmer waters and so far they were unaware of the shortages of food, which would become apparent all too soon.

Action had to be taken and it was up to commissioned officers to sort it out. The captain was quickest to react. He instructed the paymaster to gather in all food on the ship (officers' rations included) and goodies from anywhere, even the lifeboat provisions, and emergency rations which were mostly hardtack biscuits.

The small amount of fresh meat in the officers' wardroom refrigerators and fresh vegetables were set aside to make soup, which would be served with a hard biscuit. There was some flour which could be used to make bread, but there was nothing for pudding.

Breakfast was a little bit of bread served with a mug of tea with diluted Carnation milk. The midday meal was soup and water plus a hardtack ship's biscuit (a 4in x 4in x ½in thick tooth-breaker) that could only be broken by hitting it hard on the table. Teatime was lime-juice and hardtack, supper was soup and hardtack again, plus weak cocoa with watered-down milk. This regime started about the time we sailed past Nigeria, West Africa. Fortunately, fresh water was available in quantity. Bread, butter, jam, porridge and powdered eggs were rapidly running out.

The crew soon became aware of the changes of diet but they were hoping that we would put ashore soon and collect more provisions. Watching the reactions of the seven hundred-odd crew getting slowly hungry was going to be very interesting! The previous crew, and the Russians, had had months of these privations.

The non-commissioned officers swore all 'in the know' to secrecy. We could not put ashore for food because then the word would be out all over the Navy, as far as the admiral, that we had a PROBLEM! Money would rear its ugly head and add to the outstanding serious problems, as food would have to be paid for and the ship's accounts would show that all money for food had been spent earlier. As far as I knew nobody had sent any message back to Great Britain to suggest that the killick be detained.

I was so pleased to receive the captain's orders to move my gear over to the navigator yeoman's team, a real doddle of a clean job, backed up with the best position on the ship to sling my hammock, next to the junior officers' flat cabins.

It was a relief to have got away from the responsibility of six food stores below deck and the paybob.

I was beginning to enjoy being grown-up and taking responsible decisions. I had to keep reminding myself that I was still living on the *Nigeria* and was no longer a boy seaman, second class, and that, at that moment, the ship was not directly involved in the war.

We had been at sea for at least ten days since leaving the Firth of Clyde. During that time there had not been a single 'call to alarm' for enemy aircraft, surface vessels or U-boats. It appeared that our clever captain had made the right types of moves to hide his ship and crew from the enemy which was trying to destroy us. Anyone who was spying on us would have reported that we were off to the Barents Sea, or possibly Archangel, and would not have noticed that one night we altered course and turned to port at the Butt of Lewis and then turned to port again when we were well into the black Atlantic Ocean, before picking up a southerly course at our usual economical speed of 17 knots. We were told that we were heading for Colombo, Ceylon. As usual there were buzzes as to where our onward destination would be. The Indian Ocean could be a way to Burma, Malaya, Sumatra, Java, China, Australia or New Zealand. We had twelve New Zealand lads aboard manning a six-inch gun in 'X' Turret. I wasn't excited by any of these buzzes but I was interested to see where we would get to – although I was not looking forward to meeting up with the Japanese.

There were terrible stories going around the ship from some of the new crew. The worst was from a New Zealander who said that he knew of a ship which had been attacked by a Japanese pilot who landed his plane on the quarterdeck, climbed out, ran along the deck clutching a bomb and dropped it down the funnel directly into the engine room. We all laughed but a few of us felt it had a ring of truth about it.

It was getting really warm now and about the time we were passing the Cape of Good Hope (just about half way to Ceylon) we were issued with 'tropical whites', no doubt the captain wanted us to look good in whites that were 'whiter than white' when we arrived in Colombo to meet the dock commodore.

The new crew were a little confused. Here they all were on a ration of hard ship's biscuits and weak kye. They were now openly grumbling about it to the mess deck dodger.

Our Tannoy piped a: "Do you hear there, this is the captain speaking, we have to call in at Port Louis in Mauritius to land our master-at-arms and one rating. The ship's company will assume fifth degree of readiness, and anyone who is off watch and wishes to, may take shore-leave. Local currency is not available."

275

The upper deck was crowded with crew members as we were so interested in the sugar cane, there was miles and miles of it. It didn't look as if anyone lived there.

Everyone including me was over the moon. The ship arrived at about 0600 hours at a small sea wall and, waiting only long enough to deliver the jaunty and his young prisoner, who was dressed in his serge blues, complete with greatcoat and hammock. He then had to walk to town, which was three miles away, in a hot humid country! I wondered, what had he done to deserve such a punishment? This was the first time we had seen the jaunty in his whiter than whites, even his knees were white! The *Nigeria* then moored at Port Louis and having only a few hours there we rushed to the shops. The owners were as pleased as punch to see us and our lovely English money. I looked everywhere for something to buy and finally ended up in the shop where our married members had gathered and were buying up the local ladies' table cloths and so on. These two ladies were offering their handiwork at very reasonable prices; I thought what funny sailors! It seemed that sea-travelling customers were very rare and the ladies were making the most of it. All I could see worth buying were half a dozen Van Heusen separate stiff collars, a rare item, possibly left over from 1939 deliveries to that island. It was an unexpected interlude as we all enjoyed the relaxed atmosphere and a pleasant visit. We seemed to be far away from the war.

Before embarking the *Nigeria,* the crew and I could not miss seeing the paymaster, the master-at-arms and Captain S.M. Paton, RN returning together in a taxi followed by a large lorry. I wondered, after I arrived aboard, having seen the three of them in their taxi followed by a lorry if they had not pulled a fast one. The prisoner had been dumped at Port Louis to walk to a RN station, the nearest place to the UK from whence he would eventually be returned to the UK. It was just possible that there was a friend of our captain's at the RN station and that they had made up a reason for the *Nigeria* to stop here, where shopping for cheap food could be done quickly with no questions asked as to how it would be paid for, and no paperwork for the Navy. These three gentlemen ordered the duty watch to unload the contents of the lorry into our food lockers, thousands of hard, not quite ripe oranges and some thousand round, hard, two-and-a-half-inch Dutch cheeses with red rind, and hardtack ship's biscuits. Yes the jaunty had sorted his problem! The captain was soon to be relieved from his commission and he wasn't worried. The only man with a worry was the paybob.

It had taken twenty-six days to sail to Colombo from Greenock and the food situation had got worse. It was obvious that our captain, sensibly, was not interested in how or why this food shortage had happened, as some of his own staff appeared to be at fault. It looked as though the killick and his Chinese associate were going to get away with it. They were dead lucky.

My first job with the East Indies Fleet involved being collected by a young midshipman at Colombo. He was to turn up in charge of the pinnace to find me and we were to collect, from the admiral's chart office, all the charts that the *Nigeria* might need in the areas covered by the East Indies Fleet. We might sail between the East Tasman Sea, South Australia, to approximately the Arabian Sea. He was late. I was reminded of my trips in this same craft in Russia and thought of those sad laddies. It had been approximately thirty days' sailing from the other side of the world and my war was 'turned off' now.

The sun was shining and it was lovely and quiet; thirty days and no-one had died. *Nigeria* was laying off about four miles out. Standing there waiting I noticed *Nigeria*'s sailors collecting boxes of tins of evaporated Carnation milk and loading them into a duty tender for the ship. The killick in charge came over and said "'Ere Jack, come and look at this" and led me into a large cave that, over hundreds of years, had been shaped to have almost vertical walls. At the end of the cave, built from heavy cardboard cases holding two dozen tins of milk, there was a two-room dwelling with a small window; both rooms had open doorways. The first room had a table and a small chair at which sat a middle-aged man, and in the other room there was a double bed on which lay a 'tart' (as we called them) who looked old enough to be my mother. "There," said the killick, "isn't she lovely, don't you want to have a go?" "No thank you," I said, quickly moving out of the cool cave, "I've got to pick up the pinnace." It was growing up, I supposed, but it reminded me of my mother's last words to me as I left home in 1939, all those years ago.

When I came out into God's clean sunshine I found my midshipman looking very worried. "Good morning. What's your name and where's the navigation place?" I asked with a smile. He looked as young as me and I took an instant liking to him and we settled down well together. When I had told my mess mates earlier that I was going ashore to collect charts from the Admiralty building, "Lucky chap," they all said, "it's full of luscious Wrens". When we got into the building the entire place was manned by very well-dressed young Sinhalese men and women.

Having collected our charts, we partly filled the main cabin of the pinnace with them. I checked with the midshipman that we had all the necessary things for a safe journey and the chart for the route we were about to attempt. The only hazard was a small rocky area that was only visible at low tide and close to where the *Nigeria* was anchored. The midshipman had passed this area when the tide was higher on his way ashore that morning.

The young man took the steering and I let go the mooring ropes as he started the engines and off we went. I made myself comfortable in the crew seat breathing in heavenly fresh air. I looked at the 'captain and navigator' and saw him look at his chart and promptly went back to admiring the scenery. We had been travelling for some time when we came to a noisy and sudden stop and the engines were not working. Looking over the side it was easy to see that the pinnace was stuck, hard and firm, sitting on the top of a beautifully smooth, level rock about two hundred yards wide. It was one of a group called Powder Rocks which were shown on the chart. Waiting for the tide to go down further in the next two hours or so would allow all the world (and seven hundred-odd sailors from HMS *Nigeria*) to observe our forty-foot wooden boat with two handsome sailors waiting for the 0600 hours tide to allow them to float off. I thought, I bet the *Nigeria*'s crew had watched and heard us get into this mess; the officer of the watch had already known first where these rocks were, possibly checking them by Asdic and using Cockhat fixing every hour. He wouldn't want *Nigeria* floating over them! Just as these thoughts were going through my head, the Morse code message came. Neither of us could read it; the *Nigeria* duty signalman must have known that only a signalman could read at that speed. They were playing games with us both, the midshipman knew that too. I suggested that we pencilled a Morse code message on a piece of paper, by using the pinnace's code book (see Figure 47. My Signal Book) and let the signalman read it as we sent it. The middy was impressed by this solution. We sent: "Run aground, not sinking, engine failed." This resulted in the officer of the watch sending the bosun of the watch in the motor cutter to look at it all. "Idiot," said the killick. Seeing no panic, he said: "I'll go back to the officer of the watch and will be back as soon as I can. You're here for the night by the look of it. I'll bring you both an oilskin (raincoat) next time." It was not long before the cutter returned. "The officer of the watch has ordered that you two idiots will not be relieved but will remain with the boat through the night. Once an hour during the night *Nigeria* will send a searchlight signal to illuminate you, and you two will reply to that signal flash by lighting the boat's lantern. Here are two spare candles and a box of pusser's matches. Don't lose the matches, don't make any noise, don't fall overboard and don't fall asleep." The "goodnight" was accompanied by loud guffaws.

We had a few hours of daylight remaining before we had to stay awake for about eight dark hours, so it seemed a good idea to try

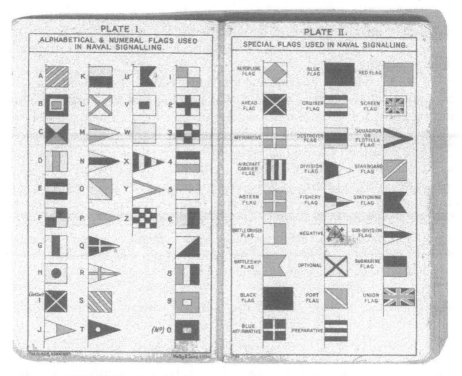

Figure 47. Signal Book

to sleep on the only small spaces available, one aft and one on the foredeck. I felt it was a good idea to tie our wrists to a fitting as we could never swim the four miles to the beach if we fell overboard.

The afternoon rest wasn't restful at all; it was not comfortable in the small areas we were using and I was pleased when we were sitting upright with our oilskins folded as cushions. I started the small-talk by volunteering to take responsibility as I had gone off the 'Andrew' anyway. The middy thanked me but laughed as he told me that his grandfather was an admiral. His father and mother had pushed him off to naval college at the early age of twelve and he had hated it. He would stand the Navy for the war, then he would buy himself out at the age of twenty. He knew just what he wanted to do with himself. He said: "The captain won't say a thing in case my grandfather hears about it and bad reports are not what grandfather wants to hear." I asked him if he had done this purposely. "No, I didn't do it on purpose, it was a genuine mistake, so don't say a word and you'll get off." I had made a life-long friend!

It was an uncomfortable night. The only comfortable cabin was full of expensive charts which made it impossible to find a 'lay down' spot for either of us, so we spent the night sitting on the low cabin roof. I recall it was a pleasantly warm night. The pair of us must have been seen clearly by anyone moving on *Nigeria*'s upper decks and, of course, we waved into the searchlight and felt silly waving our candle lantern in reply.

We were collected at 0800 by the daily watch and towed back by the motor cutter – I was amazed that nothing leaked – and we were hoisted aboard. It took about a week to repair the damage and nobody said a word to either of us; the midshipman was right.

Before Chatham Dockyard returned the completely repaired *Nigeria* back to the Royal Navy, they had installed an extra new type of press-button telephone system. This system meant that, by pressing a button, any crew member could contact any executive officer, including the admiral, whether in his cabin or at his action station. Once fitted, it was marvellous; it saved hours as it gave instant contact with the officers, but it was soon discovered that it could not be turned off. It had been designed for emergency situations.

Two days after we had arrived in Colombo the whole crew, including officers, were offered the delight of tropical food consisting of cheese and biscuits followed by fruits. This meant that we were going to be offered this fare for many more days. I had the pleasure of seeing this food being delivered to the nearest messes. Food was normally placed in special heavy rectangular tins, with two handles, about 18in x 12in and 3in deep to hold meat, gravy, potatoes and so on. These tins were apparently purpose-made for this new food. It looked as though someone was delivering a number of neatly packed dirty tennis balls. The first trayful was placed on 20 Mess table and all the sailors just looked in amazement. The second tray was taken to 22 Mess table with the same result. You must understand that all those amazed sailors had just sunk their grog. When the tray arrived at 24 Mess table, one crew member said "what's that?" and another picked up a cheese and bowled it like a cricketer up the table saying "catch – here's your dinner". It wasn't long before all the mess members, some thirty-odd men, were heaving oranges and cheeses backwards and forwards like a lot of schoolkids, but none seemed to be eating. The situation did not get any better as far as the crew were concerned with the exception that Carnation milk had been supplied from Colombo. It meant better cups of tea.

We never knew who the clever chap was who 'sussed out' that you could use the executive phone and not be traced by anyone. I suppose the paybob was the first victim when he was called dead at midnight and heard "Woof, woof, you bastard" which resulted in his name changing to 'Paybob the dog-biscuit man'. The captain found out that more of the new food went down the 'gash' into the sea than down the crew's throats, so he ordered the paybob to do something about it.

The following day the paybob ordered everyone to clear the lower decks at 1100 hours to discuss meals. "Good," said the crew's lower-deck lawyers, "we'll tell him it's unfit for human consumption, not ripe, the crew will suffer collywobbles, and so on." There are rules when a senior officer calls everyone to the quarterdeck to discuss a problem, or discuss anything. We all got there just before the due time (beware if you are late). At 1100 a bugler gave one G blast, then it was the senior officer's say. This morning it was the paybob who said immediately: "Stand at ease."

He looked angular and menacing. He snapped his fingers which brought on a corporal marine carrying a small table, followed by a midshipman with a tray which was placed on the table. On the tray was a large bone-china plate and on the plate was a complete ball of cheese and an orange. The paybob lifted the best wardroom dainty knife from the tray and, with the speed of a skilled surgeon, removed the rind from the cheese. The complete silence was broken for just a second as someone exclaimed "Ahaa" – I think for this super piece of acting, as we would all have needed hacksaws rather than dainty knives to cut through that cheese's armour plating – and then to our amazement he produced a thin slice of cheese. The paybob then completed another 'miracle' with the wardroom knife by cutting a 4in x 4in x ½in hardtack biscuit into two pieces vertically (4in x 4in x ¼in). Then he peeled the orange (no-one had been able to do this before, let alone with a tiny knife) and the inside miraculously fell into segments. Next, with his little finger cocked, he daintily placed the thin sliver of dry cheese on a section of biscuit (which must have been 'dunked' for hours to soften it) and began to chew, without water. He followed this by eating a couple of sections of green orange. I heard a brave lad mutter "de-ee-licious". When he finished there was complete silence. I felt like clapping. To this day I cannot ever remember seeing such a brilliant performance. A complete victory for the paybob!

The next statement the paybob made seemed to cement his victory: 'Would any rating like to taste this wholesome food?' There were no takers. We were then given a short talk on cold food in the tropics and how good it was for your health. He then went on to make it clear that anyone found wasting this wholesome food during wartime would be brought before the Commander's Defaulters. Then, once again, he asked, very, very slowly: "Has anyone got any questions?" There was complete silence. The paybob ordered the jaunty to dismiss the entire ship's company. The paymaster disappeared down the quarterdeck gangway to the wardroom, possibly for a couple of gins!

It was clear that the entire crew had surrendered, so they would eat the balls: that is, except for a half-dozen stubborn fellows who continued barking "woof, woof" down the executive telephone, which resulted in the commander placing a marine sentry on it.

We were settled down in Trincomalee by early April 1944 and had officially joined the sizeable Eastern fleet based there. I think perhaps I was going slowly into a religious state, I had just had the hell side of life and now I was in the heaven side. If not, whatever was Trincomalee if not heaven? This magnificent natural harbour was protected by a steel net from Foul Point to Uppervelli to prevent midget submarines entering with suicide bombers swimming to attack our ships. Small mines were also dropped by us every half-hour to deter sharks and unwelcome Japs. This harbour was populated with turtles and friendly tropical fish of different colours and shapes (I called them football fish because they were striped like footballers' jerseys). Above the water were attractive small islands, sandy beaches and green scenery, all crammed with wildlife and birds. Such a contrast to the wastelands of the frozen North. It was called 'The Second Paradise'. I called it 'My First Paradise'!

One day when we were at our usual anchorage in Trinco and everything looked beautiful as all the members of the fleet basked in the afternoon sun, I was called by the Tannoy to the commander. "Ah! Acting Petty Officer Edwards," said the commander, "I want you to pass 'Boat sailing handling' for you to consolidate your promotion." "Yes, Sir," I answered. "I also want you to contact the duty cook to make you enough sandwiches and other food to last two of you for two whole days and a night, as soon as possible. Pick either a petty officer or a killick to teach you to sail, and I want to see you sailing the whaler back satisfactorily." "Yes, Sir," I said, with a big grin. There was only one sailor on this ship to do that; he was a killick called Gus. Gus's father had taught him to sail in an old merchant ship's lifeboat fitted with a small section of a railway line to act as extra weight to the keel, on the east coast off Great Yarmouth.

Gus was delighted to be asked and he collected a clean galvanised bucket full of corned dog sandwiches and a two-gallon glass carboy of watered-down fruit juice. We loaded the whaler with our oilskins and our towels, cleared with the officer of the watch and sailed off at 0800 hours having had as much breakfast as we could find. Trincomalee harbour is roughly ten miles by ten miles and we had almost travelled that distance in the whaler on the first day, Friday. Our only instruction of 'don't do' was not to go ashore anywhere on the island or land if it was occupied by local islanders or RN Wrens. That seemed to be easily understandable.

There was a small squarish island of about two acres. This island was joined to the mainland by a rocky bridge leading to a sizeable building which was used as an RN 'Wrenery'. We sailed slowly past the island in the gentle wind, it was a quiet place, and sitting down in the whaler we could not see over the raised rocky platform at the end of the island.

I was at the tiller and Gus was moving about the boat, there was nothing else to do. I was doing all that was necessary to keep the whaler moving slowly. Gus stepped up onto the gunwale, supporting himself by the mast stays and, standing on his toes, he peered over the edge of the rock platform. He then came down with a crash and whispered "Ere, it's all bare arses!" He was a very rough matelot! I let go of the tiller and climbed up onto the gunwale, grabbed the mainstays, stood on my toes and then I saw them, but only just. We had by now lost the wind. We had turned and were now lying 'in irons' and would not be able to sail away quickly. It was obviously a Saturday-off day and I guess it was about 1100. The Wrens were lying face down on large, posh bath-towels, sun bathing. Our boat was behind them and we hadn't been seen yet. I had never seen a naked woman, other than in a magazine, and here I was counting twenty bottoms! I noticed that they were all older than me and I wondered why they were sun-bathing together. I got down, it was too much to take in all at once! I looked at Gus and put my forefinger on my lips indicating to him to be quiet and come down. Gus looked at me as though I was out of touch with reality, then without any warning he shouted at the top of his voice: "I'm not a bum man, give me tits any time!" Well, I should have known pandemonium would break out – and it did! The Wrens all got up and saw us, most of them grabbed their large towels, except for two or three who smiled at us! So I made the most of a few moments of "tits" and other bits and pieces that I had never seen before in my 'innocent' youth!

We were met by the officer of the watch when we returned in the whaler. The officer of the watch was my young midshipman friend and he gave me this message: "The commander asked me to tell you that he's been observing your sailing with his telescope and that he's very pleased with your performance." He then said, with an ear-to-ear grin: "The commander will be able to see you and Gus in person when he talks to you about another matter at Commander's Defaulters at 0900 next Monday." He then whispered "it's OK" with a smile. On the Monday I received the commander's congratulations for having passed and Gus got a "Well done" from him for his contribution. "However," he said, "I failed you both on one point; you did not know about Section No. 13 (Admiralty Regulations for small sailing

---

H.M.S. "Nigeria".

2nd March, 1944.

With reference to K. R. & A. I. Appendix XII
part 22A it is hereby certified that, Jack A. Edwards,
Acting Leading Seaman (Ty), Chatham JX.163760.

- (a) is considered competent to handle a boat
       under power, sail and oars, and
- (b) has satisfactorily completed, unaided, the
       task of splicing a thimble into the eye of
       a 3½" wire.

COMMANDER.

for CAPTAIN (Absent on duty)

Figure 48. Boat handling certificate

craft) which states that any person can contact the admiral's secretary for the serial number shown on the whaler's mainsail which enables anyone to identify which ship the whaler is registered under, K2 = *Nigeria*." At the Commander's Defaulters, Gus and I were found guilty of "disrespectful behaviour unbecoming of naval personnel", which resulted in us being fined two weeks' pay (for me, £18), and two weeks' loss of liberty.

When I complained to my mess deck pals one of them said: "Well, look at it this way, at almost ten bob per tit I think you got a bargain!"

The first job I got as an acting PO was to set up *Nigeria* with kayak patrols. These were not popular with the men although it only meant that a rating had to paddle a kayak slowly round the ship for a two-hour period on water that was invitingly warm on a warm night (possibly in the 70s Fahrenheit), not what you could in any way call hard work. You were on your own and that seemed to be the problem. I found this out when I gave the lads instructions on 'when and how' it was to be done.

The purpose of this new security procedure was to protect the ship from Japanese swimmers attaching explosives to our engine bulkhead. Our job was easy. All we had to do was find out if something was wrong, raise the alarm, then try to prise the device off or catch the saboteur before he could detonate the explosive.

To illustrate how easy it was to do, I volunteered to do the first watch. I found out what an unpleasant job it was. The kayaks gave you a trapped feeling (not like being free as in an Indian canoe) because you were tied into the kayak at the waist. Looking up, as you moved around the ship with your shoulder almost touching the ship's curved side, you could not see anybody looking down and it was difficult to see if you were being followed (you felt that you were being followed) and as it was always during the night and dead quiet, any splash and your imagination told you that a Japanese was about to sweep you into the sea as he capsized your tiny craft. It was a creepy feeling and very unnerving. Two hours was too long to be doing this job so I changed the routine to a team of four paddlers each operating for an hour, so that one paddler patrolled for only one hour. At the end of the hour he was replaced by another paddler, and he then joined the other two men on the upper deck for a rest. The other two would be positioned one at the bow and one at the stern. As the paddler passed below he could look up to see his two mates in these two positions. He was, however unable to see either of them when he passed under the bulging centre part of the ship. So that these four ratings could wander around the deck, they wore plimsolls so they didn't wake the sleeping crew below. They agreed to whistle quietly to one another which would keep them in touch and not annoy the off-watch crew.

It was some months before the admiral decided to call off this very unpopular chore as we had never had such a device attached to us. We guessed that the Japanese had been driven back so far from Trincomalee that there was little or no chance of such attacks being launched. I for one was pleased to see it go.

Mail turned up unexpectedly and one day I received a sad letter from the wife of an ex-*Nigerian* who I had sailed with on the Russian missions. The last I saw of him was during my brief Chatham stay when I visited him in hospital and met his wife. During that visit someone came round selling Irish Sweepstake tickets. They were too expensive for me to buy but he purchased one. In her letter she told me that her husband, who was about thirty-eight years old, had died. She reminded me about the Irish Sweepstake and told me that her husband had won £12,000 (a huge sum in those days) and the poor fellow was so shocked at winning that he had suffered a heart attack and died. So she became a widow and rich woman all at once! I had been warned about gambling by Mum and Auntie and how dangerous it was! When I told my mess mates about it they suggested that I wrote to her straight away and proposed marriage!

We were to take part in a carrier raid, code-named 'Operation Cockpit', on Sebang, north-west of Sumatra. We were to be part of the covering force for the carriers which were to fly off air-strikes. We left Trincomalee during the second week of April 1944. The raid was to be carried out by two task forces. We joined with the first one in company with HMS *Queen Elizabeth*, *Valiant*, and *Richelieu*, all battlewagons, together with cruisers HMS *Newcastle*, *Ceylon*, *Gambia* and *Tromp*, plus about eight destroyers. I was very content to be with such a powerful force. Two ships, *Richelieu* (French) and *Tromp* (Dutch), were new to me. The Frenchman looked huge, whereas the Dutchman was clean and unusually elegant for a light cruiser. There was another reason that I was not alarmed; that was that the second task force joined company with us comprising HMS *Renown* (battlewagon) and the carriers HMS *Illustrious* and USS *Saratoga*. The *Saratoga* seemed huge to us (I was to spend a couple of days on her later on). Also in this group was HMS *London*, a heavy cruiser (with which we had carried out convoy duty in the past) and about ten destroyers (four British, two US, a Dutchman, plus others). We were well off for admirals. Admiral Somerville was known to us from his earlier exploits. Rear Admiral Reid was also known and liked, Admiral Moody was unknown to me.

This would be my first tangle with the Nips and I had blood on my mind; I was just hoping that it wouldn't be mine! It was at about 1430 hours on the second day that nearly all of the ship's company

Photo 63. The Richelieu

congregated to look at a blue whale which was 'blowing' as it surfaced (one of the biggest blows in the business!). Everyone yelled "Thar she blows".

This was one of the largest mammals on the planet. An adult could be as much as thirty yards in length and weight up to a hundred and fifty tons, equal to the weight of twenty-four elephants. I had never come across this species of whale before during my twenty-odd Arctic convoys.

We all became aware that the large *Richelieu* was exceedingly close to the whale. This stationary blue giant would be unable to get underway again until it recharged its lungs. The Frenchman's crew must have seen it but seemed not to realise that the whale was stationary. When they did it was too late to take evasive action and they collided. The bow of the *Richelieu* at a distance looked like a very sharp plough, the poor whale was cut almost in half. Thankfully it must have been killed outright. There was blood absolutely everywhere, spreading into the ocean, staining the sea red, an awful sight. Quite a lot of us found it very distressing. I never did find out whether the Frenchman had been damaged. Some said it was a bad-luck omen. What a shame they didn't have Asdic, or did they?

When we arrived at Sebang there were salvos already being fired by the battlewagons and our cruisers had joined in.

There were a selection of planes, Avengers, Hellcats and Corsairs, but the Japanese did not seem to be putting up much resistance. There were almost two days of shelling and air attacks. Our ship saw only two Mitsubishis, and they made little or no effort to attack us, and to me they seemed so slow when compared with German planes. I was amazed how easy it had been for us.

On the first day of May 1944 I was informed by my commander that the USS *Saratoga* had just had installed British Radar 273 units. As far as I could understand, our radar was miles ahead of anything our American friends had, although we had shared with them all our secrets to enable them to manufacture their own units as they wished, to suit their gunnery. Our 273 was good and easy to understand and I had been using it for about two years in Russia. This situation can be likened to a modern young lad a few years ago setting up the TV, video and so on whilst his dad could only just about manage to switch the TV on or off and change from programme to programme. I had had training and I found the system easy to use at my action station. The commander of the USS *Saratoga* was sending a doryboat to collect me at 0800. I was stared at a bit by *Nigeria*'s crew as two cheerful Yanks and I drew away from the ship. Having spent nearly seven months in and out of an American hospital I did not feel in any way embarrassed. As we approached the *Saratoga* she looked huge, especially as the doryboat was so small.

This was the first time I had gone aboard a carrier; it was like entering a new world. My guide and I entered into an arched opening about ten feet up, and climbed up stairways until we reached the upper deck which was a long way up from the sea below. We emerged into the open air where there was a two HA four-inch gun mounting. This led to the fantastic flight-deck which was out of bounds. Whilst I was craning my neck trying to see all of that enormous flat top I could see their commander coming towards us from the pointed end on his Vespa-type motor-scooter. He was both taller and wider than me and was an impressive-looking individual. I found him pleasant too. As soon as he had dismounted from his machine he asked "Why have they sent you?" I simply said: "Because I've used 273 for over two years in Russia." He answered with a smile: "I understand, let's go." We went below to their transmitting station where I met the TS crew. I spent the rest of the forenoon easily answering their many questions. Sometimes I told them of circumstances in Russia and on 'Pedestal' where we had to make decisions to overcome a special type of attack using this radar equipment. They listened in complete silence; they had obviously never been in such circumstances.

We then adjourned for our midday meal. The mess deck was like a modern stainless-steel kitchen. I was given a stainless-steel tray moulded into compartments to contain a very large dinner. All you had to do was to ask for what you wanted and the cooks gave it to you. The many cooks were all in whites with tall hats, just like the one the Russian dentist had worn when he filled my bad tooth with gold. I followed my new-found friends with my tray as it was filled with chicken (I guessed about half a chicken), big green peas and sweet potatoes, also apple pie and ice-cream (a whole half-pint carton of it!), with a 'Coke' – named by the RN 'Jap juice'. The TS crew had found a group of tables and chairs and invited me to join them. Nobody offered to say 'Grace' so I got stuck in straight away. I had told them lots and lots about Russia, 'Pedestal' and my stay in the USA. I didn't find it difficult to eat all that wonderful food. As I finished my apple pie and ice-cream I put my hand up. "Sir," I said, "is it possible to have another carton of ice-cream?" "Yes," he said, "but you've just eaten a whole half-pint carton." I told him that the last time I had eaten ice-cream was when I was with the Mallards and before that when I was fifteen, and that was when I had joined the RN in 1939. "You can't get ice-cream anywhere at home now and we've never had it on the menu on any HM ship," I told him. There was a long silence and then one of the younger TS operators said: "You've been at sea since then?" They all stared at me as I ate my second helping. I wasn't too bothered as I had my eyes shut most of the time! Before retiring with the TS crew, I took the time to shake hands with the six white-clad cooks and thanked them for the best meal I had had for years. The captain thanked me for my time and left me with the TS chaps, to discuss communication and aircraft matters, utilising their Perspex information chart. It did not take long to complete the afternoon session. They asked if there was an agreed attack word and I told them that we used Tally-Ho as it was easy to understand. They tried it out and the afternoon was a hoot hearing an American from the Bronx and a drawl from a Southern Carolina fellow trying to sound like an upper-class Englishman on the fox-hunting field. It took time and we all became good friends. They appreciated it when I told them how grateful I was to the Mallards of Summerville for their kindness.

Back on the *Nigeria* the commander asked me how I had got on. I told him that I had had two whacks of ice-cream. I don't think that told him much! In time I was given a good report by someone on the *Saratoga*.

The *Nigeria* was to have joined HMS *Illustrious* and USS *Saratoga* and her three US destroyers on a bombing raid on the harbour at Surabaya. Two days before they departed we discovered that we were unable to use our steering which meant that we had to remain in Colombo whilst repair work was carried out. We found out after the raid that the two ships ended up in Exmouth Bay, North-West Australia. We were all sad that we had been unable to enjoy that. (See Photo 64 – USS Saratoga.)

The oranges and the cheeses were now forgotten as the normal time for re-provisioning the ship had come around. Shopping for food was done locally but it brought its own problems. The first thing we noticed was the bread; it had grey circles in each slice and when we asked why these were there we were told that one of the hazards of the tropics was weevils. To start with we were fussy and picked out these marks (about the size of a new 5p piece) but when people said "oh, what the hell, they're dead" and "they are extra protein and they haven't done us any harm" we forgot about them and ate the whole slice without thinking.

Another problem that came onto the ship with these new provisions was cockroaches. I had seen the occasional one or two when we were in the Arctic but these here were pretty numerous. They scuttled about in and out of small crevices but the main problem was that when we fired our guns, especially a broadside, they were shaken out of their hidey-holes, particularly in the galley where they would drop into the

Photo 64. USS Saratoga

food, especially into the soup. Again, at first we fished them out and put them on one side, but after a while we forgot about fishing about and just ate the soup, cockroaches and all. The captain decided that we should try to eliminate the cockroaches and issued a promise that there would be a reward for the sailor who invented the best 'cock-a-trap'. This gave crew members plenty to think about in off-watch moments. Some ideas were quite clever. I remember seeing one device which was a glass container on which had been placed a bit of jam; the device had an intricate cats-cradle made from string which the cockroach could climb across to get down to the jam but there was no way out!

Even worse were the rats. Again I had seen the odd one on the *Nigeria* earlier but because they were a rarity some sailors almost made pets of them but now they were not easy to ignore.

XVII

Whispering Death

We spent the whole of May 1944 in Colombo which was for me a bore. I was not allowed leave in that large town. We just worked on the steering which involved my department and me as chief quartermaster. Whilst we were there the fleet sailed to Surabaya and then it went on for a short leave in Exmouth Bay (North-West Australia) because they had 'drunk dry' the six fleet oil-tankers and a whole water-tanker. Whilst this tanker filling was done they had local leave, lucky fellows!

We returned to 'Trinco' (as we called it) where we had some relaxation. It was nice and clean compared to Colombo. We also felt safer amongst the Sinhalese, whereas there was an uncomfortable tension between the Tamils and Sinhalese in Colombo. In this heaven we could swim and I was able to dive without any equipment to observe the coloured fish. Other crew members didn't seem to want to fish. What would you do with a fish if you caught it? You couldn't get it cooked! Once every six months we managed to see the latest cinema film arrival, a five-year-old 'flick' at a cinema show, either on board or at the shore canteen. The shore canteen was a very large bamboo building with what looked like banana leaves serving as roof tiles.

Each week we were allowed one journey ashore on our motor cutter. To get this trip we obtained a ticket which entitled us to the trip and a half-pint bottle of beer that looked like English beer. It took half an hour to get there in the cutter, half an hour in the queue to pay for the cooled bottle, half an hour to find a seat to drink it and chat, and sometimes there was a half an hour wait for the return trip in the cutter. I found that a bore. At least when I went to the 'flicks' it sometimes had the Pathé or Movietone news. With our rudder and steering sorted out, and having returned to 'Trinco', we found out that my newly-made friends aboard the *Saratoga* were off to the Pacific with an escort of three US destroyers. We were in time to wave them 'goodbye and good luck' as they sailed away. The buzz was that some of our cruisers were going with her; for some silly reason I hoped it would include us.

On 20th June 1944 we sailed from 'Trinco' in company with our sister ships *Ceylon* and *Gambia* to look after the two battlewagons, *Renown* and *Richelieu*, together with the carrier HMS *Illustrious* accompanied by six destroyers, for an attack on Port Blair in the Andaman Islands. We all settled down to what became repetitive 'shoot-ups'. First our air attacks, followed by our battlewagon and cruisers' broadsides and salvos. All the Japs could cough up as opposition on these occasions were one to three old Mitsubishi torpedo planes which were unable to keep up with our aircraft. The Japanese ground defence seemed to either lack anti-aircraft guns or couldn't use them. They had been there since 1942, so perhaps they were not receiving supplies of shells; it was a bloody long way from Japan! There were lots of rumours going around on this subject whilst we were in Port Blair. We were very nervous about enemy submarines, which were thought to be ex-German U-boats. How had they got there and where had they refuelled? Where were they getting their fuel from now? The only submarine I ever saw was a Yankee one. The Americans had taken to subs like ducks to water and were now expert submariners.

Admiral Somerville's report that he had caught the Japanese commander "with his kimono up" could have been said of all five trips covered by the *Nigeria* at this time.

Corsairs were flown by a single pilot seated exactly in the centre of the plane, behind the wings. This was a gull-wing aeroplane powered by a Pratt & Whitney radial engine. The RN pilots flew Corsairs which were obtained under 'lease-lend' agreement with the USA. The Corsairs had to have sixteen inches cut from each wing, so that they could fit into our smaller height RN carrier hangars. The US Navy did not like the early Corsairs due to 'landing on' difficulties from the straight approach (as we knew on that day), because they could not see the flight-deck and so only used the early version on shore bases. The RN pilots solved the 'landing on' problem by using a curved approach whilst in the air before 'landing on', but some of the pilots didn't always get it right. Once in the air these planes were very good at what they did.

The Japanese called this plane 'The Whispering Death' because it was so quiet on approach. The Japanese did not have a sophisticated radar system to adequately warn them of enemy aircraft. It was said that every eighty-two minutes one Corsair was completed, or three hundred a month. Had the Japanese known this fact for just that one type of plane surely they would have thrown in the towel!

We understood that Japs could keep themselves well hidden and with good telescopes count the number of Corsair pilots who appeared to be committing Hara-Kiri every time they unsuccessfully tried to land on their British carrier and then report these as their successes to their High Command. I can remember that there were twenty-one Corsair losses on one occasion. It became clear that whoever was going to win this war was going to have to deliver supplies, especially fuel, and that those supplies also took more fuel to deliver.

We returned to 'Trinco'. Our old captain left us and was replaced by Captain H.A. King, RN, DSO, a man I took a liking to straight away. We were told to get ready for another similar job expected to be on or about 20th July.

On 20th July we were on course for Sebang again for the fifth time in company with HMS *Victorious, Illustrious* and with the battleships *Renown* and *Richelieu*, together with the cruisers *Ceylon* and *Gambia*, plus about eight destroyers.

As usual these trips were pleasant until we arrived at the shooting. Meanwhile I tried to spend as much time as I could in the sun to get a suntan but I could not get brown. I was slowly going yellow and so were the rest of the crew. We were having to queue weekly for yellow Methogere tablets to keep malaria away. As one rating said: "We all look like a bunch of bloody Japs."

To keep our arrival a surprise, we always took a different approach and flew off our aircraft early to catch them unawares. The Japanese did not have any sort of radar, as far as we knew, so they were forced to depend on binoculars, good eyesight and telescopes. On 25th July we settled down to our usual routine of 'open fire' which was not only annoying to the Japs but also shook dust and cockroaches loose in our mess decks. With two aircraft-carriers and two battleships to look after, our destroyers were tied down. To my delight I was pleased to learn that our captain had been given a chore which was normally undertaken by a destroyer and it couldn't have been given to a better bloke. Our admiral had ordered us to search, at speed, for one of our pilots who had come down by parachute. As helmsman, I was ordered to increase our speed to 23 knots by means of extra revolutions on the two engines. This meant that we were slowly pulling away from the fleet and were getting closer to land. The masthead lookout was ordered up. Everyone aboard knew it was up to 'all' lookouts, but of course everybody else on deck was looking too. It was the masthead lookout who saw the pilot first. He was almost straight ahead and was found easily on this clear day with the line of his parachute helping us to identify his position. The pilot was sitting on an inflatable raft which was yellow. As I expected, the order came up, "Full ahead,

293

both engines". I was now an important part of the following actions because I was at the wheel. *Nigeria* was now moving very fast. The masthead lookout now called our attention to a small fast-moving Jap boat fitted with a heavy machine-gun which was heading towards the pilot. We knew that the Japs were intent on capturing the pilot at whatever cost to themselves. If they could capture the pilot they would but if they couldn't they would shoot him there and then, even if it meant losing their own lives. The unfortunate pilot would have heard dreadful stories that Japs always wanted to capture pilots alive so that they could ceremonially behead them. We *had* to get there first.

I once had a long talk with a chief engineer about being given orders by a captain for "full speed ahead". The engineer told me that the reason why he didn't like that order was that he wasn't usually informed why it was given and he couldn't see what was happening. "Full speed ahead" might be putting the engines at risk if he put full revolutions on too quickly and might be putting too much strain on parts of his engines. So experienced engineers would keep a couple of knots in reserve. Some captains were sometimes only showing off, some were perhaps panicking. A good engineer would never want to put his engines at risk and therefore put the ship at risk and the crew too. It was up to me to steer as straight a course as possible and save precious time. Just in case there were a couple of extra knots available I called down the voice-pipe to the chief and told him that we had found the crashed pilot (possibly from the *Illustrious*) and asked him if we were we going as fast as we could, because a Jap boat carrying a large machine-gun wanted to capture the pilot before we got to him. As a result of my request the ship gained a couple of extra revolutions. It soon became obvious that we were going to get there first. I knew what the next orders were likely to be assuming that we were first. "Stop engines", then "hard to port" (or starboard) to pick up our pilot. I got that wrong because I had forgotten about the captain's DSO! What I got from the captain was what every helmsman wants to hear at least once in his lifetime, from "high speed full ahead" to "full astern" to "hard to starboard". I heard the chief engineer say, "f***ing hell, grab onto something!" I turned the wheel as fast as I could. To do this I simply turned sideways on and grabbed the brass handle on the wheel known as the midship spoke and, using my right hand and keeping my arm straight to form a fulcrum, I spun the wheel as fast as I could as far as it would go so all the gearing had to follow it. This technique I had had explained to me by Stripey a few years earlier. "Don't forget," he had said, "you'll knock everyone off their pins." There was a moment or two before the steering motor caught up with the metal gears and rods. Over she went. For me, that was the most exciting naval experience I ever had. All the crew who had never been in rough waters got a rude awakening during that minute! Those who had not stowed their china gear found them on the deck smashed. Those that had not troubled to latch their lockers found their clothes all over the place with loose water, and I suspect a lot had bruises. I thought that was a day never to forget! It wasn't my fault and I felt like shouting out "Yippee!"

Because of the accuracy of the officer of the watch and captain's orders to stop the ship (with a bit of help from me), the crews of 'A' and 'B' Turrets were able to throw out and heave in their heaving lines, onto which they had fastened metal grapnels, one of which got tangled up with the pilot's parachute, his clothing or him. So far as I know this was the first wounded person that our doctor had been called upon to deal with. He immediately treated him for two bullets in his leg and shoulder injuries, one of which may have been inflicted by a grapnel.

We hurried back as quickly as possible to rejoin the fleet, which made us all feel safer and happier. I can't help sometimes wondering "Did this poor fellow subsequently wake up in the night in a cold sweat seeing these two boats coming towards him and wondering which will get to him first?"

By August 1944 it seemed that we had got into a routine of swimming in all off-watch times, as there was nothing more pleasurable to do. The Tannoy words 'hands to bathe' meant that the motor cutter was out there in case anyone got into trouble. My swimming was improving all the time. At first, seventy-five percent of the crew went down the quarterdeck gangway to the water but more and more were jumping and learning to dive over the waist side (about an eighteen-foot drop). Later, many were risking the jump or dive from the bows, some thirty-five feet high. I never tried diving from that point. Later, there were only half-a-dozen who still entered the water by the gangway.

The floating dry dock arrived at Trincomalee during August. It had been constructed in two parts in India, towed the 1,500 miles to Ceylon and bolted together for the use of the 'Trinco' fleet.

At this time a small accident happened to me. I have included the daily orders.

We had an AB, a big fellow, a fantastic diver who, even when he was drunk, would return to the ship and dry-dive down the mess deck iron stairway on his chest, then slide along the brown thick lino until he came to a stop, and then laugh his head off. This AB's (whom I called 'Palmers Green') eyes lit up when he saw this floating dry dock. It wasn't long before he swam the considerable distance between us and it and then, to the amazement of both our crew and that of

```
Duty Lt. Cdr.      Lieut Cdr (N).    Capt of Top.     P.O. Lacey.
Duty S & S.O.      Mid (S) Dunne.    Duty G.M.        Sgt. Ray.
Duty W.O.          Mr. Harden.       Duty R.P.O.      R.P.O. Poole.
                                     P.O. of Day.     P.O. Flood.
Duty Part.         1st Stbd.         Emer. L/S.       L.S. Hook.
Leave.             2nd Port from 1325 to 2130, Ch & P.O.s 2230.
Duty Boats.        Frances Day, 1st & 2nd Motor Boats and Skimmer.
Dress.             Refitting rig.
Routine.           Saturday tropical.
```

<u>Programme</u>.
- 0710. Hands fall in.
         Paint upperworks.
- 0800. Dress ship with masthead ensigns in honour of the
         birthday of Her Majesty the Queen.
- 0845. Boat to take Commander (E) to Searcher.
- A.M.   Crane Test Party may arrive from Dockyard.
- 1400. Starboard watch carry on painting.
- 1630. Baggage Party (3) go in Frances Day to Admiralty Pier.
         Take Baggage to Regulating Office, Highflyer.

<u>G.O. & I.</u>

1.

   The accident to the motor cutter on Thursday
would never have happened if the stern fast and less
important, on this occasion, the bow line had not been
cast off before the boat was unhooked from the crane.
The boat could and should have been towed stern first
by the stern fast until the slings were clear.
   Two other points are worth mentioning.
   (a) One rating in the water, P.O. Edwards I think it
       was, was lucky to avoid being brained by a lifebuoy
       someone hurled at him. That was <u>not</u> a clever thing
       to do. (Throwing a lifebuoy like that, I mean).
   (b) The scratch crew that manned the 2nd whaler was
       dreadful. It is evident that more early morning
       boat pulling is required!

2.   <u>TABLE CLOTHS</u>.
        Leading hands of messes requiring new table cloths
     are to hand chit giving the number of the mess and the
     number in it into Lieutenant Foster's cabin (No. 29) by
     1800 today.

3.   <u>FRESH WATER CONSUMPTION</u>.
        From 0800 Thursday to 0800 Friday - 66 tons

4.   <u>SPORTS GEAR</u>.
        All Sports Gear, except that on personal loan to
     ship's team, is to be returned to the Gym Store today.

5.   <u>SPORT</u>.
        FOOTBALL - SATURDAY.

         <u>SHIP'S 1st XI</u>   V   <u>SUSSEX</u>
         R.N. 3 GROUND.   K.O. 1500.
     Team and a limited number of spectators will land at
     1430.

Figure 49. Daily Orders for Saturday 4th August 1945

the floating dry dock, he dived off the highest crane on it. It must have been at least sixty feet high. He then swam back to the ship. The commander immediately issued an order, the next day, placing the floating dry dock out of bounds.

The floating dry dock's first customer was HMS *Valiant*. This battleship was built in Glasgow, Scotland in February 1916. She was twice modernised, in 1930 and again in 1939, which may have increased her original weight of 27,500 tons. When I saw *Valiant* a few days later, up there on top of that Meccano-set contraption, she looked as though she was far too heavy to be supported twenty-nine feet above the water-level of Trincomalee Harbour.

This trim-looking battleship, HMS *Valiant*, which was some five hundred yards from our ship, moved during the night. It did not make a loud creaking or roaring noise but rather a number of curious groans. I did not see this happen as I was fast asleep. Was it the noise that woke me up, or was it the chap sleeping next to me? There it was in the morning, tangled within the damaged 'dry dock' which was not now a floating dock!

The whole of our crew were guessing as to why it had happened. Had it fallen or had it been pushed? I had this silly thought, perhaps it was 'Palmers Green'. He had swum across that night, climbed up to the *Valiant*'s DCT's top, bent his knees and pressed hard on the DCT's top to dive back into the sea – was he 'the straw that broke the camel's back'?

We never got a satisfactory explanation for what had happened to the *Valiant*, as to whether it was an accident or sabotage. She was repaired at enormous cost, but she was out of date anyway. (See Photo 65 – HMS Valiant.)

Photo 65. HMS Valiant

In late August we had started my twenty-third and very different convoy. This was my first troop convoy and was the longest journey but it only took four or five days. Some of my Arctic convoys travelled at about 5 knots, which meant that you were at sea for three or four weeks but covering only half the distance. We zigzagged over about 4,000 miles to Western Australia. It was the fastest journey I had ever made and was achieved by being oiled *en route*.

I also remember it for being one of the nicest trips. We were accompanied by aircraft-carriers, three battleships with lots of escorts, small and large cruisers, destroyers, and our own oil well in the form of three fleet oilers, and the sea was flat calm. Best of all, there was not a single Japanese submarine recorded or a single shot fired; it was like a holiday cruise.

I spent my time trying to get a suntan but all that happened was that the sun accelerated the yellowing effect of the Methogere tablets.

My only problem was that I was homesick. I felt terribly cut off from my family.

There was to be leave, according to the buzz; seven days was the possibility. Australian money would be available as soon as we arrived at Fremantle. I had a feeling that, if the opportunity arose, I would do a bunk to the outback and never be seen again, but I knew that if I got caught I would be in severe trouble!

We tied up alongside the quay at Fremantle. There were three things which were different about Fremantle compared with most European docks. It was warm, quiet and clean. It was quiet because it was Sunday and you could not buy beer. It was announced on the Tannoy that we were at fifth degree of readiness which meant that all non-duty crew could take normal daily leave from 1300 hours until midnight.

Well, it was quiet, we knew it was Sunday, but we felt sure that there was a pub or club that would be open. Not even able to find a cup of tea or a game of cricket or football, we asked a bloke riding a bicycle if he could direct us to the pub. He said: "It's Sunday. Nothing opens till eight o'clock tonight and that'll be a nightclub and they won't let you in unless you sign up and join and that'll cost you more than you would like to pay. They'll let you blokes in but it don't sell beer, only Port," he said. "Only Port?" we echoed. So we walked down to the 'pub'. It was hours until eight o'clock. There was a chap working outside, he gave us the opening hours and we had decided to return to the *Nigeria* when his lady wife said: "Oh, let 'em in! Port or Port with lemon?" I went for the Port with lemon. When we asked "How much?" she replied: "Have it on the house." We had a nice chat and, thanking her, we got back to the ship by 2000 hours and told the crew that, as the lady had said, there was nothing to do on a Sunday.

I don't remember how I heard of them but some organisation offered me the chance to go horse-riding. I had always wanted to see Australia with its open spaces. We would be using campfires for cooking and then sleeping under the stars in sleeping bags and could have a stay with a family. I went for the horse-riding, having thought that, after all, my father was an expert horseman. I signed up on the spot. This had been set up by the jaunty, who said "horses, humph!" There were eleven of us. One of the ladies owned the horses, two other ladies did the cooking, two men were married to these ladies, and one of the men was the leader. There were four beefy, boisterous Australian servicemen, and I made up the eleven. The only 'young' lady owned the gee-gees and she looked an old twenty-two!

Early in the morning we went by cars to an area past Northam and Kalgoolie where we were introduced to the horses; it was where they were kept. The four Aussie soldiers and I were invited to pick a gee-gee from a group of some twenty horses. I let the Aussie soldiers help themselves, which they did, whilst I stood back and our nice twenty-two-year-old lady asked me what was wrong. I said: "I've never ridden a horse, how do I pick one?" She said: "Don't come, take the car and go back." I said: "No way, I'll look a twit, I must go, I won't grumble." She gave in. So she picked out a small, mature horse with a special saddle and gentle attitude and I promised to keep up. The young lady helped me all the time with hints like "Keep your weight forward; stand on the stirrups and rest your bum by taking your seat off the saddle". At night she gave me hints about my sore and aching legs and what to do when sleeping, and provided straw to put under my sleeping bag. By now my bottom was sore too. I was in great pain and I must have looked odd in my naval uniform with bell-bottoms and no blue collar. It was hard to keep up but I persisted. The Aussie soldiers thought it was funny and they 'extracted the urine'. They saw me as a thin, anxious, quiet fellow and wondered where I had come from. One night I was talking to the young woman; up to that day I had hardly spoken to her, and I had only laughed and agreed with the others when they spoke to me. She asked about my age and what I did in the RN. I told her I could not talk about the Eastern Fleet. She asked about my past and I told her very briefly about the Med, the twenty-two Russian convoys and the shortages of food. The Aussies stopped 'extracting the urine' after that and seemed to show me more respect. We all became friends and I managed to keep up with the other travellers. I think it lasted for five days. We said "Goodbye" and I transferred from my friendly gee-gee to a car with these new friends for the journey to Kalgoolie. I did say a very good "Goodbye" to the young lady. After we had returned by vehicle to Northam I was taken to a lady's house for two days. She was 'old' and had a fourteen-year-old daughter called Jackie. I liked Jackie, she seemed more my age. I danced with them both at a dance the *Nigeria* gave, despite my sore bum and legs! It had been a complete change and it helped me to get over my homesick feeling. I shall never forget my 'horse-bottom', nor that 'lift and bang'! My sore bum and the raw insides of my thighs had certainly taken my mind off the war. I have never wanted to ride again!

After the three weeks' holiday in beautiful Australia enjoying good food and being looked after by kind ladies, which was a welcome change, we set sail to return to Colombo with soldiers (there were a lot of them) who were on course for Burma or European destinations. Some of these troop ships held 'crossing the line' ceremonies which we had done when we crossed the Equator whilst sailing down to Fremantle, and the troops received the same 'crossing the line' certificates to prove it as I had.

They seemed to have fun with their ceremonies as we had had with ours on 28th August when King Neptune arrived on board to call various members of the crew to trial. I have picked out just two members charged as follows:

1. Midshipman: "Did deem to plough the ocean with the marks still upon his stern, much to the disgust of the 'Denizens of the Deep'." Punishment awarded: "To be bounced, spliced, tanned and pitchforked for Bears" (tossed into the small canvas pool).

2. Paymaster commander: "Did attempt to starve your trusty tars by offering them offal and old fruit, thereby causing them to groan and growl." Punishment awarded: "To be roasted until he is dripping, to be tailed, parboiled and be served to Lusty Bears as offal."

As on our southbound journey, this return one was another perfect first-class cruise, without even a rifle shot, on a flat blue sea.

We disembarked our pongos at Colombo and we wished them "Good luck, you poor sods".

We returned to 'Trinco', arriving on 23rd October. During November we proceeded to the Arakan coast and anchored in the river between Akyab and Phapholting.

It was a confused situation; the Japanese were supposed to be moving south all over Burma. In late 1942 they had been pushing north, expecting to drive our 14th Army back into India. This would have allowed the Japanese to move in and take complete control of India with the help of local dissidents who were 'anti' the British Raj but the 14th Army had completely stopped this northern progress. By now, the 14th Army were at last getting well supplied and enjoying air support.

The enemy were now finding it difficult to remain where they were. It took a very long time for their supplies to arrive, if they arrived at all, as all Japanese supply routes were being attacked by the Allies and it was 2,500 miles from Japan by air, 4,500 miles by sea to Chittagong from Japan, and much, much further by road. The Japanese Army in Burma was lost and forgotten by the Japanese High Command, and we were about to attack them right here on the Arakan coast. I understood that we were there to help the 26th Indian Division by bombarding any enemy who came within firing distance. We believed that Akyab, with Ramree and Cheduba Islands, were all held by a considerable number of Japanese.

The master-at-arms had made it clear that his orders were that as an acting PO I was to do what he regarded as a very important job which was to get to a meeting by 0800 that day, with our motor cutter manned by two other sailors, and moor up ashore on the bank of the fast-flowing river, and wait until I found three or four local women who had his and other POs' whites for washing. "I should remind you," said the master, "that I can remove the rank of temp!" "Aye, aye, master-at-arms," I said, knowing that removing 'temporary' meant that I could be demoted to L/S. I was more than pleased to be carrying out my instructions concerning my laundry and quite a few other POs' 'whites', which were in the hands of these three or four dusky-skinned Burmese clothes 'scrubbers'. As the master had put it: "If we have to sail without them I'll have your guts for breakfast." We had used the ladies' laundry services before. They had made the clothes whiter than white with beautiful creases. They washed our clothes (or rather bashed them with one flat stone onto a larger flat stone in the river, or sometimes thrashed the washing down onto any smooth stone!). They had promised to return them dry the *next* morning. Their price had always been ridiculously low, as long as it was paid for in English, Indian or Ceylon currency (notes, not coins). They did not want us to 'see them off' by paying them with Japanese special occupation notes. (See colour photos – Japanese occupation notes.)

You had to catch them before 1000 hours, otherwise you wouldn't see them until the next morning. As far as I was concerned, I only had one set of whites. They had been laundered by these dusky ladies earlier but whilst they looked smart, they had a horrid smell. Looking at the river and what went on there I observed that people were washing their clothes and themselves and using the river as a latrine. Worst of all, this same fast-flowing river acted as a method of disposing of their dead. The bodies were floated down the river on burning rafts which broke up as they slowly burnt out, leaving all that was not burnt to find its way into the river for whatever was there. I now knew why my washing had smelt bad!

This river was home to a huge number of saltwater and estuarine crocodiles. We had been told it was possible, if they lived long enough, for them to reach nearly nine yards long and be two yards across at their stomachs, and weigh two tons. We, the RN, had been issued with some warnings about these crocs that could be found near sinking ships at sea as well as in rivers and which could be more dangerous than the large sharks. I wondered if they were here in this river today looking for remnants of bodies. With the crocodiles and the possibility of Japanese soldiers appearing, there was no way I was leaving the safety of the motor cutter. I did tell the two friendly ratings to watch out for crocodiles but I think they already knew.

It was a relief to see my four ladies in the distance with bundles on their heads. I was pleased and so would the jaunty be. They took the bundles off their heads, carefully folded them and put them in neat piles on top of cutter's seats with each person's name on top. I was always amazed to meet people in these out-of-the-way places who spoke and wrote almost perfect English. The master-at-arms would be pleased, I thought, and only one shilling and sixpence to pay, which was only one rupee for each with tip.

XVIII

Coping with Japanese

It was October 1944, very early to be doing Christmas shopping, when I was offered the opportunity to send a 'wireless telegraph' Christmas card. The card I chose was the same one the entire ship's company chose. We were also given the opportunity of choosing as many cards as we wished, as long as there were not more than two!

It also involved a day in a queue. I sent one to Mother and Auntie, and one to Joyce Dyster. Mother and Auntie did not receive this jolly Christmas card but Joyce did. I am told that this now has a value in the region of £1,000. Who knows? It's mine and I want to keep it!

I was given a health inspection certificate, a copy of which I have also kept. It states that in 1939 my chest measurement at fifteen years of age was 34½ inches. I was very thin then. My chest measurement in October 1944 (five years later) was 35 inches, whilst it measures 38 inches today, some millions of years later! The only reason I mention this uninteresting fact is that the chap in the enrolment

Photo 66. 'Happy Xmas'

office received a commission for any boy he got to 'sign on' for the RN. Enrolment officers (usually POs) could only get this money if the youth was up to a given height, with a chest measurement of around 34 inches, and was the proud owner of two of everything required. It must have been tempting for a PO to leave a couple of inches of slack in the tape and read it at the back of the boy!

Just before Christmas 1944, I was informed by the officer of the watch that I had been granted a trip to a rest-camp for a week's rest and some schooling. As this followed my medical check I asked the officer of the watch if it possible that, as I was ill, I was going to be sent home for Christmas leave, at which he and his staff fell about with laughter.

I met nine POs from all sorts of ships, and one Australian Army sergeant, at Trincomalee railway station. We were heading for Kandy, a distance of about a hundred and forty miles. We had plenty to eat in our packed lunches. The train was a troop-train which had park-type wooden benches without any cushions. They were very uncomfortable to sit on. The next part of our journey from Kandy to Diyatalawa, I think was about seventy miles in all. At about 5,000 feet, it was refreshingly cool, with beautiful scenery.

It took nearly all day to get to Diyatalawa where we were met by an English pongo, who put us and our gear into a small Army truck which was just big enough to take all of us. The road was poor, full of potholes, bends and sharp drops. It was dusk, beginning to get dark, and we drove very fast indeed. The pongo said he had been backwards and forwards so many times he could do this journey blindfold. It was the Aussie who stated: "You know he's as pissed as a coot and he's got to be doing fifty at times." We just looked at the Aussie, no-one was in charge! I often recall that terrifying journey.

It was dark when we arrived at the rest camp and I was pleased to find my bed and fall asleep. Nobody offered us food.

We were awoken by neatly dressed local waiters with trays of cups and pots of tea which they poured to your taste. The Aussie was in the bed next to mine. Like any pongo, he had his knapsack. It was open with his tins and shaving things showing, then he picked up what looked like a chameleon. He was putting this creature into one of the tins without a lid. I was amazed and couldn't think of what to say. "G'day," said the Aussie. "Good morning," I said. It was the PO sleeping next to him who said "what the f****** h*** have you got there, and do they bite?" The Aussie pointed out that in Burma one of these little beasties could rid you of all the winged biters found in the jungle, especially during dark hours. The breakfast bell stopped the conversation about geckos or whatever it was.

After a very nice breakfast we learnt that the 'rest' was not going to last seven days. Travelling had cut it to five days, and two and a half of these were for the so-called Japanese schooling, but after 1900 hours it was all our own time! There was also a club with reduced-price spirits, open until 2100.

During our free time there was little to do except walk about amongst some of the most beautiful bush scenery in the world, including the nearby spectacular Ravana Ella Falls. There was wildlife to see, especially elephants, monkeys and birds. The only complaint about that week was that at night our beds had to be covered because of the fine sawdust that fell out of the wooden roof-supports due to woodworm. It was important that we did not get up in the morning until the staff had collected the covers.

Our Japanese teacher, judging by her brogue, was obviously from Scotland. This fifty-year-old Scottish teacher had spent more than half her working life teaching English to Japanese in Japan and there was nothing she didn't know about Japan and Japanese language and culture.

When I came away after the two and a half days of lessons with the lady, I think I almost understood what she was trying to explain about the Japanese with their double talk and their two faces:

1. The Japanese lied but they didn't think of it as lying. For instance, one face said "Come out, we will not shoot you" while the second, hidden face thought "We will do something more painful than that".

2. Cruelty could be an asset and a weapon to frighten their enemies. It could also be propaganda for them and us.

3. All Japanese, without hesitation, if so ordered, would die for Japan and their Emperor wherever they were.

4. 'Loss of face' was the worst thing that could happen to a Japanese.

Mixed in with this was kindness towards one another as long as they were all obeying their orders. I was to find out later that they would not abandon injured comrades. "I think," said our Scottish tutor, "these Japanese soldiers in Burma know they're losing their war and are going through 'loss of face' and they'll find that this will affect their morale."

The other two and a half days were so enjoyable that I promised myself that I would return to Ceylon one day – but without the train journey which was hard on the horse-sore bum!

We were picked up by a different driver for the return journey. "G'day," said the Aussie, "where's our coming up driver, died of booze yet?" "Yes," said the new driver, "he overdid it a couple of nights ago with a skinful and never noticed all the leeches in the grass!"

In January 1945 we were on the Arakan coast again exercising with the LCPs (landing craft) which we and the *Kenya* had been over to Bombay to collect.

At 0830 I came across half-a-dozen pongos. They looked natty in their slouch hats, khaki long four-pocketed jackets, shorts, green webbing belts with guns in holsters and they were carrying machetes rather than rifles and bayonets.

Five of these soldiers had that Methogere-yellow look but the sixth, who was much shorter than the rest, had a rosy English face. It was obvious that he was a new arrival. I didn't find out his name but I bet his mates called him 'Shorty'. We chatted for a short time and I found out that the five 'yellow' guys had been out there for a couple of years. The new arrival had been in the Army for three and a half years, during which he had been sent on course after course until a couple of months earlier when an officer had said that unless he went somewhere soon he would miss fighting in the war, so he had volunteered to serve in Burma. "Today is my first day at war!" he said, and we all laughed. "Where are you off to?" I asked. "Over there, you can see a path we have cut through the long grass. We've been using it for months." Then they went on their way.

At about 0915 hours my five 'yellow' pongos emerged from the grass carrying Shorty in a groundsheet. His nice pink complexion was now the palest shade of white. Apparently they had had very bad luck and run into a two- or three-man Japanese patrol moving at right angles to them. Our short friend was last in the line when the enemy broke into the footpath and confronted him and before he realised that he was in the war he had had a bayonet driven into his left shoulder. Although in great pain, Shorty pushed the Japanese in the face with his left hand and moved his right to his holster to get out his revolver to shoot his attacker. The Japanese who had the hand in his face simply bit Shorty's thumb off. The pain was too much for Shorty and, in an effort to shoot his aggressor, he pulled the trigger and shot himself in his right foot, splintering bones. All the Japanese then disappeared into the long grass.

The others had put field dressings onto his wounds and when we met they told me what had happened. They were taking him to a Dutch hospital ship which was moored close by. Poor old Shorty with his forty-five minute war!

It was about twenty-five years ago whilst on holiday in Madeira, sitting round a table, that I heard my wife talking to another lady and I heard mention of Japanese and Burma. I joined the conversation, then her husband joined in too, and I noticed that this elderly man was without a left thumb – it was Shorty! He explained that he ran a business mending motor mowers. When I asked about his injuries he said that the hospital ship's staff had done an excellent job with new drugs. The shoulder and thumb had never been a big problem but his right foot gave him a lot of pain on occasions. He ended up by saying "I definitely shot myself in the foot!"

It turned out that his wife had made a study of the Japanese and she gave us the following short verse:

How courteous is the Japanese
He always bows and says "Excuse me please"
He walks into his neighbour's garden
And smiles and says
"I beg your pardon"
He smiles and grins, a friendly grin
And calls his hungry family in.
He smiles and bows, a friendly bow
And says
"So sorry, my garden now!"

During December and January we were part of Cruiser Squadron 5. This was made up of *Newcastle, Kenya* and us. We were to be available for bombarding targets indicated by the 26th Indian Division of the coastal wing of the 14th Army. They were moving south on the Arakan coast heading for Rangoon. The *Nigeria* was allocated a section of coast from Akyab covering Kyaukpyu, Ramree Island down to Cheduba Island.

There was a buzz that there were at least one and a half thousand Japanese there. I didn't like that buzz at all; neither did I like the fact that in daylight we could see, with the aid of binoculars, an awful lot of saltwater mangrove swamps which were obscuring the land. But we couldn't see any Japanese. Not only could we see these swamps, we knew that they were home to all manner of nasty wildlife.

Fifty Royal Marines from each of the ten cruisers were trained together to form a force of five hundred Special Royal Marine Commando. This short intensive training improved their fitness but I wondered if they could cope with the circumstances they might find themselves in. After all, I reasoned, could these 'bootnecks' (with this new impressive name) from our 'Y' Turret, who slept in hammocks next to us and who were occasionally attacked by cockroaches, be able to move about in mangrove swamps and take on the nasty wildlife, particularly the large crocs? It is a big step from coping with 'roaches to dealing with crocs.

By late January we were five miles off the northern tip of Ramree Island when we were ordered to go south to Cheduba. Whilst we were waiting for a landing on Cheduba we had the problem of finding the appointed landing place on this island. There were miles of low-lying, unlit, largely featureless coast which was swept by strong and unpredictable cross-currents. Radar 273 could only pick up the water and, with the mangroves, we did not know where the land was. We were making our calculations at night. Without any buildings, trees, roads or railway lines to guide us, it was an impossible situation for navigation. It was impossible to tell how deep any water was or whether solid-looking ground was possibly a swamp or even a rock. Our navigator was unable to find a permanent horizon to do his calculations. The rear admiral had got all three ships to keep precise track of our position during the night by taking star-sights every hour using the direction layers' crossed-wired telescope with its Gyro stabilised horizontal to provide an artificial horizon. (I bet none of them had ever done this before!) By this means we found the landing beach.

We sent a barge full of two-and-a-half-inch rockets over to it and at 0500 they went off. The noise was deafening even though we were some distance from the barge (I had never seen this done before). We then fired forty-eight six-inch shells from our four turrets onto the beach. At 0630 hours the Special Royal Marine Commando unit landed from the LCPs onto this now pot-holed and deeply cratered beach. They searched hard but they couldn't find any Japanese soldiers. What an anti-climax! Eventually a local boy of about sixteen came onto the beach and later two men joined him. They greeted the marines and told them that the Japanese soldiers had gone, to which we all said "Hooray!" and silently said to ourselves "thank God we haven't got to pick up dead bodies or deal with screaming wounded (Japanese or ours)".

In late January 1945 we sailed to Bombay in company with *Kenya* to collect six LCPs.

Armed with my pass No. 639295 (see Photo 67, of pass), a group of about thirty or forty of us walked into town at 1000 hours. We walked past the big dusky-grey granite-type building known as 'The Gateway to India' and found our way to the bazaar that sold everything.

Amongst the stalls were locals giving shows like mongoose and cobra fighting. After a while the creatures were put back into sacks to wait for the next show!

Passing through the market we wandered from one stall to another; these stalls were a real jumble laid out without any order. We had been warned that there would be hundreds of people milling around

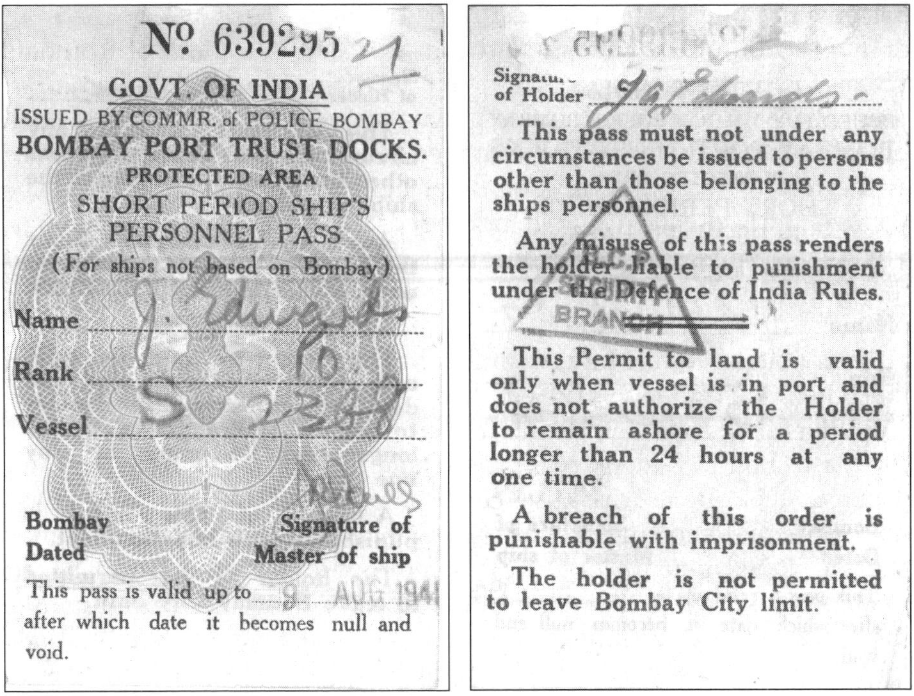

№ 639295

GOVT. OF INDIA
ISSUED BY COMMR. of POLICE BOMBAY
BOMBAY PORT TRUST DOCKS.
PROTECTED AREA
SHORT PERIOD SHIP'S
PERSONNEL PASS
(For ships not based on Bombay)

Name

Rank

Vessel

Bombay   Signature of
Dated   Master of ship

This pass is valid up to ___ AUG 194
after which date it becomes null and
void.

Signature
of Holder

This pass must not under any
circumstances be issued to persons
other than those belonging to the
ships personnel.

Any misuse of this pass renders
the holder liable to punishment
under the Defence of India Rules.

BRANCH

This Permit to land is valid
only when vessel is in port and
does not authorize the Holder
to remain ashore for a period
longer than 24 hours at any
one time.

A breach of this order is
punishable with imprisonment.

The holder is not permitted
to leave Bombay City limit.

Photo 67. Bombay Dock Pass

and we could be pick-pocketed without even noticing it. We found it impossible to keep together and were soon reduced to a group of five or six. I purchased a book, for one rupee, at a bookstall. It was about 8in x 8in x 1in and had a clean, dark red cloth cover. It was called *Constructive Thinking* and was the first book I had ever bought. Books were so rare on the ship. I bought it because it was the cleanest book on the stall. The chap who sold it to me said as I paid "Woo a man of education, Sir, and thank you". (I was reminded of him when I heard Peter Sellars sing 'Goodness gracious me'!) Anyway, the bookseller was a happy man.

I enjoyed Bombay. I found the people cheerful with a sense of humour rather like Cockneys. We went on to Bombay's Harley Street; it was a nice city street. Each doctor had a brass plate or two outside his surgery. It was different from Harley Street in London insofar as each of the Indian-trained doctors had a queue outside. Easily the longest queue was in front of the doctor who had on his brass plate 'MD Cambridge (failed)'.

The other street all of us wanted to see, for some reason or another, was Grant Street, where there were two-storey buildings with normal windows and doors on the ground floor, whilst the first floor had a balcony running the whole length of the block. Each flat opened out onto a section of the balcony and was enclosed in a mesh of iron bars giving the impression of a prison cell. In each of these 'cells' sat a girl dressed in a decorated dressing-gown. Anything these girls did took place in the back room, the entrance to which was through a door at the rear of the building. The older ladies were on the left and the younger girls on the right. It reminded me of my mum's warnings. Thinking about Mum made me realise how long it was since I had thought about her and Auntie, and even longer since I had seen either of them.

Then I began to feel hungry and turned around to discuss food with the others. I suddenly realised that I was alone. I wondered where the others had gone! I joined a queue outside the only air-conditioned cinema in Bombay (perhaps in the whole of India). The bloke in front of me in this queue was a merchant skipper. He, like me, was lining up for the first showing of *Yankee Doodle Dandy* starring James Cagney and we hoped that we might get some food and drink. We managed to obtain tickets but all we could get to eat was a bag of peanuts. We sat down in the air-conditioned cinema and stuck *Yankee Doodle Dandy* for about an hour before we thought of a better idea which was to find a restaurant. We ordered curried something. The food came on a woven bamboo tray; there were no plates. The curry was on leaves about 8in x 8in with upturned edges so that the food did not run off. I looked at the captain, he looked back at me and said: "I don't think so." I agreed, we took money out of our pockets, paid and left. I think two young Bombay fellows got stuck into our food!

We walked past the closed Bank of India which was a large building of white stone; it looked new. It had large recesses with two-and-a-half-foot-wide windows on the ground floor. The area in front of these windows was taken over by a family every night; one such family of mum, dad and two children was settling down there as we passed. I was told that these bays, with their overhangs, kept these families dry despite any heavy rain.

After a while we got a gharry (two-wheeled horse-drawn job) which took us back to the dockyard to go to the captain's ship. My pass got me in. The ship had just been built; it was the latest Liberty ship from the USA. The captain took me to his quarters where he had a whacking great refrigerator with two doors. It was full of tins of ham and tins of Budweiser beer (I had never seen canned beer before). He offered bread, ham and a can of beer which was a bit fizzy but pleasant. During the course of this beautiful meal we chatted about South Carolina and a couple of PQ Russian convoys he had been on. After the meal the captain saw me safely out of the dockyard gate and saw that my pass worked, we shook hands and I soon found myself back at the Gateway to India. It was very dark and I became aware of my full bladder (beer!) so I peed up the Gateway which looked strong enough to stand it. I made my way back to the harbour and took a transfer boat back to the ship which cost me one chip (local currency worth 1/6).

Some idiot brought a small monkey (unknown make and it would grow!) back to the ship. I never knew whether it was forced on him while he was pissed or why he bought it. Anyway, it didn't stay with us long. Whilst scampering about amongst the hammock supports during 'Rounds' (a senior officer's evening inspection) it managed to pee on the first lieutenant who was not pleased! The sailor was ordered to "get rid of it – not tomorrow but now". There was not a single animal-lover on board who would plead the monkey's case. What a good thing we had arrived back at 'Trinco' by then. The monkey was set free in the bush before we sailed on to the Arakan coast with the six LCPs.

We were anchored off Ramree Island to provide low-angle six-inch bombardment to help the 26th Indian Infantry Division who were doing a good job of 'knocking seven bells' out of the Japanese who were well dug in on a line between Kyaukpu and Leikauay (going inland eastwards for about fifty miles) and were thus protected from attacks by our combined forces. The whole of that area, approximately five hundred square miles, was mangrove swamp with its indescribable horrors. Dark during the day, as well as at night, this area consisted of impenetrable forest and miles of deep black mud which were full of leeches, frogs, mosquitoes, flies, deadly scorpions and weird insects by the billion (there was one large beetle, I remember well, we called it the 'flying walnut'!), but worst of all were the big saltwater estuarine crocodiles. The thing I remember most about them was the noise, particularly at night. Orders had been put up on the ship's notice-board saying that if you found any seawater adjacent to mangrove you were not to wade or swim in it as it was sure to be full of sharks coming in from the sea and these would be 'biters'. (These days we might be told that these species are not dangerous!)

This mangrove swamp protected the rear of the Japanese and it appeared almost impossible to attack their front. The monsoon rains were due which would make moving about very difficult. This stalemate had held up the Allies' advance. A Captain E.W. Bush, DSO, DSC, RN organised a pincer attack which was successful and now the Japanese had to make up their minds about what to do. 'Loss of face' would come into their thinking as my Scottish teacher in Ceylon had said. They couldn't even think of surrender although they were short of ammo (or so we were told) and couldn't continue fighting. They could cut inland and try to dodge the five British Army units which were backed up by air cover but it would be hard for them to hide so they chose to try to reach the western coast through the mangrove swamp which would hide these thousand-odd Japanese, plus their bleeding wounded and sick for whom they hadn't got any medicines.

A discussion arose during the watch on the subject of how the Japanese could live in the swamp, now that they had moved in with the big crocodiles for neighbours, when one of our bright seamen remarked: "The Japs will eat those 'neighbours', they're used to eating raw fish and whales." Someone else said he could imagine a Japanese sergeant saying "It's a bit big, lad, you can kill it with a hand-grenade and eat the pieces, they say croc is tender and tastes just like chicken". None of us had any intention of getting off our ship to find out if that was true. Although I was up to my ears in this rotten war, I was only certain of what was going on in my own back yard (the *Nigeria*).

The end of Ramree Island for me was the end of what I had been doing in 'X' Turret. So, is the story of one thousand-odd Japanese escaping into the swamp and subsequently being gobbled up by its ghastly wildlife true? All I can add is that during the fighting at Ramree we heard the cries of the wounded Japanese soldiers as they were attacked by the huge crocodiles in the swamps as they tried to escape. The Guinness Book of Records states that this was the largest loss of human life caused by animals ever recorded. It is estimated that about 1,000 Japanese troops were killed there by saltwater crocodiles in those few days in February 1945. In finally removing the threat posed by that Japanese force, the crocs could be said to have completed the task for us. That was the only time I felt sorry for the Japanese but it was their own miscalculations that got them into that mess. It appeared that our help was no longer required at Ramree Island by the 26th Indian Infantry Division, so we pulled up our two hooks and set south for 'Trinco' in early March. Well, at least I liked 'Trinco'.

XIX

Wildlife

We arrived back at 'Trinco' during Ceylon's monsoon season. Because 'Trinco' harbour had been invaded by deadly poisonous sea-snakes, there was no bathing allowed until the monsoon season had finished and the tides returned to normal. It was hot and sticky, making it difficult to sleep at night.

Our experience on Ramree Island had left us unhappy and disgusted by what we thought the Japanese had done to themselves there. News was coming through about the fall of Germany. This news unsettled all the HOs, many of them had not looked on the Japs as a direct threat as they did the Germans, and they felt that this part of the war should be fought by career sailors. The buzz of what was going to happen was overtaken by the official plans which were on the notice-board! Now Germany was out of the picture powerful navies (ours and the US) plus large combined armies and air forces joined in the Pacific to bring the war with the Japanese to an end. This looked as if it would take a long time and was not popular with HOs as well as me. Huge numbers of casualties on both sides (20 percent was rumoured) could be expected. The whole of the ship's company seemed to have had a change of attitude towards rules, not all bad in some cases.

Together with my friend the midshipman (who had run the motor cutter aground when we first arrived at Colombo), we were carrying out the duties of the officer of the rounds and I was the duty PO of the day. This was an evening inspection of the forty-odd messes. During these rounds, the officers of the rounds and the duty PO went from mess to mess to see that they were all clean and tidy for personal health and safety reasons. The group (like an old-fashioned hospital matron's round) was led by a bugler who blew a sharp 'burp' when they arrived, everybody in the mess would stand up and turn off the radio. The killick in charge of the mess would stand to attention and salute, give the number of the mess with a "Sir", and wait for the duty PO to say "Stand easy" and then everyone would sit down. The officer would then look at the condition of the mess deck and, finding that everything was OK and clean, he would say "Carry on" to whoever was in charge (usually it was a killick). Then the PO would say "Thank you, stand easy lads" and they would head for the next mess deck.

On this occasion we came up to a mess which had a two-badge AB in charge, who had a reputation for being a lower-deck lawyer. I would like to have warned the midshipman that there would be trouble but I didn't want to risk someone hearing me so I had no choice but to keep quiet. I needn't have worried. The bugler sounded the usual 'G', and the mess crew all stood to attention. The two-badge AB (acting as a killick) said "Mess deck clean and correct, Sir". At this stage I said "Stand easy, lads". The midshipman replied "Thank you, leading seaman" (the midshipman had said that purposely). "Sir," replied the two-badge AB, "I'm not a leading seaman but an able seaman with two good conduct stripes." "Of course, able seaman," said the middy, without any further comments. The AB didn't know how to argue with that, so nothing was said about the absence of a killick. There was a long pause as the midshipman looked around what was an especially untidy mess deck; it was obviously a set-up. There were smirks on everyone's faces as they watched the midshipman, who seemed to be taking his time. By now we were well aware that in the corner was a very big dusty spider's web, not a new perfectly constructed one, but a very dusty job obviously found and re-hung to trap this 'wet behind the ears' middy who, in the AB's mind, was getting far too much money and a large shared cabin as well. After what seemed to us a long time, the midshipman said: "Ah, leading seaman, can you tell me what that spider's web is doing up there?" "Yes," said the AB, who thought he knew this was his ace (his put-down for the young 'snotty'), "well Sir, you see we're badly troubled by flies, so of course we've left our spider's web up, in an effort to get them trapped." All the mess, including the AB, had big smiles on their faces. The 'snotty' took his time again and looked carefully (possibly noticing that the two other mess crews close to this mess deck were taking an interest in the 'web' conversation). "I see, leading seaman," the middy paused again. "What a clever idea but you know how fussy our commander is; leave it up but always take it down for the commander's rounds and then be sure to put it up again each time and, while you're at it, get this mess deck tidied up." There was complete silence from all three messes until it hit home, then there was outright loud laughter. The midshipman looked at me and I ordered "stand easy".

Once we were clear of the mess decks I wanted to say: "Ten out of ten; your grandfather would have been proud of you and the way you handled that situation." Anyway, his reputation had gone up in everyone's eyes and they now knew for certain that he was not 'wet behind the ears'!

In late March we were delighted to learn that we were off to Cape Town. We called at Diego Suarez for oiling on the way. We arrived at Simonstown, South Africa for refitting which we knew would take some time. I drew out what was for me big money – £75! My first port of call was to get a new suit. I had now been confirmed as a PO, so I went to have a uniform made. The tailor promised me that it would be ready in twenty-four hours. I suspected that he had several already half made and just adjusted them when an order came in. When I collected my suit I was very impressed with the gold work on the left arm with the PO and gunnery badge, so I had a studio portrait photo taken to send to Mum.

The photographer and I had a conversation about my youthful looks. To make me look older he suggested that I should be photographed with a pipe in my mouth – so that was done with a studio prop. I have never smoked a pipe!

This business of my age should be explained. I ceased to be a boy seaman when I was eighteen and for seven months I was an O/S. I stayed as an AB for fourteen months and became an acting L/S. At nineteen and a half I was promoted to L/S and just over a year later (at twenty-one) acting PO. When I was twenty-two, I was made up to full PO. My time through the ranks had taken four years.

In the normal peacetime Royal Navy, I would have spent about

Photo 68. My studio portrait

two years getting to the next rank, so I wouldn't have been a PO until I was twenty-four or twenty-six.

The local equivalent of the WVS in Simonstown made arrangements for the ship's company leave and we were given a choice of where to go. One of the first opportunities I had to enjoy some of this hospitality was when I went with PO Cowling to have tea with a very pleasant lady in Cape Town. I dressed in my brand-new uniform and put a clean handkerchief into my pocket. During the tea I pulled out this hanky and horror ... out of it fell two cockroaches, which scuttled away. Our hostess was horrified; she knew that they would be full of eggs and she would now have a problem.

Having chosen to go to Johannesburg for our leave, Cowling and I were given our own compartment on the Blue Train for the twenty-four-hour journey through the Hex river valley and across the Karroo 'deserts'. There was beautiful scenery and interesting wildlife for us to enjoy as we passed. We had discovered that South African brandy was good value so we had bought some and, after our meal, we started on the bottle. There was a huge bottle of fresh water available in our compartment, it was to last for twenty-four hours, but the brandy gave us such a thirst that it was drained rapidly and then we slept well in our nice bunks! The landscape became ugly and dreary near to Johannesburg with the huge spoil heaps from the gold mines in Kimberley and on the edges of Jo'burg.

In Jo'burg we stayed in a nice posh hotel and were looked after by a helpful Indian waiter who insisted in making sure that we

Photo 69. D. Cowling (left) The Cook (centre) Jack (right)

'didn't let the side down'. He whispered, when he brought us each course, which bits of cutlery to use!

One day we picked up two young Jewish girls who said that they would like us to take them to the air show in the park, so we took them there. At one point there was a plane due to fly over and drop hundreds of envelopes. One of these had a considerable amount of money in it. So we got ready to 'scramble', when one of the girls told us to stop. When we asked why, she said: "The pilot will've removed the winning envelope anyway, so don't bother!" After the show we were all waiting for a bus back to town when a car stopped and two young Jewish men hailed our lady friends who immediately jumped into the car and were driven off leaving us alone!

Another outing we went on was to a gold mine. We went down and down in one of the cages to the mine face; it seemed miles down. We listened to a short talk by a mine official who offered us a gold bar and said: "You can have it, just pick it up and it's yours." Of course we couldn't even lift one, they were so heavy! I was very glad when we had come back up again by lift into the fresh air.

It was a good leave, the journeys north and south on the Blue Train were very comfortable and we really enjoyed the impressive scenery and splendid wildlife. Mum and Auntie were fascinated when I told them about it, when I eventually got back home.

Whilst we had been travelling, a routine disinfestation of the ship had been arranged. Five lorry-loads of cockroaches and rats were removed from the ship. When questioned, the operators said that the rats were about the usual number for such a ship but the cockroaches were a large infestation! They also told us that the loads would be spread on fields as a type of manure. We asked if birds would eat the bodies and they said "Yes, they do". We were also pleased to be rid of nasty small red bugs which had lived in the cushions we sat on and bit the backs of our knees; they had persisted despite our efforts with Jeyes Fluid.

During the last few days in South Africa we had heard news that the war in Europe was nearly over; the Germans were being pushed back into their own land.

Having arrived at Trincomalee, I was still thinking about South Africa less than eight days ago. We sailed immediately after oiling, in order to join in the chase of the Japanese heavy cruiser *Haguro* which was discovered steaming up the Malacca Straits. We had now become flagship of 5th Cruiser Squadron.

When the news of the surrender of Germany came through, we were oiling at Diego Suarez and on the day officially appointed as 'VE Day' we were once again underway. Our celebrations were curtailed and we had to content ourselves with 'Splicing the mainbrace' and 'Big Eats' if you were not on watch. On the 9th of May I remember a short prayer service on the quarterdeck which was timed when the whole world was supposed to be enjoying celebrating peace in Europe.

I was sixteen when I started fighting away from England and that had continued for five years (one quarter of my life!) and in that time the Navy had given me one free rum!

When I joined up, I was offered what I thought was a free meal, only to have the cost of it removed from my first pay. I had been fed corned dog till I was sick of it, I had had a few weeks of reduced rations and hard oranges, harder cheese and hard ship's biscuits, and now I missed the 'Big Eats' because I was on watch. The war was getting at my guts as well! If only the Allies had put an end to the war in Europe eight days earlier we could have joined in the fun and games and *food* in South Africa.

It all started in late April 1945, while were we anchored off an island in the Car Nicobar group. I was summoned by the Tannoy to report to the gunnery officer on the quarterdeck. "Ah! Edwards," said the gunnery officer, "I've been informed by the GI (gunnery inspector) that you're fully qualified in the uses of the three-Fs time fuses." "I am, Sir, what's the "free-Fs", Sir?" I replied, not quite realising what he was referring to. "Come, come, petty officer, we have paid you four guineas every year, in case there are any scares involving our 6in Mark XXIII time and percussion fuse or 4in Mark XVI time fuses," said the gunner. "Oh, that, Sir!" I replied, remembering the course I took to earn four guineas, three for Mum and a guinea for me. "Are these scares in the turret or four-inch?" I asked. "Not our problem," he said, "they want you ashore. Get yourself organised and take the motor cutter and a couple of ABs as soon as you can manage." "Aye, aye, Sir," I said. As there was no mention of food I didn't ask any more questions. There were no grumbles from the two ABs I chose; any AB would enjoy a trip like this. I changed into my whites (the normal routine of dressing smartly before going ashore, that would be expected of a PO). Some of these islands had been occupied by the Japanese for about two years but we had been assured that they had gone. I signed for permission to leave the ship and, approaching the island in the motor cutter, enjoying a flat-sea day, I was thinking it would be a good day for swimming unless the sea was full of sharks or sea-snakes! As we got nearer it was easy to see that there was a sandy beach which disappeared under the jungle leaves of the land behind, these cast a shadow as though someone had drawn green net curtains, and there we could just make out the outline of a concrete pillbox with a domed roof under which we could see a heavy-machine gun's barrel. Following the single path up the hill, where the trees thinned out we could see a group of about six or seven matelots, dressed in overalls, and a 'Wavy Navy' lieutenant obviously setting up some sort of camp. As we approached, the officer turned round and spoke to me. "Petty Officer Edwards?" "Yes, Sir," I replied, "what's it all about?" I didn't think I had to give him another "Sir". "Come over here and I'll show you," he said, and led me back to the concrete pillbox with its heavy machine-gun. "In the interest of safety, and in case the locals might pinch them, I've been given instructions to disconnect and store safely any of these guns whenever we come across them," he said. Then he added: "Would you disconnect this one and my lads will collect it?" I replied: "I will; send my chaps back to the *Nigeria* with the cutter, they can pick me up later".

The entrance to the pillbox was through a low metal door and down one step to its floor. The officer had moved off quickly. Perhaps he was worried that the Jap who had pushed that door shut had left us a nasty surprise! I didn't like anything about it. I didn't like it even though I had been sent with the help of two of the officer's lads. We picked up a heavy piece of timber and gently levered the door with it. The door opened outwards without any trouble. It was dim inside. I have a dislike of spiders – I hadn't liked going down to our cellar at 10 Elm Park Road, Winchmore Hill when we were children; we knew it was the home of beasties. The two matelots didn't like the look of it either. After I had stood in the dim light for a couple of minutes I could then see that the machine-gun was supported by what looked like a bit of one-inch gas-pipe and it would only be necessary to undo the securing two-inch nut. The light seemed to improve the longer I was in there. I looked all round in case there was a suspended hand-grenade or other booby trap. The inside of the pillbox was clean white concrete. There were some Japanese printed instructions stuck to the walls but I could see nothing except a small amount of earth that had fallen in through the gun loophole, which let a certain amount of light through. The gun barrel protruded from this loophole, which was about nine inches deep and two feet across.

Having made sure the gun wasn't loaded, and that there were no spare bullets for the gun anywhere, I wanted to get out. I ordered the two lads to support the heavy weapon at each end to take the weight, whilst I undid the two-inch nut, then we could all "get the hell out of here!" I worked hard and had just released the gun, saying "Take the weight, watch my fingers, it'll be heavy for all of us" when one of the lads said: "It moved." "Watch it, it's heavy. What moved?" I asked. "Just there," the older lad said, "underneath the window." "Don't let go of anything, you'll kill someone," I said. "What was it?"

319

asked the other chap. "It's hairy, something big," replied the older lad. "Let's get this gun off the plinth and get it to that bloody door before I end up with a bad back," I snarled nervously. They did as I asked and we lowered the gun down just inside the pillbox and stretched our backs. "I didn't see anything move, just fur," said the older chap, who was having another look. "It's a big furry spider; yes, it's the biggest f*****g spider I've ever seen." That was enough for all of us. Reacting to the news about this giant spider, I shouted: "Let's get out of this place. Grab hold of that bloody machine-gun, lift it up and pull it outside." This involved crouching and lifting as the lintel to the door was so low. All three of us were so pleased to get out and away from that bird-eating spider. A local told us about them (with a laugh) the following day. "They can't kill you but can scare you to death." I couldn't have agreed more!

I was pleased to be picked up by our motor cutter and, back on board, enjoyed a shower in the PO's bathroom. I was not looking forward to another day on that island. As I fell asleep, I wondered how many days would it take to complete the job and how dangerous might it be?

The next day I felt better and, having put on my old working shorts, arranged three packed lunches so we wouldn't be hungry. I was more cheerful than I had been the day before, as the cutter dropped us at the same spot, with our food packs. I met the lieutenant, saluted and said: "Sir, did you know there were big spiders in that pillbox?" "No," he said. I had to believe him. "What else have you got for me?" I asked. "I'll show you," he replied, as he led me to a collection of three three-inch shells standing up on a paving-slab which had been set level. Two of these shells appeared not to have any fuses fitted but each of the plugs had been drilled with an eighth-inch hole. The third shell had what looked to be a standard percussion fuse. These three shells had been tied tidily and secured together. To complete this construction, there was a small piece of five-ply wood cut into a triangular

Barbie Edwards

Figure 50. Birdeating spider ¼ actual size

shape with one-foot sides. "Bloody hell," I said, under my breath, "and all for four guineas." "What do you mean?" asked the officer. "Oh," I said, "they pay me four guineas a year extra for this sort of dangerous work." This brand-new officer in training, with no knowledge whatsoever of explosives or fuses, put his fingers onto the triangle of plywood. "Don't touch it!" I shouted, which annoyed him. "But I've taken one of these three shells to pieces up the road," he insisted, "nothing happened." By this time one or two of the matelots had wandered up to listen. I immediately ordered them back to where they had come from 'at the double'. I could see that this also annoyed the lieutenant.

"Sir," I said, "by the look of the paintwork and printing on these shells, they're British but they're old and I can't tell what they're filled with and what fuses have been fitted. Can you tell me that?" He didn't answer. "Are any of them fitted with rear fuses?" Again, he didn't answer. "When did you move these ancient shells? Could you tell me why those two plugs are drilled with eighth-inch holes, possibly leading into the cordite, Sir?" Again, he didn't answer. "Sir," I said, "do you think you may have been dead lucky? What is now worrying me is, what has this nasty little yellow fellow been up to here, can you please tell me? I'm more than a bit worried about this lot, Sir." "I'm sorry, petty officer, you're right, and I may have been dead lucky," he replied. "Sir, percussion direct-action fuses are the simplest kind of fuse. They screw into the noses of high explosive shells and burst on impact. Ones like this have been set up to explode when we step heavily on them or drive a vehicle over them. When the nose of the shell makes contact with the target, or if it's hit hard, a small striker in its nose is forced into the detonator, which fires and detonates the fuse magazine, and thence the exploder and the shell filling. So we've got to find out if our Japanese is a clever Jap and included something unexpected to add to that."

I found out that I was to work with this officer for as long as it took. I considered the situation. Here I was in the wrong place, doing very dangerous work. If the Japanese was an explosives expert, what chance had I got? After all, I had only taken a five-day course (even if I had passed the exam with an 'excellent' on the certificate). I could be dicing with death here for four guineas a year! Whilst I sat on the beach with the two lads enjoying our corned dog sandwiches with water and fruit, I decided to investigate the second home-made anti-personnel mine, which had not been messed about with before we had arrived. I would dismantle it whilst the two ABs watched and they would only come near when I instructed them to. I had come to the conclusion that this was the safest way of tackling the problem.

On arriving at the second site, it looked exactly the same as the first, but there was far more vegetation surrounding it. I asked for a sharp seaman's knife, then all alone I got down on my knees and had started to cut back the shrubbery when I felt a very sharp stab of pain halfway up my shin. I didn't get up, but looked at my leg and found that my sock had fallen down to my ankle. I looked at my right shin and noticed a small red dot next to what looked like a bruise. Whilst staring at this small wound I suddenly became aware of a very thin leaf-green snake about three feet long with a very small head. I called across to the two ABs and said: "I've been bitten by a green snake, it's just gone that way," pointing to a tree by the road. They both came across and looked at my leg which by now had a very dark mauve, enlarged vein showing on it. The swelling was moving up towards my knee. Both ABs were very concerned but more with the fact that there might be lots of snakes that would bite them too! "You two help me to walk to the lieutenant," I said. One of the ABs then said: "Sit down, don't walk, one of us will find the officer," which was sensible. The lieutenant, with half-a-dozen matelots, came running back to look at me. I showed them my leg; the dark discoloration had moved up a couple of inches higher along the vein. "It's all right," said the now extra-friendly officer, "there's a hospital ship less than two miles away, moored at the Point, and the hospital boat is on its way (probably a lie, but he was trying to cheer me up), we're sending them an SOS signal now". They had brought two planks on which to carry me to the small jetty on the beach. I don't know how long the boat took to come but in the meantime the black mark had got up to my groin and I seemed to be producing a third testicle which was also turning mauve! I found myself in a panic situation again.

All I remember about my transportation to the hospital ship was that it didn't seem to take long to get there. My leg hurt now but I was no longer having to constantly look at my groin to see if the swelling was getting bigger because my shorts had been pulled up and I couldn't see my groin any more. I was placed on a small trolley when we arrived. A tall, slim, dark-haired man of about forty wearing a white coat, who I assumed was a doctor, came to see me. He spoke what I took to be German to the two ladies dressed in nun's habits which were partly red in colour, who responded in the same language. These ladies, who were older than me, removed my tatty, dirty working shorts, underpants and socks as if they had been doing it all their lives. The tall, healthy-looking man smiled and said to me in perfect English. "Hello, what bit you?" "A snake," I said. "I may not have a lot of time, so think hard," he said. "What colour was it? How long was it? How thick was it? What sort of head had it?

Think hard, was there anything that you noticed about it? I tell you now, it's terribly important to know anything that you can tell us." I told him again, after trying really hard to think about it. "It was three foot long, it was plain leaf green, without any shades or other colours, its head looked very small and flat and it was climbing in a low bush. I'm sorry, that's all I can remember." "Well, OK, we'll know by tonight," he said with a smile. He then spoke to the two ladies in 'German' again. These ladies called in a third nurse who spoke English. I asked her: "Are you English?" "No," she said, "Dutch. We're all Dutch; this is a Dutch hospital ship." Then the three ladies took off my dirty old shirt and proceeded to give me a blanket bath whilst I was lying there in the nude. I was very embarrassed indeed. I was lying there thinking that I had been fired at in the crotch by an Italian submariner; I had burnt myself in the same spot with hot shell cases whilst firing at a Heinkel; and now a thin green snake had taken sides with the Japanese and bitten me causing my crotch to swell. On each of these three occasions I had had ladies who were complete strangers attending to my private parts which hurt like hell – is this 'bit of green string' going to kill me? Is this war directed against my crotch? What sort of medal will I get? The three nurses washed me and I was given a gown. They then hoisted my right leg up into the air using a sling and left me comfortably supported with three large cushions and pleasantly bade me "good night".

The tall, dark Dutch doctor looked in during the first watch and decided that I had 'made it'; I was going to live and they kept me there for about five days.

I was the only patient in this particular twelve-bed sickbay and I don't recall seeing any patients in the second sickbay, nor do I recall the name of the ship. It could have been the *Oranje* or *Ophir* (Dutch flag); whichever it was, they looked after me well. I have never forgotten that they saved my life.

I found out later that a Wrangler viper's bite will kill a pig or child but a healthy twenty-year-old man should recover. Years later, when working at London Zoo, I came face-to-face with another such viper which gave me a nasty feeling but, on reflection, that 'bit of green string' had saved me from being blown to bits by a booby-trapped Japanese bomb! I do not know who got lumbered with the bomb-disposal job but I hope he survived!

XX

Final Chapter

We had left Simonstown in the Cape on 1st May 1945 with instructions to proceed to Ceylon as we were to become flagship of the 5th Cruiser Squadron (well, we had a cabin for an admiral!). Trincomalee looked nice now the monsoon was over. After we had oiled there we sailed and picked up Rear Admiral W.R. Patterson at sea. The *Nigeria* was ordered to join in the chase for the Japanese heavy cruiser *Haguro*. I didn't like that news; the *Haguro* was a ten eight-inch gun job. It could be anything up to ten minutes from their firing at us before we got near enough to them to return fire. We were at sea when we received an Admiralty signal saying that the Germans had capitulated. It was curious to see how the crew and I received this signal. There was no cheering. It was as if we didn't quite believe it, and anyway, how was it going to affect us here? J.T. Box, other boy seamen and Russians were all dead – so what! I couldn't alter that, it was a feeling of sadness. I felt as I had in Russia, I was looking over my shoulder again. This ten eight-inch gun job was out there somewhere. This was the war we were in now.

Our new admiral instructed us to proceed (without any destroyers) to approximately eighty miles north of the Andaman Islands group where there are two tiny islands called Preparis (some two hundred and fifty miles from Rangoon). All the islands in this chain, the Andamans, and Nicobars, might have been evacuated by the Japanese. Photography from Army Lysanders had confirmed that the Japanese had abandoned them. Two RN fleet minesweepers had been instructed to clear the area of mines laid by the Japanese. We proceeded to Preparis because one of the minesweepers had requested help as they were being attacked by a Japanese unit with a tank while they were working near the shore on an island that the Japanese were supposed to have evacuated. We arrived at Preparis at 1530 and found a reasonably safe anchorage in the bay behind a promontory so that we

324

couldn't be seen from the sea. The captain of the minesweeper came alongside in his boat and was piped on board for a meeting with the Admiral. This sort of meeting always produced a buzz. This one went that about a thousand Japanese had been transferred by small boats from Rangoon when it fell to our 14th Army. These Japanese, with tanks, were waiting to be picked up by the *Haguro* which would take them back to Japan.

Whilst we were hiding behind the promontory we kept up enough steam for a five-minute getaway. Double lookouts were posted: one group looking out to sea and the other looking across the bay into the 'bush'. Radar and Asdic were in use too. Just as it was getting dark we hoisted our anchor and went out to sea assuming second degree of readiness throughout the night in case the *Haguro* or a submarine turned up. It seemed ages since we had had an 'alarm to arms' for submarines.

In our present situation we asked ourselves, was there a little yellow officer in this 'bush' in charge of one or two thousand Japanese soldiers who were hiding whilst waiting to be picked up by the *Haguro*, or was there a little yellow chap trying to look after two dozen tired Jap soldiers? If he was waiting to be rescued by their cruiser it was to his advantage to let the minesweeper clear the last of the mines to let the *Haguro* get as close in to the shore as possible to pick them up quickly. It was difficult to see why he was 'playing games' with this one very small tank unless he was trying to warn the *Haguro* not to try to collect them and put the cruiser at risk. The fact that they had attacked the minesweeper was the reason why we had come here. The buzz about this movement was that the Japanese had deliberately given away their position to draw our ship away whilst the *Haguro* was heading for another position. If true, it was a clever move. Our Rear Admiral Patterson was not taking any risks. He had signalled for a Westland Lysander army aircraft to photograph whatever was there and drop leaflets, printed in Japanese, telling them that the Germans had 'packed it in' and there was no way that they could get back to Tokyo.

The Westland Lysander came back a second day to make another leaflet drop. The pilot, possibly not seeing any Japanese, did the same run again, but came in much lower. As a result, the Japs shot down the two-man plane. The same day, the Japanese heavy cruiser sailed for the Andaman Islands to evacuate the garrison. She was seen by one of our submarines in the Malacca Straits and Admiral Walker set out with his escort carriers to catch her. They were sighted on the 11th and *Haguro* turned back. She tried again a few days later. This time the 26th Destroyer Flotilla (Captain M. Power) with five destroyers

Photo 70. Westland Lysander

was waiting off Penang and, in a classic night torpedo attack, they sank the *Haguro*. She went down at dawn on 16th May.

Was this little action, giving himself away, an example of a Japanese helping his fellow countrymen and their ship to get to Japan to protect the Emperor (just as our Scottish teacher had told us)? This island would have been cleared by the 14th Army, no doubt with casualties.

This was the beginning of the big drive which would take us, the Allies, down through Sumatra to Singapore or through Sumatra towards Java and on to Timor following the retreating Japanese. (That was what was posted on our notice-board.) Where to after that was not mentioned anywhere.

All the Japanese were moving as fast as they could from Burma and cutting across Thailand and Laos to South Vietnam. This was going to be an awful job of pursuit with possibly many casualties. I had that Russian feeling all over again. I felt that there was going to be more sadness. We were hearing rumours about half a million 'crack' trained Japanese soldiers waiting to meet any Allies who got to Japan and that all Japanese planes would be manned by Kamikaze pilots. Worst of all, all Japanese women and children over the age of ten were to be 'called up' to fight for Emperor Hirohito. It sounded like a bloodbath ahead.

Japan had only been attacked by air once, until June 1944 when regular bombing was commenced, by sixteen B25 Mitchell (medium size) bombers. The raid was not a success due to bad weather but on

6th August 1945 we heard that an 'Atom Bomb' had been dropped on Japan. None of us knew what that was. Everyone was asking, "What's an atom?" It was an HO who was a schoolteacher in civilian life who told us that 'atom' was derived from the Greek word *atomos* meaning small or indivisible, but nobody really understood how that tied up with a bomb. When we saw the official notice it stated that a US B29 Superfortress flying from Tinian had dropped the first atomic bomb from a great height on Hiroshima (the arsenal of Japan). This atomic bomb was the equivalent of 20,000 tons of TNT and it had completely destroyed the huge Japanese arms factories and stores. We understood why this had been done; we all knew that it would save thousands of Allied lives, many Japanese too, and as a result of this perhaps the war would be finished more quickly and we could go home at last.

Japan had been fighting China since 1931 and the Allies from 1942. The Japanese had an unmatched record of cruelty towards the Chinese. In eight weeks in early 1938, they had savagely hand-butchered 300,000 men, women and children in the city of Nanking to teach the rest of the Chinese population a lesson. I couldn't feel sorry for the Japanese, especially if this new weapon would help to stop this war and perhaps save my life.

The fact that Russia had declared war on Japan on 8th August 1945 and then invaded Japanese-held Manchuria the next day, swamping the Japanese defences there, made us feel more confident that the end was even nearer.

We heard, on 9th August, as we were heading for 'Trinco', that a second A-bomb had been detonated over Nagasaki. It was a direct hit and destroyed the enormous naval base as well as many naval manufacturing plants.

VJ Day (Victory over Japan) came on 15th August when Emperor Hirohito broadcast Japan's unconditional surrender, although the actual signing of the document was not until 2nd September. It took place on US battleship *Missouri*.

In Trincomalee Harbour on VJ night, all the ships were floodlit. 'V' signs in electric lights hung from every masthead, searchlight beams played across the skies and rockets and coloured Very lights contributed to a carnival effect: The fleet was 'all lit up'. It was a night of great rejoicing but there was nothing to compare with the wild frenzy which was displayed in England. One might explain it by saying that it was difficult to become ecstatically 'happy' on one extra tot of rum but the real reason was that all of us realised that the road to victory had been hard and long. Many of our friends had been lost on the way and there was still more work to be done.

Photo 71. HMS Nigeria *with crew*

That night I was duty watch and it was my job to collect all the off-watch sailors who had gone ashore to the canteen for their one bottle of free beer; even those who hadn't got a beer ticket had joined them. I was coxswain of a drifter which was used to transport large numbers of sailors. I was to pick up all crews of any ship, including the *Nigeria*, as they turned up at the temporary pier made of scaffolding and transport them back to their ships. The job was scheduled to last until two or three in the morning.

When I arrived to pick up all these crews I could see that they had helped themselves to all the beer they could find and, having found that there was none left, they had set fire to the thatched roof of the canteen. They were as 'pissed' as you can get and had started to bend over all the jetty's round upright scaffolding poles, making it impossible to drive anything along the pier.

I waited for the hundreds of matelots to reach the end of the jetty, shouting at them to "Take it easy". They were not in the mood to listen; the war was over and they wanted to go home. They had been bending the iron tubes as they came along and every now and then some fell over the side of the jetty. For us in the drifter it was dangerous. I ordered the four ordinary seamen (two either side of the boat) to disconnect the two fore and aft stays and take a 'dry turn' which would enable us to let go fore and aft in a hurry, as the sailors

YOU KNOW, SOMETIMES IT DOESN'T SEEM THAT I'VE BEEN OUT HERE SO LONG...........

SYMPHONY IN 'Y'

You've all heard the tale of Dan McGrew,
Of Nell and the rest of the boys,
But here is a tale that is perfectly true—
A tale of excitement and noise.

A bunch of the boys from the Quarter-deck part
Closed up in a gun-house called 'Y'.
A bit of a shoot was going to start.
At least, they were going to try.

They closed the door on this iron shed
As though they had something to hide.
The silence outside would have frightened the dead,
But oh my gosh—INSIDE !

The Captain of " Y " got up in his seat
And ordered the boys to get cracking ;
But all they could see was the soles of his feet,
For the top of his stool was lacking.

He picked himself up and roared like a bull,
And angrily glared at his men.
Then they started to ram, and he jumped off his stool,
" You idiots ! I'll tell you when."

So they loaded the gun and slammed to the breach,
And all of the chatter was stilled,
But an O.D. stood where the recoil could reach.
He was the first to be killed.

Then they loaded again, just the same as before,
Though the difference was easy to see,
For the centre of " Y " blew to bits with a roar
And slung the whole crowd in the sea.

Take heed of this warning, be kind to your men,
And this you must never forget—
Unless you are careful, you'll never know when,
Like the Centre of " Y " you'll get wet.

P.O. D.E. COWLING

OH, IT'S ONLY THE 'Q.E.' DOING A THROW-OFF......

were just pressing forwards and were not interested in stopping. If I had attempted to leave them they would have pushed the drifter under water. The whole canteen was now on fire and the staff were chasing the drunks along the jetty. When the boat was full I was happy to get clear of the pier. I picked up a couple of lads who had fallen into the water and started off to one of the larger ships because the majority of sailors were from her. I only increased the speed of the drifter when we had delivered them (I think it was to a carrier).

I learnt the following day that six ratings had managed to drown themselves. As far as I remember they never repaired or rebuilt the 'straw canteen'.

In mid-September, Royal Navy ships, together with Dominions' Navies, were involved in the repatriation of Allied prisoners of war. They were found to be in a terrible condition: they had been starved and beaten and it was obvious that most needed urgent medical attention. They were in as bad a condition as people who had been in Belsen and other concentration camps. Food and medical equipment was needed for prisoners and natives everywhere in that war zone.

On 6th September, the Australian General Sturdee took the ceremony of the surrender of the Bismark Archipelago, New Guinea and the Solomon Islands. Admiral Mountbatten took the ceremony of the surrender of South East Asia, in Singapore, and 'Swiftsure' Rear Admiral C.H.S. Harcourt (one of the rear admirals who was with us in the Mediterranean on 'Pedestal' in August 1942) accepted surrender at Hong Kong.

I was twenty-two by now and it was a time of happiness and sadness all at once. Whilst all these surrender ceremonies were taking place, we were at Sebang which is situated on the Island of Pulo We (as it was called then) at the northern tip of Sumatra, from which it is separated by the Malacca Passage (about ten miles wide). The population was about 5,000, the majority of them Malays; the next largest group were Chinese. Before the war they were under Dutch administration. Sebang was a place of some importance to the Dutch as an oiling station for merchant ships trading between the Netherlands East Indies and Europe, South Africa and the USA, thus avoiding them having to buy oil from foreign sources.

Knowing that the Japanese were going to invade the island, the Dutch carried out a policy of destruction of the oil tanks, jetties and other installations before they left. The Japanese had arrived on 12th March 1942 (at the time I was still in Russia) and imposed a harsh routine.

Having landed on Pulo We, we made our way to a mission. I was accompanied by five young ABs. The beach was such a pretty place

– it looked like a holiday-maker's paradise. Steps led from the beach up to the cliff-top, a path continued over the top and down the other side to a depression where there were eleven bungalows forming a circle. Three of these buildings were the homes of the Catholic priest, the senior doctor and the almoner. These three men had not been seen since 1942. On our way down to the bungalow we passed an eight-by-twelve-foot building like a large garden shed; it was painted green and had two eight-by-four-foot doors. There, early that morning after the war was finished, we found a young white man nailed to these doors, he had been crucified. He had no identification of any sort on him and was not in any type of uniform. We guessed that he had been killed just before peace had been agreed. It appeared that the Japanese had sat on rows of chairs (which were still there) and watched him die, and to hasten his death he had been filled up with water until his abdomen was distended. He must have been in intense pain and was utterly helpless and could do nothing to save himself. This seemed to be some sort of amusement for the Japanese spectators. My five ABs found all this very distressing and, as I couldn't find any means of identification on the man, I sent a signal for the PMO (principal medical officer) to give me instructions. I was ordered to send my ABs to join the midshipman in another part of the camp.

The PMO and I went down into the woodland behind the bungalows where we found half a dozen locals hanging from the trees. They had been hung up by one leg and left to die. They had been dead for some time but their relatives had not been allowed to come in and cut them down. There was more horror but as I promised the PMO to keep silent about what I saw I cannot say what we found. Even if I could it would distress me to write about it and would horrify anyone reading about it.

The misery of cleaning up after the war and the Japanese being found and sent home lasted for nearly two months. It was a depressing time for us all as we were only interested in getting back home.

The war was over, or so they were saying; all we were thinking about was going home and seeing our families. HOs were thinking about getting out, back to their working lives as they used to be, but for so many of us we were still being given unpleasant tasks as there remained groups of Japanese soldiers who were still fighting, some possibly because that was what they wanted to do, others just didn't know that the end had come. The rest were ignoring leaflets and they knew nothing about atom bombs.

Until our daily orders stated "prepare to weigh anchor and proceed to the UK", we couldn't leave. This order came on 1st September 1946 and we left 'Trinco', Foul Point and headed for home via the Gulf of Aden, the Red Sea, Gulf of Suez, Great Bitter Lake and Ismailia, where as CQM I took the ship's wheel (with the Egyptian canal pilot in attendance) and we went through the Suez Canal and, despite the locals on the banks turning their backs and raising their gowns and showing their bare bums (doing their best to put me off my course!), we brought the *Nigeria* safely into the Mediterranean. We then proceeded to Malta, where we spent a relaxing month in Valletta Harbour.

Then via the Sicilian Channel to the Straits of Gibraltar (scenes of my nightmares on 'Pedestal') and into the Atlantic. After arrival in Britain we were sent to Chatham Docks and de-ammunitioned the ship; more hard work, this time carried out with pleasure.

After this we all left the ship for leave. Mother and Auntie were very pleased to see me well and alive, they had so many questions. They kept on repeating how thin I was and asked me what I had been eating. Auntie kept asking me about girls but I could only think about Joyce, so I replied: "What ladies? There are no girls at sea." I found out whilst I was there that Auntie had been very ill. The fourteen days went by so quickly and we returned to the *Nigeria*, ammunitioned the ship and sailed it to the Plymouth Devonport dockyard for a refit. It was then sold to the Indian Navy and renamed the *Mysore* – I thought, my sore what!

Having arrived at Chatham, *Pembroke V* Depot I found that there was a controversy going on between HOs and long-service sailors. The HOs were intent on getting out with their demob suit, shirt, Trilby hat, woolly socks, shoes tie and mac, whilst the Admiralty were set on bagging anybody they could to send aboard any ship as they were desperate to replace the HOs. I quickly caught on to this situation and signed on to spend the next eighteen months taking a course at St Mary's Gunnery Unit next to *Pembroke V*, living in the POs' mess. As long as I could keep up with the course it would give me every weekend off in London N21 to see Joyce. I would have nearly every weekday evening free in Whitstable (where Mum and Auntie were living). The Navy needed gunnery instructors, otherwise known as gunner's mates, as many fully-qualified personnel were well over the age-limit, so I settled down to this quite difficult GI course. I had also been instructed to take ET2 (higher educational test). I didn't want to do that; it sounded like an officer's course.

It was whilst I was talking to a PO oppo, telling him how fed up I was with the 'Andrew' and that I really wanted to 'chuck in' my naval career, that I laughingly added "I wish I could ask my mum to 'sell the pig and buy me out'" as the joke went. "Don't laugh," my friend said, "they were discussing this in Parliament the other day. They said that if you'd been serving in 1941 and you were eighteen years of age you could apply for release. I'll ask the jaunty in *Pembroke V*, if you give us two neat tots." I gave him two tots in a small brown bottle. He came back to me within the week. "It's possible; the jaunty found that the Admiralty Instructions are: That you must have been *under* eighteen on joining the Navy, as long as that was before 1941, then you have to apply to the commander's 'request and defaulters' at 0900 on Monday where you ask to see the captain representing the Admiralty and pay, in advance, about £50 cash. All of this will cost you another two neat tots. You've only got one problem," my friend said, "you will not be able to apply to your commander at St Mary's as you have just volunteered to take this GI course." My face dropped. "There's only one way round it," he said. "How?" I asked. "Well, lie," he said. "Say that you're staying in Chatham, *Pembroke V* and put your request in at *Pembroke V* and take a chance that with this overcrowding no-one is going to spend hours and hours finding out where you're eating and sleeping. If you do get found out it's your GI course that will go and you'll be back to a new draft to a ship. You're going to have to supply two tots in your brown bottle again when he tells you that he's received your first request to the Admiralty and two tots for the jaunty's runner to bike over to St Mary's to see the jaunty who'll tell him if your request has been received at the Admiralty. Then repeat the tots for the jaunty and messenger to tell you to go to see the jaunty with your £50 to buy yourself out."

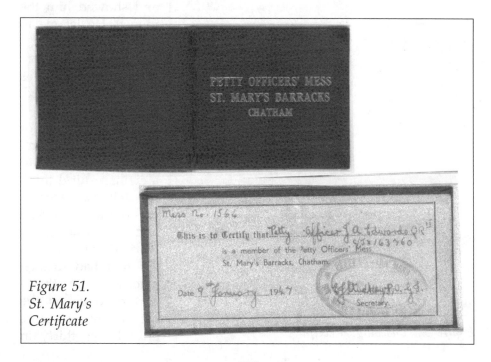

Figure 51.
St. Mary's
Certificate

Whilst I was waiting for all this to-ing and fro-ing it was a terribly cold winter and our accommodation was in a stark barrack room which contained one small coke-burning fire and, as fuel was rationed, we only had one shovelful of coke each evening. One evening, during the 'evening rounds', the officer asked if there were any complaints and one fellow remarked that it was warmer outside than in the room. "Right," said the officer, "everybody out!"

Eventually my draft came through; the tots had done their job! I was called to collect the paperwork and I even had change from my £50! The jaunty said: "Why don't you nip over there, lad, and say the jaunty sent you to collect a set of demob clothes." These I got in a brown paper bag and I ran to the exit gate. The guard there said "where are you going?" I replied: "I'm going home." He told me to hang on whilst he saw the chief. A taxi pulled up just as he had turned and walked away. I said to the taxi driver: "Take me to the station, Whitstable side please," to which he replied "Got the fare?" I said "Yes" and showed him the money. He let me in and off we went.

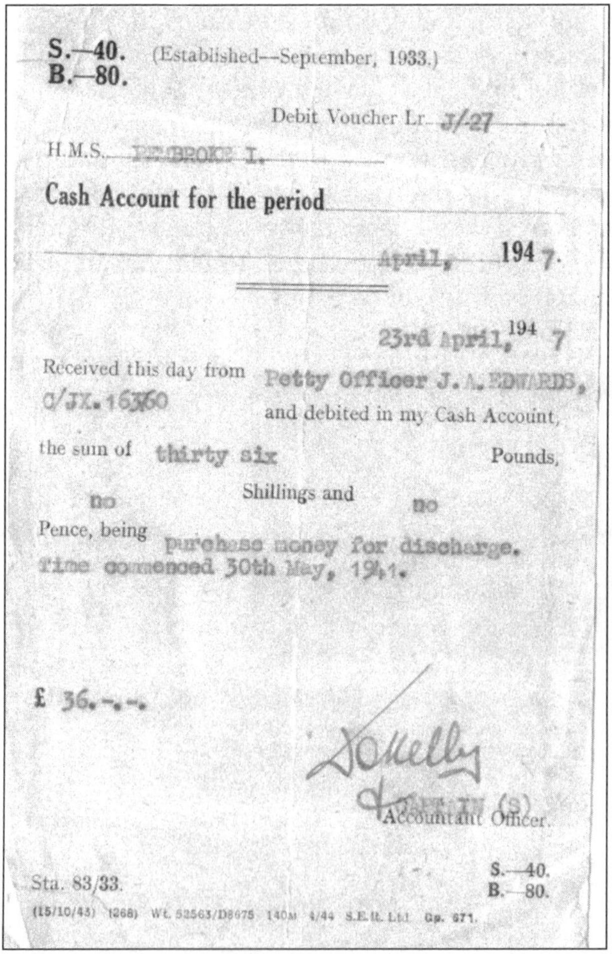

When I got to Whitstable, Mum was terribly confused. She thought that I was in the Navy for ever and couldn't take it in that I had a civilian suit. I think she felt that what I was doing was illegal and she was really worried.

I had had to sign a form to say that I agreed to be on the list of naval reserves until I was thirty in

Figure 52. Discharge Receipt

case there was another war but I was certain that there wouldn't be one. Ha, ha . . .

Whilst I was contemplating all this, Joyce and I decided to get married. The great day was to be in late 1946 and I had managed to get three days' leave. I wore my South African-made PO's uniform for the marriage, which was held at St Stephen's Church, Enfield.

We caught the 4pm train from London Bridge to go to Auntie's bungalow where we were to spend our honeymoon. We had taken one of Auntie's front door keys with us to let ourselves in as she had arranged to stay with a friend whilst we were there.

When we arrived, at about 7pm, we found we couldn't get in as the front door was locked from the inside – Auntie had been taken ill during the night and, as a result, had not left that morning. On breaking in I found the dear lady unconscious in bed. It was a Saturday and it took us some time to contact Auntie's doctor. He arranged for Auntie to be taken into the local hospital on the Monday morning and, in the meantime, we were supplied with some wooden spatulas so that we could depress her tongue to ease her breathing whilst she was unconscious. The ambulance man arrived as arranged on Monday morning, only to find that she had sadly passed away during the night. My mother and sister took over the arrangements from us newly-weds but I was so sad that another death had occurred for me to come to terms

Photo 72. My wedding

with. This nice lady had done so much for me. In the circumstances we had to postpone our honeymoon.

After I had been discharged I had to find work. This was difficult because there were so many others looking for jobs too. To make a good impression, Joyce removed the ribbons and badges from my PO's uniform jacket and sewed turn-ups onto the trousers – a job she hadn't learnt to do at Bletchley! This meant that I could now wear this revamped suit and my naval shoes when I went for interviews. I found a job with the Tottenham Gas Company and purchased a second-hand bicycle to get me to Tottenham and back, from Winchmore Hill, to save on fares.

Although I was now earning £2 10s a week (£2.50 decimal), we were still hard up, and we hadn't anywhere to live. The RN Reserve added another 10/6d a week, and Joyce earned £6 a week as a high-speed shorthand typist – that made our total weekly income £9 0s 6d. At this time there was severe rationing of food, clothing, furniture and fuel but we could just manage.

It wasn't until 1st October 1951 that I had to worry about changing my suit back to a Navy specification again – when I was called back into the Royal Fleet Reserve as a Korea situation loomed. My ribbons had gone astray somewhere – maybe the children had had them! In any event, as soon as I arrived at Pembroke Barracks without my ribbons I was arrested at the gate for not having them with me! I immediately realised that I shouldn't tell these snotty young POs that I had lost them.

(It was going to be strange, even for a short period, to be back in a Royal Navy environment again. At best I could hope to be helping to train recruits, but knowing my luck I would probably be back at the 'sharp end'!)

I was only there for three weeks. I started this training with a feeling of unease. The training included a dash round the assault course – a test which I passed! This was followed by another request for me to pass the higher educational test. At the end of the first week I was asked to meet the commander that Friday afternoon. I thought it would be because of the lack of ribbons, but no – he was reading my Gunnery History Sheet with its four SUPRs (superior). The Navy was short of gunner's mates. The commander was very friendly, and said: "How are you getting on in Civvy Street?" I remember thinking 'what are you after?' "Well, OK, I suppose," I replied. "Had you thought of coming back permanently?" he asked.

I told him that I didn't realise it was possible but he told me that, although I had bought myself out, the Navy could reinstate me for another five years – giving me £700 when I signed up plus reactivating

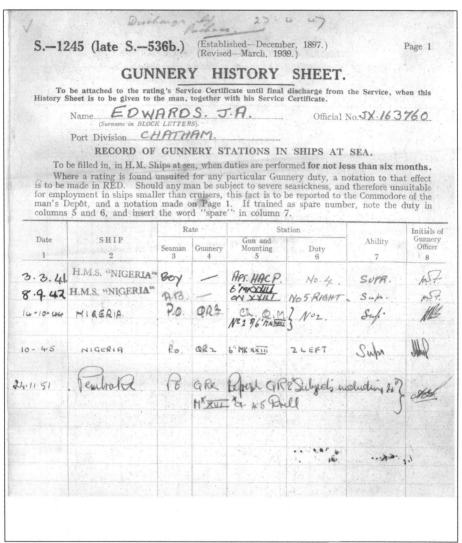

Figure 53a. Gunnery history sheets

my pension. "Think about it," said the commander, "there'll be a meeting to explain things to you all before you go home."

I phoned Joyce and asked how she felt about £700, which in those days would buy a very nice house and furniture. Joyce was straight to the point. "I don't trust the Navy! You're out – stay out!"

I did! Even though I might have earned as much as £7,000 by the time I would have served my time!

I was honoured to be asked to write to the USSR Embassy in London in 1985 following which I received a letter dated 16th December 1986 from Mr Alexey Nikiforov. In April 1987 I received a

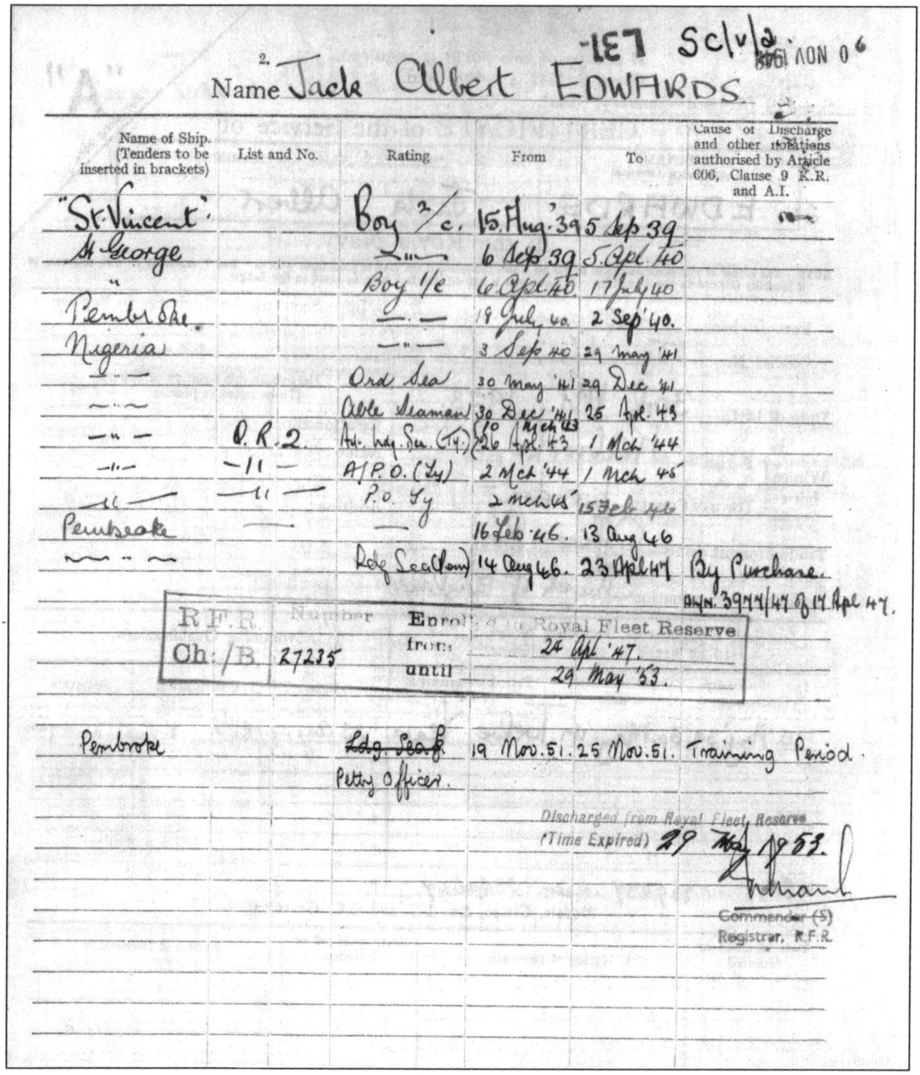

Name *Jack Albert* EDWARDS

Name of Ship. (Tenders to be inserted in brackets)	List and No.	Rating	From	To	Cause of Discharge and other notations authorised by Article 606, Clause 9 K.R. and A.I.
"St. Vincent"		Boy 2/c.	15 Aug '39	5 Sep 39	
St. George		— " —	6 Sep 39	5 Apl 40	
"		Boy 1/c	6 Apl 40	17 Jul 40	
Pembroke		— " —	19 Jul 40	2 Sep '40.	
Nigeria		— " —	3 Sep 40	29 May '41	
— " —		Ord Sea	30 May '41	29 Dec '41	
— " —		Able Seaman	30 Dec '41	26 Apl 43	
— " —	P.R.2	Ad. Hy. Sea (Ty)	26 Apl 43	1 Mch '44	
— " —	— " —	A/P.O. (Ty)	2 Mch '44	1 Mch 45	
— " —	— " —	P.O. Ty	2 Mch 45	15 Feb 46	
Pembroke		—	16 Feb '46	13 Aug 46	
— " —		Pelg Sea (Tem)	14 Aug 46	23 Apl 47	By Purchase. AWN 3944/47 of 17 Apl 47.

<table>
<tr><td colspan="2">R.F.R. Number</td><td colspan="2">Enrol... Royal Fleet Reserve</td></tr>
<tr><td>Ch:/B.</td><td>27235</td><td>from:
until</td><td>24 Apl '47.
29 May '53.</td></tr>
</table>

Pembroke		Ldg. Sea.	19 Nov.51.	25 Nov.51.	Training Period.
		Petty Officer.			

Discharged from Royal Fleet Reserve
(Time Expired) 29 May 1953

Commander (S)
Registrar, R.F.R.

Figure 53b. Service Record

Russian medal (made from gold) and a citation dated 30th November 1986.

(See copies of Mr Alexey Nikiforov's letter and the Russian medal)

As I have already stated, I was honoured to receive this medal. I know I had had to suffer on twenty-two Russian convoys and spend seven and a half months stationed ashore in Murmansk to earn it but at least the Russians presented a medal. My own country didn't manage to honour any of us who were there during those terrible years.

L-UFFIĊĊJU TAL-PRIM MINISTRU   **MALTA**   OFFICE OF THE PRIME MINISTER

L-Uffiċċju tal-Kabinett   *Cabinet Office*

                                        March 1993

Mr Jack A Edwards
33 Moreton End Lane
Harpenden
Hertfordshire AL5 2EY
UK

Sir,

NATIONAL COMMEMORATIVE MEDAL

I have the honour to inform you that the President of Malta has
been pleased to approve the Prime Minister's recommendation
that **"The Malta George Cross Fiftieth Anniversary Medal"** be
awarded to you. Your name will, in due course, appear in the
List of Awards to be published in the Government Gazette.

A number of Presentation Ceremonies, presided over by the
President of Malta, are being held at the Palace, Valletta,
Malta, while other Award Ceremonies will be held in London by
Malta's High Commissioner. Where it shall not be convenient or
practical for the presentation to be made in person, the Medal
may be delivered by registered post or such other means as may
be considered expedient.

To facilitate the presentation arrangements, you are cordially
requested to complete and tick as appropriate the enclosed blue
card and to forward it at an early date to:

            The High Commissioner of Malta
            16, Kensington Square
            London W8 5HH

Yours faithfully,

Ms C Attard
Honours and Awards Co-ordinator

Enc.

AUBERGE DE CASTILLE, VALLETTA
TEL: 225231, 220460; FAX: 244922

339

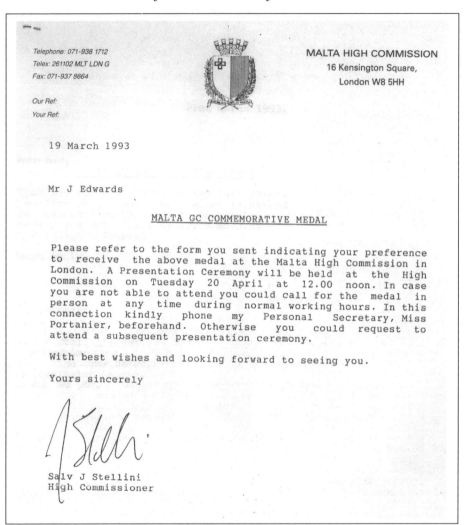

Telephone: 071-938 1712
Telex: 261102 MLT LDN G
Fax: 071-937 8664

Our Ref:
Your Ref:

MALTA HIGH COMMISSION
16 Kensington Square,
London W8 5HH

19 March 1993

Mr J Edwards

MALTA GC COMMEMORATIVE MEDAL

Please refer to the form you sent indicating your preference to receive the above medal at the Malta High Commission in London. A Presentation Ceremony will be held at the High Commission on Tuesday 20 April at 12.00 noon. In case you are not able to attend you could call for the medal in person at any time during normal working hours. In this connection kindly phone my Personal Secretary, Miss Portanier, beforehand. Otherwise you could request to attend a subsequent presentation ceremony.

With best wishes and looking forward to seeing you.

Yours sincerely

Salv J Stellini
High Commissioner

Figure 54/55. Letters re Malta Medal

The medal came with an invitation to visit Russia. Although Joyce and I had to pay our fares, the trip was fantastic and exciting. Joyce went on Russian TV in Tbilisi and we visited two universities where most of the students we met spoke very good English. At this time President Reagan, and his wife Nancy, met with President and Mrs Gorbachev – the reception they were receiving could not have been any better than the one the Russians gave us!

The special treatment given to us by the Maltese in March 1993 was equally as warm as the one the Russians had given us in 1986. (See Malta High Commission letters 8th–19th March 1993.)

I never met any *Nigerians* on either of these two occasions.

To the participant of war on the occasion of the 40th Anniversary of the Victory in the Great Patriotic War 1941-1945

СОЮЗ
СОВЕТСКИХ
СОЦИАЛИСТИЧЕСКИХ
РЕСПУБЛИК

УДОСТОВЕРЕНИЕ
К ЮБИЛЕЙНОЙ МЕДАЛИ
„СОРОК ЛЕТ ПОБЕДЫ
В ВЕЛИКОЙ ОТЕЧЕСТВЕННОЙ
ВОЙНЕ 1941—1945 гг."

Figures 56 (a & b).
Letter re Soviet Medal

ПОСОЛЬСТВО
СОЮЗА СОВЕТСКИХ
СОЦИАЛИСТИЧЕСКИХ РЕСПУБЛИК

13,Kensington Palace Gardens
London W8

16 December 1986

Dear Sir,

I have the honour to acknowledge your letter regarding the Soviet medal.

You might be aware that during the war in 1941-45 hundreds of British servicemen were awarded Soviet decorations, both orders and medals.

On the occasion of the 40th anniversary of the Victory a special medal was struck to commemorate the contribution of those who took part in the efforts which finally brought about the defeat of our common enemy. In 1985 as well as this year the Soviet Ambassador presented a great number of those medals to British citizens as recognition of their contribution to our common victory in the war. The decision to award medals was in each case taken in Moscow by the Presidium of the Supreme Soviet of the USSR, our highest State authority.

It gives me great pleasure to inform you that your letter will be properly handled. You will appreciate that the consideration of many applications regarding the medals might take some time. As soon as the Embassy gets the reply from Moscow you will be duly posted.

Sincerely Yours,

Alexey Nikiforov
Counsellor
USSR Embassy

My wife sadly died shortly after that. I have to say that this book would never have been written if it hadn't been for her support. I regret I cannot tell the world of Joyce's war at Bletchley Park. All I have managed to find out about Bletchley is that it was a terrible place to work. I only found out that Joyce worked there just before she died when the Official Secrets Act restrictions had run their course. She had never spoken about working there before that.

XXI

Tailpiece

Having read Jack's account of his six and a half years in the Navy, it might interest readers to know what followed.

His job with the Tottenham Gas Company involved starting at the lowest task which was digging holes for pipes. This was not so arduous as it was for others, since Jack was very fit and used to heavy work. He managed to pass the necessary exams and graduated from fitter's mate to the Tottenham Gas Showroom and promoted onwards to Hoddesdon showroom manager. Again, some of his Navy experience with routine bookwork and the bookkeeping training at Pitmans College came in useful. Wages did not rise greatly until May 1959 when he was promoted within the Eastern Gas Board to Norfolk as a central heating representative. In 1964 he rose to senior technician for Watford District, again responsible for central heating.

In May 1968 he was promoted to senior officer in central heating sales and given the whole area from Barnet to Haverhill with responsibility for nineteen showrooms, fifty outside salesmen, and fourteen private contractors with about eighty subcontractors. Again, naval experience had equipped him for taking responsibility for organising groups of men into various duties, keeping accurate records of materials and jobs in progress and, above all, after climbing the mast he was confident about climbing up skeletons of buildings and high-rise blocks of flats (which councils were putting up) to inspect gas installations.

At the age of fifty-three, Jack accepted a golden handshake from the Gas Board and took early retirement.

Whilst pursuing his career, he had maintained his earlier interest in astronomy and when he left the Navy he was able to take advantage of the provision it had made for ex-naval personnel to take further education. Jack chose astronomy evening classes and joined the Junior Astronomical Society in North London. He built his own six-inch Newtonian reflector telescope with equatorial head and was delighted when he was involved with Patrick Moore in tracking the journeys of the Russian Sputnik, containing the dog Leika, as it passed over London. Also, they took part in a project recording the occultations of the moons of Jupiter, tracing their journeys and timing their appearances as they came into sight from behind the planet until they disappeared around the back again.

The pleasure of using the telescope waned as the nights became polluted with street lighting and other astronomers became more demanding, wanting space and asking for a regular supply of cups of tea all through the night, so the telescope was sold!

He then built a boat which was taken to the Broads or up to the Lakes for a few years. He enjoyed sailing that but the family lost interest and Joyce found it hard work, so that was stripped of pieces for sale, then cut in two. One half is still in the garden as a garden seat!

The thing which Jack managed to do for many years, and is particularly proud of, was being a blood-donor. By the time he finished he had given a total of sixty-six pints of blood.

After retirement, Jack was immediately offered a job by Whipsnade Zoo and quickly became involved in all manner of duties there. As a volunteer, he organised a group of volunteer ladies as guides/lecturers to visitors (mostly school groups). He also helped keepers with their jobs and got to know a great deal about various creatures in order to answer children's questions. His favourite animals were the elephants, hippos (particularly Henry) and white rhino. In the winter, there was shovelling, feeding, counting of heads and general helping with animal husbandry.

Jack attended the University of Hertfordshire, as it is now known, studying zoology and passing his exams, which enabled him to become a Fellow of the Zoological Society, so even the education he had had in the Navy on the subject of whales came in useful when Whipsnade had a dolphin for a short while.

The job also included regular working visits to London and Twycross Zoos where he met delightful young apes and fell in love with a baby gorilla.

Sadly this job came to an abrupt end as a result of two things: the Government of the day decided that they would cease funding animal breeding projects, and then Joyce became very ill – so Jack left the zoo and nursed her to the end.

Jack now lives quietly in Hertfordshire with his second wife but he still plays badminton regularly!

One friendship which continued to give Jack a warm feeling was the one he had with Bill Chick (see Photo 73), whose naval career

Photo 73. Commander W.E. Chick DSC RN (ret'd)

he followed with interest. Bill was the engineer officer who managed to save the lives of the crew of the *Nigeria*, on the two occasions when she was badly damaged in the war, with his expert repairs. He went on to become a damage control expert and there is a plaque on HMS *Belfast* acknowledging his contribution to the Navy. Sadly, just as the finishing touches to this book were being completed, Jack learnt that Bill had died peacefully at the age of ninety-four.

In one of those peculiar coincidences in life, one of the lady volunteers Jack worked with at Whipsnade was Bill Chick's daughter.

knots, 0835 Sirius, Phoebe and tug Jaunty join company, 0930 sighted four Hunt destroyers 080 degrees, 1120 Speed 12 knots, 1126 Emergency turn to port, 1129 Enemy sited, turned to port 11 knots, 1320 HMS Eagle hit by two or more torpedoes, 1321 Emergency turn to port, Emergency turn to starboard, 1345, 14 knots, 1406 Emergency turn to port, emergency turns to starboard, 1538 12knots, 1605 Emergency turns, 1635 7 knots, 1640 streamed PVs 1657 12 knots, 1715 Z/Z, 1908 13 knots, 2100 course and speed as required for air attacks, 2102 opened fire, 2115 ceased fire, 2119 Speed 12 knots, 2120 re opened fire, speed 12 knots.

12th August, Wednesday. 1942. 0500 10knots, 0530 12 knots, 0651 Emergency turn, 0652 (ET), 0636 (ET), 0711 (ET), 0751 (ET), 0750 14 knots 0820 (ET), 0904 (ET), 0916 Opened fire, 0919 Ceased fire, 0924 (ET), 0932 (ET), 0940 (ET), 1027 Abeam declination, 1035 (ET), 1135(ET), 1140 (ET), 1153 (ET), 1155 14 knots, 1214 Opened fire, 1214 Ceased fire, 1216(ET), 1217 (ET), 1243 Opened fire with close range weapons, 1215 (ET), 1252 Ceased fire, 1309 (ET), 1317 Open fire, 1318 (ET), 1324 Ceased fire, Galita island bearing 148 degrees, 1342 15 knots, 1356 (ET), 1500 14 and a half knots,1502 (ET), 1557 (ET), 1603(ET), 1622(ET), 1641 (ET), 1840 Open fire, 1840(ET), 1843 (ET), 1849 (ET), Ceased fire, 1956 HMS Nigeria torpedoed amidships port side, 2010 ship stopped, 2015 HMS Ashanti secured alongside, Amiral Burroughs and the Tenth Cruiser Squadron's Commanders and staff boarded HMS Ashanti. The Admiral whished HMS Nigeria and its crew "Good Luck". 2030 Ashanti cast off. 2033 HMS Nigeria using "A boiler room only" and hand steering, in company of HMS Birchester and HMS Wilton started up engines and got underway.2220 Passed destroyers HMS Forthright and HMS Tarter.

13th August, Thursday.1942. 0025 HMS Birchester in contact, 0400 estimated speed 16-17 knots. 0052 Estimated casualties at least 52 dead. 0850 Birchester joined company. 1034 sited Bengalie on the beam, 1108, 3 aircraft in sight, 1110 Beaufighter over head, 1429 Destroyer opened fire on shadowing aircraft, 1512 Opened fire on three Vichy torpedo aircraft, 1528 Ceased fire, 1737 sighted HMS Tarter.

14th August, Friday 1942. 0325 sighted searchlights bearing 160 degrees 3 or 4 miles, 0725 (et), 1054 11 knots, 1205 HMS Wrestler, Keppel, and Valetta joined company, 1218 HMS Tarter along side (ET), 1448 HMS Malcolm, HMS Bicester reported torpedo approach, took

Log record for August to October 1942

avoiding action, 1730 passed fishing vessel. Clock put back a half an hour, Course as required for fishing vessel.

15th August, Saturday. 1942. Arrived Gibraltar, 2000 Alongside Port light at 43 berth, 0700 Colours, 0750 Ammunition lighter secured starboard side, 1250 Cast off ammunition lighter, 1430 Embarked 132 gallons of petrol, 1535 Ithurio alongside, 1595 Dead Officer taken to Minkway for burial, 1620 Argus underway, 1635 HMS Camalen left harbour, 1720 HMS Bicester secured along side 1840 Admiral Burroughs returned on board, 1845 Five absentee's returned to ship, HMS Kenya entered harbour,

16th August, Sunday. 1942. HMS Ashanti left harbour, 0310 HMS Rodney, Derwent, Bicester, and Malcolm, left harbour, 0905 Admiral Burroughs and Captain to HMS Nelson, 0955 Idomitable undocked, 1100 Ithuriocast off, 1120 HMS Phoebe underway, HMS Sirius underway, 1210 Admiral Burroughs to Kenya and returned to ship, 1555 Corvette K16 along side, 1830 Midshipman to HMS Nelson, 2000 Admiral Burroughs left the ship.

17th August, Monday. 1942. 0800 Colours, 0950 Ammunition lighter secured, 1505 Ammunition lighter secured, 1730 Ensign half mast, 1800 Ensign hoisted, 2050 HMS Westall left harbour, 2011 sunset, lowered Tenth Cruiser's Squadrons C and C's Flag 2030 Ammunition lighters leave ship.

18th August, Tuesday. 1942. 0800 Colours, 0900 HMS Furious, Charybdis, Ledbruy, Eskimo, Derwent, Bicester, Somali, Wishart, Lightning, Keppel, Lookout, Antelope, and Venomous, entered harbour.

19th August, Wednesday. 1942. 1120 Seven Bodies of the late Marine Musicians leave the ship; Three Lieutenants leave the ship,

20th Thursday, August. 1942. 0212 HMS Augus, Furious, Nelson, and Kenya leave harbour, 0930 Tugs secured along side, 1030 Secured Nigeria in No 2 dock, 1545 Engine room ratings muster at top step of dry dock to support 95 station, 1750 Ship settled in dry dock, 1945 21 ratings discharged for UK.

21st August, Friday 1942. 0801 Commence pump out dock, 1045 Dock dry, 6 bodies landed for burial, 1200 Air attack unable to open fire, 1300 Funeral party for burial

Log record for August to October 1942

from HMS Laurel, 1400 Colours half-mast, 1500 Colours
hoisted. 1525 HMS Laurel returned with funeral party,
1745 Funeral party for burial of four from HMS Laurel.
2030 Landed shore party, 2250 Shore party returned, 2303
Dock yard party returned

22" August, Saturday. 1942. Bodies of 4 ratings to HMS
Laurel for sea burial, Colours at half- mast, 1000
Colours hoisted. 1 145 One offender and escort left ship,
1800 Bodies of 3 ratings to HMS Laurel, Colours lowered,

23rd August, Sunday. 1942. 1724 Body of one rating to HMS
Laurel, 1848 Funeral party returns, 1002, Bodies of 15
ratings to HMS Laurel, 1795 Town funeral party landed,
1830 bodies of 15 ratings to HMS Laurel, 2003 Funeral
party returns,

24th August, Monday. 1942. All hands to clearing damage
sections and cleaning oil fuel spillage,

25 August, Tuesday. 1942. All hands to clearing damage
sections and cleaning oil fuel spillage,

26th August, Wednesday. 1942. 0900 Body of unknown person
on board HMS Laurel for burial, 1095 Funeral party
returns, 1715 leading signalman to UK. 1735 landed shore
patrol, 2215 Shore patrol returned,

27th August, Thursday. 1942. All hands digging out rubble
from damage amidships section,

28th August, Friday. 1942. 0957 Fire in A Boiler room,
1077 Commence flooding dry dock 1045 Fire under control,
1101 Stopped flooding, 1115 Midshipman left for UK. One
rating to the military hospital, 1795 Shore patrol, 1930
Dock empted,

29th August, Saturday. 1942. 1855 HMS Ramillies entered
harbour, 2000 HMS Malaya left harbour,

30th August, Sunday. 1942. 0900 Prayers on the Quarter
deck, 1735 Ships safety patrol, 2125 Boat patrol,

31st August, Monday. 1942. 11 15 Monthly payment, 1330
Payment, 1615 Soap and tobacco issue on the quarterdeck.
2045 Dockyard patrol, 2330 Clocks put back half an hour,

Tailpiece

Log record for August to October 1942

1st September, Tuesday. 1942. Dockyard routine 1330 Air attack, 1440 Rating for HMS Malaya, 1600 Warrant No 95, 1700 Gibraltar council complain about smell.

2nd September, Wednesday. 1942. 1600 Warrant No 95 read,

3rd September, Thursday. 1942. All hands to clean and clear damaged amidships sections,

4th September, Friday. 0020 three ratings attacked in their hammocks, 0050 Duty hands muster and search organised,

5th September, Saturday. 1942. 0130 1s Starboard watch fall in and carry on search, 1200 Hands to make and mend. Warrants 96 and 97 read, Engine room artificer accidentally drowned.

6th September, Sunday. 1942. 0710 Holy Communion in chapel, 1055 Prayers, Divine Service, 1310 Commander Perry arrived on board, 1615 Funeral for engineer artificer, buried with firing party at La Linea, Spain,

7th September, Monday. 1942. Small fire in damaged compartments, 1003 fire under control, 1 150 Captain of HMS Malaya arrived on board, Capatin of Malaya left ship, 1430 Air attack,

8th September, Tusday.1942. 2 ratings left ship for rest camp, Royal marine detachment returned from rest camp,

9th September, Wednesday. 1942. 0800 Hands to clean damaged compartments, 1330 Rating returned from hospital, 1630 two ratings left for rest camp,

10th September, Thursday. 1942. 0800 Hands to clean damaged compartments, 1745 Air attack,

11th September, Friday. 1942. 0800 Hands to clean ship, 1720 Air attack, 2345 Army Escort for one other rank.

12th September, Saturday. 1942 Nil work, Epidemic of Levant stomach,

13th September, Sunday. 1942. 0800 Two rating transfer to Newfoundland trawler Tyne Castle, to act as range party, 0930 Church parties for the starboard hanger and ashore,

Log record for August to October 1942

1115 Bugler discharged to hospital, 1610 Ratings for rest camp fall in,

14th September, Monday. 1942. 1639 Air attack, Tyne Castle return damaged after attacked by Heinkel 111, Seamen range party claimed to have shot it down, one Nigerian rating hit in the foot, 1825 Range party returned with injured seaman,

15th September, Tuesday. 1942. 1 130 Payment on quarterdeck

16th September, Wednesday. 1942.0915 Air attack, 1257 Air attack,

17th September, Thursday. 1942. 1345 One rating injured on Tyne Castle to hospital, 2029 Air Attack,

18th September, Friday. 1942. 0700 First concrete,

19th September, Saturday. 1942. 1200 HMS Lowestoft arrived in No 2 dock,

20th September, Sunday. 1942. 1100 Church service,

21st September, Monday. 1942. 0700 Concrete and shuttering,

22nd September, Tuesday. 1942. 1730 One rating returned from hospital,

23rd September, Wednesday. 1942. 1000 Air attack, One rating injured by falling off moving lorry, 1830 Air attack,

24th September, Thursday. 1942. 0700 Concrete, 1515 Engineer returns from hospital,

25th September, Friday. 1942. One rating to hospital, 1605 Two ratings to shore signal station,

26th September, Saturday. 1942. 2125 Commander "E" joined ship,

27th September, Sunday. 1942. 1100 Church Services,

28th September, Monday. 1942.0930 Board of enquiry, Rating deserted ship on the 12th August, 1800 Band of the